D1496232

studies in jazz

Institute of Jazz Studies, Rutgers University
General Editors: *William M. Weinberg & Dan Morgenstern*

Metuchen, N.J., London, 1986 Studies in Jazz No.4

The Scarecrow Press and the Institute

James P. Johnson

A Case of Mistaken Identity

SCOTT E. BROWN

A James P. Johnson Discography 1917-1950

ROBERT HILBERT

of Jazz Studies, Rutgers University

The author wishes to thank the following persons and firms for permission to reprint extracts from previously published articles and/or books:
Martin Williams, editor of Jazz Review, for quotations from Tom Davin's "Conversations with James P. Johnson."
William Morrow & Co. for quotations from LeRoi Jones' Blues People.
W.W. Norton & Co. for quotations from Frank Tirro's Jazz--A History.
Oxford University Press for quotations from Gunther Schuller's Early Jazz.
Music Sales Corporation (Oak Publications) for quotations from Rudi Blesh and Harriet Janis, They All Played Ragtime, 4th ed.
New York Amsterdam News for quotations from news stories.
To the following for permission to reproduce photographs: William P. Gottlieb, from the Edward J. Gottlieb Collection.
The New York Public Library at Lincoln Center for materials from the Otto Hess Collection, Performing Arts Research Center.

Library of Congress Cataloging-in-Publication Data

Brown, Scott E., 1960-
    A case of mistaken identity.

    (Studies in jazz ; no. 4)
    Includes lists of compositions and indexes.
    Bibliography: p.
    1. Johnson, James P. (James Price), 1894-1955.
2. Johnson, James P. (James Price), 1894-1955--Discography.
3. Jazz musicians--United States--Biography. I. Hilbert,
Robert, 1939-   . James P. Johnson discography, 1917-
1955. 1986. II. Title. III. Title: James P. Johnson
discography, 1917-1955. IV. Series.
ML417.J62B76 1986   786.1'092'4 [B]   86-3830
ISBN 0-8108-1887-6

Manufactured in the United States of America

DEDICATION

To Judi, who listened to "Backwater Blues" in her youth, and Milton, who played "If I Could Be With You" with his band every weekend forty years before they ever heard of James P. Johnson. Thank you, Mom and Dad.

CONTENTS

v

Part II

THE RECORDED WORKS OF
JAMES P. JOHNSON:
A DISCOGRAPHY
by Robert Hilbert

FOREWORD

Thirty years after his untimely death, James P. Johnson, one of the great seminal figures of jazz, is at last receiving some of the recognition he so richly merits: Scott Brown and Bob Hilbert have left no stones unturned in their effort to unearth as much information as possible about the life, career, works and recorded legacy of this important but neglected artist.

Scott Brown's meticulously researched text and impressively detailed supplemental apparatus began as a Senior Honors project at Yale University. It speaks well for the author (and for Yale) that it easily equals much of the best postgraduate work being done in jazz academia. In preparing the work for publication, Brown did much additional research and writing, with a dedication the more admirable when one considers that he was in the throes of medical studies--a pursuit allowing for little (if any) spare time.

That a discography of some sort would be needed was evident, but the task of undertaking a complete one seemed, under the circumstances, forbidding. It was the veteran Duke Ellington expert, record producer, collector and audio engineer, Jerry Valburn who brought on board his friend and fellow collector Bob Hilbert, who, though already involved in a Pee Wee Russell project (in collaboration with British researcher David Niven) scheduled for this series, volunteered to also take on Johnson, whose work he much admires. There was a previously published

Johnson discography, which proved helpful as a guildeline, but we are pleased to note that Hilbert's work supersedes it, and also pleased to point out that it is based on the computer-facilitated model and high standards established by Arnold Laubich and Ray Spencer's Art Tatum: A Guide to His Recorded Music (Studies in Jazz, No. 2) and also emulated by James M. Doran in his Erroll Garner: The Most Happy Piano (No. 3 in this series). Much that had been obscure and misleading in the attempted documentation of Johnson's recordings--especially those from the 1920s--has here been clarified, and while a discographer's work is never done, Hilbert's work is a great step forward.

James P. Johnson was born in New Brunswick, so it is entirely appropriate and gratifying that this book is published under the joint auspices of two New Jersey-based entities, Rutgers and Scarecrow Press. The editors of this series have by now become accustomed to the empathy and expertise of Scarecrow's dedicated staff, but by no means take it for granted. All of us take pride in this "homecoming" for James P. Johnson, and we look forward to the projected study of his music by Willa Rouder which will further flesh out this richly detailed portrait of a great artist and his works.

DAN MORGENSTERN

Director
Institute of Jazz Studies
Rutgers University

Part I

A CASE OF MISTAKEN IDENTITY:
THE LIFE AND MUSIC OF JAMES P. JOHNSON

ACKNOWLEDGEMENTS

Unlike my predecessors in this Studies In Jazz series, I was not fortunate enough to hear my favorite musician play in person, being born a decade after James P. Johnson's paralyzing stroke. The ragtime revival of the early 1970s provided my introduction to his music through what has since become a welcome flood of LP reissues spanning the entire history of jazz. The intensity, sparkle and pure swing of his playing were what first captivated me. A good friend aptly described it as "happy music." As I read more about James P., the same adjectives appeared again and again: underrated, overlooked, neglected. While the names of Scott Joplin, Eubie Blake, and Jelly Roll Morton were becoming increasingly familiar to the general public, (and deservedly so), James P. Johnson seemed, once again, to be passed by. Like many an ardent fan, I resolved to bring together as much information as I could find. With the addition of Bob Hilbert's excellent discography, I consider this book an overdue tribute to a great man of jazz. I hope it will lead many others to discover the joy of the music of James P. Johnson.

This work would not have been possible without support from the Scholar of the House committee of Yale College. By accepting my proposal to research the life and music of James P., they gave me the opportunity to spend my senior undergraduate year working exclusively on this project. The Scholar of the House program supplants all other undergraduate requirements for the year and is considered a major course of study in itself.   One might say I majored in James P. Johnson in college.

I am grateful to Beekman C. Cannon, then chairman of the Scholar of the House program, and Frank Tirro, my advisor and dean of the school of music, for guidance and encouragement in undertaking this project.   During production of my original thesis, William R. Bennett, master of Silliman College at Yale, made available to me the xerox machine and computer.   Elizabeth Sledge, the writing tutor in Silliman, was patient and thorough in reviewing the manuscript for grammar and construction.   Professor Arnold Rampersad in the Department of English at Stanford University graciously allowed me access to the Langston Hughes files in the James Weldon Johnson Collection at Yale.   I spent an enjoyable afternoon with Johnson's youngest child Lillie Mae McIntyre who, although only 13 years old when her father died, conveyed her memories of their home life.   Thanks also go to David Cayer, Derek Coller, Anthony Davis, Henry Gates, Bob Hilbert, Michael A. Lang, Willa Rouder, Mark Smith, Murray Stopol, Larry Thompson, Dan Morgenstern and the staff of the Rutgers Institute of Jazz Studies for information and assistance otherwise unavailable.   For the generous use of their photographs, thanks to William P. Gottlieb and Duncan P. Schiedt.

A special note of appreciation goes to Jamie Z. Chesman for her diligence and expertise in processing the manuscript for publication.

INTRODUCTION

James Price Johnson was born on February 1, 1891 (Russell), 1894 (Blesh), and 1897 (Peck). To the readers of the New York Amsterdam News during the 1920s, he was known as James P. Johnson, James Johnson, Jimmy Johnson, Jimmie Johnson, and James J. Johnson. He died on May 5, 1954 (Down Beat) and November 17, 1955 (Queens General Hospital). The inaccuracy and inconsistency in these biographical tidbits is indicative of the treatment given to the life and career of a musician whose far-reaching contributions to American music should have earned him the greatest popular and critical acclaim. The composer of perennial popular hits like the "Charleston" and "If I Could Be With You" was not elected to the Songwriter's Hall of Fame until 1973. Considered by many the first to record a "jazz" piano solo, "Carolina Shout," he is not even mentioned in several of the early works on jazz.[1] Hailed as the composer of the first genuine Negro Rhapsody, "Yamekraw," he is never considered alongside other "serious" black composers like William Grant Still and J. Rosamond Johnson. Furthermore, though 30 years have passed since his death, posterity has been remiss in defining the full range and depth of his career and making clear the diversity and significance of his efforts.

"James P. Johnson, often called the 'grandfather of hot piano,' is a discouraging subject for a biographer, which may explain why he has been overlooked so often by critics and historians of

jazz."[2]   These words, written in 1941, express
sentiments that have been reiterated countless
times since then in nearly all references to
James P. Johnson.   This author can attest to the
difficulty in doing biographical research on
Johnson.   It is a problem which, contrary to the
inference of the quotation, is not the cause of,
but is caused by the neglect of Johnson by the
public.   Possibly the greatest sources of confusion
and misinterpretation concerning the life and
music of James P. Johnson have been the
numerous and varied attempts at resolving "the
difficulty of tying him in with the tradition."[3]   It
is not simply a matter of finding a term to
describe his playing style, defined by the music
that came before and after.   Contrary to
popular opinion, his musical achievements extend
far beyond his playing ability.   In addition,
tradition, especially in reference to folk, popular,
and jazz music, exists on many different levels:
musical, historical, sociological, and humanistic.

        Ultimately, it is as a pivotal figure in the
history and development of jazz piano that James
P. Johnson is best known.   He created a
prototypical and cohesive piano style out of the
disparate musical elements of his youth and became its most accomplished practitioner.   Because
of this patriarchal role in the development of
American black music, he is affectionately
referred to as the "Father of Stride Piano."   Yet,
it is just this title which has fostered many mis-
conceptions about the man and his music.   Too
often his place in jazz history is thought to be
adequately covered by citing him as "the stride
pianist James P. Johnson," a convenient cliché
which has allowed critics to reduce his playing to
a phrase.   (Often it seems that only the so-called
"individual stylists" are considered worthy of
serious discussion.)   Although Johnson's musical

philosophy was consistently grounded in what he perceived to be the important fundamentals, his pianistic ability was of such high caliber that he was able to express the widest range of ideas. In no way can one consider his style to be musically incarcerating or expressively limited.

Being the "Father of Stride Piano" and a great stylistic inspiration for many subsequent pianists should have secured for him a permanently visible place in the literature. However, the word "stride" itself has led to interpretations which have contributed to the continuing neglect of Johnson. The term was coined long after the heyday of the music itself. It had previously been called shout piano, rent-party piano, parlor social piano, and several other empirically derived terms. It is considered to be something of a transitional style, thus making Johnson a transitional figure. Herein lies one point of controversy which has led to ambiguity. Some credit Johnson and his contemporaries with the creation of jazz from various musical antecedents, primarily ragtime. Others consider their music to be only a sophisticated offshoot of ragtime, not yet embodying the true spirit of jazz. Many writers place Johnson in both camps: ragtime and jazz.

The development of a clear-cut distinction usually leads to the question "When is a ragtime player not a ragtime player?"[4] Attempting to resolve this question leads to additional problems in perspective, since it has not been convincingly established that ragtime is independent from the jazz tradition. Although it is impossible to discuss music without it, terminology should not be used to wrap music into neat little packages. The question is not whether stride is ragtime or jazz, but how James P. Johnson's piano music, by whatever name, fits into the development of Afro-American creative music. Both James P. Johnson and stride piano have been hopelessly mired in this semantic argument.

Closely tied to the shroud of terminology is the overemphasis on geography. One of the most egregious myths, which has only recently been challenged, maintains that New Orleans is the undisputed birthplace of jazz. Johnson (and many of his contemporaries, for that matter) is put at an additional disadvantage in the battle for fame, not having been born or raised anywhere near New Orleans. The musical environment of Johnson's home in the northeast was hardly less diverse than that of New Orleans; it was just different. The types of music known as jazz which emanated from New York and New Orleans were grounded in a different mixture of fundamental musical principles. They were both a means of expressing elements from the American black folk music tradition.

Johnson had no greater success in gaining the attention of the general public at the height of his career than impressing the jazz historians later in life. He was not a uniquely colorful individual like many of his friends, such as Willie "The Lion" Smith, Fats Waller, and Duke Ellington. In a tradition of nicknames, he had none. The details of his life are not an array of chimerical anecdotes that would make a good storybook tale. Although for many years he was very active in the afterhours night-life, he also led a stable family life with his wife and three children. Johnson was by nature shy, patient, considerate, and perhaps even too easily manipulated. He was not a self-promoter, and while many of his contemporaries were building national reputations as performers and entertainers,

Johnson remained unrecognized for his own work as a composer.

One should not get the impression, however, that Johnson was a failure. As a performer, he was held in the highest esteem by his fellow musicians and quite honestly considered to be the best player. The success he did achieve provided him with ample security. He never had to seek non-musical work, as was the case with so many musicians who experienced early success only to die poverty-stricken. Johnson's story is that of a pioneer whose goals and dreams became an important, if not always celebrated, reality. As a boy, he drove himself to become a keyboard virtuoso. He next turned to writing for the musical theater and the popular music market. His most ambitious goal was to conduct his own symphonic works in brightly lit concert halls. For a while, this too he achieved.

Johnson's growth as a musician is a reflection of the extent of his musical curiosity and his ability to assimilate elements from diverse musical climates, both abstractly and through other musicians who had an impact on him, stylistically and personally. The success of his many musical pursuits and his ability to maintain the stylistic integrity of each is, to an extent, historically apparent. When the facts derived from the overall historical picture are considered, one is led to the unsurprising realization that " ... the slender threads in the disorganized pattern came to acquire lasting form and color after the rest of the picture had blurred off."[5]

1

New Brunswick, 1894--1902

There has always been a great deal of confusion
and inaccuracy concerning the details of James P.
Johnson's life. The published literature, in the
form of periodical "feature articles" and jazz history text chapters, has perpetuated misinformation
ranging from his early recordings and compositions
to lofty declarations of collaborations with George
Gershwin. One such disputed detail has been
Johnson's exact birthdate.

Recent evidence proves beyond reasonable
doubt that James Price Johnson was born on
February 1, 1894. (Ironically, the year 1891 was
commonly offered even while Johnson was alive.)
Johnson believed himself to have been born in
1894. He gives this date in two separate
interviews, one for the Library of Congress in
1938, and one with writer Tom Davin conducted
shortly before his death. A handwritten note,
probably dating from sometime in the 1940s, re-
lates Johnson's family background and reconfirms
his birthdate:

> On a cold morning in February 1894, I
> came into this world in a house in City
> Alley, an inconspicuous and plain dwelling
> in a section of New Brunswick, New
> Jersey, long ago torn down and now extinct
> as a living quarters and the neighborhood
> forgotten.
>   My father was a store helper and
> mechanic named William Johnson and worked

for a man by the name of Price whom I was named after. My grandfather on father's side had been a soldier in the Civil War and, through some unexplained circumstance had lost his company papers and my father never received his pension. He was born in New Brunswick, New Jersey. Mother's father was a Negro of half American Indian extraction who had bought his freedom. Mother was born in Petersburg, Virginia.

James P. Johnson
Dean of Jazz Pianists[1]

As a parenthetical note, Johnson took to signing most of his correspondence as "Dean of Jazz Pianists" in his later years. Very little else could be added to this concise family history. The copy of the birth information from the Bureau of Vital Statistics in Trenton, New Jersey corroborates his father's name (William), his birthdate, and his place of birth. The original record of birth in the Bureau of Statistics in New Brunswick spells out the name William H. Johnson and that of James P.'s mother Josephine Harrison. Neither source indicates that he was named at birth.

Documentation of the first 25 years of Johnson's life comes from the best possible source, James P. himself. The interview with Tom Davin recounts in uncanny, although sometimes jumbled detail the years up to Johnson's more widespread success around 1921.[2] In an almost month-by-month account, Johnson describes the music, the people, and the places which had an impact on his development. Unless otherwise noted, the details concerning Johnson's life in this section are taken from this interview.

This copied birth record from the original microfilm entry in the files of the New Jersey Department of Health, coupled with Johnson's own statements, corroborates his birthyear, 1894.

James P. Johnson was the youngest of five
children, four boys and one girl. His sister Belle
preceded him into the family by eight years. His
mother Josephine, who worked as a maid, was
very active in the Methodist Church, particularly
singing in the church choir. When she had saved
some money, Josephine was able to buy an
upright piano from one of her employers. While
she taught herself to play church hymns and
several other simple melodies, James P. played
with the pedals of the piano. When James was
four years old she began to teach him to play
"Little Brown Jug," one of her favorite tunes.
Meanwhile, his sister Belle evinced at best only
lukewarm interest in her piano lessons. James,
however, took a strong interest in the sheet
music of the popular songs his sister and brothers
brought home to play. By the time he was six
years old, his high soprano voice was sufficiently
good to wangle ten or fifteen cents from pas-
sersby on the street for his singing of popular
favorites like "There'll Be a Hot Time in the Old
Town Tonight" and "I'm Looking for That Birdie."

One of the musical fads prominent at the
turn of the century was the marching, military-
style brass band. Many of these bands paraded
through the streets of town heralding a traveling
circus, vaudeville company, or minstrel show.
There were also local "Good Will Bands" and instrumental units connected with various clubs and
fraternal organizations. As a child of six,
Johnson was struck more by their fanciful
uniforms and hats than by the music, admitting
that their playing was probably bad.

At the opposite end of the musical spec-
trum from the "popular" brass bands was a style
of dancing that had a tremendous impact on
James P.'s music, the "shout" dances. His father

and mother would often entertain friends at social parties in their home. Country, set, cotillion and, most importantly, "shout" dances were performed, having been carried north from Virginia, South Carolina, and Georgia.

> The Northern towns had a hold-over of the old southern customs. I'd wake up as a child and hear an old-fashioned ring-shout going on downstairs. Somebody would be playing a guitar or jew's-harp or maybe a mandolin, and the dancing went to "The Spider and the Bed-Bug Had a Good Time" or "Susie, Susie." They danced around in a shuffle and then they would shove a man or a woman out into the center and clap hands. This would go on all night and I would fall asleep sitting at the top of the stairs in the dark.[3]

The shout dances were the main attraction at these parties. To liven the atmosphere even more, prizes were awarded for the best dancing and the most colorful and stylish clothing, such as fancy ribbons, pantalettes or petticoats, and funny patches on pants and coats. The music and dancing of the shouts, which had undergone fascinating transformations by the time they emerged in the Johnson family parlor, left a deep impression on young James. They are a musical form with strong roots in African customs that became the ethnic foundation of a much later jazz style, stride piano, and deserve a closer examination.

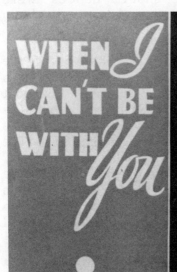

WHEN *I* CAN'T BE WITH *You*

SOUTHERN MUSIC PUB. CO. INC.
1619 BROADWAY...NEW YORK

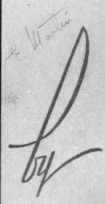

by

ANDY RAZAF
and
JIMMY (J.P.) JOHNSON
WRITERS OF
AINT MISBEHAVIN'
MY FATE IS IN YOUR HANDS
IF I COULD BE WITH YOU

2

The Ring-Shout

Before the term "stride" was widely used to describe the playing style of Johnson and his cohorts, it had, for a long time, been called the "shout" style. Willie "The Lion" Smith provided a somewhat romantic explanation for the connection. "Shouts are stride piano--when James P. and Fats and I would get a romp-down shout going, that was playing rocky, just like the Baptist people sing. You don't just play a chord to that--you got to move it and the piano players do the same thing in churches, and there's ragtime in the preaching."[1]

Shouts, before they became stride piano, were emotionally intense, highly rhythmic dances, almost narcotic in their effect. They are, in form and intent, strongly African in origin. Part of the etymology of the word shout, as determined by L.D. Turner, can be traced to West Africa. In the Arabic lexicon of the Mohammedans, the word saut (pronounced "shout") meant to run and walk around the deity Kaaba.[2] In other parts of Africa, the worshippers circled only counter-clockwise around the deity, since it was tabu to direct the right shoulder to the god.[3] Several observers who have travelled in Africa have noted the remarkably close similarities between these religious, tribal dances and the American "shout." In form, melody, and choreography, the American dance is a direct holdover from the original African custom.[4] The manner in which this transplant was accomplished is a fine example of the cultural adaptation of a displaced people.

The daily existence of the slaves in America was, due to the nature of the system, essentially restricted to only two pursuits: work and religion.   In order for an African custom to be preserved in this country, it had to be incorporated into one or both of these outlets.   The closer the process came to superimposition, the more successful the survival of the tradition. "Thus, a Dahomey river god ceremony had no chance of survival in this country at all unless it was incorporated into an analogous rite that was present in the new culture--which is what happened.   The Christians of the New World called it baptism."[5]   In similar fashion, the shout became an integral part of the church service. In their religious fervor, the participants worked into the dance the Bible, the pulpit, or the leader of the service, often creating the appearance of hysteria.   The only compromise that seems to have been made was the substitution of Biblical verse for the original African lyrics.

As the black churches became more established, the leaders began to view the white church as a more tangible model.   The black religious leaders began to shape their goals for their people with a greater awareness of the conduct of white society.[6]   At first, primarily secular music (fiddle songs, devil songs, jig tunes, and corn songs) was outlawed by many churches. They soon began to view dancing as a diversion into evil, and thought it was necessary to exorcize this transgression from the religious services. Dancing was too firmly rooted in African culture, however, to be easily removed.   To save the custom, they redefined their terms.

The "ring shouts" or "shuffle shouts" of the early Negro churches were attempts by the black Christians to have their cake and eat

> it: to maintain African tradition, however
> veiled or unconscious the attempt might be,
> yet embrace the new religion. Since danc-
> ing was irreligious and sinful, the Negro
> said that only "crossing the feet" con-
> stituted actual dancing. So the ring shout
> developed, where the worshippers link arms
> and shuffle, at first slowly but then with
> increasing emotional display, around in a
> circle, singing hymns or chanting as they
> move.7

Several first-hand accounts of the religious
ring-shout during the mid-nineteenth century have
been documented. Henry George Spaulding
described the scenes on the South Carolina Sea
Islands in 1863.

> At the "praise meetings" on the plantations,
> one of the elders usually presides and con-
> ducts the exercises with great solemnity.
> Passages of Scripture are quoted from
> memory, and the hymns, which constitute
> the principal feature of the meeting, are
> deaconed off as at church. Sometimes the
> superintendent or one of the teachers at-
> tends these meetings, and is then expected
> to conduct the exercises and make an
> address. After the praise meeting is over,
> there usually follows the very singular and
> impressive performance of the 'shout,' or
> religious dance of the Negroes. Three or
> four, standing still, clapping their hands and
> beating time with their feet, commence
> singing in unison one of the peculiar shout
> melodies, while the others walk round in a
> ring, in single file, joining also in the song.
> Soon those in the ring leave off their
> singing, the others keeping it up the while
> with increased vigor, and strike into the

shout step, observing most accurate time
with the music. This step is something
halfway between a shuffle and a dance, as
difficult for an uninitiated person to describe as to imitate. At the end of each
stanza of the song the dancers stop short
with a slight stamp on the last note, and
then, putting the other foot forward,
proceed through the next verse. They will
often dance to the same song for twenty
or thirty minutes, once or twice, perhaps,
varying the monotony of their movement by
walking for a little while and joining in the
singing. The physical exertion, which is
really very great, as the dance calls into
play nearly every muscle of the body,
seems never to weary them in the least,
and they frequently keep up a shout for
hours, resting only for brief intervals between the different songs.[8]

This quotation was originally published in the
August 1863 issue of Continental Monthly as part
of an article entitled "Under the Palmetto."
Spaulding was a Unitarian minister and a member
of the U.S. Sanitary Commission during the Civil
War, visiting the Sea Islands during a Navy
stopover.

Once slavery had been abolished, new outlets appeared for the proliferation of black
secular music. Although the ring-shout was a vital part of the religious service, it became increasingly associated with the "devil's music" as
the churches strove for artificial respectability.
The shouts were gradually displaced from their
focal position in the praise meetings. Spaulding's
account describes a shout which, although still
religiously oriented, commences after the formal
praise meeting is over. The ring-shouts began to

appear in the non-religious social gatherings which
had been difficult to arrange under slavery. The
newly found leisure time was now occupied with
the increasingly secularized variety of the shout.
This is not to say, however, that the shout was
completely eliminated from worship. Nor did the
non-ceremonial shouts cease to include religious
motifs. Its underlying principles of spirited participation and original religious intent could never
be totally divorced from any performance of a
shout.

The shout dances were once thought to be
confined to South Carolina, Georgia, and other
southeastern areas. It is now known that the
shout was not unique to any particular region.
Various forms were known throughout the southern
states, including the ring-shout in South Carolina,
reel-shoutings in Virginia, camp meeting and
Pinkster dances, and the dances of La Place
Congo in New Orleans. The occurrence of the
New Orleans versions of the shout dances represent perhaps one of the few social gatherings allowed slaves, aside from church. Every Sunday,
in a square known as La Place Congo, the slaves
were allowed to congregate. They were free to
entertain themselves as they pleased, and they
chose to let loose with shout dances. The most
famous was the Bamboula. Louis Moreau
Gottschalk, child piano prodigy and established
Creole composer, wrote the difficult piano fantasy
"La Bamboula--Dance des Negres" based on the
events he witnessed in La Place Congo. His
work represents an early attempt at "classicizing"
the roots of Afro-American music. The dancing,
unlike the ring-shout, was accompanied by many
instruments and fanciful costumes. The
Counjaille, Calinda, Chacta, Babouille, and the
Congo, all cousins to the Bamboula, could be
found in many southern states.

In 1909, Lydia Parrish made her way to the Georgia Sea Islands, establishing close contact with the people of this area, known as Gullahs and Geechies for their distinctive dialects of the same names. She described the type of shout dancing she saw, the true ring-shout. In format and presentation, the shouting Parrish encountered was very similar to the religious rituals described by H.G. Spaulding. "The feet are not supposed to leave the floor or to cross each other, such an act being sinful. The shouting proceeds with a curious shuffling but controlled step which taps out with the heel a resonant syncopation fascinating in its intricacy and precision."[10] By the early part of this century, the ring-shout had become very much a non-religious diversion. Unlike many of the other shout dances, the ring-shout maintained a cohesive structure, which is probably the reason that the dance survived in recognizable form.

Two dances which Parrish describes show the shout as entertainment and artistic expression. The "Down De Mire" ring-shout involves the physical rendering of its title. One member is enclosed in the center of the ring on his hands and knees. The shouters move around the circle, pushing down the head of the person in the middle. They push his head "down to the mire." "The several arms reaching out to give a push make an unusually picturesque pattern.[11] "Oh Eve--Where Is Adam" shout is an example of dancing and pantomime. The dance, in typical ring-shout fashion, starts slowly as the shouters swing around the circle. When the pace quickens, the dancers go through the motion of picking up leaves as they sing the refrain, "Oh Eve--where is Ad-u-m? / Oh Eve--Adam in the garden / Pickin' up leaves."[12]

Parrish also noted that in North Carolina and Virginia, the ring-shout seemed to be unknown. The solo "shout" performance predominated in this area. "It is, however, an interesting fact that the term 'shouting' is used in Virginia in reference to a peculiar motion of the body not wholly unlike the Carolina shouting."[13] James P. Johnson gives us some indication of the nature of these shouts, which he called "real shoutings." They are the basis for the southern set or square dances and cotillion music Johnson saw his Virginia-born mother and her friends perform in New Brunswick.

> One of the men would call the figures and they'd dance their own style of square dances. The calls were ... "join hands" ... "sashay" ... "turn around" ... "ladies right and gentlemen left" ... "grab your partner" ... "break away" ... "make a strut" ... "cows to the front, bulls stay back" ..... When he called "do your stuff" or "ladies to the front," they did their personal dances. The catwalk, for instance, was developed from the cotillion, but it was also part of the set dances.[14]

Musically, the secular shouts retained many of the elements of the original religious shouts. They were based on short, repeated refrains which revolve around equally short melodic statements. The most important aspects are the rhythmic variation and intensity, the patterns for which are often produced spontaneously (i.e., improvised). In essence, "the 'shouts' were little more than highly rhythmical lyrics."[15]

Years later, Johnson began to devise a compositional philosophy based very much on the characteristics of the shouts. From the time of

his parents' parlor get-togethers, to the dance
halls of "Hell's Kitchen," through the rent parties
of the 1920s, Johnson's playing incorporated many
of the musical features of the dances, and began
to mirror them in a purely instrumental form.
"A lot of my music is based on set, cotillion and
other southern dance steps and rhythms," he said.
"I think the 'Carolina Balmoral' was the most
spirited dance in the South.   I find I have a
strong feeling for these dances that goes away
back--and I haven't found anyone else with it
yet."   How the shout manifested itself in his
music will be evident later.   Willie "The Lion"
Smith was, in fact, both figuratively and literally
accurate when he said, "Shouts are stride piano."

3

Jersey City, 1902--1908

In 1902, when Johnson was eight, the family moved to Jersey City. Although his mother was a religious woman, they settled in a tough Jersey City neighborhood on Monmouth Street near the Dixon Pencil factory and many barrelhouses. Johnson told of the non-pianistic musical exploits he practiced, since the family was forced to sell the piano to cover the costs of moving. Because he was still young and "in short pants," he was not allowed to go inside any of the saloons. Instead, he developed his buck-dancing, singing, and guitar playing, performing outside the sporting houses. He was able to pick up the popular tunes of the day by listening to the music coming from inside. "Don't Hit That Lady," "She Got Good Booty," "Left Her on the Railroad Track," and "Baby, Let Your Drawers Hang Low"--all popular tunes Johnson recalled--suggest the low element of the bawdy houses. Many sexually suggestive verses would be adapted to the melody. The entertainment inside the saloons was usually supplied by an individual known as a "tickler," and it was a tickler that James P. Johnson knew he wanted to become.

A tickler was a ragtime piano player, so named for his manner of handling not only the ivories but women as well. In Jersey City, Johnson came into contact with many ragtime players who were friendly with his older brother. The lives of most of these men were strongly tied to the black underworld. The tenderloin areas offered not only music, but gambling, drugs,

prostitution, and various types of swindling,
gouging, and hustling. Almost every American
city had an area such as this, often known
euphemistically as "the district." Probably the
most famous district of this period was Storyville
in New Orleans. Unlike the larger tenderloins of
New York, St. Louis, and New Orleans, the Jersey City district served as a temporary settlement for ticklers (and other transients) as they
moved north on their way to the good life in
New York. Many of these players came from
such southeastern cities as Baltimore, Norfolk,
Charleston, and Atlanta.

        Many ticklers did not make much money
playing the piano, working 12 hours a day for ten
dollars a week, with as much more in tips.
There was more money in hustling, an endeavor
made easier for musicians because women liked
their music and preferred to work for them. The
girls usually travelled with their pimp/tickler.
Johnson related that the measure of a good girl,
not surprisingly, was how much money she could
bring in. The best were also thieves.
"Sometimes, a girl would roll a live one and get
$500 or $1,000. This usually brought a complaint
to the police, so the girl and her tickler friend
would have to leave town. They'd head north
and east to New York, and the last stop on the
railroad was Jersey City."[1] The final jump to
New York involved more than just crossing the
Hudson River. The black tenderloin in New York
around 1905 was not situated in a bustling community like Harlem, which was then in an
embryonic stage of development as a black
community. In addition, many of the established
hustlers paid protection under the table, and
didn't appreciate transients who might attract too
much attention from the police. The ticklers in
Jersey City had to work their way slowly into

the New York district, playing piano at night while their girls hustled.

Johnson was taken with the superficially glamorous lifestyle of the ticklers. In the days before the phonograph, radio, and television, a piano player was socially important. He was always welcome at parties to provide entertainment. "They were popular fellows, real celebrities. They had lots of girl friends, led a sporting life and were invited everywhere there was a piano. I thought it was a fine way to live, just as later kids would think singers like Crosby or Sinatra were worth copying."[2] Here an important distinction was made. Johnson wished to make his living as a musician, not a pimp or drug pusher. His contemporaries and he, not only on the east coast but across the country, began to see their music as distinct from the criminal element. Although many older players were involved in some kind of illicit activity, the younger generation began to legitimize the image of the "tickler." This new orientation did not change the social status of the piano player; he remained an integral part of the black community for many years, continuing into the period of rent parties during the depression. There were always women, food, and hospitality available for a high-class tickler.

Johnson jokingly recounted the story of his first job as a "tickler." When he was eight years old in Jersey City, a woman approached him and asked if he was interested in making a quarter. Anxious for the extra spending money, he agreed and followed the woman into a parlor. She had heard that the youngster could play the piano and requested that he do so. He sat at the piano for a few hours playing simple variations on "Little Brown Jug" and nursery rhyme tunes. He was instructed not to turn around, so that he wouldn't see the people entering what was probably a bordello. Johnson did not consider this experience to be a professional job, saying "it didn't count."

The players Johnson encountered in Jersey City offered him not only places to play but the benefit of their knowledge and experience. One such player, Claude Grew, bore the distinguishing mark of a good cabaret player. He could play anything in all keys, a requirement for accompanying singers. Johnson picked up this skill and was later renowned for his facility in transposing and modulating through many keys. A large part of the Jersey City ticklers' repertoire was ragtime but Johnson was quick to point out that it was not ragtime as most people consider it today. It was "mostly popular songs with a strong rhythm and with syncopated vamps, not a whole composition or arrangement."[3] Even the rags of Scott Joplin were played piecemeal as part of this aural tradition.

In 1905, when Johnson was eleven, he began to attend New York symphony concerts. A friend of one of his older brothers worked as a waiter, and was able to get tickets from Josef Stransky, the Symphony's conductor. It was his first exposure to the old masters. "I didn't get much out of them," said Johnson, "but the full symphonic sounds made a great impression on me."[4] They obviously struck some internal sensitivity, as he later utilized the forms of Western art music to compose his own rhapsodies, symphonies, and concertos based on Afro-American musical themes.

In 1908, the Johnsons moved to the San Juan Hill section of New York, west and north of

Columbus Circle in the lower Sixties. This area, also known as the Jungles, constituted the northern border of Hell's Kitchen, the notorious tenderloin district which ran from about 30th to 70th St., between Eighth and Tenth Avenues. Johnson describes the Jungles: "This was the Negro section of Hell's Kitchen and ran from 60th to 63rd St. west of Ninth Ave. It was the toughest part of New York. There were two to three killings a night. Fights broke out over love affairs, gambling, or arguments in general. There were race fights with the white gangs on 66th and 67th St. It was just as tough in the white section of Hell's Kitchen."[5] While attending P.S. 69, Johnson played for school assemblies and minstrel show productions. Still possessing a high soprano voice, he took part in the school production of Haydn's "Creation." The show was organized by Frank Damrosch, brother of the conductor Walter Damrosch, who presented Johnson with a bronze metal for his participation.

"In New York I got a chance to hear a lot of good music for the first time," including the New York Symphony, classical piano in cafés, the operettas of Victor Herbert and Rudolf Friml, popular music of the day, and "real ragtime." By far the most important musical style to contribute to the development of stride piano was ragtime. In both form and conception, stride derives from antecedent characteristics in ragtime. Yet, there are many types of music which fall under the "ragtime" designation. Almost all the popular music of the early 1900's was in some way associated with ragtime, in either name or spirit. Ragtime was not exclusively piano music intended to be played as written, nor was it just "Alexander's Ragtime Band." The history of ragtime reveals the existence of music at various conceptual levels. Ragtime, in all its incarnations stood at the forefront of popular musical culture. It also remained the cornerstone of an ethnic piano style. James P. Johnson was exposed to both worlds and eagerly assimilated elements from both traditions. A closer look at the history of ragtime is necessary to reveal the divergent styles, the style/genre dualism (i.e., improvised vs. composed music) and the contribution of each to Johnson's music.

4

Ragtime

Ragtime is an amalgamation of African and European elements. It is both an ethnically Afro-American and a nationalistic American music. Its origins lie primarily within the sphere of black folk music. Ragtime's exuberant feeling derives from folk sources connected with the various shout dances--the Counjaille, Bamboula, Calinda, and Ring-shout. In addition to the black dance forms, the slave musicians were exposed to the European folk dances of their white owners. When requested to perform, black musicians often played the Western schottisches, reels and jigs. Before the word ragtime came into use, the term "jig" piano was used to describe the spirited sound of syncopated piano playing. The jig is an Irish dance, not an African dance. "Jig" piano developed as instrumental music, unlike the blues, which was conceived and constructed to complement the voice.

One of the instruments often used to accompany these dances was the banjo. This instrument is genuinely African in origin. It (or, more correctly, the conception of a banjo) was brought to the United States by the slaves, who, when the opportunity arose, devised homemade versions. Made from gourds and cat-gut, these instruments were probably very similar to their original African precursors. Before emancipation, the banjo became very popular with black musicians. On many sheet music covers in later years were scenes depicting blacks singing and dancing to the accompaniment of a banjo player. A

highly rhythmic, fully textured style of "picking"
developed. A goal was to fill in all the spaces
in the music with melodies based on arpeggiated
and broken chord figures. Musical economy and
vocal expressiveness were not stressed; rather,
players relied on the percussive aspects of
playing. Some slaves were able to gain access to
a piano, and began to transfer many of these
ideas directly from the banjo.[1]

"Many country dance tunes are simply the
same melody repeated over and over, ad
infinitum, or until the dancers tire.... The form
tends to be brief, simple and highly repetitive.
Themes, once stated, are repeated literally with
little variation or embellishment."[2] Since the
African musical tradition is aural and not written,
to claim that variation or embellishment was absent is a distortion. Yet, many rhythmic patterns
became standard and are commonly associated
with banjo playing and the subsequent piano style.
Many of the right hand, treble parts of later rags
are characterized as "banjo" styled.

With emancipation, these folk origins of
ragtime spread across the country primarily by
two means. Probably the most important institu-
tion to disseminate the styles of the black musical subculture was the "itinerant musician." With
freedom and the difficulty of attaining steady
work, many musicians took to a life on the road,
traveling from one black settlement (usually associated with a tenderloin area which provided
work) to another. The piano assumed a more
important role, as many bawdy houses often supplied an upright for entertainment. There was
also no reason or practical method to carry one's
instrument around from place to place. The environment of "the district" was very conducive to
competitive musical interaction. The best of the

local players were constantly put on their guard to prevent out-of-town musicians from taking their jobs or their girls. The atmosphere of the tenderloin was jovial and required music suited to the uninhibited carousing with alcohol, gambling, and prostitution. The traditions and lifestyle of tenderloin entertainers were maintained through the 1920s when many red-light districts were closed and black music by black musicians became big business. Many of the players Johnson encountered in Jersey City belonged to this itinerant breed. The New York tenderloin was much less hospitable toward strangers, an attitude which pervaded all levels of black music in the city, not just in the sporting belt. This arrogance had a dramatic effect on the musical development there for many years.

While many black musicians followed an independent career, others joined the minstrel shows. A combination of musical and variety show entertainment, minstrelsy shines as the first unique American contribution to the musical theater, but is also clouded by tragic irony. The form was conceived by whites and emerged as a recognizable genre during the 1820s. Comic songs based on parodies of black figures were known for many years. As whites took closer notice of slave lifestyles, music, and dancing, consistent pictures began to emerge. Made-up in burnt cork and other distinctive garb, and accompanied by "bones" (actual animal bones used for percussion), tambourines, and banjos, whites staged musical exaggerations of black stereotypes.

"Two basic types of slave impersonations were developed: one caricature of the plantation slave with his ragged clothes and thick dialect; the other portraying the city slave, the dandy dressed in the latest fashion, who boasted of his exploits among the ladies. The former was referred to as Jim Crow and the latter as Zip Coon."3 The white minstrel show derived its humor from the racist portrayal of blacks. The first level of irony can be traced to these apparent adaptations. Many of the dances the white minstrels exaggerated were, in fact, initially exaggerations by the slaves mimicking their masters' dances. One such dance, the cakewalk, grew to its own flowering as a style years later.

The music in the minstrel show was thought to be based on black folk materials, but actually bore little resemblance to black music. The Irish ballad formed the underlying framework, not the spiritual. Daniel Decatur Emmett and his Virginian Minstrels are credited with having staged the first full-length minstrel show in New York in 1843. The standardized format consisted of two parts: the first was dominated by jokes and songs, the second contained more involved ensemble numbers, skits, and acts. Shortly after Emmett's success, a large number of imitators arose to ride the wave of popularity enjoyed by the minstrel show.4

Opportunities for black performers in organized entertainment were scarce. After the Civil War, the minstrel show provided steady (albeit self-denigrating) work and experience. In the performance, the black entertainers contributed music, dancing, and humor of generally good quality. It is unfortunate that the thematic emphasis perpetuated sordid stereotypes. Burnt cork had become an established part of the show. All performers, regardless of the color of their skin, were required to use it. For blacks to wear burnt cork compounds the irony, for now, as the line of development is often stated, blacks

were imitating whites who were imitating blacks
who had initially imitated whites.

During the latter part of the nineteenth
century, the tone of the humor took on a very
different and sharper character.   The racist
stereotypes became more cruel and blatant.   The
increase in anti-black sentiment during the 1880s
and 1890s manifested itself in over 1700 lynchings
between 1889 and 1899, in the enactment of dis-
enfranchisement and segregation laws,[5] and in
minstrelsy insuring that "the image of the happy-
go-lucky, wide-grinnin', chicken-stealin', razor-
totin' darky became rigidly embedded in the
psyche of white America."[6]

From this showcase for racism rose three
important musical forms.   Two were first introduced in the minstrel show, but each became an
independent fad near the turn of the century.
The first of these was featured in the finale of
the minstrel show, which spotlighted a "walk-
around" dance.   The members of the company
would promenade across the stage in a high-
stepping manner.   These dances were those copied
by the slaves when they saw their white masters
strutting in fine fashion.

The cakewalk was originally a plantation
dance, just a happy movement they did to
the banjo music because they couldn't stand
still.   It was generally on Sundays, when
there was little work, that the slaves both
young and old would dress up in hand-me-
down finery to do a high kicking, prancing
walk-around.   They did a take off on the
high manners of the white folks in the
"big-house" but their masters, who gathered
around to watch the fun, missed the point.
It's supposed to be that the custom of a

prize started with the master giving a cake
to the couple that did the proudest
movement.[7]

The mid-1890s saw the cakewalk blossom into a
national fad. Contests, stage shows, and gala ex-
travaganzas promoted the dance. Bert A.
Williams and George W. Walker streamlined the
cakewalk of the minstrel show. Williams, playing
the Jim Crow character, and Walker, playing the
Zip Coon role, engaged in a two-couple routine,
which as part of a vaudeville sketch, made the
cakewalk fashionable. In 1898, they starred in
"Clorindy, or the Origin of the Cakewalk," the
first of several all-black shows featuring the
dance. John Philip Sousa brought the cakewalk
to Europe, where it enjoyed phenomenal success.

Early cakewalks were published unsyncopated. Structurally, they are similar to the
march. They are in effect marches written
specifically for the cakewalk dance. Their
popularity grew around the time of the beginnings
of ragtime. Cakewalks began to take on the
characteristics of ragtime (namely syncopation, as
they are both similar in form) as it gained in
popularity. By 1900, cakewalks and rags had become indistinguishable from one another. The
cakewalk, however, was not a progenitor of
ragtime. They are based on similar musical
forms, but developed independently of one another. Eventually the term cakewalk came to
mean a lightly syncopated rag. Kerry Mills, one
of the most prominent cakewalk composers, set
the standard for the cakewalk rag in 1897 with
his "At a Georgia Camp Meeting."

Like the cakewalk, the coon song grew
from minstrelsy and experienced a wave of
popularity near the turn of the century. The

lyrics of the coon songs conveyed the image of the "darky" stereotype:

> The term "coon" is scarcely less opprobrious today than "nigger." Yet the word "coon" in 1848 was merely one of a whole variety of designations for the Negro. Besides the dignified "Ethiopian," which appears on the covers of the Glee Books, other song titles in the series were: "The Jolly Darkey," "Virginny's Black Daughter," "Yaller Girls," "De Nigger's Banjo Hum," "De Cullered Cokett," "Dinah Doe and Mr. Crow."[8]

Most of the coon songs published prior to the mid-1890s were unsyncopated, but were soon available with ragtime accompaniments as the two forms intermixed. The images of black Americans portrayed in the coon songs enjoyed a life-span of over one hundred years, since the same vicious stereotypes remained a part of American musical and dramatic theater into the 1930s. The process of eradication of the racist basis for entertainment was painfully slow, and James P. Johnson saw it succeed only near the end of his career.

Three notable coon songs are interesting for historical perspective. The first of these was "Old Zip Coon," first sung by George Washington Dixon in 1834. Although the lyrics have long since been forgotten, the melody was published with the alternate title, "Turkey in the Straw," a commonly recognized tune which gives the musical flavor of the coon songs.[9] A song written by the well-known black comedian Ernest Hogan in 1895, "All Coons Look Alike to Me," was one of the most popular coon songs of the 1890s and the most misinterpreted of any. The title was adopted by white racists as a cruelly derisive comment conferring formless, sub-human characteristics on blacks. "Quite different was the song's intention, as the words reveal. A Negro girl jilts her lover because she has fallen in love with another. The key line of the song is her declaration that all Negroes except the new one look alike to her, sentiments obviously shared by all women in a similar situation."[10]   In 1896, Benjamin Robertson Harney, a white itinerant musician from Kentucky, became the first person to publish a syncopated arrangement using the word ragtime. At Tony Pastor's Theater in New York, Harney introduced his coon songs, "You've Been a Good Old Wagon But You Done Broke Down," and "Mr. Johnson Turn Me Loose."[11] Like the cakewalk, the coon song was not a progenitor of ragtime, but the use of ragtime piano arrangements projected the songs into a sphere of ragtime. Harney's forerunner songs were a tremendous success and initiated the ragtime craze.

"It is clear that all of the structural and harmonic practices of ragtime stem from the march. The rhythmic character of the rag, too, except for the one defining factor of syncopation had its precedents in the march."[12] Marches accompanied the minstrel troupes when they paraded through the streets of town. The history of this form needs little elucidation. Suffice it to say that by the turn of the century, military brass bands were very much in vogue. Along with the ballads, popular favorites, and light classics, their distinctive sound was that of a march. The cakewalk, the rag, and the march were all forms designated to accompany a popular dance called the two-step. Little distinction is made between these forms in many titles: "A Tennessee Jubilee; Rag-Time March and two-step," "Big Foot Lou; Cake-Walk-March-And-Two-Step," "The Rag-

Time Sports; CakeWalk-March and Two Step."
The march and the rag share a common formal
and tonal structure, differing only in the use of
syncopation in the rag. In summary, if a march
is syncopated, it becomes a rag.

In 1897, the white bandleader William H.
Krell became the first to have an instrumental
piano rag published. His "Mississippi Rag" began
the trend of purely instrumental ragtime, composed as a finished product independent of other
forms such as the Coon Song. Scott Joplin soon
became the "King of Ragtime Composers" with
his "Maple Leaf Rag," published in 1899. The
"Maple Leaf" was the first instrumental piece to
sell over one million copies of sheet music,
making it the prototype of composed ragtime and
the anthem of the style. Here a distinction must
be made, since the term ragtime came to encompass many things. Crucial to an understanding of
the formative essence of stride piano and a partial reconciliation of terminology is the delinea-
tion of the two lines of conceptual development
of ragtime.

> Ragtime is properly viewed not as a single
> unified tradition, but as two commingling
> and cross-pollinating traditions: one,   a
> commercial, notated music, developed to a
> sophisticated level by some composers, well
> known today because of its ample repre-
> sentation in surviving sheet music;   the
> other, a more complicated, improvised
> music--essentially a jazz piano in every
> respect except name--but lost to us for the
> lack of recordings.[13]

The distinction between these two traditions might
best be explained by considering what Edward
Berlin has called the genre and style of ragtime.

The ragtime genre is characterized by all
the published music bearing either the name or
spirit of ragtime. This would include everything
from Scott Joplin's piano masterpiece "Maple Leaf
Rag" to Irving Berlin's commercially successful
but virtually unsyncopated popular hit "Alexander's
Ragtime Band." Contrary to the current belief
that ragtime is exclusively piano music, the genre
includes both vocal and instrumental forms. Although the general public knew both forms as
ragtime, "it is evident, viewing the style
historically, that despite the ties existing between
vocal and piano strains of ragtime, a split
occurred; vocal ragtime merged with the
mainstream of popular music, while piano ragtime
inclined toward what became known as jazz."[14]

The mainstream of popular music was directed by the American music publishing industry,
given the figurative name of Tin Pan Alley. In
actuality, there were certain areas of New York
where publishers concentrated their offices. Originally centered on Times Square, 28th St. between
Fifth Avenue and Broadway soon became known
as Tin Pan Alley. The name is thought to be
literally derived: the sound of a dozen upright
pianos being played by song pluggers along this
block sounded like rattling tin pans.[15] The
tremendous success of this business was due in
large part to the widespread popularity of ragtime. Hailed as the first truly American music,
it combined the right mixture of black ethnic
feeling and standard dance forms to appeal to a
large audience. Its heyday coincided with the
dawn of the modern age, and with it came the
technology to mass produce and disseminate popular culture on an unprecedented scale. In the
hands of Tin Pan Alley, vocal and instrumental
ragtime was simplified, diluted, and cheapened to

the point of producing period pieces, most of
them soon dated.

The predominant vocal form exploited by
Tin Pan Alley was the coon song. Although the
form itself had waned by 1902, it had a great
effect on later forms. The introduction of a less
genteel vocabulary into popular songs was a radi-
cal departure from the sweet sentiments of
Victorian, romantic imagery. "The words of the
new black music were as different from the
words of the waltz-tragedies as was the music of
those waltzes from the jagged melodies of the
raging 'rags'.... The temperature of our popular
song shot up to the top of the thermometer."[16]
Two specific examples of the modification of
common lyrics were the replacement of babies
and mammies by babes and mammas. "Every
conceivable formula for capitalizing on ragtime
was attempted--synthesis with oriental motifs,
Spanish rhythms, patriotic themes, every standard
novelty device."[17]   Indian motifs became very
popular, surviving as Indian intermezzos to 1910.

The instrumental product of Tin Pan Alley
drew on many of the same resources as its vocal
counterpart. Since ragtime presented vast technical difficulties for the average pianist, the publishers on Tin Pan Alley generally issued simple
rags that were easily manageable by the local
dime store pianist. The chief priority of the
popular music industry was, after all, to make
money. These popular rags constitute one of
eight types of ragtime compositional sub-forms as
outlined by David Jasen.

In addition to the cakewalk, another early
form is the folk rag. "In the beginning, ragtime
compositions consisted of the stringing together of
assorted syncopated themes. These tunes were

played by wandering musicians who drifted from
town to riverboat, from saloons to sporting
houses."[18]   "Some folk rags are original creations,
but others have floating folk strains--not simply
folk songs, but favorite instrumental music passages which pop up in many rags.   It is not
known where they originated or who just used
them."[19]   The most striking examples are two
"medleys" conceived by John W. (Blind) Boone, a
black virtuoso concert pianist.   His "Rag Medley
#1," subtitled "Strains from the Alleys," includes
a strain captioned, "Make Me a Pallet on the
Floor."[20]   This tune is an example of a folk
melody which circulated through the black musical
tradition, surfacing in various places.   James P.
Johnson recorded "Make Me a Pallet on the
Floor" as a piano roll in 1926 and with the Rod
Cless Quartet in 1944.   (He is erroneously
credited as its composer in the introduction to
the Davin interviews.)

A fourth type of ragtime may be geographically defined as New Orleans ragtime.   The va-
lidity of attributing a regional style to New
Orleans is somewhat tenuous, as the style is ostensibly known only through the work of Jelly
Roll Morton.   Its published history is virtually
non-existent.   Even Morton published many works
years after they were composed.   The New Orleans piano tradition, then, should be considered
from a different perspective.   It belongs more to
the performer-oriented, improvisational style of
ragtime playing than to the written genre.   In
1911, Johnson recalled sneaking into Barron
Wilkins' place, a Harlem cabaret.   Jelly Roll
Morton "had just arrived from the West and he
was red hot.   The place was on fire!"[21]   Although Johnson was not yet sufficiently skilled to
"steal his stuff," he remarked that he was picked

to impersonate Morton's style in 1943 at the New
Orleans Jazz Carnival.

Perhaps the most well-known form is classic ragtime. It may be defined operationally "as
the piano rags of Scott Joplin, James Scott,
Joseph Lamb, and their immediate collaborators,
students and followers. The term classic was
promoted vigorously by John Stark, who published
the main work of these composers, to offset the
widely held conception of ragtime as a low-class
and shoddy musical product."[22] A more analyti-
cal approach takes into consideration what is
"classic" about this body of music. The "Maple
Leaf Rag" is considered to be the epitome of
classic ragtime. In the true sense of a classic,
it is the best or finest work of its kind and established a model for subsequent compositions.
Classic ragtime is thoroughly composed music:
the melodies, harmonies, counterpoint, and rhythms
are worked out in advance and notated as they
are meant to be played.

The works of Scott Joplin were very
popular with ragtime players, several of whom
Johnson credited with having taught him the clas-
sic rags they knew. Charley Cherry corrected
Johnson as he copied his Joplin rags. Alberta
Simmons taught Johnson the full "Maple Leaf,"
"Sunflower Slow Drag," and James Scott's "Frogs
Legs Rag." Ernest Green played Joplin's
"Gladiolus Rag." By 1912, Johnson remarked,
everybody knew the "Maple Leaf." "Scott Joplin
was a great forerunner. Joplin was fifty years
ahead of his time. Even today, who understands
'Euphonic Sounds'? It's really modern."[23]
Johnson was the first to record this Joplin
masterpiece--in June 1944.[24] He follows the
printed score much more closely than one would
expect of an improvisationally oriented musician.

His respect for Joplin's art is reflected in his strict rendition.

Closely tied to classic ragtime of the Joplin tradition is a form that might best be called "advanced" ragtime. It exists as the logical extension of the earlier classic form. Advanced ragtime compositions reveal more complex harmonies, greater variety in form, and a much more eclectic approach. Artie Matthews, a prominent composer of this era (1910-1920), worked with a variety of musical materials. His pastime rags reveal folk lyricism, explosive breaks, habanera (tango) rhythms, and other typical and very atypical ragtime devices. He composed and arranged blues tunes as well as Luckey Roberts' "Junk Man Rag." In 1919, while in Cleveland, Johnson met and became a very close friend of Charles Thompson. Thompson, another important composer of advanced ragtime, was strongly influenced by Johnson's playing.[25] Roberts, and Johnson (in the early part of his career), belong to another group of ragtime composers, the Eastern School. Their music experienced the most direct transformations to a jazz style in later years, when they took notice of a wider range of musical traditions.

The last category worth mentioning is the novelty rag. During the 1920s, when jazz had virtually replaced ragtime as the latest exotic popular music, the novelty piano solo remained as the last vestige of composed ragtime. "The novelty rag blended the earlier Tin Pan Alley ragtime with the tricks of the player piano riffs and embellishments to show off the technical virtuosity of the performer."[26] Zez Confrey's "Kitten on the Keys" was to novelty ragtime what Joplin's "Maple Leaf" was to classic ragtime. The novelty piano solo was very popular

during the 1920s and considered by some to be
jazz piano.[27]   The music of Confrey, Roy Bargy
(Paul Whiteman's pianist), Billy Mayerl and others
bore little resemblance to ethnically black music.
Although musically interesting of and by themselves, the novelty rags of these white piano virtuosos reflect a complete break from the Afro-
American musical tradition.   At best they are
derivative ragtime and certainly do not fall within
the sphere of jazz.   Yet, James P. Johnson wrote
and recorded many tunes which, for the sake of
marketability, were tagged as novelty piano solos.
"High Brown--Novelty Piano Solo," "Jingles--
Novelty Piano Solo," "Jungle Nymphs--Novelette,"
all retain the distinctively ethnic qualities which
are the hallmark of truly inspired Afro-American
music.

These, then, are the eight types of ragtime
which characterize the instrumental, composed
ragtime genre.   Conceptually distinct but historically connected are the various styles of ragtime
playing.   Each of the eight sub-forms mentioned
above spawned a related style of playing based on
corresponding notated devices.   In reality, each
performer had his own personal style of playing
that distinguished him from other players.   However, the individual stylistic differences between
the early players were not greatly distinctive or
completely confined geographically, as has been
generally assumed.[28]   The general features common to most styles of ragtime playing have been
determined by the published incidence of the
characteristics most deeply rooted in the Afro-
American musical tradition.   These had the most
profound effect on Johnson's playing.

"Piano Ragtime is separated into at least
three distinct sub-groups: piano renditions of ragtime songs; 'ragged' versions of pre-existing un-

syncopated music; and original, dance-oriented ragtime compositions."[29]   The first group mentioned
existed as both printed, syncopated arrangements
of popular songs and as personal renditions of
particular performers.   The printed music was a
product of Tin Pan Alley cashing in on ragtime
as a popular craze.   The latter styles were probably the ragtime Johnson first heard in Jersey
City, "mostly popular songs with a strong rhythm
and with syncopated vamps."   By 1912, Johnson
played "generally popular stuff," not surprisingly
since New York was the popular music capital.

> I played "That Barbershop Chord" ... "Lazy
> Moon" ... Berlin's "Alexander's Ragtime
> Band."
>   Then there were "instrumentals";
> piano arrangements of medleys of Herbert
> and Friml, popular novelties and music-hall
> hits--many by Negro composers.
>   Indian songs were popular then, and
> the girls at Dan Williams' used to sing
> "Hiawatha" ... "Red Wing" ... "Big Chief
> Battleaxe" ... "Come with Me to My Big
> Teepee" ... "Pony Boy"--all popular in the
> musical halls then.[30]

This tradition overlaps with the second type
of piano ragtime: "ragging" unsyncopated music.
This is ragtime's closest link with jazz.   Folk
songs, popular tunes, marches, and classical pieces
were all subjected to various syncopated renderings. Walter "One-Leg Shadow" Gould, an old
player himself, recalls even older players: "Old
Man Sam Moore was ragging the quadrilles and
schottisches before I was born.   He was born
'way before the [Civil] War."[31]   This tradition is
the essence of ragtime and what became jazz.
"Ragging" a tune, although not known by that
name, was known long before the first published

reference to ragtime.   James P. Johnson incor-
porated many classical pieces into his repertoire:
"Once I used Liszt's 'Rigoletto Concert
Paraphrase' as an introduction to a stomp.... I
did rag variations on 'William Tell Overture,'
Grieg's 'Peer Gynt Suite' and even a 'Russian
Rag' based on Rachmaninoff's 'Prelude in C Sharp
Minor,' which was just getting popular then."[32]

The third type of piano ragtime includes
the eight categories of published piano works.
The composers of classic ragtime hoped for accurate renderings based on the notated music.
Edward Berlin asserts: "While much of the
music-buying public probably did play the music
as written (or at least made an attempt to do
so), it is unlikely that professional ragtime
musicians, accustomed by training and inclination
to ragging all kinds of musical material, would
slavishly adhere to a printed score."[33]   The formal elements of written ragtime reveal the
general characteristics of the process of "ragging"
any type of music.

The structure of an original ragtime composition, like that of the march, is based on 16-bar
strains.   Each is a complete and independent unit,
generally divisible into 4-bar phrases.   The first
two 4-bar phrases combine to form an 8-measure
antecedent phrase to the combined second two 4-
bar phrases, which form an 8-measure consequent
phrase.   The march and the rag string the 16-bar
strains together in an A-B-C format.   The A and
B strains are in the tonic key, while the third
strain, commonly known as the "trio," is usually
in the subdominant key.   Various introductions,
bridges, and interludes are also included.   Although the AABBACCDD form is usually given as
the standard pattern of a rag, "looking at Joplin's
total output of piano works, around fifty-five in

all, there are at least twenty-four different
forms. And a similar variety of structures can
be found in the works of other major rag
composers."34

Harmonically, ragtime relies on "pure"
chords, as opposed to the substituted and embellished chords of later jazz styles. Tonic,
dominant seventh, and diminished chords predominate. The harmonic speed is somewhat slow.
A single harmony usually spans at least two
measures. Melodies are built on broken or arpeggiated chords. Eli Newberger refers to the ar-
peggiations which break up the main melodic line
as "pivot" notes,35 which are derived from earlier
banjo tunes. Although they often imply melan-
choly or reflective moods, ragtime melodic lines
remain distinct from blues elements. "In pre-1912
rags, blue notes are found most often--but not
exclusively--in rags by black composers.... To
retain perspective, it must be recognized that
these passages are exceptions; generally, the blues
influence in ragtime prior to 1912 was slight.
About 3 percent of the rags of this period have
been found to exhibit blues characteristics."36

By far the most striking characteristic of
ragtime is its rhythm. A steady, even beat
maintained in the left hand is juxtaposed against
a syncopated melody in the right hand. The tension created by these two different rhythms
makes ragtime instantly distinguishable from other
music. (The difficulty, of course, is distinguishing
music based on ragtime from the original form.)
Most ragtime made use of one, or, less frequently, a combination, of four rhythmic devices
which gives the music its animated character:
untied syncopation, tied syncopation, secondary rag
(or a "3 over 4" pattern), and dotted rhythms.37

1) Untied Syncopation   2a) Tied Syncopation

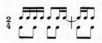 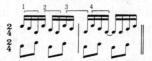

2b)   Tied Syncopation   3) Secondary Rag
      Across the Bar Line

4) Dotted Rhythm

The first two devices are actual syncopated motives, forcing the emphasis of normally unstressed beats. The second two are not. The secondary rag pattern displaces the normal accents not by syncopation, but by the superimposition of a one-two-three pattern over a one-two-three-four pattern, using the same submetric time intervals (i.e., these are not triplet figures). Dotted rhythms create their own momentum by disrupting evenly distributed time intervals (i.e., four sixteenth-notes in the example above).

While the right-hand treble part weaves melodies around these rhythmic figures, the left-

hand bass part maintains a steady beat and fur-
nishes the harmony. The characteristic pattern of
the ragtime left hand is that of an oom-pah. A
single note or octave is struck on the first beat,
and a chord or two-note interval is struck on the
second beat. This pattern is repeated for beats
three and four. The standard oom-pah is not a
rigid pattern. Various combinations of octaves,
single notes, and chords are present in the written ragtime repertory, ranging from walking octaves spanning several measures (Joplin's "Weeping
Willow"), to an entire strain of march-like chords
(Joplin's "Paragon Rag"). Regardless of the combination used, the feel is always that of a march;
one-two, one-two. It is important to realize that
ragtime oom-pah bass variations do not disrupt
the rhythm.

     In addition to admonishing performers to
play rags as written, classic ragtime composers
urged moderate and consistent tempos. "The
tradition of playing indicates that ragtime...was
based on a steady dance tempo, which creates a
subtle sensation of forward momentum through the
elasticity of inner rhythms, not through gross
shifts in tempo."[38] Ragtime became and
remained popular for 20 years because, in addition
to its refreshing sound, one could dance to it.
Sheet music covers reveal subtitles such as
cakewalks, two-steps, fox-trots, turkey-trots and
tangos.

     The various rhythmic characteristics, al-
though preserved in written form, existed before
the first rag was published. "In essence, the entire structure of ragtime represents a compromise
and regularization; its symmetry and order are
imposed, after the fact. It is not an exact
transcription of played ragtime of the 1890s but
a deliberate expurgation and correction of some

practices and a simplification of others...."[39] The practices of ragtime style were used differently by each player in adapting whatever musical material he happened to be playing. Ragtime devices could be used to play Chopin, Berlin, and even Joplin. So why then, is ragtime not generally considered to be part of the jazz tradition? One argument stems from rhythmic considerations. Jelly Roll Morton noted that "Ragtime is a certain type of syncopation and only certain tunes can be played in that idea. But jazz is a style that can be applied to any type of tune."[40] Perhaps he was referring to the four rhythmic devices and their close derivatives listed above. "As a style, it is dependent on repetition of rhythmic conventions, whether read strictly from a score or repeated in a 'head' arrangement. The style stresses a pattern of repeated rhythms, not the constant inventions and variations of jazz."[41]

As time progressed, musicians of James P. Johnson's generation began to reshape the rhythms of ragtime, expanding their potential rhythmically, harmonically, and melodically. Their music became more eclectic as increased cultural crosscurrents were whipped up by the modern age. By 1910, Johnson was starting to come into contact with people from very different musical and cultural backgrounds. New York jazz was at the point of conception.

IVY

(CLING TO ME)

WORDS BY
ALEX ROGERS

MUSIC BY
ISHAM JONES
AND
JIMMY JOHNSON

Irving Berlin, Inc.
MUSIC PUBLISHERS
1607 Broadway   New York

5

The Jungles, 1910--1913

In 1911, the Johnson family moved farther uptown to 99th Street. James P. was still in school and not quite old enough to patronize the cabarets of Hell's Kitchen or the few establishments in Harlem. An Irish Society Hall called McFarland's or the 100th Street Hall (located at 100th Street and Third Avenue) was approachable territory for Johnson. Run by a heavy drinker from Jersey City named Harry Souser, this basement dance hall featured four- or five-piece orchestras (such as the New Amsterdam Orchestra and Hallie Anderson's Orchestra). After the band was finished, Mr. Souser rolled an upright piano onto the floor and displayed his own ragtime stylings. When he was through, Johnson and other pianists played until four or five o'clock in the morning. James kept his books in the coal bin, and after a few hours of sleep went on to school. By this time, he was certain he was going to be a pianist and was waiting for the right opportunity.

During the summer of 1912, Johnson made his way out to Far Rockaway, a beach resort near Coney Island. He found a job in a place run by one Charles Ett. "It was just a couple of rooms knocked together to make a cabaret. They had beer and liquor, and out in the back yard there was a crib house for fast turnover.... It was a rough place, but I got nine dollars and tips, or about eighteen dollars a week over all. That was so much money that I didn't want to go back to school."[1] Far Rockaway had its own notables. At a place called "The Cool Off," one could find various Clef Club members, musicians who belonged to the black entertainers union established by James Reese Europe in 1910. Now forgotten characters like Kid Sneeze and Dude Finley were among those who played alongside Johnson in the Rockaway dives.

"That fall, instead of going back to school, I went to Jersey City and got a job in a cabaret run by Freddie Doyle. He gave me a two-dollar raise. In a couple of months, Doyle's folded up, and I came back to Manhattan and played in a sporting house on 27th St. between 8th and 9th Avenues, which was the Tenderloin then. It was run by a fellow named Dan Williams, and he had two girl entertainers that I used to accompany." They sang the popular Indian songs as well as most other popular hits of the day. Johnson played these, the popular instrumentals and semi-classics, and rags--his own and others. Besides Joplin, he recalled playing "Maori" by Will Tyers, and "The Dream" and "Peculiar Rag" by the legendary pianist Jack the Bear.[2]

Gotham and Attucks was the preeminent black publishing company in New York around 1912. Many great black musicians and performers gathered around the firm--Bert Williams, George Walker, Scott Joplin, Will Marion Cook, Joe Jordon, Tim Brymm. Its president, Cecil Mack (whose real name was R.C. McPherson), would later collaborate with Johnson, writing the lyrics to Johnson's music for Runnin' Wild, probably the second most popular black musical of the 1920s. Out of this show came the "Charleston," which became the theme song of the roaring twenties. In 1912, however, Johnson was still working out his first rags and had yet to learn musical notation. Although Johnson recalled Gotham and Attucks' interest in publishing his music, he could

not write it down and he knew no one who could
take the time to do it for him.

Johnson remained at Dan Williams' place
for only a few months.   During the winter of
1912-13 he held several jobs.   "One was playing
movie piano at the Nickelette at 8th Avenue and
37th Street.   They had movies and short acts for
short money.   Many vaudeville acts broke in
there, Florence Mills first sang there I recall....
In the spring of 1913, I really got started up in
the Jungles."[3]   Johnson was hired to play at Jim
Allan's place at 61st Street and Tenth Avenue.
He used to sneak into Allan's when he was younger by rolling down his knickers.   Allan's was a
remodeled cellar, with a bar upstairs and gambling downstairs.   James Weldon Johnson, in his
book The Autobiography of an Ex-Colored Man
which was published anonymously in 1912, describes the reaction of the novel's protagonist
upon his first encounter with a cabaret that
might easily have been patterned after Jim
Allan's.   It is an early reference to black music
in black literature and, in many ways,
foreshadows similar references in Harlem Renaissance literature of the 1920s.

We at length secured places at a table in
a corner of the room and, as soon as we
could attract the attention of one of the
busy waiters, ordered a round of drinks.
When I had somewhat collected my senses,
I realized that in a large back room into
which the main room opened, there was a
young fellow singing a song, accompanied
on the piano by a short, thickset, dark
man.   After each verse he did some dance
steps, which brought forth great applause
and a shower of small coins at his feet.
After the singer had responded to a rousing

encore, the stout man at the piano began
to run his fingers up and down the
keyboard. This he did in a manner which
indicated that he was master of a good
deal of technique. Then he began to play;
and such playing! I stopped talking to
listen. It was music of a kind I had never
heard before. It was music that demanded
physical response, patting of the feet,
drumming of the fingers, or nodding of the
head in time with the beat. The barbaric
harmonies, the audacious resolutions, often
consisting of an abrupt jump from one key
to another, the intricate rhythms in which
the accents fell in the most unexpected
places, but in which the beat was never
lost, produced a most curious effect, and
too, the player--the dexterity of his left
hand in making rapid octave runs and jumps
was little short of marvellous [sic]; and
with his right he frequently swept half the
keyboard with clean-cut chromatics which
he fitted in so nicely as never to fail to
arouse in his listeners a sort of pleasant
surprise at the accomplishment of the feat.[4]

In addition to cabarets that featured entertainment much like this, there were other outlets for
active entertainment.

One night a week, Johnson played for
Drake's dancing class on 62nd Street. It was actually just a dance hall, but at that time it was
easier and cheaper for a black establishment to
get a dancing school license than a dance hall
license. Also known as the Jungles Casino, it
was another basement establishment. There were
no decorative fixtures, and it came complete with
furnace and coal bin, where patrons could hide
their liquor. The floor was cement with poor

drainage. When it rained, the dancing had to be
interrupted periodically so the floor could be
mopped. Willie "The Lion" Smith recalled that
the piano was surrounded with candles to keep it
dry in the dank atmosphere.[5] The majority of
the clientele of the Jungles Casino hailed
originally from the southeastern seaboard--Georgia
and South Carolina. Many were Gullahs and
Geechies who had come north to work as
longshoremen. There were no teachers. People
came to dance as they pleased to the piano accompaniments of Johnson and his colleagues.
Two-steps, waltzes, schottisches, and the latest
popular dance craze, "The Metropolitan Glide,"
were all "taught" to anyone who cared to watch.

At various points in his playing, Johnson
incorporated ragtime. The older dancers, he said,
didn't care for it, but the young arrivals from
the South enjoyed it and used the opportunity to
display their dancing prowess. These people were
from the ring-shout region of the South. Although the formal ring might no longer have been
maintained, their dancing drew on elements of the
ring-shout. As Johnson recalled:

> The dances they did at the Jungles Casino
> were wild and comical--the more pose and
> the more breaks, the better. These Charles-
> ton people and the other southerners had
> just come to New York. They were
> country people and they felt homesick.
> When they got tired of two-steps and
> schottishces (which they danced with a lot
> of spieling), they'd yell: "Let's go back
> home!" ... "Let's do a set!" ... or "Now put
> us in the alley!" I did my "Mule Walk" or
> "Gut Stomp" for these country dances.
> Breakdown music was the best for
> such sets, the more solid and groovy the

better. They'd dance, hollering and scream-
ing until they were cooked. The dances
ran from fifteen to thirty minutes, but
they kept up all night long or until their
shoes wore out--most of them after a
heavy day's work on the docks.[6]

The "Mule Walk" and "Gut Stomp" mentioned are
Johnson compositions. They are, as he puts it,
ragtime arrangements of set dances. They are
also, as he played them in 1913, the beginnings
of the stride idiom. Other cotillion steps gave
rise to the "Charleston" rhythm. Johnson said he
composed eight "Charlestons" (so named, of
course, for the home of the people he played for)
at the Jungles Casino. One became the famous
"Charleston." Johnson's playing at this time was
still very much a ragtime style, although the
Jungles Casino provided ample experience for him
to develop facility with instantaneous invention
(i.e., improvisation). In addition, another musical
tradition was just beginning to make its way to
New York, one that did contribute to the formation of jazz from ragtime in the Northeast.

6

The Blues

The blues has always followed and is still following an independent path through musical history.
The subcultural survival of the blues as a distinct
idiom through the years illustrates an important
aspect of the black experience in America.   The
harsh realities of life, particularly in a racist
society, have been expressed best in a vocal form
like the blues.   Ragtime and the blues were, as
folk music, manifestations of two different emotional forces.   The basis for the development of
jazz was the synthesis of these two traditions:
the instrumental felicity of ragtime and the vocal
pathos of the blues.

The place of the blues in the New York
musical scene of James P. Johnson's youth was
somewhat tenuous.   The presence of ragtime was
obvious, but the impact of the blues, as either
composed, commercial music or a folk form has
been disputed.   Gunther Schuller contends that
one of the innovations in James P. Johnson's
music was the incorporation of various elements
of the blues.[1]   Others, like Max Harrison, take
an opposing view: "For the New Yorkers it involved almost everything except the blues...."[2]
Harold Courlander points out that "in reality,
there are few individual elements found in the
blues that may not be found somewhere else, in
other kinds of Negro singing."[3]   Since the blues
has become the prototype for American black vocal music, similar characteristics evident in other
types of singing have thus been denoted as blues
elements.   These characteristics were eventually

absorbed in instrumental music and became one of
the hallmarks of jazz.   The features Johnson assimilated into his playing have their roots in
much older Afro-American musical forms to which
he was sensitive.

The development of the blues reflects the
nature of the black vocal tradition in general,
which ultimately derives from the music of the
slaves.   It is sometimes claimed that the blues
derive directly from the spirituals.   While it is
true that the spirituals contributed greatly, other
non-religious music also shaped the form and
function of the blues.   In addition to the
spirituals, the "slave seculars," shout songs and
work songs were primary antecedents of the
blues.   The work songs developed from the need
to ease a difficult situation.   By accompanying
their work with song, the slaves offset the stul-
tifying routine and helped them endure.   The
functional basis of the work songs is characteristic of other Afro-American music, including
ballads, slave seculars, and the blues.   "The
secular songs of slavery were 'non-religious,' occasionally anti-religious, and were often called
'devil songs' by religious folk.   The 'seculars'
expressed the skepticism of black slaves who
found it difficult to take seriously anything sug-
gesting the religious faith of the white
preachers....   The blues reflect the same exis-
tential tension.[4]

From a different theological perspective but
in a similar way, the blues issue from the
spirituals.   Since their earthly existence was almost uniformly miserable, the slaves imbued their
religious music with thoughts of salvation.   The
goal was to eventually reach Jordan (i.e., heaven),
where they would finally be free.   "The blues is
formed out of the same social and musical fabric

that the spiritual issued from, but with the blues the social emphasis becomes more personal, the 'Jordan' of the song much more intensely a human accomplishment,"[5] observes LeRoi Jones.

Like the spirituals the shout songs contributed much to the form the blues took. As Jones puts it:

> Blues issued directly out of the shout and, of course, the spiritual. The three-line structure of blues was a feature of the shout. The first two lines of the song were repeated, it would seem, while the singer was waiting for the next line to come. Or, as was characteristic of the hollers and shouts, the single line could be repeated again and again, either because the singer especially liked it, or because he could not think of another line.[6]

Common to both the shout and the spiritual, directly descended from African music, is the call-and-response pattern. A short "call" phrase, usually of two bars duration, is answered by an equally short "response" phrase. These may be either vocal or instrumental. The repeated phrase evolved into what is called a "riff" in instrumental blues and jazz, although the term is also used more generally to refer to any short, repeated rhythmic phrase.

The evolution of the blues as a recognizable phenomon parallels that of most other black secular music. Emancipation catapulted blacks into a self-sufficient life. They had more time for activities other than work or religion. With the responsibility of caring for themselves and their families came the realization of the difficulty of existence in American society. The blues became the outlet for this worldly, secular frustration. Where the spiritual looked toward heaven, the blues looked toward satisfaction of earthly needs and desires. They express the truth of emotional and physical circumstances that seemed inescapable. "Freedom took on historical specificity when contrasted with legal servitude. It meant that simple alternatives, which whites took for granted, became momentous options for newly 'free' black slaves."[7] Frank Tirro remarks, "Blues are not intrinsically pessimistic even though they often tell of defeat and downheartedness, for in expressing the problems of poverty, migration, family disputes, and oppression, the blues provide a catharsis which enables the participants to return to their environment with resignation, if not optimism."[8] James P. Johnson said: "The Blues are the feelings of people, their protests, hopes, loves, hates; a mingling of feelings all rolled together."[9] Blues are often upbeat and filled with humorous innuendo and double entendre, an approach which the poet Langston Hughes referred to as "laughing to keep from crying."

LeRoi Jones called the blues "primarily a verse form and secondarily a way of making music."[10] Seen in this way, the functional basis of the musical attributes of the blues becomes apparent. The blues is not so much a musical form as a vehicle for expression of the lyrics. What is characteristic of all black singing is particularly important in the presentation of the blues. There is scant evidence to pinpoint a time or place which produced the first blues. "In New Orleans an old fiddler said, 'The blues? Ain't no first blues! The blues always been.'"[11] Its inception is clearly post-bellum and firmly rooted in rural musical origins. The blues takes its shape and style during the performance. It is the personal creation of the individual, reflecting his response to a particular situation. It seems logical that the first instrument to convey successfully these individual feelings would be the voice. Its expressive range is limited only by the emotional intensity of the performer.

The blues makes use of one technique which gives the music recognizable character (aside from structural forms)--the use of the so-called blues scale or blue notes. Many writers have characterized the essence of this melodic basis of the blues. Suffice it to say here that the "blue notes" are considered to be the flatted third and the flatted seventh scale degrees.

The Blues Scale[12]

(The square note head indicates a blue note, whose pitch may vary by more than a half tone, ranging between a sharp and a flat intonation of the designated pitch.)

The blues scale "developed out of melodic-harmonic practices peculiar to African music only upon contact with European harmony."[13] However, merely introducing these accidentals into an otherwise diatonic scale is neither the feature of the blues that makes it successful or distinctive, nor an accurate analysis of melody in black vocal music. There are examples of other flatted scale degrees in black music. Rudi Blesh mentions the use of the flatted fifth. In addition, "the American composer, Lou Harrison, has extracted a composite scale from a number of blues performances. In this the added intervals of the fourth and sixth are shown flatted."[14] Although the flatted third and seventh are predominant, the "blues scale" is by no means absolute. "One may ask whether certain 'true' tones according to our scale are not regarded by at least some traditional singers as centers of gravity around which there is a microtonic play. One informant, a country-style blues singer in Alabama, explained that he 'played with the notes' in the same manner that he 'played with the beats.'"[15] The incredible flexibility of the human voice, through portamento, undulation, vibrato, falsetto, and assorted shouting, whining, moaning, and growling, enables the performer to construct his own "scale" to suit his emotional purpose in singing the blues.

Among the first significant blues compositions published were the works of the noted composer and orchestra leader William Christopher (W.C.) Handy. He combined elements of ragtime, minstrel songs, and the blues in many themes, such as "Memphis Blues" and "St. Louis Blues," which have become jazz standards. A standard blues pattern emerged which served as the scaffold for subsequent works: 12 bars constitute a chorus. Each is broken into three 4-bar phrases. The lyric form adheres to an AAB format, with the actual words falling on only the first two bars of each 4-bar phrase. The remaining two bars allow the "response" of the accompaniment to the "call" of the singer. The basic harmonic outline is tonic, subdominant, tonic, dominant, and tonic: I IV I V I.

Typical Blues Pattern[16]

Measure	1 2 3 4	5 6 7 8	9 10 11 12
Singer	a——rest	a——rest	b——rest
Instruments	back-break-	back-break-	back—break—
Harmony	A	B	C
	I———————	IV—— I——	V—IV—I———

Although this is only a schematic, most of the commercial published blues which soon followed adhered strictly to this format, while the country blues of southern rural areas continued to place emphasis on individual conception.

The effect of the blues on black music in New York was, to a large extent, determined by sociological attitudes. There is a formidable body of evidence that suggests that the blues was in no way indigenous to New York. The blues had successfully propagated itself throughout the South from mid-reconstruction (1880) to the present. Yet, there was, before the advent of jazz, some sociological or psychological filter which managed to prevent the heritage of the blues from germinating in northern cities. Garvin Bushell gives some indication of the attitudes of the black community around 1910-15.

Most of the Negro population in New York then had either been born there or had been in the city so long, they were fully acclimated. They were trying to forget the traditions of the South; they were trying to emulate the whites. You couldn't deliver a package to a Negro's front door. You had to go down to the cellar door.

And Negroes dressed to go to work. They
changed into work clothes when they got
there. You usually weren't allowed to play
blues and boogie-woogie in the average
Negro middle class home. That music supposedly suggested a low element. And the
big bands with the violins, flutes, piccolos
didn't play them either.[17]

Any movement by blacks from the South to the
North before World War I triggered in them a
middle class ethic. "Negroes appeared whose
Promised Land was where they were now, if only
they could 'save a little money, send the kids to
school, get a decent place to live...'"[18] To be
successful, it was necessary for them to reject
all southern cultural habits. Their model, as with
the earlier churches established in the South, was
white society. The blues, with its vulgar imagery
and crude musicianship, was scorned as part of
this cultural rejection. The society bands of
James Reese Europe's Clef Club orchestra, Will
Marion Cook, and Ford Dabney played their ragtime orchestrations of the popular favorites, but
avoided the lowly elements of the blues. Their
interest was in gaining recognition by all of
society as respectable musicians. There was not
yet a market for the distinctively ethnic black
folk music.

James P. Johnson cited the blues of W.C.
Handy as his first significant exposure to the
form.[19] Its emergence on the scene in 1912 did
not dramatically change the orientation of New
York musicians. In the years just before World
War I, a significant wave of migration to northern cities from the rural South began.

The largest mass migration of Negroes
northward occurred during the First World

War, which greatly increased the demand
for labor in the production of war materials at the same time that it reduced the
labor supply in the North by cutting off
immigration. The migration of Negroes to
the North was originally stimulated by
northern employers who sent labor agents
even to the deep South, and it was furthered by letters from Negroes who had mi-
grated. This migration, which began in
1916, reached its maximum in 1917, and
largely ended in 1918, involved about
500,000 Negroes.[20]

The new arrivals, having brought with them their
country blues, sought out a forum for expression
in the cities. "You could only hear the blues
and real jazz in the gutbucket cabarets where the
lower class went.... Gradually, the New York
cabarets began to hear more of the real pure
jazz and blues by musicians from Florida, South
Carolina, Georgia, Louisiana, etc. What they
played was more expressive than had been heard
in New York to that time."[21] James P. Johnson
called this music the "natural blues."[22] By 1920,
the blues (along with other forms of black
country and folk music like the ring-shout) had
settled in New York.

There is an interesting parallel between the
development of jazz in New York and that in
New Orleans in the previous decade.[23] In New
Orleans, prior to 1894, a social hierarchy existed
that maintained a cultural separation between the
lower class, "uptown" blacks and the refined
"downtown" Creoles of color. With the enactment
of the Louisiana Legislative code no. 111, any
person of any African ancestry was considered to
be a Negro and treated in a discriminatory
manner. This constraint of segregation destroyed

the economic and social order of the Creole community. They tried to maintain their cultural integrity by insisting on retaining their old life-styles. This was difficult in view of their drastically lowered economic and social station. In 1897, city alderman Sidney Story proposed Section I of Ordinance 13,032 C.S., restricting prostitution (which by this time had become a major industry) to a thirty-eight block area. This district became known as Storyville, and opened up a new, large market for musicians and entertainers. Both the self-taught musicians and the classically trained downtown Creoles found work. Paul Dominguez, a Creole violinist, described the plight of the Creole:

> You see, we Downtown people, we try to be intelligent. Everybody learn a trade, like my daddy was a cigarmaker and so was I.... See, us Downtown people, we didn't think so much of this Uptown jazz until we couldn't make a living otherwise ... they made a fiddler out of a violinist--me, I'm talking about. A fiddler is not a violinist, but a violinist can be a fiddler. If I wanted to make a living, I had to be rowdy like the other group. I had to jazz it or rag it or any other damn thing.[24]

The Creoles of color were forced out of necessity to work alongside the uptown blacks. Many were eager to learn from each other; the blacks introducing the Creoles to the blues and ragtime, and the Creoles inspiring the blacks with classical technique and conception. Many Creoles became leading figures by 1922 (Sidney Bechet, Jelly Roll Morton). An important point, and one which makes New Orleans music distinct from New York music, is that the classically oriented Creoles had to compromise their values. The black musician and his earthy, blues-based approach were the dominant and driving forces behind the evolution of jazz music in New Orleans.

In New York, a similar process was taking place, but the circumstances of the conflict were different. The distinctions between the classes were not ethnic, but socio-economic. The older established musicians wished to maintain their respectability and resisted making their music too ethnic. The exponents of the rougher music were forced to keep to themselves, creating a subculture of their own. Just as the younger Creoles in New Orleans expressed curiosity about the lower class music, so did younger musicians in New York try to pick up on and incorporate elements of the blues. However, the classically oriented musicians had the upper hand. James P. Johnson recalled how the classical approach contributed to the distinctive sound of New York piano:

> The other sections of the country never developed the piano as far as the New York boys did. Only lately have they caught up. The reason the New York boys became such high-class musicians was because the New York piano was developed by the European method, system and style. The people in New York were used to hearing good piano played in concerts and cafés. The ragtime player had to live up to that standard. They had to get orchestral effects, sound harmonies, chords and all the techniques of European concert pianists who were playing their music all over the city.[25]

Some northern musicians were not eager to resort to the vulgarities of the lower class.

James P. Johnson was of a different mind. He
recognized the value of the ethnicity in the folk
forms and made a conscious effort to assimilate
the qualities which were scorned by others.   The
expressive qualities associated with the blues pervade all Afro-American folk-oriented vocal music.
This quality of vocal phrasing had a profound effect in subsequent instrumental forms.   The approximation of the qualities of the human voice
on an ostensibly percussive instrument like the
piano is more difficult than the same transforma-
tion on other instruments.   Structurally, perhaps,
Johnson's blues adhere to the commercial format
of Handy's prototypes.   Some consider his work
with the blues (and the blues of most stride
pianists) less authentic than the blues of the
Midwest.   Johnson's appreciation and understanding
of the blues as a distinct folk idiom may not
have been as successful as his grasp of other folk
forms (e.g., the ring-shout and cotillions).   Yet,
Johnson made innovative efforts to expand the
expressive possibilities of the piano and introduce
the "blues feeling" into his music.   The trend
toward vocalization and the emotional character
of Johnson's playing are clearly adopted from the
blues and not polite society music.   His use of
riffs, blue notes, approximating quarter-tone
changes with blues clusters, and call-and-response
patterns are characteristic of not only the blues
but most black vocal music.   Although tempered
by the intrumental, pianistic sound of ragtime,
the fusion of all these elements represents the
formative essence of jazz.

7

The Ticklers, 1913--1916

In 1913, the synthesis of a more expressive musical conception was just beginning. The blues was not yet popular, and the influx of Southerners had not yet reached its peak. Yet Handy's blues were being played, and places like Allan's and George Lee's (another cabaret where Johnson played) provided a forum for entertainers to try the latest music. In 1944, Johnson and his New York Orchestra recorded what he considered to be a sampling of the music heard in the Jungles around 1913. In addition to "Euphonic Sounds" by Scott Joplin, the group waxed "The Dream--Slow Drag"[1] and W.C. Handy's "Hesitation Blues."

Johnson recalled playing his first "Pigfoot Hop" in 1913. At Phil Watkin's place on 61st Street he was paid $1.50 to play for the night, plus all the gin and chitterlings he could consume. "This was my first 'Chitterlin Strut' or parlor social, but later in the depression I became famous at 'Gumbo Suppers,' 'Fish Fries,' 'Egg Nog Parties,' and 'Rent Parties.' I loved them all. You met people."[2] The generous hospitality offered at these all-you-can-eat festivals had their unfortunate side-effects. "At an all-night party, you started at 1:00 A.M., had another meal at 4:00 A.M., and sat down again at 6:00 A.M. Many of us suffered later because of eating and drinking habits started in our younger socializing days."[3]

Johnson soon undertook his first formal musical training. He had become friendly with

Ernest Green, a cabaret tickler who was also very proficient in the popular classical repertory. Johnson recalled his virtuoso renditions of the "William Tell" and "Light Cavalry" Overtures. Green's mother encouraged Johnson to study formally with an Italian music teacher named Bruto Giannini. "Ernest's mother got opera lessons from old professor Giannini by doing his housework, and she got him to teach me my harmony and counterpoint for just a dollar a lesson. He taught me for four years. I had to throw away my fingering and learn to put the right finger on the right note. I was on Bach, and double thirds need good fingering."[4]

Although some sources indicate that Johnson studied with Giannini while still in Jersey City, there is evidence to the contrary. In his conversation with Tom Davin, Johnson implies that he started with Giannini in 1913; 1914 is given by Charles Edward Smith in his liner notes to Johnson's "New York Jazz" album. Johnson also refers to Ernest Green as "a new friend of mine" after he had moved to New York.[5] It is therefore more likely that Johnson's training with Giannini began sometime around 1913 and lasted to 1916 or 1917. The time sequence is important, as it appears that Johnson began serious study not as a child of eight or nine, but after playing many professional engagements and building groundwork for his own style.

Johnson continued to listen to, admire, and steal the tricks and effects of other players. Most of these players never published anything or recorded a piano roll or phonograph record. Their names linger only in the recollections of their more famous contemporaries. Sam Gordon, Johnson recalled, played at the Elk's Cafe at 137th Street and Lenox Ave., an early Harlem

club. He was classically trained in Germany and
picked up syncopation in the United States. "He
was a great technician who played an arabesque
style that Art Tatum made famous later. He
played swift runs in sixths and thirds, broken
chords, one-note tremolandos and had a good left
hand.... Fred Bryant from Brooklyn was a good
all-around pianist. He played classical music and
had a velvet touch. The piano keys seemed to
be extensions of his fingers. Incidentally, as far
as I know, he invented the backward tenth. I
used it and passed it on to Fats Waller. It was
the keynote of our style."[6]

Other players Johnson remembered included
Fats Harris, who played in Chelsea. He had an
original stomp tune called "Fats Harris Rag" that
especially struck Johnson. Bob Gordon played at
Allan's before Johnson. He was called the March
King, and wrote "Oh, You Drummer," a popular
tune then. Freddie Singleton relieved Johnson at
the Jungles Casino occasionally. One of the most
cryptic but nonetheless original players was Kitchen Tom, who played quadrilles, set dances, and
rags, in addition to an original left-hand rhythm
that was later named the walking, Texas, or
boogie-woogie bass. Johnson heard Kitchen Tom
(whose real name Johnson could not recall ever
having known) play it years before it became
popular in the Midwest. Many jazz instrumen-
talists got started with a group from Charleston,
South Carolina, called the Jenkins Orphanage
Asylum Band, whose membership consisted of
black orphan boys aged eight to eighteen. The
band toured the black areas of many Northern
cities, passing the hat after each performance.
Most of their repertoire consisted of marches,
minstrel, and cotillion tunes.

The playing of Richard "Abba Labba" McLean had a profound influence on Johnson, who had met him playing in Chelsea in late 1914. Abba Labba was a favorite with many working girls. He played for laundresses and cooks, who supplied him with fancy clothes (pilfered from their customers' laundry) and good food. The cooks salvaged what was called cold kina (keena). The cook was entitled to leftover food from the white family's meal, so there was plenty of cold kina, or good leftover food, for the cook's family. Living so well off his women friends, Abba Labba was never forced to take a steady job. He often made only a brief appearance, playing just long enough to impress everyone, and then left.[7] "Abba Labba had a beautiful left hand and did wonderful bass work. He played with half-tone and quarter-tone changes that were new ideas then. He would run octaves in chords, and one of his tricks was to play "Good Night, Beloved, Good Night" in schottische, waltz and ragtime. I fell on his style and copied a lot of it."[8]

Johnson met three men in 1913-14 who were not only great inspirations to him, but who became his close friends and well-known figures in their own right. In 1913, while Johnson was playing at Allan's, he met "Luckey" Roberts. They were introduced at a party by their mutual friend Ernest Green. Charles Luckeyth Roberts was born in Philadelphia in 1887. He started to learn to play the piano at age five, but spent a large part of his youth touring with vaudeville and minstrel shows, performing as singer, dancer, and expert tumbler. Born a Quaker, Roberts stayed clear of alcohol, tobacco, and drugs all his life. He did have his vice, however. Much to the chagrin of his friends, Roberts was a pool shark who hustled many Harlem thugs and gangsters. The course of his career in music is similar to Johnson's. In addition to possessing superlative keyboard technique, Roberts composed the music for many musical shows and revues, several popular hits, and symphonies and other fully orchestrated works.

Roberts's most successful venture by far was the society orchestra he led during the 1920s. Roberts and his dinner-jacketed orchestra were the favorite entertainers at private parties on Fifth Avenue, in Palm Beach, and Newport. Among their clientele were the Astors, the Warburtons, the Wanamakers, the Goulds, and the Vanderbilts. Roberts commanded fees of a thousand dollars and more a night, a sizable jump from ten dollars a week in the dives of Philadephia and Baltimore. With the Second World War came the end of the big parties. Roberts bought the Rendevous restaurant in Harlem which he ran from 1942 (with singing waiters and his own occasional piano playing) until his retirement in 1954.[9]

"In the beginning he could only play in one key, F sharp. He used to play for a singer; they'd say it was too high and he'd play the same thing an octave down."[10] By 1910, Roberts had become New York's premier player, holding the piano chair at Barron Wilkin's club. He was unusually short, only four feet ten inches, but had large and powerful hands that could stretch an interval of a fourteenth on the piano. Johnson recalled that " ... he played tenths as easy as others played octaves. His tremolo was terrific, and he could drum on one note with two or three fingers in either hand. His style in making breaks was like a drummer's: he'd flail his hands in and out, lifting them high. A very spectacular pianist."[11] He was capable of playing lightning fast chromatic runs stretching several octaves, a

trick no one else seemed able to copy. Roberts
also has the distinction of being the first New
York ragtime pianist to have a composition
published.   His "Junk Man Rag," published in
1913, is undoubtedly a simplified arrangement, as
Roberts's recorded performance is immensely more
complicated and difficult.   His "Pork and Beans"
was a favorite with Eastern players, having a
third strain that rhythmically simulates a rubber
band stretching and then snapping.[12]

Johnson became friendly with Roberts, and
studied his playing.   Abba Labba and, a little
later, George Gershwin on his frequent trips to
Harlem were also "students" of Roberts.   Though
Johnson learned a great deal from Roberts, particularly about keyboard showmanship, he was
looking for a more solid piano style, grounded on
fundamentals as well as eccentric technique.

Roberts is one of the two most renowned
early New York ragtime players.   The other
Johnson met during the summer of 1914 when he
made his way to Atlantic City.   He stopped at a
place called the Belmont where Eubie Blake was
playing.   Johnson recalled how he "caught" one of
Blake's rags on this visit.   Blake is a little more
dramatic in his account of their first encounter:

And James P. Johnson!   Black James we
called him.   I wrote "Troublesome Ivories"
to have a number to cut everybody with.
It was even hard for me to play.   Black
James, he was only sixteen years old, he
came by where I was workin' in Atlantic
City and he heard me play the piece twice
and he had it.   Only sixteen!   He was still
drinkin' sarsparilla then.   Greatest piano
player I ever heard.   I let him sit in for
me for twenty minutes while I took a

break.   I come back and he's playin'
"Troublesome Ivories" without no mistakes.
I make mistakes, but not him.[13]

Of course Johnson was a little older than sixteen,
but the point of the story is not changed.

James Hubert Blake was born in Baltimore
in 1883. He began organ and piano lessons at an
early age and, like Johnson, listened attentively
to the syncopated sounds emanating from local
saloons. As he practiced, he experimented with
his own syncopated variations.   "One day my
mother came home from work early and heard
me playing like that. She said, 'Take that ragtime out of my house!' That's the first time I
ever heard the word ragtime."[14]   Blake was
especially impressed by "Florodora," a light opera
of English origin by Leslie Stuart. The show featured music that moved through many different
keys, a characteristic Blake incorporated into his
own playing and composing.   As an adolescent,
Blake played at Aggie Shelton's bawdy house,
moving into prize-fighter Joe Gans's Goldfield
Hotel in Baltimore in 1907. From 1910 to 1915,
he spent his summers in Atlantic City and the
remainder of the year in New York.

In 1915, he teamed with lyricist Noble
Sissle, forming one of the most productive
songwriting teams of all time. Their traveling
act, "The Dixie Duo," was very popular and
played top-rank vaudeville theaters. In 1921, the
team of Sissle and Blake (along with the comedy
team of Miller and Lyles, who later worked with
Johnson) produced the most successful of all black
musicals of the decade, "Shuffle Along." The big
hit from the show, "I'm Just Wild About Harry,"
was later used by Harry Truman in his presiden-
tial campaign. Blake continued to compose, going

in and out of retirement several times through
the years.   Before his success as a popular song
writer, he was, as Johnson put it, "one of the
foremost pianists of all time."

In addition to "Troublesome Ivories," Blake
composed many rags of pre-World War I vintage.
Most were not published until he had the opportunity to start his own music company in the
early 1970s.   One of these, later known as "The
Charleston Rag," was recorded by Blake in 1921
as "Sounds of Africa."   It is an excellent example
of East coast ragtime.   Boogie and standard rag
dominate the bass patterns, and a variety of syncopated figures and expressive devices mark the
treble part.   These were all techniques Johnson
picked up and expanded.   Rudi Blesh has said
that in the course of research for his historic
book, They All Played Ragtime (written with Harriet Janis), he was not aware that Eubie Blake
had ever been a preeminent "tickler."   It was
James P. Johnson who mentioned Blake's piano
skill to Blesh, a tip-off that probably initiated
Blake's return to an active career performing
ragtime.

Later, during the summer of 1914, Johnson
won a piano contest in Egg Harbor near Atlantic
City.   He played his own "Twilight Rag," and
"Steeplechase Rag" which he recorded as piano
rolls in 1917.   The latter was published in 1939
under the title "Over the Bars."   The original
title may have been a reference to either the
great rollercoaster at Coney Island, called the
Steeplechase,[15] or the Steeplechase amusement
pier on the Boardwalk in Atlantic City.   Johnson
mentioned another of his compositions, "Night-time
in Dixieland," which was never recorded or
published, and remains only as an obscure
reference.

After a brief return to New York, Johnson
went to Newark, New Jersey in the fall of 1914.
There he met Willie "The Lion" Smith, a first-
class tickler who came to be one of Johnson's
closest friends.   Smith was playing in a place
called Randolph's, located in the tough section of
Newark known as the Coast.   Johnson was traveling with a singer-dancer named Lillie Mae Wright,
who later became Mrs. James P. Johnson.   Her
first husband had been a piano player named Fred
Tunstall, better known as "The Tonsil."   He was
a pimp who preferred to live off his girls rather
than take a steady job.   "He was a sporty
dresser: green ties, high stiff collars, and a Norfolk coat with pleats that spread out when he
took his seat at the piano.   He was a piano
player worth hearing if you could catch him when
the mood was on him."[16]   Lillie Mae Wright was
not partial to Tunstall's assertive manner, as
Smith recalled, and left him for Johnson, a man
she could easily manage.

Lillie Mae and James P. stopped in at
Randolph's hoping to find jobs working together.
She was hired as an entertainer, but the manager
insisted he already had a piano player, Willie
Smith (he was not yet known as The Lion).   As
Smith recalled, "Lillie figured the way to get
Jimmy in on the deal was to give me a hard
time."   This she did by singing in the wrong key.
She and Smith argued, and Lillie started hollering
for a pianist who could accompany her properly,
all the while motioning James P. to the piano.
Willie refused to concede.   "After she ran out of
excuses I said, 'Come on, what can you sing?'
She said she'd like to do 'That Funny Man from
Dixieland' and this time we really got together
and had all the customers clapping their hands
right along with us."[17]

After her first set, Lillie introduced the two pianists, who began to exchange ideas. "Although Johnson was actually a shy, retiring type, we immediately hit it off. In later years I did a lot of his fighting for him as he never seemed to want to bother. That is, I helped him out in the brawls around the saloons.... Back in 1914, Jimmy and I were just two young boys who played piano by ear. We couldn't read or write music, but we were to both learn very soon. As the years went by we became like twins and came up together."[18] Johnson was able to get a job at the Kinney Hall. When Smith left Randolph's (renamed Lewis's Saloon), Johnson took his place at the piano.

William Henry Joseph Bonaparte Bertholoff Smith, born in 1897 in Goshen, New York, was one of the most colorful players and personalities to spring from the jazz tradition. He too was given instruction by his mother on the piano and organ at an early age. Much of his childhood was spent in Newark and the surrounding area. In his autobiography, Music On My Mind, written with George Hoefer, Smith tells many of the same stories as Johnson about the early days of black music in New York. He, too, became a fixture in cabarets in the Jungles and Harlem. In 1917, Willie Smith enlisted in the army and sailed to France with the all-black 92nd Division, 153rd Brigade, 350th Field Artillery, Battery A. True fighter that he was, Smith volunteered to fire the French 75s, huge cannons perched at the front line. "I shot those 75s at the Fritzies for forty-nine days without a break or any relief. Word got back about the several hits I had to my credit and a colonel came up and said, 'Smith, you're a Lion with that gun.' Before long everyone was calling me 'Willie the Lion,' a name that has stuck with me ever since."[19]

Willie "The Lion" Smith had a very long and active career in music. He recorded first in 1920, as part of the accompaniment to the first vocal blues recording by a black singer, Mamie Smith. He had an unusually inquisitive mind, exploring the world around him for qualities he could assimilate, which included everything from music to religion. Smith, who credited the strength of his left hand to playing Bach, also played ragtime, developed into a superb stride player, and became a prolific and original composer. Many of his works exhibit impressionistic and romantic melodic and harmonic ideas. He embraced Christian and Jewish theology, wearing both a St. Christopher's medal and a Star of David. He was vigorously opinionated, fancying himself as a fighter, an intellectual, an all-around entertainer, and a first rank piano player who was always ready to prove it. He, James P. Johnson and Fats Waller are thought of as the "big three" of stride piano.

"Willie Smith was one of the sharpest ticklers I ever met--and I met most of them," Johnson said of his close friend. "He was a fine dresser, very careful about the cut of his clothes and a fine dancer, too, in addition to his great playing.... When Willie Smith walked into a place, his every move was a picture."[20] Such a studied entrance had become a very important part of a musician's demeanor. "Yes, every move we made was studied, practiced, and developed just like it was a complicated piano piece."[21] Johnson recounted a lengthy, detailed description of the stylish clothes and show business mannerisms of the highest class players. The following is his description of a tickler's routine from the time he entered a place to the completion of his performance.

When you came into a place you had a
three-way play.   You never took your overcoat or hat off until you were at the
piano.   First you laid your cane on the
music rack.   Then you took off your
overcoat, folded it and put it on the piano,
with the lining showing.

You then took off your hat before
the audience.   Each tickler had his own
gesture for removing his hat with a little
flourish; that was part of his attitude, too.
You took out your silk handkerchief, shook
it out and dusted off the piano stool.

Every tickler had his special trade-
mark chord, like a signal ... players would
start off by sitting down, wait for the
audience to quiet down and then strike
their chord, holding it with the pedal to
make it ring.

Then they'd do a run up and down
the piano--a scale or arpeggios--or if they
were real good they might play a set of
modulations, very offhand, as if there was
nothing to it.   They'd look around idly to
see if they knew any chicks near the
piano.   If they saw somebody, they'd start
a light conversation about the theater, the
races or social doings--light chat.   At this
time, they'd drift into a rag, any kind of
pretty stuff, but without tempo, particularly
without tempo.   Some ticklers would sit
sideways to the piano, cross their legs and
go on chatting with friends near by.   It
took a lot of practice to play this way,
while talking and with your head and body
turned.

Then, without stopping the smart talk
or turning back to the piano, he'd attack
without any warning, smashing right into the

regular beat of the piece.   That would knock them dead.

After your opening piece to astound the audience, it would depend on the gal you were playing for or the mood of the place for what you would play next.   It might be sentimental, moody, stompy, or funky.   The good player had to know just what the mood of the audience was.

At the end of his set, he'd always finish up with a hot rag and then stand up quickly, so that everybody in the place would be able to see who knocked it out.

Every tickler kept these attitudes even when he was socializing at parties or just visiting.   They were his professional personality and prepared the audience for the artistic performance to come.   I've watched high-powered actors today, and they all have that professional approach. In the old days they really worked at it. It was designed to show a personality that women would admire.   With the music he played, the tickler's manners would put the question in the ladies' minds: "Can he do it like he can play it?"[22]

Most of the clothing styles were adopted from white society.   The Clef Club orchestras were engaged to play at private society parties where the musicians were exposed to the finest in fashion and deportment.   The older Clef Club members had developed the most refined manner- isms which the younger players of Johnson's gen- eration copied.

From the beginning of this century, a group of thoroughly schooled musicians undertook the difficult struggle of legitimizing black music in New York.   They accepted the mystique and the

image of the black performer as untrained and
innately talented.   One early organization called
the Frogs (which took its name from the Aris-
tophanes play) was dedicated to the advancement
of black arts, both musical and theatrical.   Its
members included Alec Rogers,   J.   Rosamond
Johnson, Jesse A. Shipp, R.C. McPherson (Cecil
Mack) and James Reese Europe, all of whom
would later work with James P. Johnson.   In
1910, these same men, led by Europe, organized
the Clef Club.[23]

        The primary role of the organization was
as a booking agency, representing and promoting
the interests of black musicians.   Working within
the framework of an organization like the Clef
Club, Europe was able to make dramatic changes
in the working conditions of black entertainers.
His orchestras played only in finer establishments,
with wages and hours set by contract.   They
dressed well and carried themselves as properly as
their employers, projecting an image of the black
musician as much more than a banjo-picking
bumpkin.[24]

        The Clef Club had a central office where
the musicians gathered, often to be sent out on a
"quick call" assignment.   The Club maintained
several orchestras, any of which could be sent to
play for the parties of the very rich in Newport
or on Park Avenue, or for an Ivy League prom.
Europe paved the way for Luckey Roberts's
success in the same market after the demise of
the Clef Club in the mid-1920s.   Many of the
orchestras were very large groups with somewhat
odd instrumentation.   Mandolins, violins, banjos,
harps, and as many as ten pianos were common
sights in a Clef Club concert ensemble.   The
emphasis was not on improvisation or exploring
folk-musical materials (like the blues), but on

producing good dance music and a show for their white clientele. Although they often played without written music, since their employers expected them to be musically illiterate, the players maintained the highest standards of social deportment. James P. Johnson played on many Clef Club dates from 1914 through the early 1920s. The upper-class manners of the established musicians influenced Johnson in developing his own manner of carrying himself. The conservative society music he was required to play, however, began to frustrate him in his search for a more meaningful conception.

In 1914, Johnson was still playing regularly at Allan's and, as he says, "visiting around." New York ragtime had taken on a distinctive character. Although the few published works of Luckey Roberts ("Junk Man Rag," "Pork and Beans") and Eubie Blake ("Fizz Water," "Chevy Chase") lay somewhere between classic ragtime and popular semi-classics, the playing tradition in the East required far more of the performer than the published score. As Johnson put it:

> New York developed the orchestral piano--full, round, big, widespread chords and tenths--a heavy bass moving against the right hand. The other boys from the South and West at that time played in smaller dimensions--like thirds played in unison. We wouldn't dare do that because the public was used to better playing.
> We didn't have any instruments then, except maybe a drummer, so we had to use a solid bass and a solid swing to get the most colorful effects. In the rags, that full piano was played as early as 1910. Even Scott Joplin had octaves and chords, but he didn't attempt the big hand

stretches.   Abba Labba, Luckey Roberts and
later ticklers did that.
          When you heard the biggest ragtime
specialists play, you would hear fine harmony, exciting touch and tone, and all the
themes developed.[25]

The phrase "orchestral piano" is an accurate description of the style.   The goal was to recreate
the sound of an entire orchestra: a solid bass to
simulate the rhythm section, and a thickly textured melody in the right hand.   Johnson continued to work at developing his playing ability
and the orchestral sound he desired.

          In addition, Johnson began to view compos-
ing and songwriting more seriously.   He had by
this time (1914) arranged several "homemade
blues" tunes for the piano from the vocal renditions he had heard.   One of these, "All Night
Long," was later made into a song by Shelton
Brooks, another popular black composer.   Four
rags from this period Johnson did retain and later
recorded: "Carolina Shout," "Steeplechase Rag,"
"Daintiness Rag," and "Caprice Rag."   He had
also met a man named William Farrell who
taught him how to write down his pieces.   They
formed a partnership and launched full force into
popular songwriting.   "Mamma's and Pappa's
Blues" was their first published composition.
They sold it, along with "Stop It, Joe" (and probably "Boys of Uncle Sam," since all three were
published by F.W. Haviland in 1917) for $25
apiece.   Johnson put the money towards a down
payment on a baby grand piano.   The two opened
an office together to make contacts in the entertainment field, since Johnson was especially interested in writing for the theater.

Johnson and Farrell composed and performed for a variety of musical productions.
"Producers in those days would round up a couple
of clever girls, work up an act with scenery and
costumes, promote the music, and then try to sell
the whole unit to a circuit. We'd get paid for
performing (not for composing). It would get our
songs heard--and maybe published. All composers
and lyric writers started out that way then, even
those that became the biggest in their field."[26]
Through their office, they were approached for
many jobs. They wrote music for social club
shows, industrial and convention shows, and topical
songs to advertise something like the first production numbers in revues. They played one-night
shows and dances as well as week-long engagements at the Lincoln or Crescent Theaters in
Harlem. Several contracts included road tours.
Johnson paid particular attention to the audience
reaction to his music. "We'd get the Negro
reaction in the South and the opera house, white
reaction in upper Pennsylvania, Connecticut, and
New York State. I was learning how to do show
music, and it was all a new experience."[27]

Johnson also had occasion to work with Ben
Harney, the prominent vaudeville ragtime player
who was the first to introduce ragtime piano to
New York and the American public, in a song
and dance act. Johnson recalled Harney's trick
of playing two pianos at the same time, one with
each hand. He continued to play the vaudeville
circuits as "the inventor of ragtime," but by the
mid-1920s he would be another forgotten and
neglected figure. At the time that Harney's
career was on the decline, Johnson's was just
beginning to climb. Soon after his tour with
Harney, he wrote the music for a tab show (short
for "tabloid," a type of musical variety show),
"The Darktown Follies," produced by the well-

known Frank Montgomery and J. Lubrie Hill.
"Follies" is the first show known by name to
which Johnson's contribution was significant.
However, no details are known as to the extent
of his participation. It is the first credit in a
long list of revues, stage shows, and musicals
which would occupy a large part of Johnson's
time and energy for the rest of his life.

This period was crucial to the course of
the rest of Johnson's musical career as he moved
swiftly upwards in the popular music field. He
could, like other musicians-turned-popular-
composers, have made less of an effort to improve his playing ability while composing
prolifically. But Johnson was a "tickler," and
thought at least as much about playing as
composing. He was, in 1915, apparently still
taking lessons from Giannini. Although from the
European tradition, Giannini did not squelch
Johnson's desire to play ragtime and blues. He
did, however, insist on proper fingering and
technique, and taught Johnson many concert
effects. While continuing to explore his folk
roots, Johnson imposed on himself the strict dis-
cipline of the trained musicians. He would
"woodshed" the tunes he heard others play; that
is, he would play them in every key and experiment with substitute chords and harmonies.

I was starting to develop a good technique.
I was born with absolute pitch and could
catch a key that a player was using, and
copy it, even Luckey's. I played rags very
accurately and brilliantly--running chromatic
octaves and glissandos up and down with
both hands. It made a terrific effect.
I did double glissandos straight and
backhand, glissandos in sixths and double
tremolos. These would run other ticklers

out of the place at cutting sessions. They
wouldn't play after me. I would put these
tricks in on the breaks and I could think
of a trick a minute. I was playing a lot
of piano then, travelling around and listening to every good player I could. I'd steal
their breaks and style and practice them
until I had them perfect.

From listening to classical piano
records and concerts, from friends of Ernest Green, such as Mme. Garret, who was
a fine classical pianist, I would learn concert effects and build them into blues and
rags.

Sometimes I would play basses a
little lighter than the melody and change
harmonies. When playing a heavy stomp,
I'd soften it right down, then I'd make an
abrupt change like I heard Beethoven do in
a sonata.

Some people thought it was cheap,
but it was effective and dramatic. With a
solid base like a metronome, I'd use chords
with half and quarter changes. Once I
used Liszt's "Rigoletto Concert Paraphrase"
as an introduction to a stomp. Another
time, I'd use pianissimo effects in the
groove and let the dancers' feet be heard
scraping on the floor. It was used by
dance bands later.

In practicing technique, I would play
in the dark to get completely familiar with
the keyboard. To develop clear touch and
the feel of the piano, I'd put a bed sheet
over the keyboard and play difficult pieces
through it.

I had gotten power and was building
a serious orchestral piano. I did rag variations on "William Tell Overture," Grieg's
"Peer Gynt Suite," and even a 'Russian

Rag' based on Rachmaninoff's "Prelude in
C-Sharp Minor," which was just getting
popular then.

In my "Imitator's Rag," the last
strain had "Dixie" in the right hand and
"The Star-Spangled Banner" in the left. (It
wasn't the National Anthem then.) Another
version had "Home Sweet Home" in the left
hand, and "Dixie" in the right.

When President Wilson's "Prepared-
ness" campaign came on, I wrote a march
fantasia called "Liberty."

From 1914 to 1916, I played at
Allan's, Lee's, the Jungles Casino, occasionally uptown at Barron Wilkins',
Leroy's, and Wood's (run then by Edmund
Johnson.) I went around copping piano
prize contests and I was considered one of
the best in New York--if not the best. I
was slim and dapper, and they called me
'Jimmy' then.

In 1916, Johnson was given the opportunity to
prove his keyboard prowess to a mass audience by
making his first recordings.

8

First Recordings, 1917

In early 1916, Johnson received a message to see
a Mr. Fay at the Aeolian Company. Fay wanted
Johnson to cut some ragtime piano rolls. From
1916 on, Johnson made one or two rolls a month
for Aeolian and several other companies, usually
of his own compositions. He believed himself to
be the first black composer to record his own
compositions on piano rolls, but several rolls supposedly hand-played by Scott Joplin predate
Johnson's efforts.[1] What is important about these
recordings is that they offer a view of Johnson's
playing before the blossoming of the stride style,
and provide a basis for comparison with recordings of these same pieces made later in Johnson's
career.

A piano roll recording is not an analog
recreation in the modern sense of electrical technology which makes use of vinyl discs and mag-
netic tape, or even in the sense of acoustic
recording. The process was mechanical from
beginning to end. The pianist played through the
desired piece on a special piano. As he played,
the hammers drew marks on a roll of paper
pulled through the mechanism. Afterwards, the
marks on the paper were cut to form notched
holes, varying in size depending on the duration
of the note. This master roll would then be
used to produce copies. It was necessary,
Johnson recalled, to write out everything that was
played so that the rolls could be corrected for
mispunched holes. The finished product was a
"hand-played" piano roll which could be run

through a player piano. As the roll worked its way through, the holes caught small levers which caused the keys to depress, and the hammers to hit the strings.

The authenticity of a piano roll as the reproduction of a performance is disputable. There is, in actuality, only one aspect of the performance reliably represented, and it too may not be completely accurate. The physical phrasing and voicing of the notes is nearly all one can extract from a piano roll, and these too may have been changed by sloppy editing or the addition of extra notes. There is no sense of shading, contouring, tone, attack, or nuance, which are the truly distinguishing features of a performer's style. Dynamics and touch are absent. Even rhythmic phrasing suffers, since it often derives its most subtle effects from the qualities mentioned above. The tempo is determined by the person replaying the roll, not the pianist who recorded it. A piano roll is, in many respects, merely "animated sheet music."[2]

The overall effect of a piano roll is flat, two-dimensional, and mechanical in delivery. "It's all too easy, one supposes, to dote on phrases such as 'imitation of life' in trying to peg the medium down. It is James P. Johnson and it isn't, depending on how you hear it."[3] It is most useful and productive, when listening to piano rolls, to suspend all the above criticisms and appreciate what exists. A Chopin sonata is distinguishable from a Johnson rag, even on a piano roll.

Twenty known hand-played Johnson piano rolls were released from May 1917 to February 1918. Of these, seventeen are recordings of original Johnson compositions. Five of the twenty

rolls remain unaccounted for, their existence sub-
stantiated by listings in catalogs and advertise-
ments.   Johnson recorded for four piano roll
companies which distributed their product under a
variety of labels.

Number of rolls released	Manufacturer	Recording location
10	Aeolian	New York, NY
4	Standard Roll Co.	Orange, NJ
4	Artempo	Newark, NJ
2	Rythmodik	Belleville, NJ

The dates associated with each roll represent the
date of release, not of recording.   There is no
way to determine the actual recording date, as
this information was not kept as part of the
cataloging files.   It is safe to assume that rolls
were cut at least two months prior to the
release date to allow for editing, reproduction and
distribution arrangements to be completed.[4]   It is
possible that Johnson cut several rolls at each
session, although he stated, "I cut one or two
rolls a month of my own pieces at Aeolian."   It
is also possible that many rolls Johnson recorded
were never issued.

        Three of the rolls released during these
years were duets.   Johnson recorded "After Tonight (Universal, May 1917)[5] with his partner and
collaborator, Will Farrell, who also composed this
tune.   Johnson also made two rolls with Edwin E.
Wilson, who was not a collaborator of Johnson's,
but apparently a member of Aeolian's recording
and editing staff.   His name appears frequently in
Aeolian cataloges both in combination with other
artists and as a soloist.[6]   The remainder of the

rolls are Johnson solos and reveal a variety of stylistic characteristics.

Johnson maintained that he had written rags in every key of the scale. This claim is certainly supported by the piano rolls. The keys of B-flat, D, E-flat, E, F, F-sharp, and G are all represented in his compositions.[7] Johnson used tougher keys to discourage others from copying his work too easily. His playing on these recordings is distinctly ragtime, dependent on the general generic devices of the style. The fundamental left hand oom-pah maintains the distinctly march-like, 2/4 rhythm which Johnson alters infrequently in these recordings. The melodic lines are syncopated with broken and arpeggiated chords and "pivot" notes. The formal structure of his rags--"Daintiness," "Caprice," "Innovation," "Steeplechase"--adheres to the standard ragtime format of AABBA, followed by a trio of varying lengths. Also interspersed are introductions, interludes, and bridges common to many ragtime compositions. Johnson probably refrained from introducing variations on repeated strains since, as he stated, corrections were made from written transcriptions of the tunes.

Some of these recordings reveal hints of Johnson's later style and an attempt to break from many stylistic conventions of ragtime playing. "Mamma's Blues" (Singa-Word Roll,[8] Sept. 1917), Johnson's first published composition, follows W.C. Handy's format for a popular blues. The first strain, A, is 16 bars. The B strain is the blues, 12-bar length. The complete layout is AABB AABB. The A strain exhibits an interesting call and response pattern. The 16 bars are divided into four 4-bar phrases. Each 4-bar phrase is divided in half. The first 2 bars employ a melody played over a standard ragtime bass. The second 2 bars completely dispense with either melodic or rhythmic accompaniment, resembling more a break than a part of the melodic continuity. What emerges is a 2-bar "call" phrase followed by a 2-bar "response" phrase. This pattern repeats three times over the course of the chorus. This call and response pattern, one will recall, is like that of a traditional blues, where the first 2 bars of each 4-bar phrase is answered by the second 2 bars.

"Innovation" (Universal, Oct. 1917), which survives only in this piano roll recording, and "Twilight Rag" (Metro-Art, Nov. 1917) display a compositional device Johnson used in many pieces. He suspends the "oom-pah" bass line at the beginning of each B strain for 4 bars. The effect is striking, as the ragtime bass is interrupted for this brief period, setting this section of the rag apart. The return to the march-like bass in measure five is also accentuated by the immediately preceding disruption. "Twilight Rag" is also filled with sixteenth-note triplet figures in the A strain, a device which was used with increasing frequency in later years by many pianists. Its use is an adaptation of the African musical principle of superimposing a triple meter over a duple meter. It appears very seldom in printed ragtime and came into common use as jazz developed. One might thus consider it a distinctly "jazz" development.

"Caprice Rag" (Perfection, July 1917) is another example in which Johnson uses extensive triplet figures. The sweeping, ascending melodic line of the A section differs markedly from the somewhat reserved folk melodies of classic ragtime. (Such a line was later paraphrased by Fats Waller in his stride composition, "Handful of Keys.") There is also a hint of rhythmic phrasing which formed the basis of many later stride styles. In the repeat of the B strain, at measures 11 and 12, Johnson employed off-the-beat block chords in the right hand. They are not arpeggiated or embellished by pivot notes. Instead of merely dividing the beat with tied and untied syncopations, Johnson shifts rhythmic emphasis by playing around the beat maintained by the left hand.

The beginning of the B strain in "Steeple-chase Rag" (Universal, May 1917) also sports a suspended ragtime rhythm for two bars. The most interesting feature of this rag is the C strain. It is not 12, but 32 bars in length, with a 12 bar interlude before the repeat of the entire 32 bars of C. It is constructed almost entirely of one rhythmic figure. With fully voiced chords in the right hand, Johnson plays this figure set against a ragtime bass. This rhythmic device reappears in several later recordings (most notably in the final chorus of "You've Got To Be Modernistic," recorded for Brunswick in 1930).

"After Tonight" (Perfection, June 1917), Johnson's solo version, includes a device that, as he claimed, became the keynote of his and Fats Waller's style. "After Tonight" is a popular song with a standard format. A 4-bar introduction is followed by one statement of a 16-bar verse. One 32-bar chorus is then played and repeated:

INTRO   A   B   B

  4   16   32   32

In measures 7-10 of each B chorus, Johnson uses a bass figure known as a broken tenth. It is achieved by striking one note of the interval of a tenth slightly before the other. In this case,

Johnson strikes the upper note first, creating a backward tenth, his stylistic keynote. The jagged effect breaks up the monotony of a straight oom-pah and creates a fuller harmonic sound.

Johnson uses another tenth device in "Stop It" (Universal, Aug. 1917--later recorded with the title "Stop It, Joe"). The A section has a standard oom-pah rhythmic character, but harmonic tenths replace what would normally be octaves in this pattern. Instead of "breaking" the tenth, Johnson plays the notes of the tenth interval simultaneously. The following is an outline of the bass line of the first three measures of the A section (notes do not represent specific pitches):

oom-pah   walking tenths

The sound is much fuller and relieves the relentless march feeling. The walking tenths (consecutive ascending and descending tenths) create more of a four-beat feeling instead of the traditional two-beats.

The most interesting roll, historically and stylistically, is "Carolina Shout" (Artempo, Feb. 1918). It is the first recording of what became James P. Johnson's most famous stride composition. As it exists, it appears to be flawed by what was probably sloppy editing and a developing (but not yet cohesive) conception. The piece may be outlined:

INTRO	A	A	O	B	C	D	E	D
4	16	16	23	16	16	16	16	14

The O strain is an odd 23 measures long and appears nowhere else in any other recording of this piece. The second D strain is an anomalous 14 measures, considering that the first D strain was a full 16 measures. These aberrations, completely out of Johnson's phrasing character at this time, could have been the result of careless and/or hurried editing to get the roll on the market quickly.[9]

The "Carolina Shout" is much less melodic in conception than the other rags recorded and a world apart from a Joplin rag. With the exception of the A strain, which employs a descending folk strain paraphrased in several other compositions[10], the emphasis is on powerful rhythmic figures. The inspiration for this work was the dancing of the Gullahs and Geechies in the Jungles Casino. The rougher, frenzied sound is Johnson's attempt to capture with music the fantastic dancing he accompanied. It is, in many ways, a regression to the initial conception of ragtime as dance music. Joplin tried to classicize ragtime by refining its compositional aspects. Not satisfied with merely notating the dances musically, Johnson strove to convey their emotional intensity as well. Two expressive devices appear in his attempt to loosen the melodic confines of ragtime. Johnson uses the dissonance of the blues cluster (striking simultaneously two notes a half tone apart, an element notably lacking in most ragtime) in the introduction and again in the C strain. In the opening of the D strain, Johnson uses another of what became a standard stride device. He strikes an octave three times with his right hand. In addition, he strikes the note a half step lower a fraction of a second before he strikes the octave. Johnson uses this filip or grace note to kick off the strain with a pianistic approximation of microtonal play around the pitch of the octave, an expressive element probably derived from vocal music (like blues singing).

The piano rolls of this period show Johnson to be a ragtime player of great proficiency. At times, his playing sounds restless as he tries to break from the rhythmic and melodic formalisms of ragtime. His rhythmic vocabulary and facility were becoming increasingly sophisticated, enabling him to convey the full intensity and range of expression of the shout dances. "Carolina Shout" became a stride classic, yet these early recordings indicate that stride, as a distinct style, had not yet fully developed. It would take several more years for Johnson and the other New York pianists to polish their virtuosity and use it to break away from ragtime's formal rhythms.

Alabama Stomp
Lyric by
HENRY CREAMER
Melody by
JIMMY JOHNSON
as featured in
EARL CARROLL'S
"VANITIES"
5th EDITION
With Ukulele Arrangement
Staged by
DAVE BENNETT
ROBBINS-ENGEL, Inc.
New York
MADE IN U.S.A.

9

The Giggin' Years, 1916--1918

Johnson called the 1916-1918 period "The giggin' years." He had by no means retired to recording only piano rolls. 1917 proved to be a very busy year. He made his first phonograph recording for a company that started in the same building as his office. He cut "Caprice Rag" for this company, which later became Okeh records. There is no indication that the record was ever issued. Johnson commented that the recording companies did not yet have much confidence in recordings by black musicians. Bert Williams was the only black singer in Columbia's catalogue. James Reese Europe's orchestra recorded for Victor in 1913-14. Wilbur Sweatman and W.C. Handy, with their orchestras, recorded lightly syncopated dance music.

Meanwhile, Johnson was rehearsing with groups of three, five, seven or 14 players. He wanted to be leader as well as arranger, experimenting with contrasting melodies and counterpoint in his head arrangements. He continued to play engagements through the Clef Club, specifically with a drummer named Happy Rhone. Johnson soon formed his own group to play jobs alongside Rhone. The Jimmie Johnson Trio worked as often as three times a day. The musicians, all virtuosos, included Nelson Kincaid on sax and clarinet (he "could reach E above altissimo" and "transpose from trumpet parts on sight," recalled Johnson), Shrimp Jones on violin, and Clarence Tisdale, the relief man on alto saxophone. All were well schooled and had no

trouble learning the music Johnson prepared, with
all the parts written out.   They played arrangements of "The Crocodile," "The Vamp," "The
Sheik," and "La Vida."   In keeping with the image
of the black musician, they learned everything by
heart so that they did not have to be seen
reading.

The best Negro band in New York, according to Johnson, was Ford Dabney's orchestra.   As
with many other black entertainers, Dabney
secured his job with the help of Jim Europe.
Dabney's orchestra of 16 musicians played at the
Ziegfeld Roof.   For the most part, they played
straight Broadway, popular, and show tunes.   The
pianist and violinist with Dabney's group was Allie
Ross.   He was a good friend of Johnson's, and
enthusiastically spoke of transcribing Johnson's
piano pieces for chamber orchestra.   These ambitions never materialized, however.

Johnson also worked as an accompanist to
a blues singer named Reece Dupree.   They
worked at the Crescent Theater, a hole-in-the-
wall vaudeville house on 135th St.   Johnson was
called to put together a five-piece band for the
play What's Your Husband Doing.   Johnson and
the band had a five-minute scene on stage.
After a run on Broadway, they took the play on
the road to Boston.   In the evenings, when the
show was over, Johnson played at Lucas' Place, a
"hangout for professionals."   He played with Louis
Mitchell, a classical violinist from the Boston
Music Conservatory.   Johnson also met Flournoy
Miller and Aubrey Lyles, a comedy team with
whom he would collaborate on many shows.
When Johnson returned to New York, he found a
new musical climate developing.

The Original Dixieland Jazz Band, commonly referred to by its acronym ODJB, had reached New York. They played at Reisenweber's cafe in New York and made many recordings. Although their position in jazz history has been argued, they were the first group to record jazz music. The ODJB was an all-white group from New Orleans. The Dixieland style they played was very different from the arrangements used by Clef Club bands. The ODJB consisted of five instruments: cornet, clarinet, trombone, piano and drums. The polyphonic effect of the cornet, clarinet, and trombone weaving their melodic lines in and around each other was an alien sound to New York. When James P. Johnson returned from his road tour, the ODJB had made a big hit, thrilling large audiences.

Johnson recognized the appeal of this new and energetic style, and tried to organize similar groups through the Clef Club. The older members would have none of this "lower class" music. They reflected the same prejudices against the New Orleans jazz style as had been used to thwart the country blues influence. "They thought that kind of playing was vulgar compared to what they were trying to do. This experience, and others, was an example of their not encouraging the younger musicians. As a result, their membership fell off."[1] The obsession with respectability died hard in New York.

Meanwhile, Johnson continued to be an active part of the night club scene. The movement uptown of the New York black community was proceeding at a much faster pace by 1917. The area around 135th Street between Lenox and Seventh Avenues had become a new residential and social center for blacks. This movement into Harlem, which had begun the decade before, was

initially triggered by a glut of unoccupied housing
in this area.   Stanford White,   the   famous
architect, had designed and built rows of beautiful
brownstones to attract affluent white families to
the serene environment of Harlem.   But in 1907,
Harlem was situated on the upper fringe of Manhattan life.   Transportation downtown to the
heart of New York's business and entertainment
worlds was not adequate to satisfy the tenants
that the realtors hoped to attract.   A black real-
tor named Philip Peyton saw this as an opportunity to provide better housing for middle-class
black families.   As a preferable alternative to
empty buildings, he convinced the other realtors
to rent to black families.   A real estate war
ensued as whites in the surrounding areas attempted to prevent the formation of a black
community.   These efforts failed, and by 1917
Harlem was swiftly on its way to becoming the
world's most renowned black ghetto.[2]

One of the most famous of the early Harlem cabarets, recalled by several musicians, was
called The Rock or The Garden of Joy.   It was
in fact, built on top of a shelf of rock in a
vacant lot at 140th St. and Seventh Ave.
Decorated with Japanese lanterns and cooled by
breezes from the Harlem River, the Rock looked
like a summer resort, with a kitchen and dance
floor, situated in the middle of the city.

On weekends, the dictys would hold their
socials, but on weekdays us musicians had
it to ourselves.   Piano players would come
up there to improvise and show off their
latest riffs afternoons and evenings: lots
of small bands (many of them became
famous outfits later) worked out their arrangements on The Rock, or sat in with us
piano players developing new music.   It was

a lively little musical mountain, visited by
all the talent in Harlem.

Some years later, Willie "The Lion"
Smith, Fats Waller, Willie Gant and myself
hung out there regularly, knocking each
other out with rags, stomps, shouts and
every wild chorus and freakish break we
could think of. It was an odd place for
an academy of music, but very relaxing;
and there was always an intelligent and appreciative audience to follow us.[3]

Another Harlem cabaret was the Livia,
built on a vacant lot on 139th Street. Many
female vocalists were fond of the Livia; Ethel
Waters, Bessie Smith, Florence Mills, Gertrude
Saunders, Adelaide Hall, and Martha Copeland
were among many singers who performed there at
some point in their careers. It was a good place
to hear the latest blues and ballads. Also on
139th Street, below the Rock, was the 101
Ranch. Many small bands played there, most
without written music. They played by ear, improvising new and original ideas. They "...just let
go with natural blues, hot stomps and all sorts of
wild rhythms and sounds that popped into their
heads and right out through their instruments
without the benefit of formalities."[4] Willie "The
Lion" Smith recalled Lottie Joplin's boardinghouse
as another after-hours watering hole. Lottie
Joplin continued to run the establishment, located
at 163 W. 131st Street, for many years after the
death of her husband Scott in 1917. She allowed
only musicians and theater people to stay there.
"It was a common occurrence to stop in at six in
the morning and see guys like Eubie Blake,
Jimmy Johnson, and The Lion sitting around talking or playing the piano in the parlor."[5]

Johnson invented a term for the playing of
the most accomplished pianists. He called "fancy
piano" the superior technique and sophisticated use
of classical themes by the better players. Willie
"The Lion" Smith was known for his renditions of
"The Sheik of Araby" or "Moonlight," using
elaborate concert-style introductions based on
classical themes like Schubert's "March Militaire."
Donald Lambert, who studied Johnson's playing
and became an excellent stride pianist (and one
of the most obscure), was known for his use of
passages from Grieg, Massenet, and Beethoven.[6]
Johnson's playing continued to evolve from similar
sources: "I used to like to rip off a ringing
concert-style opening using Liszt's 'Rigoletto
Paraphrase for Piano' that was full of fireworks
in the classical manner and then abruptly slide
into a solid, groovy stomp to wake up the
audience and get a laugh."[7]

Johnson was not a fighter like his friend
Willie "The Lion" Smith, of whom Johnson said,
"He was always a fighter; and he fought a lot of
my battles over the years. I remember the first
thing he ever said to me when I met him and
played after him on The Coast over in Newark.
He said: 'Well, you may be able to play better
than I can, but I'll bet I can beat you fightin'.'"[8]
During the First World War, Johnson had no intention of enlisting in the army like his friend
Smith. Johnson often misplaced his draft card,
an oversight that almost cost him some time in
jail. "One night, when I didn't have my card on
me, I was in a place when the MPs raided. I
knew what it meant, so I just jumped out a
window: it was only on the second floor."[9] To
avoid being drafted, Johnson took a job in the
Quartermaster Corps warehouse. The physically
exhausting job he had pushing a one-ton hand
truck didn't keep him from staying out all night

playing piano. Johnson took a significant step in
1917:   "That year I married Lille Mae Wright,
whom I met at Allan's in 1913.   We've trouped
together for years and have seen lots of things
change."10

          After the Armistice, Johnson returned to
playing with drummer Happy Rhone. Johnson gave
the piano the lead and began to take charge of
the group.   He also played further Clef Club
jobs, using bands ranging from trios to 40 men.
"In these days the Clef Club used to give big
concerts in which all the good musicians played.
I was ambitious to conduct one of these concerts
and worked hard at it.   But I didn't get it, and
it broke my heart.   I quit the Clef Club and
returned to rehearsing my own group."11   Johnson
continued to experiment with different breaks and
instrumentations.   He copied the Dixieland style
in his arrangements to get attention.   Johnson
composed "After Hours," a piece eventually published in 1923, describing it as "a good instrumental that had a blues in the last strain with a
slow, sobbing end that was muffled."12   He took
the piece to Columbia and Victor records, who
both rejected it.

          Later in 1918, Johnson and his wife worked
with a touring show, the Smart Set Revue, which
traveled across the country featuring black acts
and entertainers.   The show played a week in
Philadelphia, and one and a half weeks in
Wilmington, Baltimore, Norfolk, and Atlanta.
After the tour, Johnson made his way farther
west.   In the course of his travels, he met
several musicians who, like him, would be leaders
in jazz music.   The first stop, in Philadelphia,
had the group playing at the Standard Theater, a
haven for black performers run by John T.
Gibson.   Benton Overstreet, the director of the

orchestra for many years, later composed "There'll
Be Some Changes Made," a popular favorite,
especially with jazz musicians.   In the Philadelphia Dancing Class, a young girl named Ethel
Waters was thrilling audiences with her comic
personality and dancing.   She eventually landed in
New York, and teamed with James P. Johnson on
several superb recordings in the late 1920s.

After playing in Wilmington and Baltimore,
the company headed for Norfolk aboard the
Chesapeake Bay Ferry.   Johnson told of an unfortunate incident that occurred on the boat, and
how he and his wife, through their musical
versatility, made the best of the situation.

> I had a few drinks and dozed off.   When I
> woke up, I found that somebody had taken
> all my money and my collar buttons, which
> were gold.   Others had been robbed too, by
> the lush-rollers.   We wouldn't have a cent
> when we got to Norfolk.
> There was a piano on the boat, so I
> sat down and started to play, and my wife,
> who was with me, began to sing and dance.
> Pretty soon money started dropping.   When
> the boat tied up, we had enough to eat in
> Norfolk.[13]

In Atlanta, the <u>Smart Set</u> show played the
81 Theater on Carter Street.   At 91 Carter
Street, Bessie Smith and her trio were singing.
At a party, she was introduced to Johnson, who
played behind her as she sang one of her
homemade blues tunes, "Alcoholic Blues."   Johnson
improvised his accompaniment since every natural
blues has the same harmonic sequence.   "To be
real blues, it must follow that plan," he noted.
The fine blues and ragtime pianist Eddie Heywood

Sr. also played at 91 Carter St., but was off
during Johnson's stay and the two never met.

        After the Smart Set tour was completed,
Johnson traveled to Toledo, Ohio, for a brief
stay.   There he met Johnny Waters (this may
have been Ethel Waters' half brother), who played
"Western" piano, a designation for playing that
was not up to New York standards.   Johnson
recalled Waters' fine piano playing, which included
slow blues and tenths.   He taught his tricks to
Roy Bargy, who was later the featured pianist in
Paul Whiteman's orchestra.   While in Ohio,
Johnson undertook study in composition with Jan
Chiapuse at the Toledo Conservatory.   In addition,
he was playing a club called The Lion's Jaw.   It
was here that a nine-year-old Art Tatum got his
first glimpse of the master Eastern pianist.
Tatum later told Johnson that he had heard him
play and studied his style.   Johnson also met the
prominent ragtime composer and pianist Charles
Thompson on this trip.   He, too, listened attentively to Johnson's playing and learned from him.

        Johnson returned to New York toward the
end of 1919.   He made the rounds of the clubs
and cabarets, and picked up any playing jobs that
were offered.   This included Clef Club fast calls,
although he was probably no longer a full-time
member.   Several clubs Johnson remembered
began to feature more structured and elegant
entertainment.   Edmund Johnson's place, located
at 132nd Street and Fifth Avenue, featured singing waiters and the finest rising female singers.
Ethel Waters had come up from Philadelphia.
She sang Johnson's "Stop It, Joe," with Johnson
often accompanying her.   Mattie Hite, whom
Johnson remembered as one of the greatest
cabaret singers of all time, and Josephine
Stevens, a coloratura "able to hold a note while

the rhythm strode through and then pick up the
rhythm without a break," also sang at Edmund
Johnson's.   Another prominent club was Small's
Sugar Cane Club located at 135th Street and
Fifth Avenue.   Charlie Small ran it and took on
most of the help from the old Jungles neighborhood.   They worked as singing and dancing
waiters who performed little side shows while
they served the customers.   One of the most
popular was a man called "Whistling Seath."   He
was able to whistle the blues through his teeth,
producing a fine tone.

        Several musicians have recalled in memoirs
and interviews the fast growth of Harlem night
life.[14]   The environs of Harlem in 1920 were the
area from 130th to 140th Street between Fifth
and Seventh Avenues.   125th Street was still part
of a white neighborhood.   Many cabarets opened,
concentrated along 135th Street, still Harlem's
main artery (the fashionable street to walk down
was Seventh Avenue).   The Orient on 135th between Lenox and Fifth Avenues, Jerry Preston's
on 135th near Lenox, Leroy's on 135th and Fifth
Avenue (down in a cellar), and the Band Box on
131st and Seventh Avenue were all popular.   Most
cabarets began to feature a five-piece band and
seven or eight singers.   The pianists were often
called upon to play long hours, which provided a
lot of practice in improvising.   Black stage shows
were performed at the Lincoln Theater on 135th
St., succeeding the older Crescent a few doors
away.   Johnson played there for shows, but in
1920, 16-year-old Fats Waller was the regular
pianist and organist.

        By 1920, two events in particular had a
strong effect on the perspective of black musicians.   These were the advent of Prohibition and
the coalescing of feelings of ethnic pride.   This

latter attitude fostered a surge of artistic, creative effort within the black community.   The
period of this development, roughly from 1917 to
1933, is called the Harlem Renaissance.   Although
the black intellectuals who forged this cultural
rediscovery were not all from New York, Harlem
served as the physical and symbolic center of the
movement.   Black leaders were trying to fan the
flames of a new black consciousness, to prove to
white Americans that Afro-Americans had a
legitimate, distinctive cultural heritage.   These
feelings of racial pride manifested themselves in
many organizations and movements.   Marcus Gar-
vey and his black nationalist "Back to Africa"
movement represented one extreme.   The NAACP,
founded in 1910 as a coalition of liberal white
groups and black civil rights groups, had, by 1917,
appointed its first black executive secretary in
the person of James Weldon Johnson.   Johnson's
interests were by no means restricted to political
issues.   He had already achieved renown in music
and literature, and would continue to advance the
idea of the "New Negro" in both political and artistic contexts.

        The Harlem Renaissance as a movement
was primarily concerned with producing and dis-
playing the new art of the modern American
black man.   The folk elements of Afro-American
history were the seeds of this renaissance, resyn-
thesized by black intellectuals into a high art
form no less sophisticated and "cultured" than
those of Europe.   Visual arts, poetry, and music
were all infused with these ideas of racial/cul-
tural identity.   The merit of these works is still
being debated by scholars.   The important point,
however, is that such a strong effort was made
by black men and women to achieve the best.

The black intellectual musical world still seemed to suffer from the same urban snobbery that had informed the views of James Reese Europe and Will Marion Cook, who continued to strive for greater recognition of black music. In July 1919, the National Association of Negro Musicians held its founding meeting, at which the delegates resolved to work for a "truer appreciation of Negro music."[15] However, their view of "Negro Music" did not include jazz, which they saw as destined to remain mired in lower-class vulgarities. Not only did the musicians disdain it, but almost all black intellectuals of the time did not see jazz as part of the high art form they hoped would emerge.

> Harlem intellectuals promoted Negro art, but one thing is very curious: except for Langston Hughes, none of them took jazz--the new music--seriously. Of course, they all mentioned it as background, as descriptive of Harlem life. All said it was important in the definition of the New Negro. But none thought enough about it to try and figure out what was happening. They tended to view it as folk art--like the spirituals and the dance--the unrefined source for the new art. Men like James Weldon Johnson and Alain Locke expected some race genius to appear who would transform that source into high culture. It is very ironic that a generation that was searching for a new Negro and his distinctive cultural expression would have passed up the only really creative thing that was going on.[16]

During this period, however, jazz had its own renaissance, completely independent of the intellectual world.

Throughout the country, the response to jazz was widening. To most Americans, however, jazz was the music of white groups like the ODJB and Paul Whiteman's orchestra. Its novelty appeal pervaded vaudeville and popular entertainment. "Blues" songs were established features of stage shows and were cheapened by popular song writers in the same way that ragtime had been a decade before. Yet, the black community was exposed to a different music, and cabarets in areas like Harlem burgeoned as the concert halls of true jazz. A segment of white society has always existed which has sought out black entertainment. Most members of this group were merely fascinated by an alien culture, patronizing and condescending toward rather than truly appreciative of what they saw and heard. Black people and jazz were to them the latest exotic fad, and Harlem provided the right environment to indulge in a little vice and be entertained. Many Harlem cabarets had already begun to pander to the white clientele who came uptown for exotic and illicit entertainment. (This trend continued through the decade, and was epitomized by the Cotton Club, which employed only black help and entertainers--like Duke Ellington's orchestra--but catered to all-white audiences.)

In 1920, recording companies were still reluctant to record black jazz artists. However, in that year, a record was made which opened up an as yet unexploited market, the black community itself. Perry Bradford, a black songwriter and promoter originally from Alabama, had arranged for blues singer Mamie Smith to record several tunes for the General Phonograph Company, producers of Okeh records. Mamie Smith and General Phonograph's five-piece band, the Rega Orchestra, recorded two popular songs-- "That Thing Called Love" and "You Can't Keep a

Good Man Down." Although these recordings met
with only marginal success, Bradford was able to
secure a contract for a second session at which
Mamie Smith recorded two Bradford compositions.
In August 1920, Mamie Smith and her Jazz
Hounds, a black group, recorded "Crazy Blues"
and "It's Right Here For You." This record did
phenomenally well. It sold 75,000 copies in Harlem within several weeks. "Crazy Blues" is the
first known blues recording by a black vocalist.
This record, released by Okeh, became the first
"race" record, aimed primarily at the black
music-buying public. Soon many record companies
began to record black jazz artists, now that they
were sure there was a market.[17]

In 1920, James P. Johnson had not yet had
a phonograph recording released. According to
his own recollection, he recorded additional piano
rolls of blues tunes for Aeolian in 1920. He
recalled meeting George Gershwin, who was cutting "Oriental" numbers for piano rolls at Aeolian.
The two men exchanged ideas and spoke about
their mutual interest in the blues and other indigenous American music, and their "ambitions to
do great music on American themes."[18] Another
facet of Johnson's musical personality began to
take shape. Like Gershwin, he aspired to writing
music on a higher level, so-called "serious" music.
It was, in fact, the type of music the Renaissance intellectuals were waiting for. Johnson had
attained his boyhood goal of becoming a first-
class tickler. He now dreamed of conducting
symphony orchestras in large concert halls, playing
his works based on native Afro-American musical
themes. The products of this dream were still
many years in the future. But as his career
during the 1920s expanded more into the popular
and show music worlds, Johnson never let go of
this desire to compose concertos that would be

respected and honored alongside the works of
Bach and Mozart.

The year 1921 proved to be very successful
for Johnson in the recording field. He became
one of the first black staff artists for QRS
(Quality Reigns Supreme) piano roll company.
(Luckey Roberts also joined their staff around this
same time.) The QRS company had featured
many novelty players, one of whom was Max
Kortlander. He eventually became general
manager of the company's recording laboratories
and, probably following the lead of the "race
record" phonograph recording companies, began to
use black pianists. In May of 1921, five Johnson
piano rolls were released: "Carolina Shout,"
"Eccentricity," "Don't Tell Your Monkey Man," "It
Takes Love To Cure the Heart's Disease," and
"Loveless Love--A Blues Ballad." The most interesting of this group is the recording of "Carolina
Shout," the sequel to Johnson's 1918 recording of
the same tune. The QRS version had a much
wider distribution than the earlier roll and became well known throughout the Northeast. It is
considered the definitive version of "Carolina
Shout," which was soon to become the prototype
for stride piano, just as "Maple Leaf Rag" had
been for ragtime.

In August of the same year, the first
phonograph record including James P. Johnson on
piano was released. Singer Alice Leslie Carter
was accompanied by Jimmie Johnson's Jazz Boys
on a recording released on the Arto label. In
September, Johnson made several more records
accompanying vocalists Carter and Lavinia Turner
with his Harmony Seven. Also in September,
Johnson cut his first recorded piano solo, "Harlem
Strut," issued on the Black Swan label. The
Black Swan label was the product of the first

all-black owned and operated record company, the
Pace Phonograph Corporation.   Harry Pace, W.C.
Handy's partner in the publishing firm of Pace
and Handy, started the firm in 1921.   Pace saw
the need to record and promote music by black
musicians.   Since black music by black performers
was swiftly gaining in popularity, the advertise-
ments for Black Swan records emphasized the
fact that its recordings were made by blacks and
not whites attempting to imitate blacks.   (Ironically, performances by white artists were nonetheless issued by Pace.)   In 1923,   the Pace
Phonograph Corporation expanded and changed its
name to the Black Swan Phonograph Company,
Inc.[19]   In April of 1924, Black Swan was ac-
quired by Paramount Records.   Johnson accompanied a few other vocalists with an orchestra
for Black Swan, but "Harlem Strut" was his only
piano solo released by that label.

On October 18, 1921, Johnson recorded
again for the General Phonograph Corporation on
its Okeh label.   (In 1917, he had recorded a test
of "Caprice Rag" for the same company.)   He
made two of his own compositions as piano solos,

Facing page:
Happy Rhone, with whom Johnson worked ca.
1920, led one of the most successful early Harlem bands.   This concert program promotes
Rhone's orchestra with several special guests, including Johnson, who was already an exclusive
recording artist with QRS.   Also on the bill is
William Farrell, Johnson's old partner.   Farrell
had since teamed with Ike Hatch to form a two-
man vaudeville act.   Farrell and Hatch toured the
country for many years on the vaudeville circuits.

PROGRAM

MANHATTAN CASINO. FRIDAY EVE. APRIL 22nd, 1921

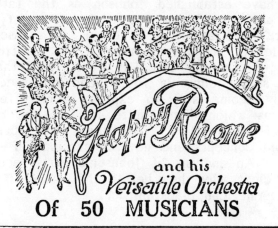

and his Versatile Orchestra

Of 50 MUSICIANS

Dance Musical Numbers Furnished By

Pace & Handy, Jerome H. Remick, Foster Co., Perry Bradford, Sam Fox, Will Rossiter, Sherman Clay, Leo Feist, Shapiro Bernstine, G. Ricordi, Daniels & Wilson, Watherson Berlin synder, G. Schirmer, Jack Mills, Broadway Co., Harry VonTilser, Stark & Cowan, Chappell, T. B. Harms, Belwin, Boston Music Co., Maurice Richmond, Jenkins & Son, Edward Marks, Walter Jacobs, Van Alstyne & Curtis, Joe Morris, Reed Music Co., L. Wolfe Gilbert, Warren Short, McKinley, Seidel Music Co., Irvin Berlin, Witmark Co.,

PROGRAMME

Broadway Jimmie
In Songs
Late of "See Saw Co."

Miss Lucille Hegamin
"The Chicago Cyclone"
Courtesy of the
Arto Phonograph Co.

Farrell & Hatch
Singing Their Latest Song Success
" I LIKE YOU"
Assisted by
Mr. Wilbur White

Mr. James P. Johnson

Courtesy of the

Q. R. S. Piano Rolls Co.

Assisted by His Four Piano Fiends

The Misses Ruby Mason

Alice McDonald

Bertha Lindsey

and

Geneva Batman

Pianos from Mathushek & Co.

Decorations by Theodore Gunsel's & Co.

Staff Officers And Committee

Mr. Cassio Norwood	Mr. Walter Tate	Mr. John Barnes
Mr. Keily Thompson	Mr. Sidney Helm	Mr. C. A. Parker
Mr. W. F. Patrick	Mr. Ras. Johns	Mr. Wilbur White
Mr. R. Keys	Mr. A. A. Dismuke	Mr. C. H. Hines	Mr. R. Ross

Elkie Print. 104 West 53rd Street. Tel. Circle 6722

"Keep Off The Grass," and "Carolina Shout."   "If
he had recorded nothing else, these two sides
would have established Johnson as the father of
stride piano.   All the essentials of his style are
present.... What we are hearing is a fascinating
example of the transition from ragtime to
jazz...."[20]   In the three to four years that had
passed since Johnson's first piano roll recordings,
he had become able to express more effectively
the ideas which didn't quite fit into the ragtime
style of his youth.   These ideas were based on
both old concepts and new conceptions of expression.   An analysis of Johnson's early recordings
makes clear why they herald the dawn of a new
age in American black music.

The Original
CHARLESTON
WITH
UKULELE
ACCOMPANIMENT
The original of
all Charlestons,
first introduced
in "Runnin' Wild"
WORDS AND MUSIC BY
CECIL MACK
AND
JIMMY JOHNSON
HARMS
NEW YORK

CHARLESTON FOX TROT

DANCE DIRECTIONS

BY

OSCAR DURYEA, "AMERICAN AUTHORITY ON MODERN DANCES"

The Ballroom, Hotel Des Artistes, One West 67th Street, New York.

To learn this dance, first practice the Charleston step—Place the feet as in illustration No. 1, man's left foot behind the right, left toe at the heel of the right, both toes turned out,—his partner's right foot in front of her left, her right heel at the toe of her left foot, both toes turned out.

The man raise the left foot and **at the same time** rise on the toe of the right, turn both toes in, twisting on the ball of the right foot —his partner raise her right foot, and **at the same time** rise on her left toe, twisting on the ball of her left foot, turn both toes in, as in illustration No. 2. For 4/4 time music, in counting Fox Trot, count and.

With the feet in this position, twist both toes out, with the man's left heel in front at his right toe—his partner's right heel in front at her left toe. For 4/4 time music, in counting Fox Trot, count 1.

Man raise his left foot **at the same time** rise on the ball of the right and twist both toes in, then put left foot behind right, and on the balls of both feet twist both toes out,—his left toe behind at the right heel—his partner raise her right foot, **at the same time** rise on the ball of her left foot and twist both toes in, then put her right foot in front and on the balls of both feet turn both toes out —her right toe in front, at her left heel. For Fox Trot, count and 2. This is the SINGLE CHARLESTON and is done on one side with one foot (the same one) moving forward and backward. After practicing with the foot described, **then** practice with the other foot, moving it forward and backward with the same movements and counts. A toddle movement (a double rise or jiggle of the body up and down) is taken throughout all the "CHARLESTON" steps, on the foot on which the weight is.

For the DOUBLE CHARLESTON start as before, the left foot for the man, the right for his partner, and take the count "and 1" as before, then step back on the left foot for the man and on the right foot forward for his partner, putting the weight **on it**, but doing the turning in and out and the toddle with the weight on the left behind for the man, his partner with the weight on her right in front. Count and 2. Then the man "CHARLESTON" with the right foot, moving it back behind the left foot and forward again in front, finishing with the weight on the right foot in front of the left—his partner moves the left foot in front of the right and back with the same foot, finishing with her left foot in front of the right with the weight on it, Count and 3, and 4

FOX TROT ROUTINES WITH SINGLE AND DOUBLE CHARLESTON STEPS

ROUTINE I. Directions for the man, his partner does the same but with the opposite foot in the opposite direction. Walk 4 steps forward, commencing with the left foot, count 1, 2, 3, 4. Then SINGLE CHARLESTON STEPS with the left foot moving forward and backward twice, count and 5, and 6, and 7, and 8 ———— 4 measures.

ROUTINE II. Walk 4 steps forward, commencing with the left foot, count 1, 2, 3, 4. Then DOUBLE CHARLESTON with the left foot, moving forward and backward, then the right foot backward and forward, count and 5, and 6, and 7, and 8 ———— 4 measures.

ROUTINE III. Walk 2 steps forward, commencing with the left foot, count 1, 2, then 3 short quick steps to the left side, with the left, right and left foot (step, close step) finishing with a "kick up" with the right foot from the knee (see illus. No. 4) as the third step is taken on the left foot, count 3 and 4, and repeat the 3 quick steps to the right side with the right, left and right foot, finishing with the "kick up" with the left foot, count 5 and 6 and, then a SINGLE CHARLESTON STEP with the left foot moving forward and backward, count 7 and 8 and ———— 4 measures.

ROUTINE IV. Repeat ROUTINE III ———— —— ——— ———— 4 measures.

NOTE: Discretion should be used as to how pronounced the CHARLESTON "kick up," and "toddle" movements are made for ballroom dancing.

HARMS, Inc. - - - 62 West 45th Street, N. Y. C.

10

Harlem Stride Piano

Harlem stride piano immediately strikes the listener when it is introduced in the course of a performance. At its most fierce, it surges forward furiously like a raging bull or a barreling freight train. It can also be delicately expressive, proving that momentum and lyricism need not be mutually exclusive. As is the case with any term, any strict definition has a tendency to compound confusion and perpetuate oversimplification. Stride derives from the synthesis of four elements that have already been discussed in some detail: ragtime, the blues, "shout" dances, and pianistic virtuosity. Stride may indeed be considered a type of ragtime, depending on how loosely one defines ragtime. When the term stride was mentioned to Eubie Blake, he replied, "My God, what won't they call ragtime next?"[1] Willie "The Lion" Smith, in his inimitable manner, claims ignorance of the term stride (beyond his comment that "shouts are stride piano"):

> The writers who make up titles for the ways of playing music have called our piano style here on the eastern seaboard Harlem Stride Piano. I am not very sure I know what they are talking about. I do know how we played here in the east. A good pianist had to be able to play with both hands, performing in perfect unison. It was like learning to walk correctly. Some people just lope along while others

> walk like they are crippled, while a good
> walker goes forth with balance and dignity.[2]

Once again Smith has offered an analogy which is
closer to actual fact than mere parallel. From a
descriptive standpoint, the term stride was probably used to describe the motion of the left
hand, appearing to walk or "stride" up and down
the lower end of the keyboard. Smith's analogy
prescribes correctly that this walking motion must
be carried off with "balance and dignity."

Many technical definitions of stride piano
dwell on the left-hand pattern. The current
popular definition asserts that "the stride effect
is produced by the left hand hitting a single note
on the first and third beats and a chord of three
or four notes on the second and fourth beats."[3]
A more thorough description includes the role of
the right hand: "Stride piano is characterized
chiefly by an oompah left hand (a two-beat
seesaw, whose ends are a powerful mid-keyboard
chord and a weaker single note played an octave
or a tenth below) and by an arabesque of right-
hand chords and arpeggios, fashioned in counter-
rhythms."[4] James P. Johnson has also stressed
the importance of both hands in making a distinction between ragtime and stride: "The difference
between stride and traditional piano ragtime was
in the structure and the precise bass played in a
rag style by the left hand, while the characteristic strides were performed by the right hand."[5]
Johnson's definition adds to the confusion by attributing the stride patterns to the right hand.
He does, however, give an indication of the difference between a stride bass and a ragtime bass.
The stride bass is played in a "rag style," probably meaning an oom-pah rhythmic pattern.
There are many different ways to produce an
oom-pah, and Johnson points out that the struc-

ture and precision of the stride oom-pah differs
from a ragtime oom-pah.

The traditional march-like bass described as
an "oom-pah" makes use of the listeners' expecta-
tion of alternating strong and weak beats of the
bass rhythm.   The strong beats are thought of as
"oom" beats, and the weak beats are thought of
as "pah" beats.   Although the most common pattern is, as the definitions contend, the consecutive placement of an "oom" and a "pah" (falling
on the expected strong and weak beats of the
measure), stride basses utilize other combinations
of these strong and weak beats.   The figures
which are thought of as strong (or "oom") beats
may be of several types.   A single note, an
octave, a broken octave, a tenth and a broken
tenth are the most common figures used.

Each of these figures is built on top of the
single bass note, which can also be played
independently.   This foundation note, whether
alone or in conjunction to form the other figures,
is played in the lower registers of the piano,
some two octaves below middle C.   In a melodic
reduction of stride bass lines, the foundation
notes tend to move in scalar and chromatic
patterns.   They often set up a melodic line of
their own, independent of the surrounding musical
environment.   Ragtime bass notes differ in
register placement (usually voiced higher) and lack
melodic contour, stressing alternating roots and
fifths of chords.   There is also virtually no written evidence of tenths in ragtime.

The weaker (or "pah") beat almost always consists of a three or four note chord. It is voiced at least an octave higher than the bass note, much closer to the middle of the keyboard. The notes are usually played as tightly bunched as possible, meaning that the chord is played in close position. When properly voiced, the rhythmic feeling of the "pah" chord is stronger, although it remains the weaker of the two beats. These chords are generally not used twice in succession, as in ragtime where the same chord may be played through two measures. Although the actual harmony of the tune may not change, a stride bass line will use the passing chords (e.g., dominant and diminished seventh chords). These also aid in supporting the chromatic motion of the bass notes.

As is the case with ragtime, stride bass lines make use of many different combinations of "oom" beats and "pah" beats. There are two ways in which a triple pulse can disrupt the march-like one-two feeling. One is identifiable in several ragtime compositions (e.g., Joplin's "Maple Leaf," D strain, mm. 1-2). In this case, substitutions are made starting with a weak beat for a strong beat (i.e., a "pah" chord is used where an "oom" bass note would normally be played). For example, if the second "strong-weak" pattern is reversed in the usual

$$\frac{4}{4} \quad \begin{matrix} 1 & 2 & 1 & 2 \\ \text{strong-weak-strong-weak} \end{matrix}$$

$$\frac{4}{4} \quad \begin{matrix} 1 & 2 & 1 & 2 \\ \text{strong-weak-strong-weak,} \end{matrix}$$

the pattern becomes:

$\frac{4}{4}$ ⌐ 1   2   3 ⌐⌐1
   strong-weak-weak-strong

$\frac{4}{4}$ 2   3 ⌐⌐1   2
   strong-weak-strong-weak.

This disrupts the binary, march-like phrasing of the bass line. The phrasing becomes divided into two groups of three and one group of two instead of four groups of two (i.e., 3 + 3 + 2 instead of 2 + 2 + 2 + 2). However, because the initial substitution is that of a weak beat for a strong beat, the rhythmic disruption is not strong enough to mask the underlying march rhythm.

The second pattern is generally attributed solely to the stride style. In this case, the pattern is also changed by a series of substitutions which create a triple pulse. However, the initial substitution is that of a strong beat for a weak beat:

$\frac{4}{4}$ ⌐ 1   2 ⌐⌐1   2
   strong-weak-strong-strong

$\frac{4}{4}$ 3⌐⌐ 1   2   3 ⌐
   weak-strong-strong-weak.

Since a "misplaced" strong beat initiates this disruption, the effect is much more pronounced. The resulting phrasing is also different. The eight beats are divided into a 2 + 3 + 3 pattern. This rhythmic disruption is much stronger and gives the impression of having turned the beat around. The march-like, binary pulse is not only rephrased to a triple pulse, but the accents of the triple pulse itself are changed. The usual triple pulse is strong-weak-weak (as is created in case 1). The stride triple pulse is strong-strong-weak, an uncharacteristic accent pattern. This left hand device is known as "change-step"[6] or "back-beat"[7] and is a notable bass characteristic employed in varying degrees by most stride pianists.

The traditional "oom-pah" bass line has a distinctly two-beat feeling, and is thus the under-lying rhythm associated with ragtime. The stride bass line takes the same principle of weak and strong beats of fundamental duration (i.e., the beat is kept by quarter notes in $\frac{4}{4}$ time) and re-arranges them to produce often complex patterns of 2, 3, and 4 beats. Back-beats, parallel tenths and octaves, as well as non-"oom-pah" bass figures serve to break up the unremittent two-beat feeling. The latter group of figures includes various boogie-woogie patterns, sustained chords, and variations on "shuffle-rhythms" which require both hands playing in an alternating fashion. The essence of the stride bass remains the "oom-pah." The wide stretch between the bass notes and chords gives stride its full sound, and enables the player to activate the overtones of the piano by specific pedalling techniques.[8]

One other aspect of a stride bass distin-guishes it from a ragtime bass. "The oom-pah-oom-pah left hand is merely necessary, not sufficient, for stride piano. No ordinary left hand will do, for stride must swing. Rather, if it does not swing, it is not stride."[9] The ele-ment of swing is commonly assumed to be the hallmark of all good jazz. It has defied accurate definition or description. Schuller comments:

Like the description of a primary color or the taste of an orange, the definition takes on full meaning only when the thing defined is also experienced.... In analyzing the swing element in jazz, we find that there are two characteristics

there are two characteristics which do not
generally occur in "classical" music: (1) a
specific type of accentuation and inflection
with which notes are played or sung, and
(2) the continuity--the forward-propelling
directionality--with which individual notes
are linked together.[10]

An element implicit in the latter of these two
characteristics is momentum.   The propelling
force behind the linear continuity of music that
swings is momentum. Traversing the distance between the bass note and chord in the course of
playing stride creates a strong feeling of propul-
sion.   This is especially noticeable when single
notes are used in the bass, since the momentum
is maintained with more of a springing than
pounding feeling.

Part of the reason that a stride bass
swings is the four-beats-to-the-bar feeling created
by the various bass patterns and counter melodies
employed.   "Further, as the left hand began to
develop its own cohesive line, the beat began to
be felt independently between the two hands."[11]
Although the rhythmic phrasing can often create
very complex patterns, the time of the performance must always be kept by the left hand.

To a non-performer, the left-hand domi-
nance probably seems either unimportant or
self-evident, but it is the crux of a successful stride performance. If, in the heat
of battle, the time switches to the right
hand (because perhaps of a series of
heavily accented figures), leaving the left
hand merely to wag, then the momentum
goes out the window. The left hand must
always be the boss and leave the right

hand free to use whatever vocalized inflections the player desires.[12]

Although the left hand can swing independently, by itself it is only half of a stride performance.

One noticeable break from the characteristics of ragtime in the stride right-hand patterns is their fluidity and smoothness. Many of the earlier pianists were well known for one or two particular tricks. By the time stride piano blossomed, the best pianists were gifted with enough facility to employ many figures. There are a few general characteristics upon which the stride pianists built their individual styles. " ... [T]he characteristic rhythms of stride are provided by the right hand, not the left. It is possible to play an otherwise impeccable stride bass and ruin it by playing inappropriate right hand patterns. By pulling and tugging at the rhythms of the left, the right hand provides the swing."[13]

There has always existed the problem of accurately representing what is actually played in written notation. The trend toward greater accuracy can be seen in the development of published ragtime. The straight eighth-note pattern, ♫ , gave way to the increasing use of the dotted rhythm ♪. ♩ . The stride pianists tempered each of these rhythmic extremes. Notated as ♩ ♪ , it expresses more accurately the sound of³ the unevenness in playing eighth notes, a technique which creates a forward pull and adds to the swing. It confers the duration of 2/3 of a beat on the first "eighth note," as opposed to 1/2 of a beat in the square ♫ and 3/4 of a beat in the jerky ♪. ♩ .

One particular figure is prevalent in the playing of all stride players. It is a see-sawing figure utilizing these "swinging" eighth notes.

This figure may be played using a variety of melodic or harmonic ideas, since the order and structural organization (voicing) of the notes gives it a distinctive sound. This rhythmic pattern is called a riff. It and others tend to dominate the right hand. Since the heart and soul of stride piano derives from the rhythms of the shout dances, the tendency is toward expanding rhythmic as opposed to melodic ideas. Several critics have noted Johnson's use of such figures. "Many of his [Johnson's] 'melodies' are essentially rhythmic figures that happen to have pitches attached to them."[15] The " ... improvised figures gravitate about small discrete snatches from the melody."[16] "He keeps repeating little figures or riffs, especially ones that center around one particular note, so that the momentum builds through repetition over changing harmonies."[17] The adaptation of riffs from the shout dances into instrumental forms is one of the greatest achievements of the New York musicians, a conception first employed extensively by the pianists.

An important feature of the stride right hand is its ability to create a nonsynchronous rhythmic pulse without impinging on the time-keeping function of the left hand. " ... [W]hile the striding left hand defines the beat, the right hand leads or lags it and in so doing creates in effect another beat of the same tempo but displaced in time."[18]   Ragtime juxtaposed two different rhythms (syncopated and even); stride adds to this the juxtaposition of two different beats. The right hand is free to approach the beat, established by the left hand, from any rhythmic angle; before it, with it, or after it. Embellished with riffs, triplet figures, chromatic runs, and dramatic register changes reaching to the upper end of the keyboard, the stride right hand weaves in and around the pulsating left hand, which itself is shifting rhythmic emphasis from a 2 to 3 beat feeling and back again.

The expressiveness of the blues enters into stride playing and provides the proper inflection and accentuation which, when coupled with the swinging rhythms, drives the music in a linear direction. This aspect, which makes up the complementary characteristic to momentum of swing, is called vocalization. One method of "bending" notes on a piano in an approximate manner is accomplished by playing clusters. Two adjacent notes are struck some small fraction of time apart, ranging from the duration of a normal grace note to simultaneous attack. Through appropriate use of touch, attack, and dynamics, the music can be given an expressive quality very uncharacteristic of ragtime. "Stride is perhaps the most earthy non-blues piano style in the history of jazz; it is as savage rhythmically as the blues are harmonically and melodically."[19]

The improvised style of ragtime playing was probably confined by the limited rhythmic devices the early players were able to recreate on the piano. The stride pianists incorporated "improvisation within a broad compositional frame of reference."[20]   The exact nature of the improvisations varies. "The stride players were, as a group, not great improvisors. The idea with them

was to compose an original piece or perhaps
make an arrangement of current show tunes, and
then to wow the folks with it, night after
night."[21]   It is probably not likely that fast
stride passages were spontaneously improvised,
considering the complexity of the style.   From
listening to a large cross section of recordings by
many stride pianists, one gets the impression that
many of the phrases were worked out in advance.
This is true to the extent that there is a specific musical vocabulary from which the pianists
drew.   Yet, these elements in themselves provided
only a framework for individual interpretation.

If there is one particular trait of James P.
Johnson's playing which, by most contemporary
accounts, sets him apart from the other pianists,
it was his consistent ability to work out original
and inventive ideas within formal stylistic con-
straints. In his own words, "I could think of a
trick a minute."   The European tradition of technical virtuosity had, after years of practice,
enabled him to project the varied rhythmic potential of the shout dances onto the piano keyboard.

... for Johnson and the other most advanced New York pianists, as for Liszt,
Alkan, Chopin and the other Romantic
piano composers almost a century before,
the point of virtuosity was not the chances
it offered for display but that it was a
catalyst, a means of extending the
instrument's scope and hence their music's
range of expression. The audience could be
dazzled if it liked, yet what mattered to
the pianists was bringing fresh resources--
rather literally--into play.[22]

Along with the quality of swing, improvisation is
considered to be of paramount importance in

characterizing music as belonging to the "jazz"
tradition.   Johnson's use of pianistic invention
certainly qualifies his music as part of this tradition.   He along with the other more accomplished pianists in New York make up the first
generation of true jazz virtuosos.

Certain attributes of Johnson's playing make
it distinctive.   He took advantage of the upper
end of the keyboard, where the riff figures take
on a ringing or chiming character.   His touch
varied from light and springy in the upper
register to rather heavy handed.   Overall, his
playing reveals " ... crisp delicacy and incom-
parable imagination of a playing that, like the
ring-shout, sang while it danced."[23]   Johnson was
a master at devising new and startling rhythmic
fragments with which he reshaped a tune.   "He
has an almost architectural way of handling
rhythm, of placing pulses like building blocks, and
a wonderfully subtle manner of allowing different
rhythmic conceptions to exist simultaneously in
both hands."[24]   One ragtime cliché Johnson
retained in his playing was the two-handed break.
It was a feature associated with piano rolls,
which Johnson recorded often through the 1920s.
Garvin Bushell described the ragtime conception
as "a lot of notes."   The implication of earlier
ragtime composers was that the style was often
sloppy and imprecise.[25]   Johnson was very proud
of the accuracy of his playing, a characteristic
that critics praised.   "Listen to Jimmy Johnson
today--and watch his fingers ... abandon and
rubato there are, in abundance; but every finger
at every note knows just where it is going.   The
blending of the improvisatory spirit with the
precision of the virtuoso makes for a delicious
uncertainty that at no moment slips out of
control."[26]

The consensus among most musicians in
New York during the 1920s was that James P.
Johnson was the best and most original player.
"James P., due to the influence of Abba Labba
and his own capacity, was one of the few great
pianists in New York.... When you heard James
P. at his best, that was Abba Labba, except that
James P., who had studied, played with a little
more finesse and taste."[27]   Stride pianist Joe
Turner recalled the first time James P. Johnson
was mentioned to him: "Frank (Johnson) was the
first one, too, who mentioned the name of James
P. Johnson to me, making clear that James P.
was known, in fact, as the greatest jazz pianist
in the world.   That happened in 1923."[28]   Other
musicians and performers have compared Johnson's
playing with that of other early pianists.   New
Orleans bassist Pops Foster spoke of Jelly Roll
Morton's playing: "It didn't swing like most jazz
and wasn't up to date like James P. Johnson's."[29]
He also comments on Willie "The Lion" Smith in
a similar manner: "Willie could play in more
keys than anyone except James P."[30]   Garvin
Bushell continued, "Willie 'The Lion' played more
ragtime than James P. Johnson.   James P. was
cleaner and more inventive, as those early QRS
rolls demonstrate.   He played things that were
very close to what pianists in Ohio and the West
were doing.   He was getting away too from the
ragtime of Joplin, adding to what he retained,
and expressing himself."[31]   Ethel Waters summarizes Johnson's influence on later players: "I
was learning a lot in Harlem about music and the
men up there who play it best.   All the licks
you hear, now as then, originated with musicians
like James P. Johnson.   And I mean all of the
hot licks tht ever came out of Fats Waller and
the rest of the hot piano boys.   They are just
faithful followers and protégés of that great man,
Jimmy Johnson."[32]

Although Johnson's early piano rolls hint at some of these rhythmic developments, the recordings which mark the start (1921) of the most fruitful part of his career are filled with the general stylistic characteristics and have thus become "classic" examples of stride piano.

> Such a Joplin rag as "Pineapple" is filled with the feeling of folkballad, schottische, and reel, and the forceful rhythms of its concluding strains recall the buck and wing and the coonjine rag of the roustabouts. In an Eastern masterpiece like James P. Johnson's "Carolina Shout," on the other hand, one can literally hear the high shout of one worshipper and the answering outburst of the ecstatic congregation. The Eastern Shout is based on a different rhythmic beat from that used in the classic Midwestern ragtime. The two beats set up for different rhythmic tensions with the conventional ragtime bass.[33]

One example of this difference between ragtime rhythms and stride rhythms can be seen in two of Johnson's recordings of "Carolina Shout." In his 1918 piano roll, Johnson uses the weak beat for strong beat substitution in the bass line of the A section. (This rhythmic pattern was used by the better ragtime composers. It appears in the D strain of Joplin's "Maple Leaf Rag.") In measure 8-9 of the A strain, Johnson uses the following bass rhythm: $\frac{4}{4}$ strong-weak-weak-strong strong-weak-strong-weak. The rhythmic phrasing works out to a 3 + 3 + 2 pattern, but the impact is not strong. In his 1921 phonograph recording of the same tune, Johnson employs the stride back-beats to give the triple-duple phrasing its greatest emphasis. In the first statement of the A strain, the bass line is phrased in 2 beat (oom-pah) and 4 beat (walking broken tenths) segments until the seventh bar. Here Johnson introduces the first back-beat. Measures 7 and 8 are divided into 3 + 2 + 3. (The initial disruption is, as should be expected, a strong beat for a weak beat on the second beat of measure 7.) Johnson plays the second eight bars of A using more 2 and 4 beat divisions. In the repeat of A, Johnson continuously turns the beat around with numerous back-beats. The rhythmic breakdown of the bass line of A repeat is:

$$2 + 2 + \overset{\leftarrow}{3} + 4 + \overset{\rightarrow}{3} + 2 + \overset{\leftarrow}{3} + \overset{\rightarrow}{3} + 2 + \overset{\leftarrow}{3} + \overset{\rightarrow}{3} +$$
$$2 + \overset{\leftarrow}{3} + 4 + 4 + \overset{\rightarrow}{3} + 4 + 2 + 4 + 4 + 4.^{34}$$

It is interesting that the piano roll recording released by QRS in May of 1921 does not show this varied a bass line.

There are other features of the phonograph recording of "Carolina Shout" that distinguish it as a masterpiece on both compositional and stylistic grounds. The first statement of the A strain juxtaposes the even bass line of broken tenths and chords against the descending folk melody in the right hand. The repeat of A shows a great deal of variation. Johnson dispenses with the broken tenths and uses single notes and octaves in conjunction with chords to construct the back-beats. His left hand is thus varied not only rhythmically, but texturally as well. Johnson also varies the melody. He starts to play it an interval of a third higher than in the first A statement. This melodic variation does not occur on either piano roll. He also introduces many triplet figures and rhythmic variants.

The B strain features a rocking rhythm in the right hand set against a stride bass. In this case, the back beats are placed to provide an interesting melodic anticipation while maintaining the supporting harmony of the right hand melody.

... the left hand line implies different harmonies than the surrounding material. Johnson uses left-hand octaves as a melodic line while the right hand joins in with its own melody in m.3. The harmonic basis for the first two measures is

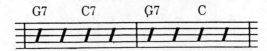

In m.3, however, the left-hand octave anticipates the repetition of the C chord on count 2. By contrast, the right hand retains the G chord throughout the measure. The left hand emphasizes the G chord on count 3 before returning to its melody note C again on count 4. The left hand, consequently, maintains two different harmo-

James P. Johnson, "Carolina Shout," mm.1-4, 3rd strain.

nies at the same time: the C chord implied in its melody line and the G chord
supporting the G harmony in the right-hand
melody.

One statement of B leads into the C
section. It was noted earlier that an important
aspect of the ring-shout was the call and
response pattern of the shouters, usually constructed in short phrases. The C section of
"Carolina Shout" is an instrumental representation
of this tradition. The call phrase is played as
two crushed clusters in the upper register. The
response phrase consists of a hand-to-hand shuffle
rhythm in the mid to lower register. This call
and response pattern, coming in two-bar phrases,
dominates the entire C strain. After the repeat
of C with slight variations, Johnson introduces
call and response patterns based more on riff
figures. In the first statement of the D strain,
Johnson contrasts dissonant chord clusters with an
arpeggiated chord riff in the right hand. The
left hand maintains a stride bass line of various
3 + 2 combinations. After the first D strain,
Johnson plays one statement of an E strain. The
riff he uses here is the see-sawing figure using
the "swing" eighth notes. It is clearly defined
rhythmically, and is without a doubt the most
universally applied riff in all stride playing.
Johnson changes the bass line in E as well, playing walking octaves interspersed with a bass syncopation during right hand breaks. Instead of
returning to the standard stride bass for the
repeat of D, Johnson prefaces the same arpeggiated chord riff from the first D strain with the
shuffle rhythm of the C strain. (This is as opposed to the dissonant chord clusters used in the
first D strain.) Johnson ends with a four-bar
coda using the traditional ragtime/piano roll

device of a two-handed break, with the hands moving in contrary motion.

This recording of "Carolina Shout" exhibits a plethora of the devices that constitute a large part of the musical vocabulary of stride style. With them, Johnson increases tension and forward pull throughout the five distinct strains. From a compositional standpoint, the use of riff, shuffle rhythms and call and response patterns are clearly worked out and defined. They form the framework for the stride style in general. Schuller contends that "the solo piano style Johnson brought to its finest flowering was made obsolete by orchestral developments in jazz...."36 This is true to the extent that Johnson's style fostered many of these orchestral developments, most notably the instrumentalization of the riff. This case can be made when it becomes clear that many of the leaders of New York orchestral jazz were stride pianists themselves.

The flip side of "Carolina Shout" was Johnson's "Keep Off the Grass." It is not a shout in the same sense as its coupling, but rather a ragtime-styled composition to which Johnson applies the techniques of stride variation. The piece is essentially a three-theme rag that may be outlined:

INTRO	A	A	B	B	A	BRIDGE	C	INTERLUDE	C'
4	16	16	16	16	16	4	16	16	16

A	A'	BRIDGE	C"	CODA
16	16	4	6	4

The A strain hints at the rural roots of ragtime melody and the transition from banjo phrasing. "The banjo-like repeated notes in the right hand, voiced above the melody, give the strain something of the quality of a folk tune, and Johnson varies it slightly each time a-round."37 Johnson's superb digital control creates the impression of two distinct voices in the right hand. The bass line moves partly in chromatic motion and establishes its own melodic line. The B strain opens with a compositional device Johnson used in his earlier rags. He suspends the stride bass and plays an arpeggiated chord figure in the right hand for two bars. He then returns to the steady left hand with striking effect.

After a brief 4-bar bridge, Johnson plays the trio or C strain. "There is not much melody in the series of descending diminished chords that form the heart of the trio, but that gives Johnson more freedom to improvise freely."38 This first statement of C contrasts a repeated right hand rhythmic pattern against an even stride bass without back-beats. Johnson plays a 16-bar interlude to highlight his virtuosity, followed by the second statement of C. The right hand figures show greater rhythmic variety, and the bass line in measures 8-16 contains back-beats. Johnson increases the complexity of the rhythms of each hand, which, when played together, increase the internal rhythmic tension--the "pulling and tugging" effect.

Before repeating the C strain again, Johnson returns to the A strain for two choruses. The first of these is very similar to the initial statements of A at the outset of the piece. The second departs dramatically. He completely dispenses with any sort of stride bass, using a series of fast sixteenth-note broken octaves reminiscent of a boogie-woogie pattern (Eubie Blake uses this figure in the opening of his "Charleston Rag"). In the right hand, too, Johnson changes the rhythmic and textural structure. He uses a pattern based on one chord without the banjo-like melodic movement of the first A strain. Johnson plays one more 4-bar bridge before launching into the final C strain, at which point he adds even greater rhythmic variety and complexity. Unlike the phrases of the "Carolina Shout" which revolve around repeated riffs in call and response patterns, the final statement of the trio in "Keep Off the Grass" shows Johnson at his best in weaving complicated rhythms by integrating the two hands. Yet one hand never intrudes or overlaps into the realm of the other. The last eight bars (before the coda) are the pinnacle of this process.

The eight bars are divided into a 2 + 2 + 4 pattern, but in both two-bar segments the left and right hands articulate two dif-

"Keep Off the Grass"

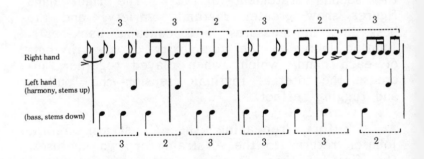

(Points marked   represent syncopated anticipation; they do not alter the basic ternary pattern.)

ferent sub-patterns in ternary units. The right hand divides the phrase into beat patterns of 3 + 3 + 2, while the left hand accompanies in 3 + 2 + 3. In the succeeding two bars the roles are reversed. A purely rhythmic distillation (no pitches are given) can be seen:

Within the compositional framework of a rag, Johnson uses his ability for rhythmic variation on a basic melodic and harmonic concept. Carried off with technical precision and sureness, his playing swings in the finest jazz tradition.

I NEED LOVIN'
LYRIC BY
HENRY CREAMER
MUSIC BY
JIMMY JOHNSON
Remick Music Corp.
219 W. 46th ST., New York

11

James P. and Fats Waller, 1921

By the end of 1921, James P. Johnson was the leader of the New York pianists, a group often referred to as the "race" pianists. Their playing was part of the black collective consciousness, and the term "race" was applied as a meaningful designation to associate the person with this cultural identity. His QRS piano roll of the "Carolina Shout" spread quickly, particularly throughout the Northeast. There was a distinct advantage to learning a piece from a piano roll rather than from a phonograph recording. The latter can not be slowed down without distorting the music. A piano roll, however, can be slowed down and even stopped without changing the sound of the notes. One can learn a piece by following the keys as they are depressed by the action of the roll. Many pianists learned to play Johnson's "Carolina Shout" and other tunes by placing their hands into the correct position at certain points in the piece. Once a phrase was memorized, the roll could be advanced and a new section could be learned.

Sometime in 1921, 17-year old Fats Waller had won a talent contest at Harlem's Roosevelt Theater by playing James P. Johnson's "Carolina Shout," which he had learned from the piano roll.[1] Johnson's reputation was great, and Waller idolized him as Johnson had idolized older players in his youth. Thomas Wright Waller was born in New York City in 1904. His father, Edward Martin, was a minister and eventually became Pastor of Harlem's Abyssinian Baptist Church.

Waller's mother was also religious and encouraged
her son to play hymns and other church music,
since he had taken to music at an early age.
The Wallers moved from their home in Greenwich
Village to the Jungles and eventually to Harlem
in the late 1910s. By 1920, Fats Waller (a nickname applied to him from elementary school days)
had developed sufficient proficiency on both piano
and organ to play the film accompaniments at
the Lincoln Theater.

        In 1921, Waller became a student of his
idol James P. Johnson.   Johnson taught Waller
the essence of stride piano, introduced him to
other great New York musicians, and made it
possible for Waller to record his first piano rolls
and phonograph records.   Through Johnson's
tutelage, Waller became the third pianist in the
triumvirate of great Harlem stride players:
Johnson, Smith, and Waller.   Waller's propensity
for showmanship and clowning eventually brought
him worldwide success in the 1930s.   He recorded
hundreds of sides with his group, "Fats Waller and
his Rhythm." He is the best-known stride pianist
and a colorful figure in jazz history.   Waller
lived more of life in 39 years than most could in
a hundred.   A voracious eater and drinker, he
rarely allowed himself time for idleness.   Waller's
relationship with Johnson was more than merely
one of student and teacher.   The two became
very close friends from their first meeting until
Waller's tragic death from pneumonia on a trans-
continental train near Kansas City on December
15, 1943.

        Several people have recalled the details of
the start of their association. The man responsible for introducing Johnson and Waller was a
fellow Harlem piano player, Russell Brooks. Waller was a friend and schoolmate of Brook's

younger brother Wilson. Russell Brooks thus had
a passing acquaintance with Waller through his
younger brother.   Waller was very anxious to
learn the new music developing in Harlem and
approached Russell, who was playing for a dance
on Lenox Ave. and 140th Street, for help.   The
"dance hall" was merely a tent, and Waller had
no trouble sneaking in under a flap and talking to
Brooks on the bandstand.   Waller confessed his
desire to learn to play rags and shouts.   Brooks
did not consider himself to be a teacher, and
half-heartedly promised to arrange an introduction
to a friend of his who might be able to help,
James P. Johnson.   Waller raced out of the tent
elated.   Before he could escape cleanly, he
managed to catch his foot in a supporting rope
and brought down the whole tent.   However,
neither Waller nor Brooks followed through on this
arrangement, and nothing came of it.[2]

A few months later, a very unfortunate
circumstance in Waller's life rekindled Russell
Brooks's interest in the youngster's music.   On
November 10, 1920, Fats Waller's mother Adeline
died of a massive stroke.   Waller was particularly
close to his mother and was devastated by her
death.   He had always been on poor terms with
his father, and argued bitterly with him after his
mother's demise.   He left home and went to stay
with his friend Wilson Brooks.   Waller's father
had no objections to his son's new residence,
which became permanent.   The Brooks family had
a player piano and several rolls of recordings by
Luckey Roberts and James P. Johnson.   Waller
began to learn them and often practiced late into
the night.   Russell, who had since married and
moved out, came to visit his family and heard
Waller playing Johnson's "Carolina Shout."   He
remembered his earlier promise and soon mentioned the boy to Johnson.[3]

Johnson knew of Fats Waller as the piano player at the Lincoln, but did not know him personally.

> A friend of mine who used to hang out with me--his brother used to bring Fats to his house--he and Fats went to school together. My friend came around one day and told me about this Waller kid who was coming to their house to play the piano. So I went down there--they lived on 131st St.--and he played a couple of things. He had fervor--he was the son of a preacher, you know--but he didn't have any swing then.
>   My friend's father said Fats had to stop coming there because he worked nights and couldn't sleep with all the noise going on every afternoon. I was living with my sister at 267 W. 140th Street. She had a piano and I brought mine there, too. Then I took Fats home. I'd get on one piano, he'd get on the other, and we'd work together. This went on for a couple of years, steady. He picked up all the stomps and rags I knew and that walkin' bass, too.[4]

Fats Waller became James P. Johnson's star pupil. The Johnson household became a second home-away-from-home for Waller, with Lillie Mae Johnson, his surrogate mother, making sure that he did not lose too much sleep practicing the piano. She gave him his first pair of long trousers, and recalled in addition:

> Right after James P. heard Fats Waller playing the pipe organ, he came home and told me, "I know I can teach that boy." Well, from then on it was one big headache for me. Fats was seventeen, and we

lived on 140th Street, and Fats would bang on our piano till all hours of the night-- sometimes two, three, four o'clock in the morning. I would say to him, "Now go on home--or haven't you got a home?"

But he'd come every day and my husband would teach. Of course, you know the organ doesn't give you a left hand and that's what James P. had to teach him.[5]

Johnson also made sure Waller was properly intro- duced and exposed to the other great pianists in Harlem.

The most notable was Willie "The Lion" Smith, who had established a formidable reputa- tion. He was the featured pianist at Leroy Wilkins' club, a favorite hangout for the black celebrities of the day. Smith recalled his first encounter with Fats Waller:

James P. Johnson brought him down one Sunday afternoon. We were all dressed in full-dress suits and tuxedos and in comes this guy with a greasy suit on, walks down to the bandstand, and says, "Hello there, Lion, what do you say?" He made me furious. I turned around to Jimmy and said, "Get that guy down, because he looks filthy." "Get them pants pressed," I said. "There's no excuse for it." From that day on, I called him Filthy.

So he sat down until I got finished and when I got finished he was insistent, very persistent. He insisted he wanted to play Jimmy's "Carolina Shout" and when I got through he sat down and played the "Shout" and made Jimmy like it and me like it. From then on it was Thomas Fats Waller.

> I gave him a listen and made my
> famous prediction: I said to James P.
> Johnson, who was in the house again that
> night, "Watch out, Jimmy, he's got it.
> He's a piano-playing cub!"[6]

After a short time, Smith left Leroy's and
Johnson arranged to have Waller take his place.
However, Waller would now have to accompany
singers, a new challenge which frightened him.
With the help of James P. and Lillie Mae
Johnson (who was one of the singers at Leroy
Wilkins's), Waller started his career performing in
the better establishments:

> When Waller got his first job, as accom-
> panist at Leroy Williams' [sic] cabaret at
> 135th and Fifth, he got stagefright and
> wouldn't go. We sat him down at home,
> my wife sang the songs and I played the
> backgrounds to show him he could do it,
> too. After that, he started going up.[7]

With Johnson's help, Waller made his first phonograph recordings in October of 1922: "Muscle
Shoals Blues" and "Birmingham Blues."[8] Through
Johnson he was introduced to Max Kortlander, J.
Lawrence Cook and others at the QRS piano roll
company. His first roll was released in March
1923.[9] At the age of 19, Fats Waller was well
on his way to a frustrated superstardom. Somewhat surprisingly, in view of their close
association, Waller and Johnson made only a few
recordings together.

Opposite: This advertisement appeared in black
newspapers in 1923. Johnson, whose picture is
largest and featured most prominently, had been
recording for QRS for several years.

Johnson might be considered the better of the two as composer and pianist, although Waller was undoubtedly the superior showman and entertainer. Willie "The Lion" Smith commented:

It is my opinion that James P. was a better composer than Fats, although Waller's tunes have had much more success.

James P. started to devote most of his time to writing show scores during the early twenties. He also got on an arranging and conducting kick. It was his hope he could become a symphonic conductor. From then on, he had no eyes for clowning or showmanship. I used to tell him that when we ran into pianos with the keys broken you had to mug your way to entertain the people. His reply was, "Lion, it just ain't dignified."[10]

Dick Wellstood compared the two as musicians:

James P. was not Pete Johnson, nor a mere "teacher" of Fats Waller. He was a much more interesting musician than Waller. His bass lines are better constructed, his right hand is freer and less repetitive, his rhythm is more accurate, and his playing is not so relentlessly two-beat as that of Fats.[11]

Eubie Blake's comment tells the story in three lines: "Fats Waller knew how to hold an audience, and he could really play too. Between you and me, though, he wasn't no James P. But he learned a lot from Black James."[12] Waller recognized his debt to Johnson and often attributed his vehement faith in maintaining melody in music to his mentor. " ... [Y]ou got to have melody. Jimmy Johnson taught me that. You got to hang onto the melody and never let it get boresome."[13]   Their   mutual   admiration   and friendship   marked   one   of   the   most   famous teacher-pupil relationships in the jazz tradition. Johnson said of his protégé: "Some little people has music in them, but Fats, he was all music, and you know how big he was."[14]

12

Plantation Days, 1923

The various recordings of "Carolina Shout," particularly the QRS piano roll, had established James P. Johnson as a most accomplished pianist. Will Marion Cook, the prominent black composer ("Clorindy or The Origin of the Cakewalk," 1898), declared Johnson to be the most versatile pianist of the race.[1] However, no Johnson phonograph recordings were released in 1922. QRS released 11 piano rolls, but there is a strong probability that they were all cut by Johnson early in the year and released at specified intervals. The dearth of Johnson recordings during this time may have been symptomatic of his increasing involvement in the musical theater. His desire to compose show music had been strong since the days of his association with William Farrell in the mid-1910s. Such work provided many benefits: it exercised his ability as a composer and orchestra leader, afforded a reasonable amount of publicity, and, in many cases, it paid well. Yet, these benefits were ephemeral and provided no real security. Johnson devoted a great deal of time to composing for shows during the 1920s and experienced the fleeting success of most popular composers.

However, his contribution to American musical theater and the popular music field was significant in both output and quality. He worked for Earl Carroll, George White, Flo Ziegfeld, and the Shubert Brothers in addition to such black producers as Frank Montgomery and J. Leubrie Hill. Johnson's music could be heard in full-

blown Broadway productions as well as floor
shows and revues in Harlem cabarets and
theaters. Several of his compositions have become classics of popular music. When appraised
with respect to his total musical output as
composer, performer, and recording musician, his
high level of activity and success in musical
theater becomes even more impressive.

Sometime during the latter part of 1922,
Johnson undertook the job of musical director for
a traveling show called Plantation Days. It is
one of the earliest and more important productions to which Johnson contributed. Details of
the show and Johnson's role in it are obscure and
have often been confused with several other
shows of that time with similar titles. Plantation
Days is thought to have had a very successful
run in the United States. It was afterwards
booked to tour Europe, where Johnson recalled
working with George Gershwin on the show. In
reality, the show was not quite the success one
might imagine. In the United States it was involved in a minor scandal concerning production
numbers, while the association with George
Gershwin in England was merely incidental. The
run in London was plagued by anti-black and anti-
American sentiment which, despite reasonable
popular acclaim, cut short its stay. The information which follows comes almost exclusively from
various contemporary periodicals and traces the
course of the show and the others of similar
name with which it has been confused.

O'Neil and Greenwald's Plantation Days
revue toured much of the mid-Atlantic and eastern United States, setting records in Detroit,
Pittsburgh, and Cleveland for the longest-running
black show. During the Chicago run, Ethel
Waters was added as a special attraction for two

weeks. In December 1922, the show was playing in Toledo, Ohio. An article in the Toledo Blade praised the show for its outstanding musical numbers and the performances of its leading men, Harper and Blanks.[2]   Charles Elgar's Chicago-based Orchestra (Joe Sudler, trumpet, Bert Hall, Harry Swift, trombones, Darnell Howard, violin, Wellman Braud, bass, and others)[3] was under the direction of James P. Johnson.   One Johnson number singled out was "Ukulele Blues," a tune copyrighted in 1922.   After what was proclaimed a very successful tour, the company arrived back in New York in mid-February 1923.

Plantation Days was scheduled to open at the Lafayette Theater the week of February 25. Staged by Leonard Harper and Lawrence Deas, the cast included Joyner and Foster, comedian Eddie Green, George Pasha, and of course the Plantation Days Syncopated Orchestra.   After their week at the Lafayette, the company was scheduled to sail for London.   However, for some unknown reason, Harper and Blanks failed to respect the contract to play at the Lafayette. In addition, they were prevented from leaving for Europe by an injunction requested by the travelling Shuffle Along company.   This show had opened originally in 1921 with a book by Flournoy Miller and Aubrey Lyles (who were also the stars) and music and lyrics by Eubie Blake and Noble Sissle.   It scored a tremendous success and set the standard for black musical productions for the rest of the decade.   The 1923 company of Shuffle Along, while on their own cross-country tour, had not been receiving the enthusiastic response they expected.   As it happened, they were following the Plantation Days show through the larger cities.   Eventually the Shuffle Along company was informed that this show (Plantation) was registering a big success with musical num-

bers taken from their show. They engaged the
services of the Keystone National Detective
Agency of Chicago (a black agency) to work on
stopping Plantation Days.

The three numbers surreptitiously used by
Plantation Days were the hits "Gypsy Blues," "I'm
Craving For That Kind of Love," and "Bandana
Days." Leonard Harper, the leader of the
company, assured the Shuffle Along people that
they would no longer use any of their material.
He also renegotiated a contract with the Coleman
brothers, proprietors of the Lafayette Theater.
The fact that the problem centered on "borrowed"
musical numbers perhaps does not reflect favorably on James P. Johnson, since he was musical
director. However, a story in a prominent paper
reported, "We understand that the colored people
in the show had no choice, as they are under
contract to white men behind the company."4

Plantation Days finally opened at the
Lafayette Theater on April 2. The cast now included the "Plantation Four," Adams and Tunstall,
Julian Mitchell, Smith and Deforrest, Ida Roley,
Daisy Pizarro and a "Peppy Chorus." Sam
Wooding's Famous Syncopated Orchestra was an
added attraction. The reviews were generally
only fair due to the deletion of the crowd-
thrilling numbers from Shuffle Along. The critics
cited two bright spots, however: the performances of comedian Eddie Green, and the
"Hawaiian Number," based on Johnson's "Ukulele
Blues." The British producer Sir Alfred Butt engaged the company to come to England after the
week's run in Harlem. The Plantation Days company of 35 became part of a larger production in
London. They filled only a 12 minute scene in a
show entitled The Rainbow, which opened at the
Empire Theater in early April. The troupe en-

countered both racial prejudice and professional resentment over American entertainers supplanting British performers. In a letter to the editor of the Amsterdam News written upon their return to the United States, Harper and Blanks declared their British engagement to have been a great success, despite various social and contractual problems.[5]

As mentioned, Johnson recalled having worked with George Gershwin on this show. Gershwin had in fact been offered $1500 and a round trip ticket to write the score for the remaining parts of The Rainbow. In three days, Gershwin produced a score that he later considered to be his weakest effort. Although Johnson and Gershwin had been acquainted since their piano roll work for Aeolian, the production they worked on, like most of the theatrical world, was rigorously segregated, preventing the two composers from enjoying professional contact. At best, their collaboration was informal and remains undocumented.[6] Writers often comment favorably on Plantation Days as a significant step in Johnson's career only because he had apparently worked with Gershwin. They seemingly found it necessary to attach Johnson's work to a respected member of the white musical world to afford it universal credibility. Such treatment is misleading and counterproductive, as Johnson's work stands on its own merits.

In addition to blatant segregation, the British resentment toward Americans mentioned by Harper and Blanks was unexpectedly incorporated into the show. An unhappy British comedian, whose part had been sizably cut, delivered an unprogrammed soliloquy just before the finale. He spoke of the poor treatment afforded English performers, and how they were in fact superior

to Americans.   The speaker was physically
removed from the stage, introducing an element
of farce into the entire production.[7] Johnson and
Gershwin's "collaboration" ran for only two
months, and the Plantation Days company returned
to New York in early June of 1923.

The show most often confused with Planta-
tion Days is Lew Leslie's Plantation Revue.
Florence Mills, one of the greatest entertainers of
the American musical theater, was the star of
this show, which ran for several months at the
Plantation restaurant on Broadway.   This show
was very successful and far better known than
Plantation Days.   The British producer Charles B.
Cochran contracted Mills and the Plantation
Revue to appear in a larger show in London, just
as Sir Alfred Butt had done with the Plantation
Days company.

The Revue opened in London on May 31 at
the Pavilion Theater.   It became part of a revue
called From Dover Street to Dixie.   The "Dover
Street" section was made up of white English actors and actresses who appeared in the first part.
The "Dixie" section followed, and featured Mills,
the company, and Will Vodery and his orchestra.
The revue scored as big a success in England as
it had in the United States.   Unfortunately, box
office receipts notwithstanding, the Ministry of
Labor subjected the black members of the company to unfair restrictions in response to the
growing antagonistic sentiment of English performers toward alien entertainers, particularly
blacks.   The Plantation Revue was withdrawn and
its members set sail for the United States in
September.

While in England, members from both Plantation productions were honored by a black social

club called "The Coterie of Friends." According
to the program of the event, the club was
"started by a small group of Students [sic] with
the object of creating a social vehicle whereby
the much isolated population of serious minded
people of colour may come into contact at
frequent intervals." On the evening of May 13,
1923, Miss Florence Mills, Mr. Will Vodery, Mr.
Shelton Brooks, Mr. James P. Johnson, and members of the West Indian cricket team were the
guests of honour. The program credits Johnson
and his orchestra "who have kindly taken charge
of the Musical Program." On an evening when
the buzz of controversy in the London theatre
was silent, truly sincere performers were able to
display their talents before an appreciative
audience.

Back in the United States, Lew Leslie, the
original producer of the Revue, had already put
together a new Plantation Revue which was playing on Broadway. This production initially featured "Hamtree" Harrington and Cora Green.
Upon her return to New York, Florence Mills was
added to the cast. To further complicate things,
the Plantation Days company split into two
separate Plantation shows upon its return from
England. Harper and Blanks were producing their
Plantation Revue at the Lincoln Theater. They
performed at the opening of the famed Connie's
Inn. In addition, the Plantation Days company,
starring Jones and Jones, Chapelle and Stinnette,
Five Cracker Jacks, Seymour and Jeanette, Austin
and Delaney, Scott, Allen and Lee, Baby Theada
Deas and the Clarence Johnson Orchestra, was
starting an extended tour through the Western
United States and Canada. Thus, in August of
1923, there were at least four shows with Plantation in their titles:

> Plantation Revue   London, England
>   with Florence Mills
>
> Plantation show   Broadway, New York
>   with Hamtree and Green
>
> Plantation Revue   Harlem, New York
>   with Harper and Blanks
>
> Plantation Days   Chicago, Illinois
>   with Clarence Johnson Orchestra

James P. Johnson was involved with none of these shows; by August, he already was busy with what would become his most successful musical show production.

13

Runnin' Wild, 1923

Consistent images arise when one speaks of the "roaring twenties." Prohibition, gangsters, and bathtub gin, prosperity and high living, flappers, and perhaps most prominently, jazz music and dancing. If there is one single tune that might be considered the theme song of the decade, it would undoubtedly be the "Charleston." Its melody and rhythm are instantly recognizable the world over, but few can name its composer. Some might credit Cole Porter or George Gershwin with this phenomenal success, or perhaps Paul Whiteman, the "King of Jazz," might be named as its creator. In reality, what white America knew as the "Charleston" in the 1920s was a descendant of a West African (Ashanti) ancestor dance.[1] The composer of the music was, of course, James P. Johnson, who had been exposed to the various transformations of the original African dance as they were executed a decade earlier in the dance halls of the Jungles. In addition to his "shout" pieces, Johnson said that he wrote eight "Charlestons" while playing for these dances, one of which became the famous song. The actual dance steps are far removed from the more authentic unstandardized renditions which spawned the Charleston rhythm. By the middle of the decade, the "Charleston" had become the most popular dance song and step America had known.

The original song and dance were first introduced to the public in the show Runnin' Wild. Its predecessor, Shuffle Along, had established it-

self as the most successful and significant all-
black musical of the decade, a position in
theatrical history from which it was never
displaced. Not since the first decade of the century had a major all-black production held forth
on Broadway with any real success. The 1920s
saw the beginnings of the fusion of various musical and theatrical forms which had previously
been distinct. Burlesque and minstrel shows
began to overlap in character, creating a revue
form of much wider scope. More importantly,
the gap between rural and urban settings for
shows was narrowing. Shuffle Along combined the
black heritage of both country and city, depicting
the agrarian roots in earthy humor and sentimental song and the urban hopes and struggles in the
blues, shouts, and jazz dancing.[2]

Specifically, the show broke with several
conventions to which previous black shows had
adhered. The majority of the cast did not wear
burnt cork, most noticeably the light-skinned
chorus line of female dancers. In the tradition
of white shows like the Follies or Vanities,
Shuffle Along presented a line of precision dancers in semi-suggestive garb. The most important
break with tradition (or tabu, in this case) was
the incorporation of a serious unparodied, romantic love element in the show. During the first
heyday of black musical theater around the turn
of the century, when women were allowed on the
same stage as men at all, strict social convention
imposed by the white audiences proscribed any
expression of real affection.[3]

Based on a comic sketch by Miller and
Lyles called The Mayor of Dixie, Shuffle Along
established a new and urbane standard for black
musicals to follow, relying less on mere self-
parody and using the nuances of life's reality.

Runnin' Wild was one of several shows to use these new conceptions of blacks on stage. Produced by George White, famous for his series of productions called the Scandals, the show featured a book by Miller and Lyles, who also played the leading roles. Eager to ride the wave of success built up by their previous show, the two comedians constructed what falls just short of a sequel. The story concerns two deadbeats from the southern town of Jimtown. They skip on their board bill and go to the frigid climate of St. Paul, Minnesota. After a fill of the cold, they return to Jimtown as spiritualistic mediums. The story line is not very deep, allowing a series of song and dance numbers and comedy sketches to serve as the framework. Miller and Lyles were the best black comedy team of their day and together with a superb supporting cast, they produced a very well-received show.

The aspect which made Runnin' Wild an important historical link was the introduction of the "Charleston" to the American public. Johnson worked with Cecil Mack on writing the tunes, while Lyda Webb staged the dances. The rise in popularity of the dance and song is not a clearly defined development. Most of the reviews singled out the song "Old Fashioned Love" as the number most likely to catch the public's favor, not the "Charleston." Although the original sheet music carries the proper spelling, many show programs, including at least one from as late as 1925, lists the tune as "Charston." Yet, by the middle of the decade, the name was applied to myriad spin-offs and imitations in addition to holding the place at the top of the dance world. Later sheet music printings included pictorial instructions on mastering the dance steps. Somehow, the "Charleston" struck at some internal sensitivity of the American public, which turned it into the symbol of an age.

The common practice for shows headed for Broadway then as now was to stage a brief tour through other eastern cities before opening in New York. Runnin' Wild opened on August 25, 1923, at the Howard Theater in Washington. The 15-piece orchestra was under the direction of Will Marion Cook. It is not known definitely whether Johnson was at the piano, though it is likely since he was in the pit when the show reached New York. The show ran successfully at the Howard for two weeks, grossing $8,000 during the first week. In mid-September, it opened at Selwyn's Theater in Boston. Reviews for the most part had been very favorable, clearing the path for a successful run on Broadway.

Opening in New York on October 29, 1923, at the Colonial Theater at Broadway and 62nd Street, it ran for 27 weeks and 213 performances. The first few weeks, the gross was $19,000 per week, a sizable sum. John T. Ricks' Orchestra played in the pit. John Hammond, later to become a famed patron of jazz and record producer, recalled meeting Johnson for the first time when he played in the orchestra at the Colonial Theater.[4] The show did very well for its entire run, its gross receipts eventually leveling off at $11,000 per week. Five of the musical numbers were copyrighted and published: "Ginger Brown," "Love Bug," "Old Fashioned Love," "Open Your Heart," and the "Charleston." ("Love Bug" was eventually dropped from the show.)

Most of the cast members were veterans of Shuffle Along and had established their reputations in that show. The feature number "Old Fashioned Love" was presented by three such veterans: Ina

Duncan, Arthur Porter, and Adelaide Hall. This
number was singled out above all others by the
reviewers as the overwhelming hit of the show.
The two biggest white entertainment publications
had this to say:

> The key song of the piece, "Old Fashioned
> Love," was particularly well done and seems
> destined for great popularity." Gordon
> Whyte--Billboard, Nov. 10, 1923

> Of the musical numbers, which are the
> work of James Johnson while the lyrics are
> by Cecil Mack, there isn't one but that
> will register. The "love number" is the
> theme song and will undoubtedly be one of
> the big sellers of the coming season.
> Meakin--Variety, Aug. 30, 1923

As the show continued its run, changes
were made in the cast, musical numbers, and
sketches. By 1925, one noticeable rearrangement
placed the "Charleston" before the finale of both
acts. In addition, the dance had been choreo-
graphed to include the entire company. After
the run on Broadway, the show travelled around
the New York area for two years, playing at
such theaters as the Shubert in Newark, The
Bronx Opera House, and Werba's Theaters in
Brooklyn and Montauk, Long Island. In May of
1928, a travelling company took the show to
London.

The duration of Johnson's role as company
pianist is not exactly known. Show programs
name only the orchestra director or make no
mention of the musical accompaniment at all.
Unlike Eubie Blake, who recorded many of the
musical numbers from his show during its run,
Johnson recorded very few of the tunes from

Runnin' Wild during the height of its popularity.
Recording royalties for the composer or performer
who was not also the copyright claimant and
record promoter were not accorded as standard
procedure.   The likelihood is that phonograph
recordings simply did not pay well enough to
make the effort worthwhile.   Perhaps a flat fee
of $30 or $50 might be offered.   Johnson was
making upwards of $100 for each of his piano
rolls, and in view of his big success with Runnin'
Wild, was in great demand to compose for other
productions, which paid better than recordings.

The show world was attractive financially
and enabled Johnson to build a backstage reputation as a composer.   His playing continued to
develop and expand, creating an additional demand
for his talents as solo performer.   The mid-1920s
(1924-1926) were busy times for Johnson, although
the details are somewhat vague.   He recorded
only sporadically, often with his friend Perry
Bradford of "Crazy Blues" fame and his various
groups: the Jazz Phools, his Gang, the Mean
Four,   and the Original Jazz Hounds.   As a
performer, Johnson did not forsake the grass-roots
influence of Harlem which pervaded all of his
work.   The world of basement saloons, backroom
cabarets, and most importantly, the rent parties
or "parlor socials" constituted a large part of the
Harlem social fabric in which Johnson, in the
words of Duke Ellington, "went right on up to
the greatest."

14

The Rent Party

Chittlin' Struts, Gumbo Suppers, Fish Fries, Egg
Nog Parties, Parlor Socials, Buffet Flats, and
Rent Parties--all are synonyms for a form of
mass cultural expression, the initial essence of
which derived from the physical and cultural dis-
placement of a race of people. The migration of
blacks before and during the First World War
from a largely rural environment to the inner
city required a means of acclimatization to a
new set of internal and external pressures.
Naturally, living in a white-dominated society
created hardships, which in the rural past were
dealt with creatively through the blues. In the
northern cities, the new breed of middle class
Negro scoffed at the unsophisticated, crude life-
styles of the newly arrived southerners. One
place where neither group could intrude was a
private residence, particularly the family parlor.
The family parlor provided a haven from racial
prejudice and class snobbery where the newcomers
and others of similar sensibility could gather
unobserved.

The phenomenon of parlor socials was nothing new. Yet, in the black areas of northern
cities they developed into a distinct phenomenon
known collectively as the rent party. Appearances may have suggested a variety of
reasons and formats for arranging a rent party,
but the necessity of communal release and
unspoken camaraderie was always the common,
underlying feature. Rent parties predominated as
middle- to lower-class private entertainment

through the 1920s, although they had existed in recognizable form as early as 1913 and continued into the depression.

The black population in Chicago, located on the famous south side, also relied on rent parties to vent the same frustrations. The music played there was often a hybrid form known as barrel-house, skiffle, or South-side piano. It was a cross between midwestern ragtime and boogie-woogie. Eventually, the style moved increasingly toward a more cohesive blues-based boogie-woogie style. In the 1920s, one could find both ragtime-oriented players such as Jimmy Blythe and Clarence Johnson as well as boogie-woogie pianists like Clarence "Pine-Top" Smith and Meade Lux Lewis playing for rent parties.[1] In New York a cohesive piano style had already been developed and perfected. At the rent parties in Harlem, one heard stride piano. Although stylistic differences did exist which varied in their degree of eclecticism, the leaders of the rent party circuit were the best stride pianists and provided the featured entertainment.

A parlor social was usually arranged as a fund-raising event and a demonstration of community support. Originally, a church group, in order to raise money to pay the preacher or help a needy congregation member, would arrange such an event in a parishioner's home. Guests payed a nominal admission charge at the door, usually 25 cents or 50 cents, and could then buy all the food and drink they could consume for a very low price. A number of singers and musicians provided the entertainment. The money taken in was used to cover expenses and finance whatever cause prompted the party.[2]

During the 1920s, these parties became a distinguishable phenomena and integral part of Harlem's social life. They eventually came to be called rent parties, since their stated function on many occasions was to raise rent money. The system worked the same way as the old church socials. During the 1920s, admission was usually one dollar. Chitterlings, hogmaws, barbequed chicken, ribs, and pork chops, and other traditional southern dishes became the standard bill of fare. The rent party also provided an easy outlet for illegal alcohol during prohibition. Sometimes a hundred people would crowd into a seven-room railroad flat, the furniture having been stored in another apartment. The kitchen was always active, as was the bedroom for serious gambling, or casual sex. The rent party was the place to pick up the latest news, jokes, and gossip.[3] Although a great many middle-class blacks disdained the debauchery they saw at the parties, the fashionable section of well-to-do Harlemites residing on 139th Street between Seventh and Eighth Avenues often featured rent parties. Johnson recalled, "It was called Striver's Row because people strived like hell to pay the rent and taxes. They were the days of bathtub gin and corn whisky and stills in the apartments and Jimmy Walker was Mayor. The parties attracted a lot of people, many white folk who were taking up the Negro."[4] Some of these curious liberal-minded whites were Carl Van Vechten, John Hammond, and George Gershwin.

Aside from the alcohol, the driving force behind the parties was the entertainment. The big three on the rent party circuit were Willie "The Lion" Smith, Fats Waller and James P. Johnson. Another player named Lippy Boyette acted as a booking agent. He contracted several pianists for each party, sometimes lining up as

many as three parties in one night for the same
players. They would make the rounds, starting in
the afternoon and continuing through late the
next day. Tickets printed to advertise the performers were sold in advance on the street.
Sometimes, to be included in a particularly good
lineup, a player would arrange for a substitute to
take his place at his regular job for the evening.
The tradition of deportment which had been a
crucial part of a player's performance was maintained in performing at a rent party.[5]

In spite of the image of elegance which
the players hoped to convey, the picture many of
the cultural highbrows painted was merely one of
decadence. Novelist Wallace Thurman depicted
what he perceived as the savagery of the rent
party, the vulgarity of the participants, and the
unappealing image of the pianists:

> When they returned to the room, the
> pianist was just preparing to play again.
> He was tall and slender, with extra long
> legs and arms, giving him the appearance
> of a scarecrow. His pants were tight in
> the waist and full in the legs. He wore
> no coat, and a blue silk shirt hung damply
> to his body. He acted as if he were king
> of the occasion, ruling all from his piano
> stool throne. He talked familiarly to every
> one in the room, called women from other
> men's arms, demanded drinks from any
> bottle he happened to see being passed
> around, laughed uproariously, and made
> many grotesque and ofttimes obscene
> gestures.
>   Emma Lou could not keep her eyes
> off the piano player. He was acting like a
> maniac, occasionally turning completely
> around on his stool, grimacing like a witch

doctor, and letting his hands dawdle over the keyboard of the piano with agonizing indolence, when compared to the extreme exertion to which he put the rest of his body. He was improvising. The melody of the piece he had started to play was merely a base for more bawdy variations. His right punished the piano's loud-pedal. Beads of perspiration gathered grease from his slicked-down hair, and rolled oleagenously down his face and neck, spotting the already damp baby-blue shirt, and streaking his already greasy black face with more shiny lanes....

A sailor had suddenly ceased his impassioned hip movement and strode out of the room, pulling his partner behind him, pushing people out of the way as he went. The spontaneous moans and slangy ejaculations of the piano player and of the more articulate dancers became more regular, more like a chanted obbligato to the music. This lasted for a couple of hours interrupted only by hectic intermissions. Then the dancers grew less violent in their movements, and though the piano player seemed never to tire there were fewer couples on the floor, and those left seemed less loathe to move their legs.[6]

The rent party was a showcase for a pianist, who knew very well that his performance at the piano determined the success of the party. His flamboyance was part of the performance.

The rent party often became a musical battleground. The party-goers, especially after several drinks, were not abashed to express their opinions about whose playing they appreciated most. The contests between pianists were, in many instances, taken more seriously by the audience than the performers, for whom the spirit of professional but friendly competition prevailed. Willie "The Lion" Smith described his approach:

> We would embroider the melodies with our own original ideas and try to develop patterns that had more originality than those played before us. Sometimes it was just a question as to who could think up the most patterns within a given time. It was pure improvisation.
>
> You had to have your own individual style and be able to play in all the keys. In those days we could all copy each other's shouts by learning them by ear. Sometimes in order to keep the others from picking up too much of my stuff, I'd perform in the hard keys, B major and E major.[7]

There was, however, a semi-official pecking order for playing time at the larger affairs. One player would sit down and "warm up" the piano with several choruses of a particular song. After a while, another player would slide in on the piano bench next to the first player, relieving him one hand at a time. This procedure continued until everyone had played. Then, only the best players (or the most daring) would vie for the greatest support of the audience. The competition often grew heated.

By most accounts, the acknowledged piano king at the rent parties was James P. Johnson. "You know," remarked Duke Ellington, "he ordinarily played the most, and in competition a little bit more."[8] Garvin Bushell described the scene:

There'd be more controversy among the listeners than the participants.   There was
betting and people were ready to fight a-
bout who'd won.   Jimmy played with the
most originality.   He'd create things the
other guys hadn't thought up.

Jimmy was on top most of the time.
You got credit for how many patterns you
could create within the tunes you knew,
and in how many different keys you could
play.[9]

The test pieces most often used were Johnson
compositions.   All the stride pianists mastered
"Carolina Shout" or "Harlem Strut." For any player to develop credibility within the guild, these
had to be performed convincingly with the right
dose of originality.

Duke Ellington, Cliff Jackson, and Joe Turner all told of the first time they played
Johnson's "shouts" for the composer himself.

Ellington:

My first encounter with James was through
the piano rolls, the Q.R.S. rolls.   There
was a drummer in Washington who told me
about them, took me home with him, and
played me 'Carolina Shout.'   He said I
ought to learn it.   So how was I going to
do it, I wanted to know.   He showed me
the way.   We slowed the machine and then
I could follow the keys going down.   I
learned it!

And how I learned it!   I nursed it,
rehearsed it....   Yes, this was the most
solid foundation for me.   I got hold of
some of his other rolls, and they helped me

with styling, but 'Carolina Shout' became
my party piece.

Then James came to Washington to
play Convention Hall. It holds maybe four
or five thousand people. I was always a
great listener. I'm taller on one side than
the other from leaning over the piano,
listening. This time I listened all night
long. After a while my local following
started agitating.

"You got to get up there and play
that piece," they said. "Go on! Get up
there and cut him!"

So you know, I had to get up there
and play it.

"Hey, you play that good," James
said. We were friends then, and I wanted
the privilege of showing him around town,
showing him the spots, introducing him to
my pals, the best bootleggers, and so on.
That, naturally, meant more leaning on the
piano. Afterwards, we were fast friends,
and James never forgot.[10]

Jackson:

It was during the prohibition. I was
making a lot of money on liquor, and I
walked into the room at this big party and
told the guys to set everybody up. I had
noticed a big fellow sleeping on a couch in
the corner, but I didn't pay him much attention until after someone asked me to
play the piano. I started playing "Carolina
Shout" and this fellow, without moving,
opened one eye and asked: "Who are you?"
I got pretty mad, because I was quite well
known in Washington and I figured this guy
had some nerve asking who I was! So I
answered him with the same question, but

when he told me he was James P. Johnson
I couldn't play any more.   He asked me to
continue, but I just couldn't.[11]

Turner:

I asked the first person I met where I
could find the colored people in town.   I
was told to take the L-train to 130th
Street in Harlem.   There I asked where the
musicians were hangin' out.   They told me
that it was a place called the Comedy
Club.
Going there, I had a drink, set my
bag down, and noticed that anyone who
wished could go to the piano and play.
Realizing that none of the pianists who had
performed before me had done anything
special, I walked over to the piano and
started to play.   After a warm-up number,
I went into the "Harlem Strut," and then I
went to the climax with the "Carolina
Shout."
When I had finished, people swarmed
around me and wanted to know where I
came from.   After I told them, someone in
the crowd reminded me that the composer
of the last two numbers I had played was
in the room--James P. Johnson!   Of course,
you can imagine how I felt!   I must have
impressed him, however, since he left his
table, came up to the piano, and played
the same two numbers as nobody in the
world could![12]

Clarinetist Milton "Mezz" Mezzrow, in his
autobiography, Really the Blues, told the story of
a fantastic "cutting contest" at a rent party.
This particular incident took place sometime
during the depression, probably the early 1930s.

Johnson had moved out of the city, but his ability at the piano was still superior.

One morning a sensational cutting contest took place, just between piano players.
Corky [Williams] sat down and started to play "Tea for Two," a number that Willie The Lion could give a fit. All of a sudden Willie jumped up and said to Corky, "Git up from there you no-piano-playin' son of a bitch, I got it," and with that he sat down next to Corky. As Corky slid over, Willie started to play just the treble, while Corky still kept up the bass, and then he picked up with his left hand too, the tempo not even wavering and without missing a beat. Willie played for a while and then Fats took over, sliding into the seat the same way Willie had done. He played for a while, looking up at Willie and signifying every time he made a new or tricky passage. It went on like that, the music more and more frantic, that piano not resting for even a fraction of a second, until finally Fats said "I'm goin' to settle this argument good." He went into a huddle with his chauffeur, who left and returned about an hour later, but not alone. Fats had telephoned to Jamaica, Long Island, and woke up James P. Johnson out of his bed. When the chauffeur brought Jimmy in he was still rubbing his eyes, but as soon as he sat down at the piano that was all. He played so much piano you didn't have to yell "Put out the lights and call the law," because the law came up by request of the neighbors. "We been sittin' downstairs enjoying the music," the cops told us, when we got a call from the station house to see who was disturbing the

peace around here. Some people ain't got
no appreciation for music at all. Fats,
just close them windows and pour us a
drink, and take up where you left off." So
for the rest of the morning the contest
went on, with these two coppers lolling
around drinking our liquor and listening to
our fine music. It was great.[13]

Both the rent party and stride piano seem to be
the two most overlooked phenomena that predominated during the twenties. Few works deal with
either beyond superficial imagery. Yet their
place in the social and musical history of the
period is of key importance and should not be
passed over lightly.

James P. Johnson's activities through the
years 1924-1926 are not accurately and specifically documented. Except for piano rolls, few
recordings were made. Johnson was, however,
continually in demand as composer and performer.
In addition to the rent parties, Johnson and the
better known of his contemporaries (like Smith
and Waller) were often invited to fashionable
cocktail parties on Park Avenue. Their white
counterparts in the music field, men like Harold
Arlen, George Gershwin, Vernon Duke and Roy
Bargy, requested their presence at formal affairs,
perhaps to pick up on new ideas from the true
jazz innovators. Smith recalled that Johnson
spoke very little about his music. His hosts
would have to rely on the sharpness of their
ears, since Johnson explained very little of what
he was doing. One such event in particular was
the celebration of the success of Gershwin's
"Rhapsody In Blue" in 1924, to which the
threesome was invited.[14]

Johnson remained active playing in numerous jam sessions, after-hours parties, sitting in with various groups, and no doubt leading some of his own bands in Harlem clubs. Virtuoso soprano saxophonist and clarinetist Sidney Bechet recalled joining Johnson's group, which was playing at the Old Kentucky Club, on Eighth Avenue off Broadway, sometime in 1924. Bechet was a New Orleans-born and bred Creole. His style was rooted in collective improvisation. Johnson was leaning more toward arranged, orchestral jazz. In a rather disdainful tone, Bechet commented that "James P. was trying to make it almost like one of those big swing bands--hit parade stuff."[15] Their stylistic disagreement eventually led to Bechet's departure from the group. Although Johnson claimed the manager of the club was more in favor of his own approach, Johnson also left the club not long after.

Johnson and Bechet for a while worked together with Will Marion Cook on a show entitled Negro Nuances. Bechet recalled that it was never completed. However, it is more likely that he gave up on the show, since it was produced by Cook in 1924. Johnson was orchestra director and, with Cook, composed the score. The story traces the musical history of the black people from its origins in Africa through the years of slavery to reconstruction. The book was written by Abbie Mitchell, Will Marion Cook's wife, a prominent singer and dancer. With Mitchell, the cast featured Lucille Handy (daughter of W.C. Handy), Flournoy Miller, and Aubrey Lyles. Also in 1924, Johnson wrote the music for Cotton Land, a show featuring Gertrude Saunders. The year 1925 saw the production of another show, Mooching' Along. Johnson's old collaborator Cecil Mack, and Jessie

Shipp, the "Dean of the Colored Theatrical Profession," also contributed to the show.[16]

Although no details concerning the musical numbers from these shows could be found, several Johnson/Mack collaborations were published in 1925. It is possible they were part of the score for Mooching Along. Johnson's total copyrighted output increased steadily through 1925, 1926, and 1927. Several of his earlier instrumental pieces, "Carolina Shout," "Eccentricity Waltz," and "Keep Off the Grass," were finally copyrighted and arranged for publication, as well as newer pieces like "Jingles" and "Scalin' the Blues." More than anything else, Johnson concentrated on writing for the popular and theatrical market. Chicago Loop: Musical Comedy in Two Acts, and Geechie: Dusky Romance in Three Acts were copyrighted in 1926. It is not known whether either was ever produced. In the same year, Johnson composed a tune which became his most popular "top-ten" hit.

"If I Could Be With You (One Hour To-night)," with lyrics by Henry Creamer, had a slow start on the popular charts. George Randol and Andy Razaf featured the tune in an edition of Irvin C. Miller's Brownskin Models.[17] Ruth Etting, the famed star of the Ziegfeld Follies, introduced it to the majority of the white music-buying public in 1930, and boosted it to the top of America's popular song market. Louis Armstrong recorded it in the same year, as did McKinney's Cotton Pickers. Its phenomenal success provided ample reason for Johnson to join ASCAP (the American Society of Composers, Authors and Publishers), the organization that protects artists' rights to the use of their works. Its members receive quarterly checks based on the number of works registered, the length of membership, and the number of performances of their works.

In 1949, Warner Bros. Pictures released the movie Flamingo Road, starring Joan Crawford, Zachary Scott, and Sydney Greenstreet. The score for the film which, according to the credits, was an original work by Max Steiner, is based primarily on "If I Could Be With You." It is interpolated in numerous ways, from Crawford's solo humming to the fully orchestrated arrangement highlighting the climax of the story. The sheet music depicts a full page photograph of Joan Crawford, with an appropriate caption describing its place in the movie. No mention is made of Johnson or the song title in the film's credits, leaving one to wonder if he was at all compensated as composer for a song still under original copyright. The royalty agreements with Jerome H. Remick, the publisher and original copyright claimant, are not known. Johnson was not a shrewd businessman and, judging from the manner in which other non-business oriented composers like Fats Waller were treated by the publishers, it is conceivable that Johnson was not offered the most equitable settlement. Curiously, Johnson himself recorded "If I Could Be With You" only twice, possibly due to lack of a recording royalty agreement. It is unfortunate that most of America, from recordings by Ruth Etting and Joan Crawford to Bugs Bunny in his Valentine's Day episode, knows the tune, but not the identity of its composer.

There is no question that James P. Johnson was a very busy man during the mid-1920s. As he often said, it was hard for him to keep up with himself. In 1926, James P. and Lillie Mae added their first child to the family, James P. Jr. The whirlwind of musical activity which laid such heavy demands on Johnson's time and physical endurance came to a head in the latter part of the twenties. In four years, Johnson produced a remarkable body of recordings and compositions which, in addition to live engagements, represented the widest cross-section of involvement in the music field. The scope, quantity, and quality of his work marks this period as the high point of his career, fulfilling many of his own important musical aspirations, but for developing what counts most to posterity, a name well known to the public.

15

James P. Johnson: The Composer

Johnson's abilities as composer are demonstrated by the diversity of his published output in 1927. Rather than forsaking one aspect of his career to pursue another, he continued to add to the laurels he had already gathered. In so doing, he compounded the conceptual complexity of maintaining the stylistic integrity of the various compositional forms he employed. Show tunes, descriptively ethnic songs, "jazz" instrumentals, and a serious, extended composition were all added to the Johnson portfolio. Remaining true to the distinct characteristics of these compositional forms while attempting to excel at them all is a formidable task in itself. Add to it Johnson's various roles as performer--playing virtuoso solos, leading orchestras and accompanying vocalists--and one may begin to see the sources of the stylistic frustration to which Johnson partially succumbed.

Johnson contributed three numbers to Rosalie Stewart's revue, A la Carte. "I'm Stepping Out With Lulu," written with Henry Creamer, was one of the featured tunes from the show and did well commercially. Most of the score was written by Herman Hupfeld, famous for "As Time Goes By," with other tunes contributed by Louis Alter, Norma Gregg, Karl Kreck, and Paul Lanin. At least 16 of Johnson's popular songs were copyrighted and/or published in 1927. Among them was a collection of "Five Descriptive Negro Songs," given the title "Dixieland Echoes." The work was co-written and published by Perry Bradford, Johnson's old friend and promoter-

exploiter of black music. The foreword to the
collection, written by Bradford, contains a brief
statement explaining the rather trite images and
meanings of each of the tunes.

"Echoes of Ole Dixieland"

We picture a log cabin scene in Alabama, with
Fathers, Mothers, Sons and Daughters after their
evening meal at sundown.

"Honey"

A crooning Negro lullaby, with love for its theme.

"Mississippi River Flood"

A Negro Musical Poem, of the Mississippi River
Flood, with style descriptive.

"Cotton Pickin'"

A descriptive gem, telling how the Negroes
celebrate the event by singing, dancing, banjo
playing and giving thanks to the Lord for their
good crops.

"Liza Jane's Weddin'"

A Terpsichorean Jazz Classic, with words that
describe the happenings at a Negro Wedding.

These introductions suggest an attempt to recast
the hackneyed and threadbare images of southern
black life which countless stale popular songs had
beaten to death. "Crooning Negro Lullaby,"
"Negro Musical Poem," and "Terpsichorean Jazz
Classic" convey a serious approach to using folk
materials as more than stereotypical pandering.
Rather than introducing any truly novel conception

however,   the   pieces   rely   on   nineteenth   century
romantic, descriptive imagery.

Bradford   published   another   collection   of
works   representative   of   a   different   contem-
poraneous   musical   conception.   "Jazzapation--A
Study   in   Jazz   by   the   Masters,"   included   "Six   Hot
Piano Solos":   two each by Johnson, Bradford, and
Fred   Longshaw.   Longshaw,   a   pianist   from   the
Midwest, is best known for his work accompanying
Bessie   Smith   and   other   blues   singers   through   the
1920s.   He   recorded   "Chili   Pepper"   and   "Tomato
Sauce"   in   1925   before   their   inclusion   by   Bradford
in "Jazzapation."   His recorded versions reveal an
interesting   blend   of   blues,   ragtime   and   novelty
effects.

"Toddlin'   Home"   and   "Scoutin'   Around"   are
the   two   Johnson   compositions   included   in   "Jazzapation."   He recorded them for the Okeh label in
1923,   the   former   with   the   title   listed   simply   as
"Toddlin'."   "Scoutin'   Around"   consists   of   two
basic   themes,   the   second   modulating   to   the
dominant   as   is   the   common   practice   in   many   ragtime   pieces.   Each   chorus   is   based   on   a   blues
progression   of   standard   12-bar   length.   The   A
theme   divides   into   one   4-   and   one   8-bar   phrase.
The   4-bar   segment   consists   of   a   descending   break
which,   when   initiated   immediately   at   the   outset
of the performance, sounds more like a 4-bar introduction   than   part   of   the   first   chorus.   This
pattern   is   maintained   for   five   choruses,   with
Johnson   varying   each   one.   He   then   swings   into
four   statements   of   the   B   theme,   varying   each   one
and   using   a   very   complex   array   of   back-beats   set
against   right   hand   counter-rhythms.   In   the   fourth
and   final   B   chorus,   the   listener   may   think
Johnson   has   lost   the   beat   and   that   he   will   end
up   with   too   few   or   too   many   beats.   With   structured   effortlessness,   he   ends   the   chorus   exactly

on time, concluding with a reprise of the 4-bar break from the A theme as a coda.[1]

As a collection of "jazz" piano solos by three composers, "Jazzapation" is and probably was more of a success than "Dixieland Echoes," at least in an aesthetic sense. Yet, the perennial conflict between composition and performance in the jazz tradition once again reminds the reader and listener that the element which makes "Scoutin' Around" a "hot" piano solo is Johnson's playing. For a more universal application of elements of the black musical tradition, Johnson turned toward projecting many of these ideas into the extended forms of serious composition.

His first and possibly his best work in this regard is "Yamekraw: Negro Rhapsody." Noble Sissle recalled Johnson's work and progress on this piece:

> When James P. Johnson got to kicking around the idea of composing a Rhapsody he first tried to use an original theme. In fact he was quite on the way with the first movement when he dropped in to Perry Bradford's office and asked a group of fellow musicians to listen to his efforts. Among the listeners was Will Vodery and Will Marion Cook both of whom were great musicians and knew construction of the classics whereas Johnson was doing a good technical job.
>   Both Will Marion Cook and Vodery suggested to the young composer, that rather than trying to compose an original theme why not get one of Perry's Spiritual and Blues and use them as to themes. Because as they both pointed out that an American Rhapsody would have to include

those great elements.   And they called attention to how Dvořák used the Spiritual
melody of "Going Home" in order to set
the mood for his "New World Symphony."
And thus this great work ["Yamekraw"] was
created.[2]

Almost 20 years before Ellington wrote his mas-
terwork of black music in extended form, "Black,
Brown and Beige," Johnson had completed this
pioneering effort to express the range of emotion
and vitality in black music.   The piece is not
strictly jazz, stride, ragtime, blues, or a spiritual,
but uses the underlying elements of black folk
and religious traditions, as Sissle pointed out, in
the same way that European masters had used
black American folk material.

The foreword to "Yamekraw" describes the
intent of the work as "A genuine Negro treatise
on spiritual, syncopated and 'blue' melodies by
James P. Johnson, expressing the religious fervor
and happy moods of the natives of Yamekraw, a
Negro settlement situated on the outskirts of
Savannah, Georgia."   The foreword also hints at a
comparison with Gershwin's "Rhapsody in Blue,"
which had already received world-wide acclaim as
an important link in American art music.   It is
more than likely that Johnson saw himself as the
black Gershwin and, with closer links than
Gershwin to the Afro-American musical tradition,
perhaps even better qualified to compose "American Music."   Many other black composers of the
period with similar aspirations, like J. Rosamond
Johnson, W.C. Handy, Hall Johnson, and William
Grant Still (who orchestrated "Yamekraw"), were
not as intimately familiar as Johnson with the
grass-roots tradition so necessary to achieve the
right tone of authenticity.

"Yamekraw" was the first realization of Johnson's desire to be considered a serious composer. Its success was not overwhelming and along with other work in this genre, is thought to be his least successful venture overall. Yet "Yamekraw" does represent a serious effort to "legitimize" American black music without sacrificing content and expression for form and structure. As Rudi Blesh comments, "These are long works with a feeling of breadth and sweep and with a racial pungency that Gershwin missed, and their African rhythms move with a forthright nobility. One feels none of these qualities as borrowed--they all reside in the dark, diminutive composer himself."[3] At the very least, the black intellectual community should have paid half the attention to Johnson's work that they did to the large volume of literary work from the period, most of which in retrospect is considered no better artistically in its field than Johnson's compositions. However, important progress was made in literature and music which established the groundwork for the success of men like Ralph Ellison and Duke Ellington in successive generations.

Perry Bradford, the publisher of the piece, outlined the thematic material which Johnson used for the four movements. The first is based on "Every Time I Feel The Spirit Moving In My Heart" and "Sam Jones Done Snagged His Britches." The second movement includes "Brothers and Sisters," a melody used independently as a separately published song. The third and fourth movements also include a theme, "Mississippi Roustabouts," which was used separately in a later show. "You Can Read My Letters, But You Can't Read My Mind" and "We Are Leaving For Yamekraw" constitute the closing sections.[4]

The rather segmented structure implied by Bradford's breakdown is the most audible weakness of the piece.   "What emerges is a collage of short themes that seem to be lifted out of context and lose all sense of spontaneity.   It's like seeing scenes from a movie in the form of 'previews of coming attractions'--intriguing, but somehow incomplete."[5]   The problem is one of structural conception.   It is the same problem that plagued Scott Joplin in his attempts to compose on a higher level, using the form of an opera. Simply transplanting musical ideas into an alien form seems destined for failure, either because of a loss of authenticity or irreconcilable incompatibility between form and content. It was necessary for a new form to evolve by itself, a process which thwarted Johnson's best and most sincere intentions. At the time, Johnson was one of the most qualified composers to attempt such an ambitious endeavor. However, the time was not right.

"CHARLESTON"
MILLER AND LYLES
(LATE STARS OF "SHUFFLE ALONG")
RUNNIN' WILD
BOOK BY
MILLER AND LYLES
WORDS & MUSIC BY
CECIL MACK AND JIMMY JOHNSON
BOOK STAGED BY
FLOURNOY E. MILLER
NUMBERS STAGED BY
ELIDA WEBB
"CHARLESTON"
LOVE BUG
OLD FASHIONED LOVE
OPEN YOUR HEART
HARMS
NEW YORK

16

James P. Johnson: The Recording Artist

The busiest years in the recording studio for James P. Johnson were 1927-1930. He was involved in 60 recording sessions, constantly in demand to cut piano rolls, record piano solos, lead orchestras, and accompany vocalists. Recording had become a much more profitable venture in the latter half of the decade.   Trumpeter Louis Metcalf, with whom Johnson recorded during this time, recalled the situation: "It happened overnight and it just boomed--records, records, records.   We used to make so many records during the day that we didn't feel like working at night.   That's where the money was and for at least three or four years I didn't bother about taking a steady job at night."[1]   The sessions themselves were very different from today, often involving pick-up musicians and compositions written in the studio with little or no rehearsal. Many masters were cut in only one take, although Johnson somehow arranged for several takes for many of his solos.

New Orleans-born bassist George "Pops" Foster claimed to recall an undocumented recording session with Fats Waller and James P. Johnson. It is very likely that his recollection is a pastiche of several occasions, some not even from record dates, but the images conveyed can be taken as typical of the two pianists and the general setting of a session.

In New York going to a recording session was like going on a picnic.   The most fun was with Fats Waller. He'd pack up a suitcase like he was going on a trip but it would be full of whiskey. When he'd get to the recording studio he'd pass bottles out to the guys. Then Fats would sit at the piano with his bottle and a big glass to drink out of. Him and James P. Johnson would sit down and fool around on the piano. They'd write and arrange the number right there in the studio. Then Fats would say something like, "Let's time this chorus." He'd have them time one chorus of what he was doing. As fast as Fats would play it, Jimmy would write it out. When Fats finished he'd go get a drink. Jimmy would write the music out and pass it around to the guys. Sometimes if Jimmy needed a note he'd go over to the piano and find it. Fats would sit down and say, "OK, fellas, b-flat we're gonna do this in." And off we'd go.

Jimmy always talked very soft and tried to help guys with their music. Jimmy would tell you when you were wrong, but if he told you, you were wrong. Then he would tell you when you were right.

Jimmy always wanted someone to come to the studio with him when he cut piano rolls or made records just to have some company. He'd want you to go out and get his booze and you'd sit and drink and joke. He used to come by the house and get me when he was going to the studio.... Sometimes Jimmy would bring four or five people with him.[2]

Johnson had gained a great deal of experience as an accompanist working with singers in cabarets throughout the East, an ability which is demonstrated on many recordings with a number of prominent and lesser-known vocalists. Evelyn Thompson, Sara Lawrence, Rosa Henderson, Martha Copeland, Clara Smith, Eva Taylor, Roy Evans, Lonnie Johnson and Spencer Williams all recorded with Johnson in the late 1920s. The two most famous singers to work with him were Bessie Smith and Ethel Waters. Within the realm of black popular music of the time, these two women performed in very different styles. Bessie Smith primarily sang the blues, while Ethel Waters was much more a singer of popular songs. Yet, Johnson's work with each includes some of the finest recordings the two women made. This is solid testimony to Johnson's versatility and sensitivity as an accompanist, enabling him to provide much more than a mere backdrop.

Bessie Smith, the "Empress of the Blues," was at the helm of the many female vocalists of the 1920s who sang what was later given the name "classic blues." The country blues was thought of as a typically male form of expression, at least in terms of a performing art. Although women certainly sang the blues before 1920, the advent of race records and the migration of the blues to the north created a new form of the music, the classic blues, a field dominated by women. The male counterpart was given the name urban or city blues. The classic blues singers found their greatest popularity during the 1920s, riding the wave of success initiated by Mamie Smith and "Crazy Blues." While Bessie Smith was not the first (an honor bestowed upon Bessie's putative mentor, Gertrude "Ma" Rainey), her outstanding talent established her as the best of the classic blues singers. Her deep, heavily resonant voice was one distinguishing feature that set her noticeably apart from the others. Her interpretation of the blues was somewhere be-

tween the rough sound of the truly earthy southern blues and the more polished "pop" blues
styles. She was the biggest seller in the Columbia race record catalogue, and recorded exclusively for that company, from 1923 to 1931.

On February 17, 1927, Bessie Smith and
James P. Johnson made their first records
together. They had met several years before,
around 1920, when they were both playing in
Atlanta. Johnson alone accompanied Smith on
two blues tunes for Columbia, "Preachin' the
Blues," and "Backwater Blues." Johnson's effec-
tiveness as an interpreter of the blues is somewhat in dispute. It is, however, rather a moot
endeavor to compare the expressiveness of
Bessie's singing and Johnson's playing only within
the context of the blues. A much more productive and enlightening view is to consider their
collaborations as duets. Johnson's playing may
not be the deepest "blues," and it is very possible
he did not intend it to be. His accompaniments
are thoughtfully constructed (in the true spirit of
a composer) and precisely executed. They
complement Bessie's singing in a way which
requires far more skill than playing earthy blues.
The greatest flaw of an accompanist is to con-
strain the singer unnecessarily by repetitive and
unimaginative playing, a very real problem in
playing blues, which has such a formal structure.
In the 14 sides Smith made with Johnson, he
never flags. It is no wonder that Bessie considered him her favorite pianist.[3]

Ethel Waters, whose success dominated a
different popular music market, expressed similar
sentiments about Johnson and some of her other
accompanists. "Men like him [James P. Johnson],
Willie (The Lion) Smith, and Charlie Johnson could
make you sing until your tonsils fell out. Be-

cause you wanted to sing.   They stirred you into
joy and wild ecstasy.   They could make you cry.
And you'd do anything and work until you dropped
for such musicians."[4]   Johnson and Waters worked
together on only one recording session on August
21, 1928, for Columbia.   The four sides produced
("Lonesome Swallow," "Guess Who's in Town," "My
Handy Man," and "Do What You Did Last Night")
are among Waters' most inspired efforts.

Although jazz singing in the 1920s was
dominated by classic blues, Waters applied her
versatile vocal style to a more varied repertoire.
Her rich tone, clear diction and theatrical air
were aimed at a middle-class popular music
market that was not partial to earthy blues.
Despite her concessions to commercialism, and
because she was not tethered to the blues,
Waters was one of the first great jazz singers.
The material she recorded with Johnson was perfectly suited to her, composed of popular songs
with a liberal dose of double-entendre lyrics.
Johnson responded to the difference in style and
material by producing accompaniments that fit
well without relying on cheap novelty and maintained a high degree of sophistication, nuance,
and taste.   Many of his accompaniments for
Waters, Smith and other singers are so finely
crafted that they might almost work equally as
well as solos.[5]

Johnson recorded no known piano solos in
the four years between August 1923 and February
1927, a time spent composing for the stage and
cutting piano rolls.   The consensus among critics,
historians, and fans is that Johnson's most
successful venture in the music world was as a
soloist.   The respect and awe his contemporaries
evinced for his solo playing is convincing support
in itself.   Posterity is fortunate to have at its

disposal a number of astounding Johnson solo recordings which provide indisputable evidence of his keyboard prowess. It is interesting to examine the effect of changing events in the music world on Johnson's playing.

As a performer and composer, Johnson must have been acutely aware of the demands of the popular music business. Two of his best friends in the commercial music business, Clarence Williams and Perry Bradford, seem to have arranged for almost all of Johnson's recording sessions. Aside from some of the blatantly commercial band sides Johnson made with them, he was able, most likely on purpose, to retain genuinely jazz characteristics in his playing and avoid the commercial. The most illuminating exercise is to compare a Johnson solo from this period with any of the immensely popular "novelty solos." Both are highly virtuosic, employing many tricks and recurring rhythmic devices. The most noticeable difference lies in Johnson's use of blues elements, namely the 12-bar form, the blues scale, blues clusters and other dissonances, and the underlying emotional character. Johnson's playing is not a blues style; it is a jazz style, which by definition incorporates blues characteristics.

One of Johnson's most successful and popular instrumental pieces is "Snowy Morning Blues." Technically, it is not a blues as it does not contain 12-bar phrases. However, the blues feeling is present, due in no small part to his manner of playing. On two sessions in February and March of 1927, he recorded six takes, one of which was finally deemed acceptable for release. The piece consists of two strains of 16-bar length, each repeated, with a short introduction and coda. It was a favorite of Johnson's, and a number he actively kept in his repertoire.   He recorded it at least five more times, last in 1947.

On the flip side Johnson recorded a Perry Bradford tune, "All That I Had Is Gone."   Bradford was known for his relentless obsession with getting his tunes recorded.   In the span of one month, including ensembles, solos, and rejected takes, Bradford had Johnson record his tune ten times.   The solo version finally released was one of five takes.   Johnson's experience in playing the tune is obvious from the masterful job he does, creating a carefully constructed set of interesting variations on an otherwise unexciting theme.[6]   Pianist Art Hodes commented on the two recordings: "Somehow I had gotten my hands on a Columbia recording, 'Snowy Morning Blues' and (on the flip side) 'All That I Had Is Gone' and believe me, I heard me some piano.   And as old as I've become, and as far as I've traveled, there's something Jimmy did on that recording that I'd still like to arrive at."[7]   John Hammond has always cited Johnson's first recording of "Snowy Morning Blues" as one of his favorite recordings of all time.

Johnson's next issued solos were made for the Okeh label two years later, on January 29, 1929.   "Feelin' Blue" is similar in conception to "Snowy Morning."   Two themes of 16-bar duration are each repeated, followed by one statement of a C strain.   The melody is filled with many blues characteristics although structurally it is not a blues.   The other tune recorded, a Johnson composition called "Riffs," was one of three "novelty" pieces recorded in 1929-1930.   "Riffs" was perhaps an attempt to appeal to both the waning market for virtuoso novelty numbers and the rising market for "modern" instrumental jazz.   As the title indicates, the piece is constructed

almost entirely of short rhythmic figures.
Johnson uses both types of riffs, the repeated and
the unrepeated, although the latter predominate.
There is little melody to speak of, since the
piece emphasizes rhythmic variation.   In that
respect it is one of Johnson's most complex
pieces.

Johnson plays many of the standard left
and right hand stride figures, plus many original
licks.   The amazing characteristic of his performance is how little time Johnson gives to each
of these figures.   The listener is literally hit by
a barrage of "riffs" at a breakneck pace.   More
so than in any other of his solos, Johnson hides
the beat by switching syncopations from hand to
hand and layering different rhythms.   The most
striking example comes at measure 17 of the
second to last chorus (the fifth 32-bar chorus).

Johnson maintains a back-beat triple pulse
in the bass relentlessly for six measures.   In the
same six measures above the bass, he plays a
series of sustained chords also phrased with a
triple pulse (i.e., three beats apart).   In addition,
he plays the chords slightly behind the newly established 3/4 beat.   The normal pulse seems hopelessly lost,   until, like a magician, Johnson makes

it reappear at measure 23.   A rhythmic picture
of these six measures is outlined above.   (The
notation does not represent specific pitches).

One of Johnson's most interesting compositions is "You've Got To Be Modernistic."   In the
two months between November 1929 and January
1930, Johnson recorded the tune four times.   The
last recording took place on January 21 in New
York at the Brunswick recording studios.   Johnson
recorded four piano solos on that date,   all of
them released and subsequently reissued.   In addition to "Modernistic," he waxed another original
"novelty" piece called "Jingles," and two popular
songs,   "Cryin' For the Carolines" and Cole
Porter's "What Is This Thing Called Love."
"You've Got To Be Modernistic" is a fast-paced
number,   modern in the sense of its unusual
harmonies.   Whole tone (augmented),   ninth and
diminished chords predominate in the first two
strains, giving rise to a series of highly rhythmic
and inventive choruses.   In the final chorus,
Johnson uses a rhythmic figure which appeared in
his early piano roll of "Steeplechase Rag,"

In its form in "Modernistic," it consists of a
chord repeated three times,   a device used by
many other players, among them Duke Ellington,
Don Ewell,   Dick Wellstood,   and Dick Hyman.
"Modernistic" was also marketed as a "novelty
piano solo," and is one of Johnson's most brilliant
performances.

The first three recordings of "Modernistic"
were all made with vocals.   The first attempt
took place on November 18, 1929, with Jimmy
Johnson and His Orchestra recording "You Don't

Understand" (another Johnson original, also recorded with Bessie Smith earlier that year) and
"You've Got To Be Modernistic." The personnel
included King Oliver on trumpet, Johnson and
Fats Waller on piano (it is difficult to tell from
the recording if one or two pianos were used),
and vocals by an anonymous "Keep Shufflin' Trio."
Keep Shufflin' was a 1928 Broadway show featuring a score written by Johnson and Waller. Since
"Modernistic" does not appear in the show, the
use of the "Keep Shufflin' Trio" was probably an
attempt to exploit the show's popularity to sell
records. In any case, the tune does not lend itself well to vocal treatment.

The next two recordings are equally unsuc-
cussful. Clarence Williams and His Jazz Kings
recorded the number for Columbia on December
3, 1929, with William's wife, Eva Taylor, featured
on vocals. The third vocal recording gives a clue
to the origin of the tune. In December 1929,
Johnson accompanied the Great Day New Orleans
Singers for the Okeh label. In November 1929, a
Johnson show entitled A Great Day In New Orleans opened in Philadelphia but never made it to
New York. It is likely that "Modernistic" is all
that remains of this show. Johnson's final
recording of it as a virtuoso solo is by far the
most successful, leaving one to wonder why he
thought it had such great possibilities as a vocal
number.

17

Keep Shufflin', 1928

The year 1928 was a big one for James P. Johnson and Fats Waller, not only as two towering figures in black music, but as a perfectly matched team. Together, they produced one of the decade's most popular black musicals on Broadway, set down more than half of their total co-recorded output and, in the spirit of friendship and respect for each other's musical talent, furthered each other's career. The spark for this flurry of co-ordinated activity was a new show being put together by Miller and Lyles in 1927. They had arranged very heavy financial backing, and set out with the producer of the show to recruit the best musical talent available.

Officially, the producer was Con Conrad. He had, however, sold the show to one of the leading figures of New York's underworld, gambler Arnold Rothstein. Rothstein used the risky but often lucrative world of show business as a means of laundering money made in illegal pursuits. He was thus interested in seeing that the shows he financed did well in return.[1] Perry Bradford recalled being approached by Conrad for help in assembling a top song-writing team.

Bradford suggested James P. Johnson and Henry Creamer write the music and lyrics. Conrad confessed that he had never heard of Johnson. Bradford reminded him of Johnson's qualifications, which, he told Conrad, could be checked with Miller and Lyles. Johnson, busy with many other projects including his rhapsody

"Yamekraw," suggested that they employ the songwriting talent of Fats Waller and his lyricist Andy Razaf to collaborate with him on the score. Johnson and Waller auditioned for Rothstein, who was very favorably impressed and signed them both.[2]

Keep Shufflin', with a book by and starring Miller and Lyles, opened at Daly's 63rd St. Theatre on February 27, 1928. The music was written primarily by Johnson and Waller, with additional numbers by Clarence Todd and Con Conrad. Henry Creamer and Andy Razaf wrote the lyrics. Will Vodery, a musician of great stature best known as writer and arranger for Flo Ziegfeld's Follies, made the orchestrations for the show. The dances and ensembles were staged by Clarence Robinson, and the overall production by Con Conrad. Johnson was the musical director of the pit orchestra, three members of which are listed on the program: "On the White Keys ... Fats Waller--On the Black Keys ... Jimmy Johnson--Behind the Bugle ... Jabbo Smith."

The reviews were for the most part very favorable, and make much greater reference to the orchestra than usual. The quality of this particular pit band was quite remarkable. If Louis Armstrong was in a class by himself, then Jabbo Smith, a "graduate" of the Jenkins Orphanage Band, was certainly ahead of all other cornet players of the period. Some have argued that he equalled Armstrong in technical skill and imaginitive interpretation. With Johnson and Waller each at his own piano, the Keep Shufflin' Orchestra astounded audiences night after night. The Johnson-Waller pairing worked so well that Conrad and Miller suggested the two pianists perform during intermissions.[3]

One of the acclaimed hits from the show was a tune written by Johnson, Creamer, and Conrad called "Sippi." Between acts, Johnson and Waller used the tune as musical artillery for a piano tandem of which only a few brief glimpses remain on their few recordings together. Other tunes which were singled out in various reviews were "Give Me the Sunshine" also by Johnson, Creamer, and Conrad, and "How Jazz Was Born" by Waller and Razaf. Another Waller/Razaf tune, "Willow Tree," was added to the production after its opening week; it is not listed in the original program but it too became a popular hit.

On March 27, 1928, four members of the Keep Shufflin' Orchestra made a somewhat obscure but most interesting recording for Victor. The group was given the name Louisiana Sugar Babes and had an unorthodox makeup: Johnson, piano; Fats Waller, pipe organ; Jabbo Smith, cornet; Garvin Bushell, clarinet, alto saxophone, and bassoon. They recorded at the former Trinity Church on Fifth Street in Camden, New Jersey, known as "Studio No. 2, Church Building." Bushell rcalled that Waller was situated at one end of the studio at the pipe organ while the other musicians set up at the opposite end, a distance of "about a city block." The group recorded four titles: "Willow Tree" and "Sippi" from Keep Shufflin'; "Thou Swell" from A Connecticut Yankee by Rodgers and Hart; and "Persian Rug" by Gus Kahn.[4] All but the last were in two takes.

In essence, these sides represent an "original cast recording" of two hits from Keep Shufflin'. The physical distance separating Waller and the other musicians in the studio seems to have had no detrimental effect as all four were obviously very comfortable with the material.

Despite the somewhat strange instrumentation and
the occasionally overpowering organ, all the songs
work well, highlighting the individual sounds of
each musician. Smith and Bushell exhibit superb
control, weaving individually conceived melodic
lines about piano and organ. It is Johnson and
Waller, however, who are most interesting to
hear. Often, dual keyboard performances tend to
sound muddy if the two players are unfamiliar
with or try to outdo each other. But Johnson
and Waller complement each other as perhaps
only they could. Their individual styles, based on
much common ground, combined with their in-
timate personal relationship, enabled them to
produce these remarkable duets.

Three months later, Waller and Johnson
again recorded together with a different group,
Jimmy Johnson and his Orchestra. On "Chicago
Blues" and "Mournful Tho'ts," the two tunes
recorded, they each play on one piano. Waller
and Johnson complement each other so well that
it is impossible to distinguish who is playing what.

The four Sugar Babes returned to the pit
of Keep Shufflin' which moved downtown and
opened at the Eltinge Theatre on 42nd St. West
of Broadway on April 23. In the meantime, W.C.
Handy was working on an ambitious project.
With the financial help of poet Robert Clairmont,
whom Handy described as "a hatless bohemian
from the 'Village'," Handy was producing a concert at Carnegie Hall to show the evolution of
black music. Clairmont had laid out $5,000 to
support the production, so Handy could contract
the best-known performers and composers. A
chorus of 60 voices and an orchestra of 30
musicians led by Handy accompanied a number of
featured soloists performing a wide range of
music.[5]

The program included a number of spirituals arranged by Handy and J. Rosamond Johnson, the former conducting the orchestra and chorus on his arrangements while the latter sang his with Taylor Gordon. Katherine Handy sang several of her father's more famous blues compositions ("Yellow Dog Blues" and "St. Louis Blues"), and W.C. Handy, Jr. performed a xylophone solo of Scott Joplin's "Maple Leaf Rag." Tenor soloists Russell Smith and George E. Jackson sang several "plantation songs" written by the prominent nineteenth-century ballad composer James A. Bland. Work songs, character songs, "descriptive instrumentals" and the cakewalk were all represented. Under the heading of "Negro Rhapsody," Handy included James P. Johnson's "Yamekraw," hoping also to arrange for the composer to play the piano part.

Johnson, however, was under contract to lead the orchestra of Keep Shufflin', a commitment Miller and Lyles were unwilling to waive. Johnson suggested that Waller lead the band for that one performance, but Miller and Lyles were adamant. Johnson must have been very disappointed, being thus prevented from performing the debut of his most ambitious work in one of America's most prestigious concert halls. It became necessary to arrange for a substitute pianist at Carnegie Hall, and Johnson recommended Waller. Miller and Lyles did agree to allow Waller to take Johnson's place at the concert, a comment on their relative importance to the show. The promoters, having never heard Waller play, suggested an audition. Waller played both piano and organ, and was so impressive that a set of Waller organ solos was programmed for the concert in addition to his part in "Yamekraw."[6]

Anita Waller, Fats' second wife, recalled
the concert, held on the evening of April 27,
1928:

> It was a Friday night, and the city was hit
> with a wild, spring storm. It rained all
> day and the streets were so windy you
> couldn't walk around. With all that bad
> weather you'd think no one would go out
> and I was surprised to see that hall filled
> to capacity.[7]

The program was very well received and did a
great deal for Waller's reputation as a serious
performer. It also marked one of the first, if
not the earliest, public performances of "Yamekraw." It was subsequently used many times in
many contexts. It was played by several orchestras, including Nat Shilkret's Victor Recording
Orchestra, Don Vorhees' Columbia Orchestra, and
the Phil Spitalny band with 48 voices. Around
1930, Warner Bros. made a movie short based on
the piece. During the depression, it was used as
an overture to Orson Welles' production of
Macbeth. Joe Jordan conducted the Negro Unit
Orchestra of the Federal Theater Project for the
production which opened at the Lafayette Theater
in 1938. W.C. Handy used "Yamekraw" many
years later on N.B.C. in a program including
Gershwin's "Rhapsody in Blue" and his own "St.
Louis Blues." It was also performed several
times on Firestone TV. In 1962, at the First
Washington, D.C. Jazz Festival, "Yamekraw" was
performed in a new orchestration for symphony
orchestra by Gunther Schuller, who also conducted.

A few months after the Carnegie Hall
concert, Waller left Keep Shufflin' to take a job
playing piano and organ at the Grand Theater in
Philadelphia. Johnson stayed with the show,

directing the orchestra, until it closed in late 1928. It is interesting to compare the musical numbers used in February and those used in September. Of the 17 numbers in each production, only five appear in both shows, "Chocolate Bar," "Where (How) Jazz Was Born," "Give Me The Sunshine," "Sippi," and "Keep Shufflin'." The 11 other numbers are different for the two programs from February 27 and September 3, yet it is the same show. The dramatic changes in musical numbers gives some indication of the flexibility of the type of musical show commonly produced during the 1920s. Sophisticated story lines which had specific musical numbers fitted to them were not yet the predominant form of stage entertainment. The threads of plot that did exist were easily adapted to new musical numbers. Composers like Johnson were often called upon to produce many more tunes for a show than were actually used at any one time. Keep Shufflin' is a specific example.

Before the end of 1928, the Johnsons added another member to the family, a daughter named Arceola. Before things began to catch up with him, most notably the economic devastation of the depression, James P. kept up the fast pace he had set for himself, producing many recordings and a number of shows.

After an initial tryout in Baltimore, Messin' Around, a show with music by Johnson and lyrics by Perry Bradford, opened at the Hudson Theater (44th St. east of Broadway) on April 22, 1929. The production was conceived and staged by Louis Isquith, the dances were staged by the renowned tap dancer Eddie Rector, and the orchestra was directed by Johnson. The show received fair reviews, and ran for a little over a month. Virtually the only aspect of the show most reviewers praised was the music.   One song in particular was singled out as a certain hit, "Your Love Is All I Crave."

Richard Watts, Jr., in the <u>New York Tribune</u> of April 23, 1929, gave a rather lengthy and perceptive description of Johnson as orchestra director.   One gets the impression that Watts spent more time watching Johnson in the pit than the show itself.

In its composer and orchestra leader, Jimmy Johnson, it has a figure with enough instinctive showmanship to make it seem unfortunate that he is not placed upon the stage, rather than obscurely in the pit. The rest of the players are, however, without the ability to make themselves inherently interesting to the expectant paying guests.

If a really adept showman had been in charge of <u>Messin' Around,</u> he would certainly have made more use of the unconscious histrionic ability of Jimmy Johnson, though perhaps, in the process, the excellences of that ebony gentleman would have been diluted.   A placid, lethargic band leader, with an apparent gift for restfulness, he seems to grow more and more excited as he leads his own compositions to victory.   Beginning with a calm crouch, he suddenly starts to expand until at the climax of his melody he seems fairly leaping upon the stage in his enthusiasm.   He is a good revue composer, an excellent leader and a marvelous instinctive showman.

Most of Mr. Johnson's music is pleasant, but certainly undistinguished, but in at least one number he has scored that

> ambition of his profession--he has written
> an authentic song hit. It is called, "Your
> Love Is All I Crave." It is more than a
> bit reminiscent, but it has the stuff of
> which triumphant Broadway melodies are
> made and its future radio popularity is
> more than ordinarily deserved.

Although the tune was used in the film "Show of Shows," Johnson never recorded it, and it seems to have faded from memory, along with the show.

In June, Johnson recorded the soundtrack to one of the better short jazz films of the day, St. Louis Blues. The film starred Bessie Smith and Jimmy Mordecai as Bessie's "Nogooder." It was written and directed by Dudley Murphy, who later directed the film version of "The Emperor Jones," and employed a wealth of musical talent to construct the score. A mixed chorus of 40 voices and an orchestra accompanied Bessie's superb voice. The chorus, which plays the role of cafe patrons, is actually the Hall Johnson choir. W.C. Handy and J. Rosamond Johnson arranged the choral parts. James P. Johnson was the musical director and assembled a band containing a few former members of the Fletcher Henderson orchestra.

The exact personnel has not been definitely identified, although a possible roster may have included: Joe Smith, Sidney De Paris, trumpets; Happy Caldwell, Arville Harris, reeds; Charlie Green, trombone; Harry Hull, tuba; Charlie Dixon, banjo; Kaiser Marshall, drums; James P. Johnson piano and leader. Only the last two and the trumpet players have been positively identified.[8]

In 1930 no fewer than three shows featuring music by James P. Johnson were produced.

Fireworks of 1930 was one of several lesser-
known stage shows for which Johnson composed
and performed the music.   In this instance, he
collaborated with his friend and student Fats
Waller.   This ad appeared in the New York
Amsterdam News of June 25, 1930.

Accurate and comprehensive details from each are difficult to ascertain, but their existence is certain. The most obscure was a revue which ran at the Lafayette Theater called Fireworks of 1930. The show featured blues singer Mamie Smith and the Fats Waller-Jimmie Johnson Syncopators, another collaboration between the two men. The show was billed as a Fourth of July holiday special and ran for only a few weeks.

At Werba's Brooklyn Theater, a show entitled Shuffle Along of 1930 was produced by Irvin C. Miller and, according to the program, featured Miller and Lyles in the starring roles. However, the two comedians who actually played the parts were not Miller and Lyles, but two other men using their names. The press quickly discovered this hoax and publicized it widely.[9] The music for the show consisted entirely of tunes written by James P. Johnson and Fats Waller, almost all of which originally appeared in Keep Shufflin'. Two numbers from Shuffle Along of 1930 were copyrighted in 1930 and may have appeared first (or with slight overlap) in the third Johnson show produced in 1930.

Small's Paradise, at 2294-1/2 Seventh Avenue, had established a formidable following with the downtown clientele during the mid to late twenties. The floor shows became a big drawing card for the finely dressed whites coming up to Harlem to see the exotic entertainment, but unlike The Cotton Club, Small's also admitted black patrons. In 1930, guitarist Elmer Snowden led the band there, which included Gus Aiken, Red Harlen, trumpets; Herb Gregory, trombone; Otto Hardwick, Wayman Carver, reeds; Don Kirkpatrick, piano; and Sid Catlett, drums. Sometime in 1930, a floor show entitled Kitchen Mechanics Revue

was produced, the musical accompaniment for
which was supplied by Snowden's band.[10]

Details concerning the musical numbers
composed by Johnson come from some interesting
copyright information. On March 14, 1930, 11
tunes written by Johnson and Andy Razaf were
copyrighted, all claimed by the Joe Davis Publishing Co. Two weeks later, two additional
tunes by Johnson and Razaf were copyrighted by
Davis. All 13 numbers, some bearing vividly
descriptive titles like "Slippery Hips," "Mammy
Land," "Bantu Baby," and "Elevator Papa-
Switchboard Mama," remained unpublished. On
May 19, one of the tunes was resubmitted as a
published listing. "Porter's Love Song to a Chambermaid" became one of Johnson's most popular
compositions, especially with jazz musicians. It
was one of the first tunes Fats Waller recorded
with his group, the "Rhythm," in 1934. The song
was listed on the copyright card as a "novelty
song from 'Kitchen Mechanics Revue'." It is also
one of the tunes from this show (the other being
"Go Harlem") that was used in the 1930 edition
of <u>Shuffle Along</u>.

The worst economic disaster America has
ever known cataclysmically interrupted the fast
pace of the twenties. As is still the case when
times are hard and jobs are scarce, those at the
lower end of the socio-economic ladder were hit
hardest. Blacks were a large part of this group,
and suffered much. Scraping together enough
money to buy food was difficult in itself; little
or no cash was available to spend on entertainment. The music business was especially hurt in
certain respects. With the introduction of sound
motion pictures and the growing popularization of
radio, many live "accompaniment" musicians were

put out of work. In addition, the race record market soon dried up.

For James P. Johnson, who was beginning to be bothered by a sinus condition and other health problems, the 1930s came perhaps as a welcome but not necessarily hoped-for rest. He and his family moved out of New York City and settled in the suburban community of St. Albans, Queens. He began to take things a little easier, devoting more time to his family and serious music study. Although he continued to compose a great deal, he recorded very little and almost exclusively with Clarence Williams. Early in the decade, he appeared regularly with Williams and his wife Eva Taylor on a morning program on WEAF radio in New York.[11] In addition, he interrupted his self-imposed semi-retirement at frequent intervals for jam sessions, rent parties, guest appearances with orchestras, and to lead his own orchestra in Harlem in the mid-thirties. At a time when many musicians were establishing national fame in a new musical idiom called "swing," Johnson seemed to have missed the boat.

Johnson's neglect as musician and composer is two-fold. In one respect he is often overlooked by jazz critics and historians, perhaps because of mere oversight, but likely because of ignorance and misunderstanding concerning his music. In another respect, Johnson's name failed to gain any popular acclaim from the general public. Johnson himself gave the biggest clue to the reasons for this obscurity:

> I had just come out of the period when I was in the show business. I looked down on dance bands. In a dance band you had to work all night. I was making big money and dance bands weren't making big

money.   Then   in   Chicago   Paul   Ash   introduced   a   new   form   of   entertainment--the
band   on   the   stage.   Well,   they   began   to
sell   bands   for   a   lot   of   money   after   that.
I   was   misplaced.   I   didn't   have   an
orchestra.[12]

It   is   somewhat   ironic   that   much   of   the
"big band" sound emanating from New York was,
to   simplify   somewhat,   the   instrumentalization of
elements   of   stride   piano.   This   should   come   as   no
surprise   when   one   considers   the   position   of   the
pianists   in   many   of   the   best-known   orchestras.
The   pianists   were   often   the   leaders,   and   the
pianists   played   stride.   Duke   Ellington,   Cliff
Jackson, and Claude Hopkins, all from Washington,
D.C.,   learned   it   from   Johnson's   piano   rolls.   So
did Fletcher Henderson, at the insistence of Ethel
Waters, for whom he played many accompaniments
on   tours   and   records.   She   badgered   him   to   learn
to   play   "'the   damn-it-to-hell   bass,'   that   chump-
chump stuff that real jazz needs."[13]   Count Basie
was also an accomplished stride pianist, who took
organ lessons from his idol, Fats Waller.   All of
these   men   were   associated   with   orchestras   for
more   than   intermittent   periods,   and   with   con-
siderable   success.   Henderson,   Basie,   and   Ellington
were   three   of   the   greatest   innovators   of   various
styles of big-band swing and are household names
even   today.

James   P.   Johnson   never   led   a   dance   orchestra for any length of time.   With a respectable   arsenal   of   original   popular   song   hits   to   his
credit,   Johnson   could   have   toured   and   recorded
with a band of his own, the best way to make a
name   for   himself   as   composer   and   band   leader.
He   did   not.   He   chose   rather   to   direct   his   efforts to the more lucrative occupation of compos-
ing   and   playing   for   the   musical   theater.   Of

course, Henderson, Basie, and Ellington were brilliant arrangers and leaders, and deserve their
place in history.   Yet, it is ironic that the
source of their inspiration and original conception,
in the person of James P. Johnson, should have
been unable to find the right niche of his own.
Schuller summarizes his plight well:

> Johnson's problem was, of course, that of
> all sensitive and honest musicians: the
> compromises he was prepared to make in
> the direction of commerical music were
> minimal and certainly insufficient to satisfy
> the demands of that market.   As a result,
> without Johnson ever quite understanding it,
> both areas, the commercial and jazz, began
> to pass him by.[14]

He was, in effect, betrayed by his own desire for
diversity in his career, producing a wide range of
higher quality music, but never amassing enough
credits in any one area to increase his public
visibility.   At least as a composer of popular
tunes, Johnson should have been better known, but
without an orchestra to plug his own work, the
success he deserved never really developed.

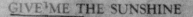

GIVE ME THE SUNSHINE

CON CONRAD, INC. *Presents*
MILLER AND LYLES IN

KEEP SHUFFLIN'

BOOK BY
MILLER AND LYLES

LYRICS BY
HENRY CREAMER
AND ANDY RAZAF

MUSIC BY
JIMMY JOHNSON
AND THOMAS WALLER

ADDITIONAL MUSIC BY
CLARENCE TODD
DANCES AND ENSEMBLES BY
LEONARD HARPER
THE PLAY STAGED BY
FLOURNOY MILLER
AND NAT PHILLIPS

Get Myself Another Jockey Now
How Jazz Was Born
'Twas A Kiss In The Moonlight
Chuckle, My Back Door Man
Give Me The Sunshine
Willow Tree
Sippi
Pining

WILL VODERY'S SYMPHONIC BAND

MADE IN U.S.A.

THE ENTIRE PRODUCTION STAGED UNDER SUPERVISION OF CON CONRAD

HARMS
NEW YORK

18

The Stormy Days, 1930s

The early 1930s is a period generally thought of as one of relative inactivity for Johnson. Although he was no longer completely immersed in the hotbed of musical activity in New York, he was by no means a recluse in his Long Island home. On December 25, 1931, another show starring Miller and Lyles with music by Johnson, Sugar Hill, opened at the Forrest Theater. The book, by Charles Tazewell, was subtitled "An Epoch of Negro Life in Harlem." Sugar Hill was the fashionable section of Harlem located on the hill between Morningside Heights and Harlem proper. The nickname came from the feeling that living in the apartments on the hill required plenty of "sugar," meaning money. The show did poorly and closed after only 11 performances.

The next year Johnson wrote the score for a much more successful production. Harlem Hotcha was the featured floor show at Connie's Inn, still one of the most popular Harlem clubs frequented by the downtown clientele, along with the Cotton Club and Small's Paradise. Johnson's music was matched with the superb lyrics of Andy Razaf, and was performed by Don Redman, one of the most outstanding leader-arrangers in the history of the music, and his fine orchestra. A substantial number of tunes from this show were published by Handy Bros. Publishing Co.

The last large-scale show of the decade using a Johnson score was produced several years later, having its first performance at the dilapidated Nora Bayes Theater on December 29, 1938. Policy Kings was written and produced by Michael Ashwood and, from beginning to end, was nearly a complete disaster. The show suffered from great pre-production chaos and adversity, the nature of which is not entirely clear. One can guess that the difficulties encountered by any show are of similar nature, and that Policy Kings struggled against more than its share of financial and contractual problems. Of the few aspects praised by the reviews was the fact that the show opened at all. The score, written by Johnson and lyricist Louis Douglass, was the only other bright spot cited almost unanimously:

Michael Ashwood wrote it and James P. Johnson composed the score. This last is not bad ... as it [the show] is--well, the music is O.K. New York Times--L.N.

Despite the fact that a large orchestra appeared to be indulging in a sort of battle royal in the pit, and most of the large chorus preferred to express their own individuality in dancing rather than to be regimented into orderly figures, James P. Johnson's music actually survived those untoward circumstances, and emerged with something of a real swing in it. New York World Telegram--S.W.

... Policy Kings, the Harlem musical comedy which opened at the Bayes last night, has a score by James P. Johnson that is worthy of a better fate than to be hitched to Policy Kings. New York Sun--Herrick Brown

The publication of most of the production numbers compensated somewhat for the failure of the show.

Policy Kings closed after three performances, running into severe financial trouble.
The book was a comedy about the numbers racket
in Harlem. It is interesting to note that Johnson
was still locked into writing for self-effacing, all-
black musicals, despite the quality of his work.
Judging from some of the comments made in the
reviews, it seems that this type of production had
run its course. Yet, the public continued to view
such productions expecting the self-parody and
stereotypes of the minstrel show. Herbert Drake,
in the New York Herald Tribune remarked, " ...
this newest sepia musical lacks nearly everything
shows of its genre are supposed to have."   He
elaborates: "You expect some fine dancing, at
least....   The comedians are expected to be
uninspiring in a Harlem show...."   Herrick Brown's
comments in the New York Sun rely more on
blatant stereotypes: "Not that there aren't some
good dusky steppers in Policy Kings, for there
are.   Here again we claim an assist for Mr.
Johnson, however, for anybody with rhythm in
them--and what Negro hasn't?--could dance to
those tunes."

Policy Kings was Johnson's last known full
stage production for more than a decade. John
Hammond, in Johnson's obituary, touched upon the
overly long-lived prejudices of Broadway and its
productions of the "blackface" genre.

As a writer of show tunes Jimmy was the
equal of Gershwin, Youmans, and Kern, but
the prejudices of Broadway producers and
publishers confined him to the all-Negro
musicals, which rarely found favor on Times
Square.
He wrote other shows, too, like
"Policy Kings," and "Sugar Hill," and all of
them had librettos that perpetuated every

miserable Negro stereotype, with blackface
comics rolling eyes and dice, wild shake
dancers, and tear-jerking scenes on the old
plantation.[1]

Whatever one may think of Hammond's compari-
sons, Johnson's talents for writing for the theater
were great and never put to the best use.

With the jazz world changing dramatically,
rendering his approach dated, and the commercial
show business world restricting his creative
outlets, Johnson rigorously pursued his most ambitious desire, the practice of extended composition.   Sometime in the mid-1930s, Johnson contacted James Weldon Johnson, asking for his help
in obtaining a Guggenheim Fellowship.   James P.
expressed his strong desire to continue his musical
education and to keep working on new compositions, an endeavor which required financial support.   No records indicate he was successful in
obtaining a grant, but he pursued his music nonetheless. "Yamekraw," his first large-scale work,
was a rhapsody, and for the rest of his life,
Johnson wrote pieces using many of the Western
"classical" (extended) forms of composition: symphony, concerto, opera, ballet, sonata and tone
poem.

In 1932, Johnson completed his "Harlem
Symphony."   The piece consists of four movements: "Subway Journey," "April In Harlem,"
"Night Club," and "Baptist Mission."   This last
movement, Rudi Blesh recalled, ends with a syncopated passacaglia on the hymn "I Want Jesus to
Walk with Me."[2]   The piece was supposedly conceived from the sounds of New York City, characteristic of various ethnic neighborhoods Johnson
may have passed while riding the subway from
Long Island to Harlem: Jewish horns at 110th

St., Spanish castanets at 116th St., and Negro basses at 125th St.[3]

Along with "Yamekraw," it was one of Johnson's most often performed pieces. The first known performance occurred in 1937 when Eugene Von Gronna used it in a ballet at the Lafayette Theater. Although it was performed several other times through the thirties and forties, the only surviving part of the score is the second movement, "April In Harlem," which was published in 1944.

Since most of Johnson's longer works were never published in any form and were probably in manuscript when performed, few have survived. "Jassamine Concerto" was copyrighted but not published in March of 1934. The second movement was published as a piano solo in 1947, and recorded under the fictitious title "Blues For Jimmy" in 1945 for Folkways Records. Another Johnson original recorded at the same session was a track entitled "Jungle Drums"; this may be part of a three-movement tone poem called "Rhythm Drums." Rudi Blesh recalled seeing the fully orchestrated score for this piece at Johnson's home in the late 1940s. Some parts, he noticed, were constructed in four-part counterpoint.[4] A second symphony, "Symphony in Brown," was copyrighted in 1935 by Johnson himself (as was "Jassamine") and never published.

A number of other serious pieces have been attributed to Johnson, but no trace of them has been found. There is one other work, however, which is of musical, cultural, and historical interest. James P. Johnson collaborated with the famous poet Langston Hughes to create The Organizer--A Blues Opera in One Act. Johnson first contacted Hughes sometime in early 1937

about the possibility of collaborating on an opera.
Hughes responded positively but nothing seemed to
materialize until a year later when Johnson again
wrote Hughes with a concrete idea.   Johnson had
apparently signed a contract with Theodore Brown
to do a grand opera based on Brown's play
Natural Man, which had already been performed
throughout the west coast.   Hughes transformed
the work into blank verse and Johnson set it to
music.   Several copies of the Hughes libretto exist, but only one piece remains from the score--
two versions recorded in 1939 of "Hungry Blues."
If the other numbers are as well written as
"Hungry Blues," (eventually copyrighted but not
published in 1962), then the entire work might
well represent Johnson's greatest "serious"
achievement.

The Organizer was performed at Carnegie
Hall in 1940 as part of an International Ladies'
Garment Workers Union convention.   The action
takes place on a backward plantation in the
South.   The characters are mostly ragged share-
croppers assigned the following vocal parts: The
Organizer, baritone; The Woman, contralto; The
Old Man, bass; The Old Woman, soprano; Brother
Dosher, tenor; Brother Bates, tenor; and The
Overseer, bass.   The sharecroppers have gathered
and await the arrival of the Organizer who will
help them establish a union.

The "Hungry Blues" is sung near the beginning of the action by Brother Dosher.   This song
establishes the philosophical and sociological ideas
the work tries to convey.   Conditions are very
hard and food is scarce.   The sharecroppers hope
that someday a world will come where "nobody's
hongry" and where there is "no color line."   The
Organizer finally arrives and shows them the way
to help themselves against the plantation owner.

The Overseer tries to break up the meeting, but is overpowered and runs out to alert the owner. However, the workers have rallied into a frenzied state and are confident they can overcome their hardships through the newfound strength of their unity.

It should be obvious from this brief plot summary that this work departs dramatically from the usual subject matter of black productions, whether they be musicals, movies, or any other form of theatrical entertainment. The Organizer expounds not only racial equality but socialist ideas involving unionization. It does not need to rely on the stereotypes maintained in the other art forms, as its purpose is not simply to entertain. Ideas concerning social reform were of great importance to Langston Hughes and pervade much of his work. Johnson's interest is more difficult to characterize since a large part of his work in musical theater was not so revolutionary as The Organizer. Johnson's interest was almost certainly more than passing. Willie "The Lion" Smith hinted at Johnson's interest in social reform and people he associated with who shared his views. It is a great loss that the score to this important work has disappeared.

As a performer, Johnson was continually drawn to the city. Pianist Joe Turner recalled that Johnson still frequented many rent-parties, despite objections from wife Lillie Mae.

James P. loved competition. Jam sessions he loved, and for this reason he would go home rather late. We would have our jam session until two or three the next afternoon. He was then living on Long Island, and his wife would come all the way to Harlem, and she would go from street to

> street until she heard the piano. And she
> would recognize his style, and then she
> would go up to the apartment to get him
> out of there and take him home. He was
> not the kind of fellow who would look
> around for women or anything. He just
> loved to play the piano.[5]

In addition to playing at rent parties, he played
guest appearances (e.g., Fess Williams, 1936) and
led his own band at Small's Paradise in 1933 and
the Apollo Theater in 1934. In 1933, he also appeared in the film "The Emperor Jones." Yet
the pace of his activity during the early and mid
thirties was not nearly so frenzied as it had been
during the twenties.

The Johnsons were often host to many
friends at their home in St. Albans, especially the
Wallers. Maurice Waller recalled the family
visits.

> Some Sundays the family would go out to
> South Jamaica to visit James P. and Lil
> Johnson. Their children, James Jr. and
> Oceola [sic], were the same age as Ronnie
> and me, so it was a trip we always looked
> forward to because it gave us the oppor-
> tunity to play in the "country" with kids
> our own age. When I was a child I never
> realized how brilliant a pianist James P.
> was. A shy, retiring man, he had long ago
> given up the clamor of the business.
> Jimmy had elected to live off of the in-
> come from his record and writing royalties.
> Jimmy Jr. played piano and we'd jam
> together just like our fathers. Oceola [sic]
> sang and danced and we had a good little
> act going there. Lil Johnson was one of
> my favorite women. Outspoken, with a

mouth capable of making any man blush,
she was also a lovable, generous woman--
who more than once belted me across the
jaw for talking out of turn or being wild.

Ronnie and I were always excited
when Buster [Shepard, a cousin] picked us
up to go to the Johnson house. It was a
special treat. Clarence Williams and Eva
Taylor lived across the street from the
Johnsons, so the entire day was a social
event. We ran through the backyards and
played up a storm. When we were called
in there were two pianos to play. We
thought the place was paradise.[6]

The slower pace of Long Island also ap-
pealed to Fats, who moved his family out of Harlem in 1938. Lillie Mae Johnson recalled how
Fats talked his way into the Johnson parlor (as
he had done 15 years earlier) to work out new
ideas without disturbing his own family. "I sold
Fats his house--just a few blocks from ours, and
every once in a while, he'd come in at four or
five in the morning to go to bed here. He'd say
'The kids are too noisy over at my house'."[7]

In the same year Waller moved out of the
city, Johnson began to surface there more often,
beginning what would amount to a second career
as interest in traditional jazz increased.

MY HEADACHE
THERE GOES MY HEADACHE
HARLEM HOTCHA
CONNIE'S INN NEW REVUE
CONCEIVED and PRESENTED by
CONNIE IMMERMAN
LYRICS BY
ANDY RAZAF
MUSIC BY
JAMES P. JOHNSON
STAGED BY
TEDDY BLACKMAN
FEATURED BY
DON REDMAN
AND HIS
CONNIE'S INN ORCHESTRA
I WAS SO WEAK, LOVE WAS SO STRONG
AINTCHA GOT MUSIC
MY HEADACHE
THERE GOES MY HEADACHE
YOURS ALL YOURS
STOP THAT DOG
HARLEM HOTCHA
SUMMER WAS MADE FOR LOVERS
HANDY BROTHERS MUSIC CO. INC.
1595 BROADWAY, NEW YORK, N.Y.

19

Rediscovery, 1938

By the late 1930s, the term jazz was beginning
to encompass a wider variety of musical styles.
Big band swing, itself a designation for different
approaches to arranged orchestral music, had
flowered and was slowly starting to decline.
While many bands featured and were renowned for
their soloists, some musicians felt that the arrangements subordinated their role and left insuf-
ficient room for individual expression.   In
addition, a following of fans had developed whose
interest was more in listening to the music than
in dancing to it.   As a result, the small clubs
with back-room jam sessions and cutting contests,
which had always been the homes of jazz
innovation, spawned a new style of playing and
composing.   The main setting for these developments, later to be known as the Bebop revolution,
was Harlem.

At the same time, there was a resurgence
of interest in so-called traditional jazz, especially
New Orleans style.   A number of younger critics
and fans, later joined by even younger players,
created a new market for older jazz styles.   In
their search for "authenticity," the historians
"rediscovered" many semi-retired musicians who
thus experienced a renaissance of playing and
recording activity.   One of the most significant
of these resurrected players was Bunk Johnson,
the New Orleans trumpeter.   Through the efforts
of ardent fans, and with the aid of Louis
Armstrong, he was found working as a laborer
and part-time W.P.A. music instructor in the

Louisiana town of New Iberia.   Johnson, who
claimed to be older than King Oliver and said he
had worked with Buddy Bolden, was first recorded
in 1942, and fed the fires of interest in revivalist
jazz.

        While it was not necessary to "rescue"
James P. Johnson, he nevertheless benefited
greatly from the growing interest in preserving
classic jazz.   Beginning in mid-1938, James P.
Johnson came out of retirement, as it were, and
started a second career.   His first opportunity
came in August, when Steve Smith, the proprietor
of the Hot Record Society Record Shop, called
Johnson to take part in a recording session.   The
Hot Record Society, as the name implies, was an
organization of collectors devoted to preserving
and studying "hot" jazz (i.e., traditional jazz) on
records.

        The personnel recruited for this session rep-
resented a wide cross-section of jazz styles.

        Trumpeter Max Kaminsky, trombonist Dicky
        Wells, and guitarist Freddie Green were all
        big-band musicians at the time, but they
        were from bands as different as those of
        Red Nichols (Kaminsky) Fletcher Henderson
        (Wells) and Count Basie (Green).   Bassist
        Wellman Braud and drummer Zutty Singleton
        were strictly from New Orleans.   Saxophon-
        ist Al Gold, then playing in Joe Marsala's
        band on 52nd Street, was strictly from
        swing.   As for Johnson, he was the very
        model of Harlem stride--and Pee Wee Rus-
        sell was, as Duke Ellington used to say,
        beyond category.[1]

Johnson also recorded a few tunes in a trio setting with Singleton and Russell.   Although these

were Johnson's first commercial recordings in
three years, his playing had lost none of its drive
or delicacy. In fact, Johnson had lightened his
touch and played more "economically," (a more
modern approach), relying less on full chords to
delineate the melody.

Although the H.R.S. session got off to a
bit of a jumbled start due to the mix of
musicians, things worked out well as they became
more comfortable with each other. Then, in the
late fall of 1938, the French jazz authority and
record producer Hugues Panassié came to New
York to record some hot jazz. The author of
the influential Le Jazz Hot, published in the
United States in 1936 as Hot Jazz, Panassié had
been anxious to undertake this project for some
time, and now arranged to record as many of his
favorite musicians as he could locate. Johnson
was prominently included, though Panassié had not
done him justice in his book. The personnel for
the Panassié sessions also consisted of musicians
from varied musical backgrounds.

Clarinetist Mezz Mezzrow, under whose
name the first group recorded, recalled that the
session did not go smoothly. The plan was to record several tunes with a strong blues feeling.
One tune, "Comin' On With the Come On," was
recorded in two parts, one a slow blues, the
other in a bright tempo. However, trumpeter
Sidney De Paris insisted on playing modern swing
riffs which, according to Mezz, did not complement the blues playing of the others. Mezzrow
recalled that Johnson and another older musician,
trumpeter Tommy Ladnier, became disgusted with
the way things were going and began drinking
heavily. "Swingin' for Mezz," the last tune, was
recorded without piano and second trumpet, as

Johnson and Ladnier walked out in a drunken stupor.2

Panassié recorded four sessions. The November 21 session was the first. For January 13, 1939, the last, he called on Johnson again to play in a very different band, trumpeter Frankie Newton and His Orchestra. Mezzrow and Johnson were the only holdovers from the first session. The other musicians Newton, Pete Brown (alto sax), Al Casey (guitar), John Kirby (bass), Cozy Cole (drums) were very much 'swing' oriented. This group worked much better than the first, not having to deal with stylistic conflicts. The tunes chosen lent themselves well to swing treatment, a style with which all the musicians were comfortable. Johnson's ability to play both on the New Orleans-style session and the one in swing style is a good illustration of his versatility.

In December 1938, Johnson was interviewed by Alan Lomax, Curator of the Folk Music Division of the Library of Congress. Lomax had devoted much of his career to recording the works and reminiscences of folk musicians. Many of his recordings were made in the field, at southern work camps, in small towns, and prisons. Lomax found Johnson easily, and at Haver's studio in New York recorded Johnson playing some of his own tunes ("Stop It Joe," "Snowy Morning Blues"), tunes by other pianists ("Bull Diker's Dream," "Pork and Beans") and reminiscing about his early life and other musicians. Always shy and proper, Johnson was reluctant to sing the bawdy lyrics to an old time blues tune. Lomax eventually succeeded in coaxing from Johnson a few of the verses, their salty phrases quite hushed, however. Johnson would no doubt have preferred to talk about his ambitions as a serious composer, but Lomax was a folklorist.

Some of the most acclaimed events in which Johnson participated were the "Spirituals to Swing" concerts produced at Carnegie Hall by John Hammond. Twice in December of 1938 and 1939, Hammond presented a line-up of performers representing nearly every phase of American black music. The first concert was a smashing success, if a little unorganized. Its emphasis was on the blues and was dedicated to the memory of Bessie Smith, who had died tragically in an automobile accident the year before. Ruby Smith, a niece of Bessie's by marriage, sang several of her aunt's tunes accompanied by Johnson. Through the course of two concerts, Johnson performed in more contexts than any other musician. He accompanied singers Ruby Smith, Ida Cox, and Helen Humes, played in the New Orleans style of Sidney Bechet and his New Orleans Feetwarmers, and performed as soloist, playing his own "shout" compositions.3

The two facets of Johnson's career obviously missing from the "Spirituals to Swing" program are his work in the popular field and his serious composing. Fortunately, Johnson had the opportunity to perform samples of these endeavors at Carnegie Hall during this same period. To celebrate its Silver Jubilee, ASCAP sponsored a full week of American music at Carnegie Hall, starting October 1, 1939. They empowered W.C. Handy to engage the most outstanding black musical artists for the "All-Negro" program scheduled for October 2. The so-called Negro Orchestra, conducted by Joe Jordan, at times joined by over 300 voices of several combined choirs, performed music ranging from minstrel tunes to symphonies.

In the first part of the program, after a rousing version of "Lift Every Voice and Sing," excerpts from three symphonies were performed,

each conducted by its composer. These were
"American Symphony" by William Grant Still,
"Sketches of the Deep South," by Charles L.
Cooke, and "Harlem Symphony," by James P.
Johnson. The second part opened with several
performances in minstrel show format, composed
of members of the Crescendo Club, an organization of song writers. Each member of the club
presented his own compositions, including Johnson's
"Charleston." The finale consisted of, as Handy
put it, "a wild orgy of blues, jazz, jitterbug and
jive, now called swing, in which the following
bands participated: Cab Calloway, Noble Sissle,
Louis Armstrong, and Claude Hopkins." This
event marked the first time Johnson led "his own
compositions to victory" on the concert stage.4

     The various performances at Carnegie Hall
allowed Johnson to demonstrate the diversity of
his musical ability. Although he had returned to
a much more visible place in the music world, he
encountered the same problems in 1939 as ten
years earlier. He recorded more than 35 sides in
1939, due mostly to the efforts of John Hammond
and Perry Bradford. Yet, many of the sides
were not issued until at least 20 years later,
since the recording company executives thought
them to be "uncommercial".

     This reaction to his playing is only further
support for Johnson's stylistic integrity. Despite
this initial corporate resistance to Johnson's
music, a number of small jazz collectors' labels
sprang up in the wake of the depression from
1938 on, run by people more interested in the
music than the marketplace. Blue Note,
Commodore, H.R.S., Asch (which later became
Folkways) and, by the mid-1940s, a number of
others, provided a non-commerically oriented out-

let for the preservation of good music. The Forties proved to be very active and rewarding for Johnson.

20

The 1940s: A Johnson Renaissance

The "Spirituals To Swing" concerts resulted in New York night club bookings and record dates for many of the performers, most of them promoted by John Hammond.   From January 1 through June of 1940, James P. Johnson led his own band at the Greenwich Village jazz club called Cafe Society Downtown.   The Organizer was performed in June, and Johnson appeared to be making a successful return to visible activity in the music world.   In late August, however, he succumbed to the first of eight strokes.   For the remainder of 1940 and 1941, Johnson once again removed himself from public activity, this time to recuperate from his illness.

Johnson had long since given up the fast pace of Harlem night life for a more sedentary existence with his family.   After the stroke he tempered his habits further.   He gave up all hard liquor in favor of champagne and beer.   The Johnsons spent a good deal of time with Lillie Mae's family in the Pocono mountain region of Pennsylvania.   James P. took up gardening, bird watching, and tended a few chickens.   In the winter, when he was feeling up to it, he indulged in a little light skiing.   By early 1942, Johnson slowly made his way back into public performance.[1]

On March 8, 1942, the Brooklyn Civic Orchestra under the direction of Dr. Paul Kosko played a program consisting entirely of Johnson's symphonic works at the Heckscher Theater.

Sponsored by Long Island University, the program was billed as the "First Concert of Symphonic Works by James P. Johnson." The title to the introduction printed in the program summed up the event well--"A Dream Realized." This concert marked the first "all-Johnson" program consisting entirely of his serious works. There were no oversize choirs or noisy jam-session recreations. It was a night for James P. Johnson, the serious composer. Included were all four movements of the "Harlem Symphony," the first and third movements of the "American Symphonic Suite--'St. Louis Blues'," several songs, two of them from his one-act opera "The Dreamy Kid," the adagio movement from "Jassamine Concerto," (featuring Johnson at the piano), and the symphonic poem "African Drums."

The beginning of 1943 saw Johnson playing with "Wild Bill" Davison and his band at the Ken Club in Boston. The band, consisting of Davison on cornet, Sandy Williams on trombone, Rod Cless on clarinet, Johnson at the piano, and Kaiser Marshall on drums, opened on February 8. After a five-week run, it played in New York, first at Jimmy Ryan's (from March 22 to May 15), then at the Onyx Club, after dropping the trombone and drums and adding bassist Al Matthews. Jimmy Ryan's and the Onyx were two of the prominent clubs on 52nd Street, best known as "Swing Street." Rod Cless had this to say about his stay with the Davison band: "This is the best job I ever had. James P. Johnson sounds like a 100-piece orchestra, and after playing all night and rehearsing in the daytime, I feel fine, because the band is such a good kick."[2]

In June, Johnson was forced to drop out of Davison's band, again because of illness. Although he was conscious of his health problems

and took some steps to relax and keep the pres-
sure low, he seemed incorrigibly drawn to increasing activity. Within two months, he was back in
the thick of things. In August, he attended a
mammoth jam session at the studio of Life
magazine photographer Gjon Mili. Some of the
biggest names in jazz were assembled, including
Duke Ellington, Billie Holiday, the Mary Lou Williams trio, the Don Redman sextet, Teddy Wilson
and his band, and Eddie Condon and his band. In
October, Johnson appeared with a new band of
his own at Small's Paradise. November saw him
tack on Sunday afternoon jam sessions at Jimmy
Ryan's (sponsored by Milt Gabler of Commodore
Records) and weekend night engagements at
Sperry's Bar and Grill, a local pub in Queens.
Also in 1943, the Johnsons added a third child,
adopted daughter Lillie Mae, Jr.

Moreover, Johnson returned to regular sessions in the recording studios. By 1940, many of
the racial barriers in the jazz world had been
broken. Johnson often participated in interracial
bands, both in live performance and for recordings. In 1943 and 1944 he recorded with
Chicago-oriented groups led by Eddie Condon,
Yank Lawson, Rod Cless, and Max Kaminsky. He
also worked with all-black groups led by Edmond
Hall and Sidney De Paris for the Blue Note label.
For the same label, in 1943, Johnson recorded a
series of piano solos on 12-inch 78 discs which
are among his best and represent a variety of
musical styles. On November 17, Johnson recorded four numbers: "J.P. Boogie," "Backwater
Blues," "Carolina Balmoral," and "Gut Stomp."
These recordings illustrate many interesting things,
one of which is the imperceptible effect of his
stroke on Johnson's playing. Friends and fans
recalled that Johnson had put on a lot of weight,

and had an increasingly difficult time speaking. Yet his playing seemed to be unaffected.

Perhaps as a concession to Blue Note's owners, Alfred Lion and Frank Wolff, Johnson recorded several "boogie-woogie" and blues tunes (four in all), which, after all, was not his most natural idiom, but one of which Blue Note was enamored. "Gut Stomp," written with Willie "The Lion" Smith, is aptly named. It smacks of the gutbucket, stomping feeling of pre-World War I vintage. "Carolina Balmoral" is a piece in a similar vein, and shows Johnson at his best in improvising on a theme. The piece consists of two similar strains which Johnson plays in no particular order. As he proceeds from chorus to chorus, the differences between the two themes become more difficult to discern. Using the basic material of these strains, he creates 17 different choruses. It was this ability for seemingly endless variation on thematic material which set Johnson apart from his contemporaries.

On December 15, Johnson recorded another four solos for Blue Note. These contain similar thematic material as the first four: two blues, "Arkansas Blues" and "Improvisations on Pinetop's Boogie-Woogie," and two shouts, "Mule Walk" and "Caprice Rag." These eight sides are perhaps Johnson's best efforts of the decade. A sad irony surrounds the December session, for on the same day that Johnson was reaffirming his title as "Dean of Jazz Pianists," Fats Waller, once his protege, and then the man who eventually eclipsed him as popular composer and performer, died of pneumonia on a train nearing Kansas City. It has been said that Johnson was unable to touch a piano for three days after hearing the news.

On December 18, Johnson paid tribute to his best friend.   He recorded a piece called "Blues for Fats," which included interpolations of some of Waller's most popular songs.   That evening, Johnson participated in one of Eddie Condon's first jam session concerts at Town Hall. He played several Waller tunes, including "Willow Tree," "Ain't Misbehavin'," and "Honeysuckle Rose," and his own "Carolina Shout."   Johnson was one of the honorary pallbearers at Waller's funeral on December 20.   Although the whole jazz world mourned the death of one of its greatest exponents, Johnson's loss was particularly personal and poignant.

Johnson was contracted by the Decca label in 1944 to record a series of Waller compositions, an opportunity he welcomed.   At two separate sessions in April, he recorded eight Waller tunes as piano solos--"I've Got a Feelin' I'm Fallin'," "My Fate Is in Your Hands," "Ain't Misbehavin'," "Blue Turning Grey Over You," "I'm Gonna Sit Right Down and Write Myself a Letter,"[3] "Keepin' Out of Mischief Now," "Squeeze Me," and "Honeysuckle Rose."   In June, in two sessions, Johnson recorded the same eight tunes again, that time with accompaniment by drummer Eddie Dougherty, "who could not recall, some three and a half decades later, exactly why a pianist like Johnson needed a drummer to back him."[4]   All 16 sides are an affectionate monument, from teacher to pupil, from friend to friend.

The month of June was a very active one for Johnson.   He recorded 23 commercially released sides for Decca, Asch, Blue Note and Commodore.   In addition to the eight Waller tunes, he recorded with his "New York Orchestra," demonstrating different styles of jazz, with Sidney De Paris, and with Max Kaminsky.

Johnson took part in another Condon Town Hall
Concert (Johnson participated in these events
throughout the decade) that was broadcast on the
Armed Forces Radio Network. He was also enlisted to play an engagement at a New York
club, which, as pianist Dick Hyman put it, "gets
more wondrous as the years go by."[5]

Early in 1944, a club on Barrow Street in
Greenwich Village was taken over by its creditors.
They renamed the establishment the Pied Piper,
but had no more success in drawing customers
than the previous owners. They approached trumpeter Max Kaminsky, offering him $55 per week
per man to assemble a band that would attract
patrons. A fringe benefit was free food and
drink for the musicians. With this to offer,
Kaminsky was able to put together a band including James P. Johnson. For Johnson, Kaminsky
had a further incentive: "I managed to talk the
bosses into investing in a Steinway baby grand,
and I took James P. up to 57th Street and
turned him loose in the store until he found one
that talked back in the right tone of voice."[6]
Johnson played intermission piano between sets
with Max Kaminsky's Orchestra. In August, Willie
"The Lion" Smith joined the band at the Pied
Piper while James P. continued in the intermission spot. Just as James P. and Fats had done
during the intermission of Keep Shufflin', James
P. and The Lion engaged in cutting contests that
packed the house. One wonders how many of the
customers understood the historical context upon
which the piano battles they witnessed were built.
By December, the pace once again became too
much for Johnson, who was forced to step out of
the Pied Piper engagement to regain his health.

On January 17, 1945, Esquire magazine held
its second annual all-American Poll-Winners

concert--an ambitious program. The first such
event had taken place at the Metropolitan Opera
House in New York, featuring musicians chosen by
a panel of experts. The second concert presented
the panel's choices in concerts held simultaneously
in three cities, each headlined by a great name:
Louis Armstrong in New Orleans, Duke Ellington
in Los Angeles, and Benny Goodman in New York.
James P. Johnson was engaged as the pianist in
Armstrong's Jazz Foundation Six. The concerts
were broadcast over national network radio.
Johnson did get to play one solo, "Arkansas
Blues," after a terse introduction as "one of the
great names in jazz piano at the keyboard, James
P. Johnson."[7]

Back in New York, Johnson was preparing
for a concert that symbolically marked the pinnacle of his career as a composer. On May 4, a
"Jazzfest and Pop Concert presenting James P.
Johnson--composer-pianist" was produced at Carnegie Hall. It was neither the first all-Johnson
concert, nor his first appearance at Carnegie
Hall, but the combination of these two circumstances marked an important night in his
career. Baritone William Franklin, soprano Edith
Sewell, guest pianist Bruce Wendell, and a chorus
and orchestra of 50 assisted Johnson in the
performance. As composer of extended compositions and popular songs, vocal accompanist,
soloist, and "jam" musician, Johnson was well
represented.

The first part of the program was dominated by Johnson's orchestral pieces, interspersed
with pieces by Josef Cherniavsky, the conductor,
and spirituals sung by Edith Sewell. "April in
Harlem" and "Baptist Mission" (excerpts from
"Harlem Symphony") and "Yamekraw" were the
Johnson pieces performed. "Reflections," a tone

poem, was listed on the program, but accounts of
the concert indicate that it was not performed.
H.J. Harrison, in his review of the concert in
The Jazz Record, commented about Johnson's approach to extended composition.

> What Jimmy has written is not arranged
> jazz.   It is not jazz with some fancy in-
> struments thrown in to make a big stage
> show.   It isn't string music with some raz-
> ma-taz stuff added.   It's music of itself.
> The jazz voice is natural to him, and he
> blends it in with the classical, using both
> to achieve the expression he wants.[8]

The second part of the program featured
Johnson and his works almost exclusively.   He
accompanied Edith Sewell as she sang "If I Could
Be with You" and "Old Fashioned Love."   With
Johnson still at the piano, William Franklin sang
the featured piece of the evening, "Ode to Dorie
Miller."   The piece is an orchestral work honoring
a 22-year-old black Navy cook, third class, who
was awarded the Navy Cross for heroism at Pearl
Harbor.   As Harrison noted, "plain old jazz didn't
get going until 10:10, when Jimmy unloosed [sic]
some solo work.   The audience had been very
happy all evening but now went wild."   Included,
according to the program, were "Caprice Rag,"
"Arkansas Blues," and "Willow Tree."   Johnson's
solos were followed by a "jazz-jamboree" and
finale with guest artists including Sidney and Wilbur De Paris, Sam Jackson, Kaiser Marshall, and
Israel Crosby, playing Johnson compositions.   This
part of the performance is supposed to have been
recorded, but nothing is known to have survived.
Not surprisingly, Johnson dedicated the concert to
Fats Waller.

On October 25th, Johnson was again the center of attention, this time at a concert at Town Hall. The emphasis was on Johnson's recollections and interpretations of musicians who had influenced him. Johnson opened with a medley of his own compositions, including "If I Could Be with You," "Old Fashioned Love," "Don't Cry Baby," "Charleston," "Carolina Shout," and the second movement of his "Jassamine" concerto. Then followed sets highlighting the work of George Gershwin, Johnson's impression of other pianists--Scott Joplin, Jelly Roll Morton, Earl Hines, Pinetop Smith, Jack the Bear, One Leg Willie (Joseph), Luckey Roberts, Willie "The Lion" Smith, and Eubie Blake--and a set of tunes by Fats Waller. Johnson was joined on several numbers by tenor saxophonist Bud Freeman and drummer George Wettling.   This concert was projected as the first in a series by Johnson, according to Jazz Record writer Lewis Eaton, but no information has been found concerning any subsequent events.

Although Johnson tried to remain as active as possible in 1946 (Jazz Society of Boston in May, Eddie Condon's Club in New York in August, a Town Hall concert in September), he spent most of the year resting while other pianists substituted for him in his regular jobs. Back on his feet in 1947, Johnson participated in the "Honky Tonk Blues at Midnight" concert, produced by Alan Lomax, at Town Hall in February.   Also on the program were Sidney Bechet, Pops Foster, and a number of blues singers including Sonny Boy Williamson, Big Bill Broonzy, and Memphis Slim.   In March, Johnson began regular appearances on Rudi Blesh's weekly This Is Jazz program, broadcast nationally over the mutual network.   Many of these broadcasts, which also featured veteran New Orleans musicians like Sidney Bechet, Albert Nicholas, Danny Barker, Pops Foster, and George Brunis, were recorded and released on LP in later years.

Johnson undertook an interesting engagement on April 13. Clarinetist and tenor saxophonist Cecil Scott, bassist Pops Foster, drummer Baby Dodds, and Johnson provided the music for a performance by Mura Dehn and the Jazz Dancers at Local 105 Auditorium of the I.L.G.W.U. at 100 East 17th Street. The performers were billed as "Harlem's greatest dancers." The program consisted of two parts. The first involved the "Jazz Vocabulary," short pieces based on popular dance steps such as the Charleston, Snake Hips, Lindy, and Shim Sham. The second part was built more on ad libbing to blues and jazz tunes.

Johnson continued to perform at jam sessions and jamborees, including those sponsored by pianist (and then editor of the Jazz Record) Art Hodes in Syracuse, New York, and Boston. In addition, he composed, with his old friend Flournoy Miller, a comic opera entitled Meet Miss Jones, which played at the Experimental Theater on 126th Street in Harlem in December.

By the end of the decade, James P. Johnson had experienced the promise of recognition and the reality of oversight and neglect. For 25 years, he seemed to be on the verge of breakthrough to public acclaim and admiration from the scholarly music world. He had also seen the music change dramatically through the years, from Dixieland to Swing, to a newly emerging form called Bebop (or Rebop as it was sometimes known then), and the revival of traditional jazz. He strove to improve his ability as composer, in an attempt to transcend the ephemeral success of musical trends by casting the fundamental elements of Afro-American music into a timeless form. He studied with pianist Leopold Godowsky, with E. Aldama Jackson in composition, Morrie Deutsch in orchestration, and E.E. Treumann, all in an after-working-hours musical education.

In 1949, Rudi Blesh spoke with Johnson about musical trends.

> The atonal and twelve-tone systems become common and monotonous. I have done six-tone atonal work myself, but they haven't dug to the bottom of the old harmony yet. They've forgotten how to use it--there was a break somewhere--so they think it's all used up. Any harmony is only so many chords unless you have a real melody. And the Schillinger system--you are supposed to have emotional intent by science. This is impossible, because true inspiration is gone. Why do these composers, and the be-boppers, too, try to get away from the melody? It shows a weakness. No melody is in them and they know it.[9]

In 1947, at the request of Art Hodes, Johnson wrote his comments on Bebop for the Jazz Record. First Johnson demurred about not being an instructor and his lack of knowledge of bebop as a style; finally he confined his comments to the music of Dizzy Gillespie.

> I say that Dizzy makes it sound agreeable and I like it. But that doesn't mean that I like it all. I like anything that's good, and some of it's good just like anything else. It's the old story of it being all according to a person's taste. As far as the big bands are concerned, I like some of the

work that the arrangers are doing. A lot of the arrangers write with reason, and that's good, but others write merely for the effect--or simply to astound.

In the classics different scholars have added, from time to time, new, theoretical harmonic effects. Up to very recently that hadn't been done in jazz. What Dizzy and his kind play is simply a new treatment of basic jazz.

I understand that J.C. Heard said in Jazz Record that no one understands rebop and won't understand it for five or ten years. I'm afraid that I have to disagree with him. I think there are quite a few people who understand it now.

As I said, it's just a different treatment of basic jazz and is still jazz. I agree that the music is revolutionary, but it's still the basic thing that counts.[10]

Johnson concluded his statements with a prediction that, had it been borne out, might have been the crucial factor in "legitimizing" Afro-American music within the context of a Western aesthetic and Western definition of a "classical" music.

The most important point that I can see is that the jazz musicians of the future will have to be able to play all different kinds of jazz--in all its treatments--just like the classical musician who, in one concert, might range from Bach to Copland.[11]

Yet two years later, Johnson was acutely aware that this intellectual understanding and apprehension of all stages of the tradition was not a dominant factor in the development of younger musicians.

They're still playing ragtime now, or trying to, but they conceal and cover it up. It's considered certain traditional figures by some, but that's wrong, it's a rhythm that you feel and work with. They're just ashamed of a name.[12]

All of his life, Johnson remained a stalwart proponent of the grass-roots heritage of jazz, maintaining a pure style at the expense of commercial success. Although Blesh recalled that Johnson was not bitter as he spoke about his music, his remarks clearly illustrate a life of frustration in adhering to ideals. Yet, even as late as 1948, Johnson continued to study music very seriously. Johnson's youngest daughter Lille Mae recalled how many hours her father spent at the piano experimenting with new ideas.

The Johnsons had been a family since 1917, when they married. With their three children, they lived in a modest home on Long Island. Although her father was often out of town, Lillie Mae Jr. recalled that he always brought gifts for everyone when he returned. "He was a good father," she said. "My parents never argued in front of us. At home, my mother was the boss, but she would always tell us not to disturb our father when he was studying." Johnson was a very religious man. He played the organ and piano for the family's congregation, and attended church services regularly when he was home. Meanwhile, his life as a performer continued between periods of illness.

From June 1948 through Februry 1949, Johnson was a regular at the Friday night jazz sessions sponsored by Bob Maltz at the Stuyvesant Casino and Central Plaza in downtown Manhattan. After rehearsing for a few months, Johnson's last show, written with Flournoy Miller, opened at the Las Palmas Theater in Hollywood, California in June, 1949. The show was called Sugar Hill, but was completely different from Johnson's first show by that name in 1931. Another all-black production, it ran for three months, but the producers could not find the financial backing to bring the show to New York. While in California, Johnson performed in a concert at Pasadena's Civic auditorium featuring the Yerba Buena Jazz Band, one of the first revivalist groups of traditional jazz and ragtime. Johnson played in a trio with clarinetist Albert Nicholas and drummer Zutty Singleton, two New Orleans veterans.

The review of the event in Down Beat sported the headline "Johnson Puts on Great Show at Coast Concert." Although Johnson and Nicholas appeared to run into some stylistic controversy, and Johnson seemed "just a little more than buoyant," reviewer Hal Holly closed his comments with the following appraisal:

> But the real highlight was Johnson's introduction to one of his own numbers: "Ladies and gentlemen, I shall now play my own original arrangement of 'Who.'" He started with a strain a few of us recognized as the verse of "Hallelujah," then went off into a musical world that was all his own. He should have introduced it as a special arrangement of "What?"
> Even so, good old James P. proved himself to be a great musician in that he never really botched it up. We'll gladly take all of our concerts from now on with James P. Johnson just as he was at this one. After all, maybe this was The True Jazz.[14]

Photo by William P. Gottlieb (Edward J. Gottlieb Collection)

A

Photo by Duncan P. Schiedt

Johnson outside his home, late 1920s.

Johnson with his son, Jimmy, Jr., and friends at the Stuyvesant Casino, 1950.   Photo by Duncan P. Schiedt

B

Johnson with Hot Lips Page (center) and Eddie Condon at the Fats Waller Memorial Concert, 1944. Photo by Duncan P. Schiedt

Johnson with Fess Williams (center) and Freddie Moore playing at the office opening of photographer William P. Gottlieb. Photo by William P. Gottlieb (Edward J. Gottlieb Collection)

C

Courtesy of the New York Public Library (Otto Hess Collection)

D

Courtesy of the New York Public Library (Otto Hess Collection)

E

Left to right: Zutty Singleton, Johnson, Milton "Mezz" Mezzrow, Hughes Panassie, and Tommy Ladnier in the recording studio, November 21, 1938.   Photo by Duncan P. Schiedt

F

Left to right: Harry Lim, Ralph Burton (?), Sidney Bechet, Johnson, Sidney De Paris, Claude Jones, Pops Foster, Manzie Johnson (?) in a jam session at the New School, New York City, mid-1940s. Photo by Duncan P. Schiedt

G

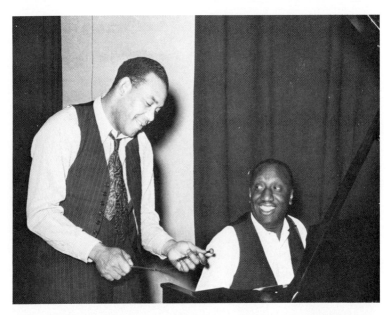

Johnson with Zutty Singleton, possibly at the Panassie recording session, November 1938. Courtesy of the New York Public Library (Otto Hess Collection)

Johnson with bass player Pops Foster, probably late 1940s. Courtesy of the New York Public Library (Otto Hess Collection)

H

Photo by Duncan Butler

I

Johnson with jazz writer Floyd Levin in front of the Las Palmas
Theater (Los Angeles) on opening night of Sugar Hill, July 12, 1949.
Photo courtesy of Robert Hilbert

Johnson with Marty Marsala (trumpet), Danny Alvin (drums), Sandy
Williams (trombone), Johnny Windhurst (trumpet, seated), Albert
Nicholas (clarinet) (?).   Photo by William P. Gottlieb (Edward J.
Gottlieb Collection)

J

<u>Left to right:</u>   Rod Cless, Sidney De Paris, Johnson, and unknown bassist.   Courtesy of the New York Public Library (Otto Hess Collection)

K

Johnson with Sidney De Paris and unknown bassist.   Courtesy of the
New York Public Library (Otto Hess Collection)

L

It's both astounding and fortunate that Johnson's
playing still showed few signs of his deteriorating
health, even when he had imbibed a bit.

In 1951, James P. Johnson suffered a massive stroke, paralyzing him and putting an end to
a career that had stretched over 35 years. He
spent the remainder of his life in either the
hospital or at home in a room specially equipped
by Lillie Mae to care for her husband, now an
invalid and unable to speak or care much for
himself. Since Johnson rated a B classification
with ASCAP, his four-figure quarterly check and
royalty payments supported the family. An article which appeared in Down Beat in 1953 about
Johnson's condition made the following point:
"Some of the younger ASCAP writers who are de-
manding that performance be made the dominant
factor in determining classification, thus increasing
their current revenue at the sacrifice of later
security, might change their reasoning if they
could drop in and see Jimmy Johnson."[15]

Johnson was now indeed a tragic figure.
He lingered through irreversible paralysis only to
witness how little attention he received. Close
friends like Willie "The Lion" Smith were still
concerned and visited often, and on September 28,
1953, Smith and other musicians organized a jazz
concert in Town Hall as a benefit for Johnson.
The list of sponsors read like a Who's Who of
jazz, both past and present. A slap in the face,
however, which quite literally adds insult to
injury, was the premature appearance of Johnson's
obituary in Down Beat, on May 5, 1954. The article by Goerge Hoefer, which employed enough
spiritualistic metaphor ("left his earthly keyboard")
and romanticized history to be distasteful, was
retracted in the next issue; the magazine apolo-
gized for its error in having failed to follow up

on a false rumor of Johnson's death. When told
of the mistake, Lillie Mae Johnson responded,
"Usually when they say somebody's passed away
who hasn't, it means that he won't." [16]

In a somewhat spiritualistic mood, Willie
"The Lion" Smith recalled the last time he saw
Johnson. James P. was unconscious and hadn't
spoken to anyone for a few weeks. Willie sat
down at a piano in Johnson's room and played
"Carolina Shout." Johnson was stirred enough to
write out a message: "They were too good to
the piano players with all that free booze and
rich food. It catches up with you."[17]

On November 17, 1955, Lillie Mae's wishful
thought was proven wrong. James P. Johnson
died as a result of a final massive stroke. He
was admitted to Queens General Hospital after
having suffered the stroke (his eighth) at home
two days earlier. All the major New York
newspapers carried his obituary, but his name
probably meant little to the general public. One
thing, however, is very interesting about these
obituaries. In their headlines and opening
paragraphs, they identify Johnson not only as a
jazz pianist but also as a prolific composer.
They are also more factually correct than the
premature obituary in Down Beat, supposedly the
leading magazine covering the jazz world.

In its December 28, 1955 issue, Down Beat
published a much-improved tribute to James P.
Johnson. In an obituary that is also a diatribe
against the music world and the general public,
John Hammond recounted the frustrations of
Johnson's career and the neglect of his talents.

James P. Johnson, one of the great figures
in American music, died in New York City

on Nov. 17. Two days later, fewer than
75 persons attended the funeral services at
University Chapel, in midtown Manhattan.
    His enormous talents as composer,
pianist, and arranger were as unappreciated
in life as now. Although he wrote such
tunes as "Charleston," "Old-Fashioned Love,"
"Porter's Love Song," and "If I Could Be
With You," the general public was ignorant
of his name. A few musicians may
remember such classics as "Carolina Shout,"
"Worried and Lonesome Blues," and "Snowy
Morning Blues," but the sad fact is that
Jelly Roll Morton was far better known.
Even as a pianist, Jimmy's fame was soon
eclipsed by his pupil, Fats Waller.[18]

Hammond further commented on the segregation
of the music field, which had confined Johnson to
the race record market as a performer and to
the all-black musical as composer. He scorned
the disinterest of the music community toward
Johnson's serious work and the "public that never
even noticed" Johnson's popular music. After a
plea to the record companies to reissue Johnson's
early recordings, Hammond concluded, "James P.
Johnson was 64 [sic] when he died, and he should
have been among the most famous and successful
of men. Let us hope that future generations will
make up for our lack of appreciation."

NOTES

Introduction

1. Le Jazz Hot, by Hugues Panassie, and Jazzmen, by Frederick Ramsey and Charles E. Smith, two historically and critically important works published during the 1930s, don't mention Johnson.

2. Ross Russell, "Grandfather of Hot Piano ... James P. Johnson," Jazz Information, (November 1941), p. 20.

3. Ibid., p. 20.

4. Humphrey Lyttelton, The Best of Jazz--From Basin Street to Harlem (New York, Taplinger, 1973), p. 23.

5. Russell, p. 23.

1. New Brunswick, 1894--1902

1. Frank Kappler, Dick Wellstood, and Willa Rouder, "Giants of Jazz--James P. Johnson," Time-Life Records (1981), insert to liner notes. The original source of this note was Lillie Mae McIntyre, Johnson's youngest daughter.

2. Tom Davin, "Conversations with James P. Johnson," Jazz Review, (June-September 1959; March/April 1960).

3. Rudi Blesh and Harriet Janis, They All Played Ragtime, 4th ed., (New York, Oak Publications, 1971), p. 190.

2. The Ring-Shout

1. Blesh and Janis, p. 188.

2. Lydia Parrish, Slave Songs of the Georgia Sea Islands (New York, Creative Age Press, 1942), p. 54.

3. Blesh and Janis, p. 187.

4. Parrish, p. 54.

5. LeRoi Jones, Blues People (New York, Morrow/Quill Paperbacks, 1963), p. 27.

6. Ibid., p. 48.

7. Ibid., pp. 42-43.

8. Bernard Katz, The Social Implications of Early Negro Music in the United States (New York, Arno Press, 1969), pp. 4-5.

9.   Blesh and Janis, pp. 82-84.

10. Parrish, p. 85.

11. Ibid., p. 71.

12. Ibid., p. 85.

13. William Francis Allen, Charles Pickard Ware, Lucy McKim Garrison, Slave Songs of the United States (Peter Smith reprint, © 1867), p. xiv.

14. Tom Davin, (June), p. 15.

15. Jones, p. 28.

16. Davin, (June), p. 15.

3. Jersey City, 1902--1908

1.   Davin, (June), p. 16.

2.   Ibid.

3.   Ibid.

4.   Ibid., p. 17.

5.   Davin, (July), p. 11.

4. Ragtime

1.   William J. Schafer and Johannes Riedel, The Art of Ragtime (New York, Da Capo, 1973), p. 14.

2.   Ibid., p. 14, f.n.

3.   Eileen Southern, The Music of Black Americans (New York, Norton, 1971), p. 100.

4.   Ibid., p. 102.

5.   James Weldon Johnson, Black Manhattan (New York, Atheneum, © 1930).

6.   Terry Waldo, This Is Ragtime (New York, Hawthorn Books, 1976), p. 12.

7.   Blesh and Janis, p. 96.

8.   Ibid., p. 86.

9.   Isaac Goldberg, Tin Pan Alley (New York, Frederick Unger, 1930, 1961), p. 37.

10. Blesh and Janis, p. 89.

11.   Ibid., pp. 210-213.

12.   Edward A. Berlin, Ragtime--A Musical and Cultural History (Berkeley, University of California Press, 1980), p. 104.

13.   Edward A. Berlin, "Ragtime and Improvised Piano: Another View," Journal of Jazz Studies, 4:2 (Spring/Summer 1977), pp. 8-9.

14.   Berlin, p. 61.

15.   Waldo, p. 79.

16.   Goldberg, p. 155.

17.   Schafer and Riedel, p. 127.

18.   David A. Jasen, Recorded Ragtime, 1897-1958 (Hamden, Ct., Archon Books, 1973), pp. 2-3.

19.   David A. Jasen and Trebor Jay Tichenor, Rags and Ragtime--A Musical History (New York, Seabury Press, 1978), p. 22.

20.   Trebor Jay Tichenor, Ragtime Rarities--Complete Original Music for 63 Piano Rags (New York, Dover Publications, 1975), pp. 33-35.

21.   Davin, (June), p. 17.

22.   Schafer and Riedel, p. 49.

23.   Blesh and Janis, p. 204.

24.   Jasen, p. 40.

25.   Blesh and Janis, p. 261.

26.   Jasen, p. 5.

27.   Henry Osborne Osgood, So This Is Jazz (Boston, Little, Brown, 1976).

28.   Joan M. Wildman, "The Function of the Left Hand in the Evolution of the Jazz Piano," Journal of Jazz Studies, 5:2 (Spring/Summer 1979).

29.   Berlin, p. 63.

30.   Davin, (July), p. 11.

31.   Blesh and Janis, p. 190.

32.   Davin, (July), pp. 12-13.

33.   Berlin, pp. 76-77.

34.   Waldo, p. 59.

35.   Eli H. Newberger, "The Transition From Ragtime to Improvised
       Piano Style," Journal of Jazz Studies, 3:2 (Spring 1976).

36.   Berlin, p. 155.

37.   Ibid., pp. 83, 131, 147.

38.   Schafer and Riedel, p. 145.

39.   Ibid., p. 101.

40.   Alan Lomax, Mister Jelly Roll (Berkeley, University of Califor-
       nia Press, © 1950), p. 62.

41.   Schafer and Riedel, p. 147.

5. The Jungles, 1910--1913

1.   Davin, (July), p. 11.

2.   Ibid., p. 11.

3.   Ibid., p. 11.

4.   James Weldon Johnson, The Autobiography of An Ex-Colored
      Man, (New York, Knopf, 1927; Avon Books, 1965), p. 447.

5.   Willie "The Lion" Smith and George Hoefer, Music On My Mind
      (New York, Da Capo Press, 1964), p. 65.

6.   Davin, (July), p. 12.

6. The Blues

1.   Gunther Schuller, Early Jazz (New York, Oxford, 1968), p. 214.

2.   Max Harrison, "James P. Johnson: A Jazz Retrospect," reprint
      from Jazz Monthly (Boston, Crescendo Publishing Co., 1976), p.
      83.

3.   Harold Courlander, Negro Folk Mysic, U.S.A. (New York,
      Columbia University Press, 1963), p. 125.

4.   James H. Cone, The Spirituals and the Blues (New York,
      Seabury, 1972), p. 110.

5.   Jones, p. 63.

6.   Ibid., p. 62.

7.   Cone, pp. 112-113.

8.   Frank Tirro, Jazz--A History (New York, Norton, 1977), pp.
      114-115.

9. Mildred McAdory, "Noted Blues Composer Writes Ode to Hero," The Worker (Wednesday, May 3, 1945), p. 11.

10. Jones, p. 50.

11. Southern, pp. 332-333.

12. Schuller, p. 45.

13. Ibid., p. 47.

14. Rudi Blesh, Shining Trumpets (New York, Da Capo Paperback, 1946), p. 106.

15. Courlander, pp. 20-21.

16. Tirro, p. 119.

17. Nat Hentoff, "Garvin Bushell and New York Jazz in the 1920s," Jazz Review 2:1 (January 1959), p. 12.

18. Jones, p. 123.

19. Davin, (June), p. 17.

20. Maurice R. Davie, Negroes in American Society (New York, McGraw-Hill, 1949), p. 94.

21. Hentoff, p. 12.

22. Davin (June), p. 17.

23. In presenting this view, I do not intend to perpetuate the cliche of New Orleans as the birthplace of jazz. I use these simplifications as a basis for comparison and illustration that jazz was conceived as a result of musical and cultural interaction and not necessarily geography.

24. Jack V. Buerkle and Danny Barker, Bourbon Street Black (New York, Oxford, 1973), p. 10.

25. Davin, (June), p. 17.

7. The Ticklers, 1913--1916

1. "The Dream" was characteristic of early Eastern ragtime. It was often played by John "Jack the Bear" Wilson, but was written by Jess Pickett, another legendary Eastern player. The piece is based on a tango rhythm. Johnson recorded it again as a piano solo in 1945. Fats Waller recorded it under the title "Digah's Stomp." Other titles include "Digah's Dream," "Ladies Dream," "The Bowdiger's Dream," and "The Bull Diker's Dream." Willie "The Lion" Smith recalled that it was dedicated to lesbians, i.e., "Bull Dykes."

2. Davin, (July), p. 12.

3.   Ibid., p. 10.

4.   Blesh and Janis, p. 203.

5.   Ibid., p. 203.

6.   Davin, (July), p. 13.

7.   Hentoff, p. 13.

8.   Davin, (July), p. 13.

9.   Blesh and Janis, p. 200.

10. Waldo, p. 113. Quote by Eubie Blake.

11. Davin, (July), p. 12.

12. Blesh and Janis, p. 201.

13. Al Rose, Eubie Blake (New York, Schirmer, 1979), p. 148.

14. Waldo, p. 106.

15. Michael Montgomery, "James P. Johnson--1917 vol. 2," (New York, Biograph, 1973), BLP 1009Q, liner notes.

16. Smith and Hoefer, p. 35.

17. Ibid., p. 36.

18. Ibid, pp. 36-37.

19. Ibid., p. 78.

20. Davin, (August), p. 13.

21. Ibid., p. 14.

22. Ibid., pp. 14-15.

23. Robert Kimball and William Bolcom, Reminiscing With Sissle and Blake (New York, Viking, 1973), pp. 10-12.

24. Waldo, p. 100. Kimball and Bolcom, pp. 58-61.

25. Davin, (June), p. 17.

26. Davin, (September), p. 26.

27. Ibid., p. 27.

28. Davin, (July), pp. 12-13.

8. First Recordings, 1917

1.   Michael Montgomery and Trebor Tichenor, "Scott Joplin--1916" (New York, Biograph, 1971), BLP 1006Q.

2.   Art Napoleon, "Record Review--Parlour Piano Solos, 1917-1921, Bio. vol. 1," Jazz Journal, 23:12 (December 1970), p. 35.

3.   Ibid.

4.   Montgomery, "James P. Johnson, 1917, vol. 2," liner notes.

5.   The name of the roll in parentheses is that of the label, not necessarily the manufacturer.   The date is the release date.

6.   Montgomery, "James P. Johnson, 1917, vol. 2," liner notes.

7.   Ibid.

8.   A word roll has the words to the song printed on the roll.

9.   Michael Montgomery, "James P. Johnson, 1917-1921," (New York, Biograph, 1970), BLP 1003Q, liner notes.

10.   Jasen and Tichenor, p. 244.   The A-strain melodic phrase of "Carolina Shout" also appears in the respective A strains of "Wild Cherries Rag," "Perfect Rag," "Buddy's Habits," and "Little Rock Getaway."

9. The Giggin' Years, 1916--1918

1.   Davin, (September), p. 27.

2.   Johnson, pp. 147-151.

3.   Davin, (March/April 1960), p. 11.

4.   Ibid.

5.   Smith and Hoefer, p. 90.

6.   Davin, (March/April 1960), p. 11.   In 1941, Donald Lambert recorded four superb examples of "striding the classics," using themes by Donizetti, Grieg, Massenet and Wagner.

7.   Ibid.

8.   Ibid, p. 12.

9.   Ibid.

10.   Davin, (September), p. 27.

11.   Davin, (March/April 1960), p. 12.

12.   Ibid.

James P. Johnson

13. Ibid.

14. James P. Johnson, Willie "The Lion" Smith, Ethel Waters, Pops Foster, Garvin Bushell (see bibliography).

15. Ronald Clifford Foreman, Jr., "Jazz and Race Records, 1920-1932" (University of Illinois, doctoral dissertation, 1969), p. 40.

16. Nathan Irvin Huggins, Harlem Renaissance (New York, Oxford, 1971), pp. 9-11.

17. Foreman, pp. 56-58.

18. Davin, (September), p. 26.

19. "Phonograph Company Changes Name and Increases," New York Amsterdam News, (Wednesday, February 14, 1923).

20. Kappler, Wellstood, and Rouder, p. 28.

10. Harlem Stride Piano

1. Dick Wellstood, "Donald Lambert--Harlem Stride Classics," (Miami, Pumpkin Productions, 1977), 104, liner notes.

2. Smith and Hoefer, p. 3.

3. John S. Wilson, "The Jazz Panorama," Hi-Fi Review Supplement (Ziff-Davis, April 1959).

4. Whitney Balliett, "Supreme Tickler," The New Yorker, 39 (May 11, 1963), pp. 153-156.

5. Smith and Hoefer, p. 85.

6. Lyttelton, p. 33.

7. Wellstood, "Donald Lambert," liner notes.

8. Ibid.

9. Henry Francis, "Musical Aspects of Stride Piano," Storyville, 42 (August-September 1972), p. 213.

10. Schuller, p. 6.

11. Wildman, p. 33.

12. Wellstood, "Donald Lambert," liner notes.

13. Ibid.

14. Francis, insert between pp. 212-213.

15. Schuller, p. 215.

16. Newberger, p. 15.

17. Kappler, Wellstood, and Rouder, p. 37.

18. Francis, p. 214.

19. Ibid., p. 213.

20. Schuller, p. 219.

21. Wellstood, "Donald Lambert," liner notes.

22. Harrison, p. 84.

23. Blesh and Janis, p. 206.

24. Dick Wellstood, "Reviews: Recordings--W.C. Handy Blues acc.
     by James P. Johnson," The Jazz Review, (December 1958), p.
     34.

25. Scott Joplin, in his instruction manual entitled "School of
     Ragtime," cautions the reader several times against "careless or
     imperfect rendering."   Artie Matthews put the admonition
     "Don't Fake" on his series of five Pastime Rags.

26. Goldberg, p. 146.

27. Hentoff, p. 13.

28. Joe Turner, "The Pianists In My Life," Melody Maker (April 25,
     1953), p. 2.

29. Pops Foster and Tom Stoddard, Pops Foster (Berkeley, Univer-
     sity of California Press, 1971), p. 97.

30. Ibid., p. 153.

31. Hentoff, p. 13.

32. Ethel Waters and Charles Samuels, His Eye Is On The Sparrow
     (Garden City, New York, Doubleday, 1951), p. 145.

33. Blesh and Janis, p. 187.

34. A left-pointing arrow indicates a point where the beat is
     turned around.   A right-pointing arrow indicates where the
     "normal" rhythmic pulse is restored.   As can be seen, the pulse
     is sometimes disrupted for several measures.

35. Wildman, pp. 35-36.

36. Schuller, p. 214.

37. Kappler, Wellstood, and Rouder, p. 28.

38. Ibid.

39. Schuller, p. 218.

11.   James P. and Fats Waller, 1920

    1.   George Hoefer, "The Sound of Harlem" (Columbia Records, Jazz
          Odyssey, vol. III), C3L-33, album booklet.

    2.   Maurice Waller and Anthony Calabrese, Fats Waller (New York,
          Schirmer, 1977), p. 26.

    3.   Ibid., p. 27.

    4.   Seymour Peck, "PM Visits: The Dean of Jazz Pianists," PM
          (Friday, April 27, 1945), p. 20.

    5.   Nat Shapiro and Nat Hentoff, Hear Me Talkin' To Ya (New
          York, Rinehart, 1955; Dover Edition, 1966), p. 253.

    6.   Smith and Hoefer, p. 99.

    7.   Peck, p. 20.

    8.   Waller and Calabrese, p. 185.

    9.   Michael Montgomery, "Thomas (Fats) Waller, 1923-1924" (Buffalo,
          N.Y., Biograph) BLP-1002Q, liner notes.

    10.   Smith and Hoefer, pp. 258-259.

    11.   Wellstood, p. 34.

    12.   Rose, pp. 148-149.

    13.   Joel Vance, Fats Waller--His Life and Times (Chicago, Contem-
          porary Books, 1977), p. 156.

    14.   Shapiro and Hentoff, p. 253.

12.   Plantation Days, 1923

    1.   James A. Jackson, "Recent Blues Craze Bringing Another Big
          Publishing House to the Fore," New York Amsterdam News,
          (Wednesday, July 11, 1923), entertainment section.

    2.   G.M.W., "'Plantation Days' Is Carnival of Jazz," Toledo Blade,
          (December 18, 1922).

    3.   Art Hodes and Chadwick Hansen, Selections From the Gutter
          (Berkeley, University of California Press, 1977), p. 5.

    4.   "Sleuth Acting For 'Shuffle Along' Spike 'Plantation'," New York
          Amsterdam News, (Wednesday, February 28, 1923), entertainment
          section.

    5.   Harper and Blanks, "Harper and Blanks Issue First Statement of
          'Plantation Days' in London," New York Amsterdam News,
          (Wednesday, June 13, 1923), entertainment section.

6.   Edward Jablonski and Lawrence D. Stewart, The Gershwin Years (Garden City, New York, Doubleday, 1973), pp. 81-82.

7.   Ibid., p. 83.

13.   Runnin' Wild, 1923

1.   Jones, p. 17.

2.   Kimball and Bolcom, p. 100.

3.   Ibid., p. 101.

4.   John Hammond, "Talents of James P. Johnson Went Unappreciated," Down Beat, 22:12 (December 28, 1955), p. 12.

14.   The Rent Party

1.   Mait Edey, "Boogie Woogie Rarities, 1927-1932," (Milestone Records, 1969), MLP 2009, liner notes.

2.   Smith and Hoefer, p. 152.

3.   Ibid., p. 156.

4.   Peck, p. 20.

5.   Smith and Hoefer, p. 153; Waller and Calabrese, p. 37.

6.   Wallace Thurman, The Blacker the Berry (© 1929 by The McCaulay Co.; Collier Books, 1970), pp. 152-154.

7.   Smith and Hoefer, p. 155.

8.   Edward Kennedy Ellington, Music Is My Mistress (New York, Da Capo Press, 1973), p. 94.

9.   Nat Hentoff, "Garvin Bushell and New York Jazz in the 1920s." The Jazz Review, 2:2 (February 1959), p. 10.

10.   Ellington, pp. 93-94.

11.   Chris Albertson, "Backwater Blues" (New York, Riverside Records, 1961), RLP 151, liner notes.

12.   Shapiro and Hentoff, p. 174.

13.   Milton "Mezz" Mezzrow and Bernard Wolfe, Really the Blues (New York, Random House, 1946), pp. 231-232.

14.   Smith and Hoefer, p. 225.

15.   Sidney Bechet, Treat It Gentle (New York, Twayne Publishers, 1960), pp. 140-141.

16.   Henry T. Sampson, <u>Blacks In Blackface</u> (Metuchen, N.J.,
      Scarecrow Press, 1980), pp. 271, 479, 481, 484.

17.   Ibid., p. 359.

15.   James P. Johnson: The Composer

 1.   Schuller, pp. 220-221.

 2.   Perry Bradford and Noble Sissle, "Yamekraw--Negro Rhapsody"
      (New York, Folkways Records, 1962), FJ 2842, liner notes.

 3.   Blesh and Janis, p. 204.

 4.   Bradford and Sissle, liner notes.

 5.   Waldo, p. 117.

16.   James P. Johnson: The Recording Artist

 1.   Kappler, Wellstood, and Rouder, p. 32.

 2.   Foster and Stoddard, pp. 150-151.

 3.   Chris Albertson, "Bessie Smith--Any Women's Blues"   (New
      York, Columbia Records) G30126, liner notes.

 4.   Waters and Samuels, p. 145.

 5.   Kappler, Wellstood, and Rouder, p. 34.

 6.   Ibid., p. 31.

 7.   Hodes and Hansen, p. 218.

17.   Keep Shufflin', 1928

 1.   Waller and Calabrese, pp. 72-73.

 2.   Perry Bradford, <u>Born With the Blues</u> (New York,   Oak
      Publications, 1965), pp. 137-138.

 3.   Waller and Calabrese, p. 74.

 4.   Roland Cooke, "Fats Waller--vol. 3, 1927-1929" (France, RCA,
      1973), 741.076, liner notes.

 5.   W.C. Handy, <u>Father of the Blues,</u> ed. by Arna Bontemps (New
      York, Collier Books, 1941), p. 219.

 6.   Waller and Calabrese, pp. 75-76.

 7.   Ibid., p. 76.

8. Chester Collins, "Black Jazz Film Shorts--Bessie Smith, Louis Armstrong, Cab Calloway," (Biograph, 1978), BLP-M3, liner notes.

9. "Belated Discovery Made That Miller and Lyle Did Not Head Brooklyn Show," New York Amsterdam News, (Wednesday, April 30, 1930), entertainment section.

10. Hoefer, "Sound of Harlem," album booklet.

11. Smith and Hoefer, pp. 208-209. "With Our Song Writers Along Tin Pan Alley," New York Amsterdam News, (Wednesday, March 26, 1930), entertainment section.

12. Peck, p. 20.

13. Waters and Samuels, p. 147.

14. Schuller, p. 223.

18. The Stormy Days, 1930s

1. Hammond, p. 120.

2. Blesh and Janis, p. 204.

3. "Jimmie," Time Magazine, (December 27, 1943), p. 41.

4. Blesh and Janis, p. 204.

5. Kappler, Wellstood, and Rouder, p. 24.

6. Waller and Calabrese, p. 168.

7. Vance, p. 121.

19. Rediscovery, 1938

1. Kappler, Wellstood, and Rouder, p. 39. Actually, Kaminsky was with Artie Shaw and Tommy Dorsey, and Wells had just joined Basie.

2. Mezzrow and Wolfe, p. 361.

3. John Hammond and Charles Edward Smith, "From Spirituals to Swing" (New York, Vanguard Recording Society, 1973), VSD 47/48.

4. Handy and Bontemps, pp. 288-289.

20. The 1940s: A Johnson Renaissance

1. "Jimmie," Time Magazine, (December 27, 1943), p. 41.

2. "Boston Is Jumping," The Jazz Record (March 1, 1943), p. 2.

3. Although Fats Waller did not actually write this tune, his rendition became one of his most popular recordings and the song inseparably associated with him.

4. Kappler, Wellstood, and Rouder, p. 50.

5. Dick Hyman, "Themes and Variations On a Child Is Born" (Chiaroscuro, 1977), CR 198.

6. Kappler, Wellstood, and Rouder, p. 49.

7. Tony Middleton, "The Second Esquire Concert" (England, Saga Records, 1974), SAGA 6924, from transcription.

8. H.J. Harrison, "James P.'s Jazzfest," The Jazz Record, (June 1945), pp. 5-6.

9. Blesh and Janis, p. 205.

10. James P. Johnson, "I Like Anything That's Good," The Jazz Record, (April 1947), pp. 13-14.

11. Ibid., p. 14.

12. Blesh and Janis, p. 205.

13. Ibid.

14. Hal Holly, "Johnson Puts On Great Show At Coast Concert," Down Beat, (July 15, 1949), p. 9.

15. Sharon A. Pease, "Johnson, Now Ailing, Sustained by Royalties," Down Beat, (May 20, 1953), p. 20.

16. "James P. Johnson Alive; Report of Death Regretted," Down Beat, (May 19, 1954), p. 1.

17. Smith and Hoefer, p. 257.

18. John Hammond, p. 12. Even Hammond was not impervious to misinformation; he gives the wrong age for Johnson.

The following is a list of all known stage productions to which Johnson contributed in some way, as performer and/or composer. These include stage and floor shows, revues, Broadway musicals, plays, operas, operettas, and ballets. Not included are concert performances. If information on a particular show was found in only one secondary source, that source is cited in parentheses after the title of the show. Otherwise, the reader may assume that several sources, both primary and secondary, corroborate the details. These are cited in the text or the reference section.

1914-1916

The Darktown Follies (Davin)

Produced by J. Leubrie Hill, several editions of this show were staged during this time period. Johnson claimed to have worked for Hill on this show in the Davin interviews. No additional information concerning Johnson's part in the show could be found.

1917

What's Your Husband Doing?

"A Farce (founded on fact)" written by George V. Hobart. Opened at 39th Street Theater, New York, November 1917.

This was a play in which Johnson led a five-piece band on stage for a five-minute scene. The music was incidental and not mentioned in the program.

1919

Smart Set (Davin; producer of the show from Sampson)

Produced by Salem Tutt Whitney and J. Homer Tutt. Opened in Philadelphia at the Standard Theater; also played in Wilmington, Baltimore, Norfolk, Atlanta.

Some sources refer to this as Sherman H. Dudley's Smart Set. Dudley was the head of the first original Smart Set company from 1904-1909. Whitney and Tutt organized the second company of the original Smart Set in 1909, and in 1916 gained full control of the production and renamed it Whitney and Tutt's Smart Set Company.

1922

Me and You (Sampson)

Principal Cast: Andrew Tribble, Alec Lovejoy, Eddie Gray, James P. Johnson, Bradford and White, Parker Anderson, Dink Stewart

1922-1923

Plantation Days

Produced by O'Neil and Greenwald; musical director--James P. Johnson.

Cast: Harper and Blanks, Dave and Tressie, George Pasha, Silvertone Four, Marjorie Sipp, Plantation Johnnies, Hula girls, Eddie Green, Adams and Tunstall, Daisy Pizarro, Smith and DeForrest, Ida Ruley, Julia Mitchell

Musical Numbers:
     Ukulele Blues (by Johnson and Merton Bories)
     Gypsy Blues (by Sissle and Blake)
     I'm Craving for That Kind of Love (by Sissle and Blake)
     Bandana Days (by Sissle and Blake)

Toured United States.   After playing Lafayette Theater in New York, became part of Sir Alfred Butt's show The Rainbow in London, April 1923.

1923

Raisin' Cain; "Cyclonic Musical Comedy"

Produced by Nat Nazarro; dances staged by Frank Montgomery; music by Jimmie Johnson.   Opened Lafayette Theater, New York, New York, July 9, 1923.

Principal Cast: John William Sublett (Bubbles), Ford Washington Lee (Buck), Emory Hutchins, Jean Starr, Coressa Madison, Sam Bilo Russell, Ruby Mason, George McClennon, Demos Jones, Tony Green, Percy Wiggins

1923

Runnin' Wild

Produced by George White; book by Flournoy Miller and Aubrey Lyles; music by James Johnson; lyrics by Cecil Mack; dances staged by Lyda Webb.   First opened in Washington, August 25, 1923; opened on Broadway at Colonial Theater, Broadway and 62nd St., on October 29.

As performed the week of December 24, 1923:

Orchestra--John T. Ricks' Orchestra

Principal Cast: F.E. Miller, A.L. Lyles, C. Wesley Hill, Arthur D.
Porter, Lionel Monagas, Revella Hughes, George Stephens, Paul C.
Floyd, Mattie Wilkes, Ina Duncan, Adelaide Hall, Eddie Gray, Tommy
Woods, Elizabeth Welch, George Stamper, Georgette Harvey

Musical Numbers (all music presumably by JPJ unless noted):
    Charston [sic]
    Ghost Recitative
    Gingerbrown
    Jazz Your Troubles Away
    Juba Dance
    Log Cabin Days
    Old Fashion Love [sic]
    Open Your Heart
    Pay Day on Levee
    Red Cap Cappers [sic]
    Roustabouts
    Set 'em Sadie
    Snow Time
    Swanee River

Additional Musical Numbers:
    Banjo Land
    Heart Breakin' Joe (by Jo Trent and Porter Grainger)
    Keep Moving
    Love Bug
    Slow and Easy Goin' Man (by Turner Layton and Darl MacBoyle)
    Sun Kist Rose
    The Sheik of Alabam' Weds a Brown Skin Vamp
    Watching the Clock (by Jo Trent and Porter Grainger)

1924

Negro Nuances (Sampson, mentioned by Bechet)

Produced by Will Marion Cook; book by Abbie Mitchell, F.E. Miller,
A.E. Lyles; music by James P. Johnson, Will Marion Cook; lyrics by
Will Marion Cook; orchestra director--James P. Johnson.

Principal Cast: Abbie Mitchell, Lucille Handy, Louis Douglass, F.E.
Miller, A.L. Lyles

1924

Cotton Land (Sampson)

Music by James P. Johnson

Principal Cast: Billy Higgins, Gertrude Saunders, James P. Johnson,
Dickie Wells, Billy Mitchell, Jimmy Mordecai, The Three Browns, Cotton Land Chorus

1925

Sunshine Sammy

Book by Jesse A. Shipp; music by James P. Johnson; lyrics by Cecil Mack (R.C. McPherson); starring Sunshine Sammy.

This show may never have been produced as such but may have become Moochin' Along (see next entry).

Moochin' Along

Produced by Billy Mitchell, Broadway Revue Company; stage manager --Dick Conway; book by Jesse A. Shipp; music by Jimmie Johnson; lyrics by Cecil Mack; dances staged by Hartwell Cook and Roscoe Simmons, Jr. Opened at the Lafayette Theater, December 7, 1925.

Principal Cast: Billy Cumby, Inez Dennis, Edgar Connors, Alonzo Fenderson, Ollie Burgoyne, Jimmy Marshall, Mattie Harris, Al Majors, Ada Rex, Richard Gregg, Izzie Ringold, Slim Henderson, Arthur Ames, Arthur Gaines, Ada Guignesse, Madge Hall and Thelma Jordan

Possible musical numbers:
Everybody's Doin' the Charleston Now (words and music by Elmore White, Cecil Mack, James P. Johnson; © 1925)
Mistah Jim (by James P. Johnson, words by Cecil Mack; © 1925)
You for Me, Me for You from Now On (by Cecil Mack and Jimmie Johnson; © 1925)

1926

Earl Carroll's Vanities, 5th Edition

Produced by Earl Carroll; staged by Dave Bennett; music by Morris Hamilton; lyrics by Grace Henry; additional music by Hugo Frey, Fred Rich, Jesse Greet, Jimmy Johnson, Lou Allen; musical number by Johnson--Alabama Stomp.

1927

Midnight Steppers (Sampson)

Produced by Leonard Harper.

Principal Cast: Billy Higgins, Paulis and Jimmie Johnson, Nina May, Joe Byrd, Dewey Brown, Three Dixie Song Birds, Alabama Four, "Midnight Steppers," and others

This Jimmie Johnson may not be James P. Johnson

A la Carte

Produced by Rosalie Stewart; sketches by George Kelly; music and Lyrics by Herman Hupfeld, Louis Alter, Norma Gregg, Karl Kreck, Paul Nanin, Creamer and Johnson; dances and ensembles staged by Sam Rose; orchestra director--Carl C. Gray.

Musical Numbers (by Creamer and Johnson):
      Kangaroo
      Stepping Out with Lulu
      Whiskers

1928

Keep Shufflin'

Produced by Con Conrad; book by F.E. Miller and A.L. Lyles; music by Jimmy Johnson, Fats Waller and Clarence Todd; lyrics by Henry Creamer and Andy Razaf; dances and ensembles staged by Clarence Robinson; orchestrations by Will Vodery; musical director--Jimmy Johnson.   Opened on Broadway at Daly's 63rd St. Theater on February 27, 1928.

Principal Cast: Evelyn Keyes, Byron Jones, Clarence Robinson, Jean Starr, John Vigal, Josephine Hall, Maude Russell, Honey Brown, George Battles, F.E. Miller, A.L. Lyles

In the Orchestra--
      On the White Keys . . . Fats Waller
      On the Black Keys . . . Jimmy Johnson
      Behind the Bugle . . . Jabbo Smith

Musical numbers from February 27 performance:
      Charlie, My Back Door Man (by Creamer and Todd)
      Choc'late Bar (by Razaf and Waller)
      Dusky Love (by Creamer and Vodery)
      Everybody's Happy in Jimtown (by Razaf and Waller)
      Exhortation (by Creamer and Conrad)
      Give Me the Sunshine (by Creamer, Johnson, and Conrad)
      Harlem Rose (by Gladys Rogers and Con Conrad)
      How Jazz Was Born (by Razaf and Waller)
      Keep Shufflin' (by Razaf and Waller)
      Labor Day Parade (by Razaf and Todd)
      Leg It (by Creamer, Todd, and Conrad)
      On the Levee (by Creamer and Johnson)
      Opening Chorus (by Creamer and Vodery)
      Pining (by Creamer and Todd)
      'Sippi (by Creamer, Johnson, and Conrad)
      Washboard Ballet (Waller)

Musical numbers from September 3 performance:
      Brothers
      Bugle Blues
      Chocolate Bar
      Deep Blue Sea
      Don't Wake 'Em Up
      Give Me the Sunshine
      Holiday in Jimtown

Keep Shufflin'
Let's Go to Town
My Old Banjo
Pretty Soft, Pretty Soft
Sippi
Teasin Baby (Mama) (by Creamer and Johnson)
Where Jazz Was Born
Whoopem Up
You May Be a Whale in Georgia

Additional numbers:
Exhortation Theme from Yamekraw Negro Rhapsody (by
    Creamer and Johnson)
Got Myself Another Jockey Now (by Razaf and Waller)
Skiddle-de-Scow (by Johnson and Perry Bradford)
'Twas a Kiss in the Moonlight (by Stephen Jones, Creamer and
    Conrad)
Willow Tree (by Razaf and Waller)

1929

Messin' Around

Produced by Louis Isquith; music by Jimmy Johnson; lyrics by Perry
Bradford; dances staged by Eddie Rector; orchestra director--Jimmy
Johnson. Opened on Broadway at the Hudson Theater, 44th St. East
of Broadway, on April 22, 1929.

Principal Cast: Paul Floyd, Freda Jackson, Monette Moore, Arthur
Porter, Cora La Redd, James Dwyer, Audrey Thomas, Billy McLaurin,
James (Slim) Thompson, Hilda Perleno, Sterling Grant, Walter
Brogsdale, William McKelvey, Olive Ball, Jimmy Johnson

Musical Numbers:
Circus Days
Get Away from My Window
Harlem Town
I Don't Love Nobody But You
I Need You
Messin' Around
Mississippi
Put Your Mind Right on It
Roustabouts
Sorry (That I Strayed Away from You)
Shout On
Skiddle De Skow
Yamekraw (Piano Symphony)
Your Love Is All I Crave

1929-1930

A Great Day In N' Orleans

Staged and sponsored by Flournoy Miller; music by Jimmie Johnson; a
company of 50 singers and dancers. Opened in Philadelphia at the
Pearl Theater, December 30, 1929.

Possible Musical Number:
<u>Possible Musical Number:</u>
    You've Got To Be Modernistic

<u>1930</u>

<u>Earl Carroll's Vanities, 8th Edition</u>

Produced by Earl Carroll.
<u>Musical Number</u> (by Johnson):
    Rhumba Rhythm

<u>Shuffle Along of 1930</u>

Produced by Irvin C. Miller; music by James P. Johnson and Fats
Waller; lyrics by Andy Razaf and Henry Creamer; staging by Irvin C.
Miller.   Opened at Werba's Brooklyn Theater in April 1930.

<u>Principal Cast:</u>   Margaret Simms, Allen Virgel, Valaida Snow, Hilda
Perleno,   Billie   Young,   Derby   Wilson,   Howard   Elmore,   Herman
Listerino, Herman Jenkins, Herman Edwards, and two men posing as
F.E. Miller and A.L. Lyles

<u>Musical Numbers:</u>
    Banjo Land
    Brothers
    Chocolate Bar
    Go Harlem
    Labor Day Parade
    Loving Honey
    Poor Little Me
    Porter's Love Song
    Rhythm Man
    Sippi
    Spirituals
    Taps
    Teasing Baby
    Willow Tree

<u>Kitchen Mechanics Revue</u>

Produced at Small's Paradise,   2294-1/2 Seventh Ave.;   orchestra
director--Elmer Snowden; music by Jimmie Johnson; lyrics by Andy
Razaf.

<u>Probable Musical Numbers:</u>
    Bantu Baby
    Elevator Papa--Switchboard Mama
    Go Harlem
    Good for Nothin'
    Kitchen Mechanic's Parade
    Mammy Land
    On the Level with You
    Porter's Love Song to a Chambermaid
    Sambo's Syncopated Russian Dance
    Shake Your Duster
    Slippery Hips

Swanee Fashion Plate
Ya Gotta Be Versatile

Fireworks of 1930

Produced by Emory Hutchins; music by Fats Waller--Jimmie Johnson's
Syncopaters.   Played at Lafayette Theater, started June 28.

Principal Cast: George Dewey Washington, Mamie Smith, 40 others

1931

Sugar Hill; "An Epoch of Negro Life in Harlem"

Produced by Moveing [sic] Day Company, Inc.; music by James P.
Johnson; words by Jo Trent; book by Charles Tazewell.

Principal Cast: Broadway (Henry) Jones, Juanita Stinnette, Chappy
Chappelle, F.E. Miller, A.L. Lyles

Musical Numbers:
      Boston
      Fate Misunderstood Me
      Fooling Around with Love
      Hangin' Around Your Door
      Hot Harlem
      Hot Rhythm
      Yes, I Love You Honey
      Moving Day
      Noisy Neighbors
      Rumbola
      Somthing's Going to Happen to Me and You
      What Have I Done

1932

Harlem Hotcha

Produced and conceived by Connie Immerman; staged by Teddy
Blackman; music by James P. Johnson; lyrics by Andy Razaf; or-
chestra director--Don Redman.   Presented as featured floor show at
Connie's Inn, 1932.   In March 1933, played four week run at the
Lafayette Theater, Harlem.

Principal Cast (at Lafayette):   Earl "Snakehips" Tucker, Bessie Dudley,
Jazzlips Richardson, Paul and Barbara Meeres, the Lucky Seven Trio,
Lilian Cowan and the Dixie Nightingales, Roscoe Simmons, the Eight
Dancing Fools.   Special orchestral arrangements by Russell Wooding.
Music played by Luis Russell's Band.

Musical Numbers:
      Aintcha Got Music
      Get Off
      Harlem Hotcha
      I Was So Weak, Love Was So Strong
      Madame T.N.T.

My Headache
Stop That Dog
Summer Was Made for Lovers
Yours, All Yours

1933

Plantation Follies (Sampson)

Produced by James P. Johnson.

Principal Cast: Carrie Marerro, Joe Byrd, Billy Higgins, Rogers and
Rogers, Three Little Words, "Snake Hips" Tucker, Bearnice and Scott,
Maitland and Wheeler, Cecilia Williams, Twelve Sepia Dancers, James
P. Johnson's Black Diamond Aces

1939

Policy Kings

Produced by Michael Ashwood; directed by Louis Douglass; music by
James P. Johnson; words by Louis Douglass; musical arrangements by
Ken Macomber; dance direction by Jimmy Payne; book by Michael
Ashwood; staged by Winston Douglass.   Opened at Nora Bayes Theater
on December 30, 1939.

Principal Cast: Billy Cumby, Frankie Jaxon, Ray Sneed Jr., Willor
Guilford, Monte Norris, Robert Mason, Norman Astwood, George
Jenkins, Enid Raphael, Edward Davis, Cora Green, Bessie DeSaussure,
Irene Cort, Herbert Evans, Margie Ellison, Henry Drake

Musical Numbers:
   Court House Scene
   Deed I Do Blues
   Dewey Blues
   Harlem Number Man
   Harlem Woogie
   Havin' a Ball
   I'm Gonna Hit the Number Today
   Prologue
   To Do What We Like
   Walking My Baby Back Home
   You, You, You

Class Struggle in Swing

Music by James P. Johnson; words by Langston Hughes

In a letter to Hughes dated October 6, 1939, Johnson says he sub-
mitted this work to the TAC (Theater Arts Committee) Cabaret.   It
is not known for certain that it was produced (see next entry).

TAC show, title unknown.   (This may be the above entry.)

Sketches and songs by James P. Johnson, Aarons and Stratton, and Lewis Allen; produced by TAC, November 7

1940

The Organizer; "A Blues Opera in One Act"

Produced by Labor Stage and Ladies Garment Workers Union at Carnegie Hall; music by James P. Johnson; libretto by Langston Hughes

Characters:
> The Organizer--Baritone
> The Woman--Contralto
> The Old Man--Bass
> The Old Woman--Soprano
> Brother Dosher--Tenor
> Brother Bates--Tenor
> The Overseer--Bass

Musical Numbers:
> Glad to See You Again (possibly)
> Hungry Blues

The score is lost.   Hungry Blues is all that remains from it, as a 1939 recording.

1941

Pinkard's Fantasies (Chilton)

Musical director--James P. Johnson.

Tan Town Topics of 1941

Produced by Irvin C. Miller; music performed by James P. Johnson's Band.   Opened at the Apollo Theater in Harlem, March 28, 1941.

Principal Cast: Flournoy Miller, 5 Crackerjacks, Juanita Hall Singers, Lilyn Brown, Flash and Dash, Winnie Johnson, John Vigal, Louis Douglass, Walter Mosby, Belle Rossette, Peppy Dancing Girls, Beautiful Models

It is not known how much (if any) of the score was composed by James P. Johnson.

1942

The Dreamy Kid

A One Act Opera based on a play by Eugene O'Neil (never produced).

Musical Numbers performed separately in 1942 at the Heckscher
Theater by Brooklyn Orchestra:
    Dreamy
    Sun Will Be Shinin' for You

1947

Meet Miss Jones; A Musical Comedy

Produced by Walter Brooks; staged by Walter Brooks; music by James
P. Johnson; libretto and lyrics by Flournoy E. Miller. Opened at Experimental Theater 126th Street.

Musical Numbers:
    Don't Lose Your Head (and Lose Your Gal)
    I've Got to Be Lovely to Harry
    You're My Rose

1949

Sugar Hill

Produced by Paul P. Schreibman and Alvin B. Baranov; music by
James P. Johnson; book and lyrics by Flournoy E. Miller; directed by
Charles O'Curran; musical direction by Dudley Brooks; settings by Les
Marzoff. Opened at Las Palmas Theater in Hollywood, California.

Musical Numbers:
    Apple Jack
    Bad Bill Jones
    Busy Body
    Caught
    Chivaree
    Don't Lose Your Head, Then Lose Your Girl
    Faraway Love
    I Don't Want Any Labor in My Job
    I've Got to Be Lovely for Harry
    Keep 'Em Guessing
    Love Don't Need a Referee
    Lovin' Ain't My Aim
    Mr. Dumbell and Mr. Tough
    My Sweet Hunk of Trash
    Peace, Sister, Peace
    Sender
    Sepia Fashion Plate
    Smilin' Through My Tears
    That Was Then
    Until You Are Caught
    We're Going to Blitz the Ritzes
    What Kind of Tune Did Nero Play
    You Can't Lose a Broken Heart
    You're My Rose

The following works remain only as listings in the sources cited next to the title.

1926

Chicago Loop (Library of Congress)

Musical comedy in two acts.
Melody by Jimmy Johnson; lyrics by H. Creamer and Ted Wing; copyright by Henry Creamer, 1926.

Geechie (Library of Congress)

A dusky romance in three acts.
Music by Jimmy Johnson; book and lyrics by H. Creamer; copyright by Henry Creamer, 1926.

1930

Three Little Maids (Library of Congress)

Musical numbers (by Johnson):
    My Idea of Love
    Never Mind

Copyright by Shubert Theater Corp., 1930.

1947

Kitchen Opera (ASCAP)

Music by James P. Johnson; lyrics by Flournoy E. Miller.

Musical numbers:
    Accusation
    At Home with My Range
    Butler and the Cook Desire
    Butler and the Handy Man
    Chauffeur
    Finale Love
    Handy Man
    Lindy Lou
    Love
    Mandy's Blessing
    Reprise Love
    Solution
    Spring Cleaning
    Where Is the Handy Man

The following works are mentioned only in several secondary sources as Johnson projects.

The Husband--an operetta

Sefronia's Dream--a ballet

Manhattan Street Scene--a ballet

James P. Johnson on Film.   The following motion pictures contain music written and/or arranged by Johnson.

1929

St. Louis Blues

Written and directed by Dudley Murphy; starring Bessie Smith and Jimmy Mordecai; choral arrangement by W.C. Handy and J. Rosamond Johnson; musical director and pianist--James P. Johnson; with members of the Fletcher Henderson orch. and Hall Johnson choir.   Recorded by RCA Photophone.

ca. 1930

Yamekraw

Warner Bros.   Based on Johnson's rhapsody of the same name.

1930

Show of Shows

Your Love Is All That I Crave, from Messin' Around; arr. by Samuel Grossman; vocal trio arr. by Bob Neilson.

1933

The Emperor Jones

Several sources indicate that James P. Johnson composed the score for this film, which starred Paul Robeson.   The Exhibitor's Campaign Book distributed by United Artists to promote the film states: "Rosamond Johnson, best known arranger of real Negro folk songs, engaged to arrange and direct the music for "Emperor Jones"....   The entire musical arrangement was handled in splendid style by Rosamond Johnson."   Johnson appears in the film as pianist in a party scene, but the score was written by Rosamond Johnson.

1936

Klondike Annie

Paramount.   Starring Mae West and Victor McLaglen; music by Gene
Austin and Jimmie Johnson.

Musical numbers (by Johnson):
          Mister Deep Blue Sea

1943

Stormy Weather

Twentieth Century-Fox.   Starring Lena Horne, Cab Calloway, Bill
"Bojangles" Robinson, Fats Waller.

Musical numbers (by Johnson):
          There's No Two Ways About Love

Extended Instrumental Arrangements and Compositions.   The following
works represent Johnson's serious composing.   Those pieces listed in
the Library of Congress, ASCAP, or known to be performed or exist
in manuscript are so noted.   Others have been attributed to Johnson.

African Drums (also known as Rhythm Drums).   Performed by Brooklyn Orchestra, 1942.

American Symphonic Suite--St. Louis Blues.   First movement exists in
manuscript (Yale U.); first and third movements performed by Brooklyn Orchestra, 1942.

Carolina Balmoral.   Arranged for symphony orchestra.

City of Steel.

Etude.

Fantasia in C-Minor.

Harlem Symphony.   Four Movements: Subway Journey; April in Harlem (Song of Harlem); Night Club; Baptist Mission.   Performed many
times; second movement, April in Harlem, published in 1944; supposedly completed in 1932.

Improvisations on "Deep River."   Published as piano solo in 1946.

Jassamine Concerto (Piano Concerto in A^b).   Copyright by Johnson in
1934; second movement published in 1947.

Jersey Sweet: Prelude.   Published as piano solo in 1944.

Mississippi Moon: Tone Poem.

Old Time Suite.

Sonata in C-Major.

Sonata in F-Major.

Sonata Form On the St. Louis Blues For Piano and Orchestra.

Spirit of America: string quartet.   Four Movements: light 'jazz'; spiritual; modern American waltz; fugal jazz rondo.   Mentioned by Johnson in an undated letter (probably mid-1930s) to Mrs. Sprague Coolidge, appealing for a performance of this work by the Coolidge Quartet.

Symphony in Brown.   Copyright by Johnson in 1935.

Two Tone Poems: Suite--Love; Reflections.   Both scheduled to be performed at Carnegie Hall, 1945; Reflections published in 1948.

Yamekraw: Negro Rhapsody.   Published as piano solo in 1927; or- chestrated by William Grant Still; performed many times.

APPENDIX TWO

The following is a list of all instrumental and song pieces known with reasonable certainty to have been composed by James P. Johnson. The sources used were the Library of Congress catalogue of copyright entries, ASCAP files, programs with specific composer citations, recordings, correspondence, and Belwin-Mills music files and MCA Music Publishing files. Not all tunes from all shows are included, since it is not clear that Johnson was the composer in every case. Not included are the extended compositions from Appendix One.

A Disordered Dream (song). Music by James P. Johnson, lyrics by Flournoy Miller. Mills Music, ASCAP, 1950.

Accusation (song). Music by James P. Johnson, lyrics by Flournoy Miller. From Kitchen Opera. Mills Music, ASCAP, 1947.

A Flat Dream (instrumental). Music by James P. Johnson. Bregman, Vocco and Conn, Inc., copyright February, ASCAP, 1940.

After Hours (novelty piano solo). Music by J.P. Johnson. Jack Mills, Inc., copyright December, ASCAP, 1923.

Aintcha Got Music (rhythmic spiritual). Music by James P. Johnson, words by Andy Razaf. From Harlem Hotcha. Handy Bros. Music Co., copyright November, ASCAP, 1932.

Alabama Stomp (song). Music by Jimmy Johnson, lyrics by Henry Creamer. From Earl Carroll's Vanities, 5th ed. Robbins Music Corp., copyright August, ASCAP, 1926.

All Night (song). Melody by James P. Johnson, words by Jo Trent. Southern Music copyright October, 1934.

Anima Anceps (or The Negro's Heart). By James P. Johnson, words by Andy Razaf; choral arrangement by Steve Stevens. Handy Bros., copyright December, 1945.

Apple Jack (song). Music by James P. Johnson, lyrics by Flournoy Miller. From Sugar Hill (1949). Mills Music, ASCAP, 1948.

At Home with My Range (song). Music by James P. Johnson, lyrics by Flournoy Miller. From Kitchen Opera. Mills Music, ASCAP, 1947.

Bad Bill Jones. Music and words by James P. Johnson. Mills Music, ASCAP, 1950.

Bantu Baby (song). By Jimmie Johnson, words by Andy Razaf. From Kitchen Mechanic's Revue. Joe Davis, copyright March, 1930.

Barbeque Song.   Music possibly by James P. Johnson, words by
    Langston Hughes.   Mentioned by Hughes in correspondence,
    1943; this may be "Alabam' Barbeque," listed in the Belwin-
    Mills files.   The title was changed to "Carolina Balmoral."

Blue Mizz (inst.).   Music by James P. Johnson.   Mills Music, ASCAP,
    1945.

Blue Moods, 1, 2, and Sex (inst.).   James P. Johnson piano solos.
    Folkways FG 3540, 1944.

Blueberry Rhyme (inst.).   By James P. Johnson.   Bregman, Vocco &
    Conn. Inc., copyright February, 1940.

Blues for Jimmy.   Recorded as piano solo in 1945, Folkways FJ2850.
    This is actually the second movement of the Jassamine
    Concerto.

Blues for Fats (inst.).   By James P. Johnson.   Mills Music, copyright
    November, ASCAP, 1948.

Bon Bon Steppers Parade (march).   Music by James P. Johnson.
    Listed in Belwin-Mills files, contract date June 7, 1945.

Boogie Dreams (inst.).   By Jimmy Johnson.   Part of "Jimmy Johnson's
    Boogie Woogie."   Mills Music, copyright December, ASCAP,
    1943.

Boogie Woogie Runaway (inst.).   By Jimmy Johnson.   Part of "Jimmy
    Johnson's Boogie Woogie."   Mills Music, copyright December,
    ASCAP, 1943.

Boogie Woogie Stride (inst.).   By James P. Johnson.   Mills Music,
    ASCAP, 1944.

Boys of Uncle Sam (march).   By James P. Johnson and William
    Farrell.   F.B. Haviland Pub. Co., copyright July, 1917.

Brothers (song).   By James P. Johnson.   Mills Music, ASCAP, 1945.

Busy Body (song).   Music by James P. Johnson, lyrics by Flournoy
    Miller.   Mills Music, ASCAP, 1950.

Butler and the Cook Desire (song).   Music by James P. Johnson,
    lyrics by Flournoy Miller.   From Kitchen Opera.   Mills Music,
    ASCAP, 1947.

Butler and the Handy Man (song).   Music by James P. Johnson, lyrics
    by Flournoy Miller.   From Kitchen Opera.   Mills Music,
    ASCAP, 1947.

Candy Sweets.   Performed at Eddie Condon's Town Hall Concert,
    N.Y.C.   June 17, 1944.

Caprice Rag (inst.).   By James P. Johnson.   Appeared first on 1917
    piano roll.   Mills Music, ASCAP, 1955.

Carolina Balmoral (inst.).   By James P. Johnson.   Piano solo, Blue
Note BN 25, 1943.   Composed before World War I; original
title was "Alabam' Barbeque" from Belwin-Mills files.

Carolina Shout (inst.).   By James P. Johnson.   Appeared first on 1918
piano roll.   Clarence Williams Music, copyright January, 1926.

Caught (song).   Music by James P. Johnson, lyrics by Flournoy Miller.
From Sugar Hill (1949).   Mills Music, ASCAP, 1948.

Charleston (song).   By Jimmy Johnson and Cecil Mack.   From Runnin'
Wild.   Harms Inc., copyright September, ASCAP, 1923.

Charleston Dance (song).   By Jimmy Johnson.   Jack Mills Inc.,
copyright June, 1923.

Chauffeur (song).   Music by James P. Johnson, lyrics by Flournoy
Miller.   From Kitchen Opera.   Mills Music, ASCAP, 1947.

Cheyenne of the Cherokees (song).   Melody by Henry Creamer and
Jim Johnson, words by Henry Creamer. Copyright May 1930 by
Caroline Meredith.

Chicago Stomp Down (song).   By Jimmy Johnson, words by Henry
Creamer.   Jack Mills Inc., copyright January, 1928, ASCAP.

Chivaree (song).   Music by James P. Johnson, lyrics by Flournoy
Miller.   From Sugar Hill 1949.   Mills Music, ASCAP, 1949.

Cissy, I Loves You (song).   Music by James P. Johnson, lyrics by
Henry Creamer.   Mills Music, ASCAP, 1962.

Clementine (song).   By Jimmy Johnson and Harry Warren, words by
Henry Creamer.   Shapiro, Bernstein & Co., copyright June,
1927.

Coming Down the Stairs (song).   Music by James P. Johnson, lyrics
by Henry Creamer.   Mills Music, ASCAP, 1962.

Congo Kate (song).   Words and melody by Jo Trent and James P.
Johnson.   Southern Music, copyright October, 1934.

Congoland Melody (song).   Music by James P. Johnson, lyrics by
Henry Creamer.   Bibo Music, ASCAP, 1927.

Cottin' Pickin' (song).   Composed by Perry Bradford and James P.
Johnson.   Part of "Dixieland Echoes" set.   Copyright December,
1927 by Perry Bradford Inc.

Couldn't Get In (song).   By Jimmy Johnson and Jimmy Butts, words
by James Crawley. Copyright April, 1947 by James Crawley,
Jimmy Johnson, and Jimmy Butts.

Court House Scene (song).   Music by James P. Johnson, lyrics by
Louis Douglass.   From Policy Kings.   Copyright December, 1938
by Joe Davis Inc.

Creola (song). Music by James P. Johnson, words by Henry Creamer. Mills Music, ASCAP, 1962.

Creole Lullaby. By James P. Johnson and Omer Simeon. Mills Music, ASCAP, 1946.

Crossover (song). Music by James P. Johnson, lyrics by Robert Hicks.

Daintiness Rag (inst.). By James P. Johnson. Appeared first on 1917 piano roll.

Darktown Huskin' Bee, The (song). Music by James P. Johnson, lyrics by Henry Creamer. Mills Music, ASCAP, 1962.

Day Dreams (song). By Jimmy Johnson, lyrics by Stella Unger and Saul Bernie. Copyright May, 1929 by Irving Berlin, ASCAP.

Deed I Do Do Blues (song). By James P. Johnson, words by Louis Douglass. From Policy Kings. Copyright December, 1938, by Joe Davis.

Desperate Blues (song). By James P. Johnson, words by Alex Rogers. Copyright November, 1922 by Sphinx Music.

Dewey Blues (song). By James P. Johnson, words by Louis Douglass. From Policy Kings. Copyright December, 1938 by Joe Davis.

Dixie Doodle Dandy (song). By James P. Johnson, words by Stella Unger and Saul Bernie. Copyright March, 1944 by Unger, Stella, Bernie, Saul and Johnson, James P.

Doin What I Please. By Jimmy Johnson, words by Andy Razaf. Copyright August, 1931 by Irving Berlin, ASCAP.

Don't Cry Baby (song). By Jimmy Johnson, words by Saul Bernie and Stella Unger. Published February, 1944 by Advanced Music, ASCAP. Copyright July, 1929 by Saul Bernie, Inc.

Don't Lose Your Head, Then Lose Your Girl (song). Music by James P. Johnson, lyrics by Flournoy Miller. From Meet Miss Jones and Sugar Hill (1949). Copyright 1947 by Mills Music, ASCAP.

Don't Need Nobody to Tell Me I'm in Bad (song). By Jimmy Johnson, words by Mercedes Gilbert. Copyright July, 1923 by Irving Berlin, ASCAP.

Don't Never Tell Nobody What Your Good Man Can Do (song). By Jimmy Johnson, words by Mercedes Gilbert. Copyright July, 1923 by Irving Berlin, ASCAP.

Dreamy (song). Music by James P. Johnson, words by Henry Creamer. From Dreamy Kid. Performed in 1942.

Dusky Rose (piano novelette). By James P. Johnson. Mills Music, ASCAP, 1945.

Ebony Dreams (inst.). By James P. Johnson. Copyright December, 1927 by Perry Bradford Inc., ASCAP.

Eccentricity (waltz). By James P. Johnson. First appeared on 1918 piano roll. Published 1926, ASCAP. Copyright October, 1925 by Clarence Williams.

Echoes of Ole Dixieland (song). Composed by Perry Bradford and James P. Johnson. Part of "Dixieland Echoes" set. Copyright December, 1927 by Perry Bradford Inc.

Elevator Papa--Switchboard Mama (song). By Jimmie Johnson, words by Andy Razaf. From Kitchen Mechanic's Revue. Copyright March, 1930 by Joe Davis.

Everybody Does the Charleston Now (song). Words and melody by Elmar [sic] White, Bud Green, Cecil Mack and Jimmy Johnston [sic]. Copyright July, 1925 by Irving Berlin Inc.

Everybody Step with Me (song). Music and lyrics by James P. Johnson and Clarence Williams. Listed in MCA Publishing files, ca. 1920.

Everybody's Doin' the Charleston Now (song). Words and music by Elmore White, Cecil Mack and James P. Johnson. Possibly from Mooching Along. Copyright September, 1925 by Irving Berlin Inc.

Exhortation (song). By James P. Johnson, words by Henry Creamer. From Keep Shufflin'. Copyright May, 1928 by Perry Bradford, Inc.

Far From Love (song). Music by James P. Johnson, words by Andy Razaf. Handy Bros., ASCAP, 1944.

Far-Away Love (song). Music by James P. Johnson, lyrics by Flournoy Miller. From Sugar Hill, 1949. Copyright 1949 by Mills Music, ASCAP.

Fascination (inst). By James P. Johnson. First appeared on 1917 piano roll. Copyright February, 1940 by Bregman, Vocco & Conn.

Feelin' Blue (inst.) By Jimmy Johnson. Copyright August 1930 by Acme Music.

Finale Love (song). Music by James P. Johnson, lyrics by Flournoy Miller. From Kitchen Opera. Mills Music, 1947, ASCAP.

Foolin Around with Love (song). By Jimmy Johnson, words by Jo Trent. From Sugar Hill, 1931. Copyright June, 1932 by Harms Inc.

Fortune Teller. By James P. Johnson. Copyright December, 1962 by Estate of James P. Johnson.

Four A.M. Shout (inst.). Possibly by James P. Johnson. Appeared as Victor test recording, January, 1922.

Four O'Clock Groove (inst.). By James P. Johnson. Mills Music, ASCAP, 1952.

Get Off (song). By James P. Johnson, words by Andy Razaf. From
    Harlem Hotcha. Copyright September, 1932 by Handy Bros.
    Music.

Get Off the Grass Liza Jane (song). Music by James P. Johnson,
    lyrics by Henry Creamer. Mills Music, ASCAP, 1962.

Ginger Brown (song). By Cecil Mack and Jimmy Johnson. From
    Runnin' Wild. Copyright October, 1923 by Harms, Inc.

Give Me the Sunshine (song). By Jimmy Johnson, words by Con Con-
    rad and Henry Creamer. From Keep Shufflin'. Copyright
    March, 1928 by Harms, Inc.

Glad To See You Again (song). Music by James P. Johnson, lyrics by
    Langston Hughes. Possibly from The Organizer. Mentioned by
    Johnson in correspondence, 1939.

Glory Shout (inst.). Possibly by James P. Johnson. Appeared as
    Columbia rejected take, February, 1923.

Go Harlem (song). By Jimmie Johnson, words by Andy Razaf. From
    Kitchen Mechanic's Revue and Shuffle Along of 1930.
    Copyright March, 1930 by Joe Davis. Mayfair Music, ASCAP.

Good for Nothin' (song). By Jimmie Johnson, words by Andy Razaf.
    From Kitchen Mechanic's Revue. Copyright March, 1930 by
    Joe Davis.

Gut Stomp (inst.). By James P. Johnson and Willie "The Lion" Smith.
    Bregman, Vocco and Conn, ASCAP, 1940.

Handy Man (song). Music by James P. Johnson, lyrics by Flournoy
    Miller. From Kitchen Opera. Mills Music, ASCAP, 1947.

Harlem Band (march). By James P. Johnson. Arr. for band by
    Michael Edwards. Copyright March, 1951 by Mills Music,
    ASCAP, 1948.

Harlem Bon-Bon Babies (song). By James P. Johnson, lyrics by Henry
    Creamer. Mills Music, ASCAP, 1962.

Harlem Choc'late Babies. Melody by James P. Johnson, lyrics by
    Henry Creamer. Copyright April, 1926 by Henry Creamer.
    Mills Music, ASCAP, 1927.

Harlem Hotcha (song). By James P. Johnson, words by Andy Razaf.
    From Harlem Hotcha. Copyright September, 1932 by Handy
    Bros. Music, ASCAP.

Harlem Number Man (song). By James P. Johnson, words by Louis
    Douglass. From Policy Kings. Copyright December, 1938 by
    Joe Davis, Inc.

Harlem Strut (inst.) By James P. Johnson. Mills Music, ASCAP,
    1974. Appeared first on 1921 phonograph recording, Black
    Swan, BS 2026.

Harlem Woogie (song).   By James P. Johnson, words by Louis Douglass. From Policy Kings. Copyright December, 1938 by Joe Davis Inc. Mayfair Music, ASCAP, 1939.

Havin' a Ball (song; fox-trot).   By Andy Razaf and James P. Johnson. Copyright December, 1936 by Joe Davis Inc.   Mayfair Music, ASCAP.

He Pulled the Temple Down (song).   By James P. Johnson, lyrics by Henry Creamer. Mills Music, ASCAP, 1962.

Heart Breakin' Sal (song).   By James P. Johnson, lyrics by Henry Creamer. Sun Music, ASCAP, 1927.

Hey, Hey, Hey, Hey, Your Cares Away (song).   Music by Mike Riley and Jimmy Johnson, words by Nelson Cogan.   Copyright December, 1936 by Leo Feist Inc.

High Brown (inst.)   By Jimmy Johnson.   Copyright September, 1934 by Joe Davis Inc.

Honey (song).   Composed by Perry Bradford and James P. Johnson. Part of "Dixieland Echoes" set. Copyright December, 1927 by Perry Bradford.

Hot Curves (fox-trot).   By James P. Johnson, arr. by Ken Macomber. Copyright November, 1930 by Alfred Music.

Hot Diggity Dog (song).   By Jimmy Johnson, words by Henry Creamer. Copyright June, 1923 by Jack Mills Inc.

How Could You Put Me Down (song).   By James P. Johnson and Willie "The Lion" Smith, words by Mitchell Parish.   Copyright December, 1945 by Mills Music, ASCAP, 1944.

How Long Is That Train Been Gone (song).   Melody by Jimmy Johnson, words by Gus Horsely.   Copyright December, 1930 by Blues Music Co., Jamaica, N.Y.

I Don't Love Nobody But You (song).   By Jimmy Johnson, lyrics by Perry Bradford. From Messin' Around. Copyright April, 1929 by M. Witmark & Sons, ASCAP.

I Don't Want Any Labor in My Job.   By James P. Johnson, lyrics by Flournoy Miller. From Sugar Hill, 1949. Copyright 1949 by Mills Music, ASCAP.

I Need Lovin' (song).   By Henry Creamer and Jimmy Johnson. Copyright November, 1926 by Jerome H. Remick, ASCAP.

I Need You (song).   By Jimmy Johnson, lyrics by Perry Bradford. From Messin' Around. Copyright April, 1929 by M. Witmark and Sons.

I Think You're Swell (song).   Music by Jimmy Johnson, words by Andy Razaf. Copyright September, 1932 by Keit-Engel, Inc.

I Was So Weak, Love Was So Strong (song).   By James P. Johnson,
    words by Andy Razaf.   From Harlem Hotcha.   Copyright
    September, 1932 by Handy Bros., ASCAP.

I'll Never Kiss Her Anymore (song).   By James P. Johnson, lyrics by
    Henry Creamer.   Sun Music, ASCAP, 1927.

I'm Gonna Hit the Number Today (song).   By James P. Johnson,
    words by Louis Douglass.   From Policy Kings.   Copyright
    December, 1938 by Joe Davis, Inc.

I'm Stepping Out with Lulu (song).   By Jimmy Johnson and Henry
    Creamer.   From A La Carte.   Copyright August, 1927 by
    Harms, ASCAP.

I've Fallen for Love (song).   Melody by James P. Johnson, words by
    Andy Razaf.   Copyright April, 1933 by Andy Razaf.

I've Got to Be Lovely to Harry (song).   Music by James P. Johnson,
    lyrics by Flournoy Miller.   From Sugar Hill, 1948.   Mills Music,
    ASCAP, 1948.

If I Can't Have All (song).   Music by James P. Johnson, lyrics by
    Henry Creamer.   Mills Music, ASCAP, 1962.

If I Could Be with You (song).   Music by James P. Johnson, lyrics by
    Henry Creamer.   Copyright November, 1926 by Jerome H.
    Remick, ASCAP.

Imitator's Rag (inst.).   By James P. Johnson.   Claimed by Johnson to
    have been composed circa 1913.   No known existence.

Impressions (inst.).   By James P. Johnson.   Copyright December, 1947
    by Mills Music.

Innovation (inst.).   By James P. Johnson.   Exists only on 1917 piano
    roll.

It Takes Love to Cure the Heart's Disease.   Possibly by James P.
    Johnson.   Exists only on QRS piano roll, 1921.

Ivy (song).   By James P. Johnson, words by Alex Rogers.   Arr. by H.
    Qualli Clark.   Copyright November, 1922 by Sphinx Music Pub.

Ivy, Cling to Me (song).   Music by Jimmy Johnson and Isham Jones,
    words by Alex Rogers.   Copyright November, 1922 by Irving
    Berlin, ASCAP.

J.P. Boogie (inst.).   By Jimmy Johnson.   Copyright December, 1943
    by Mills Music, ASCAP.

Jersey Sweet.   Recorded as piano solo in 1945, Folkways FJ2850.
    This is the same tune as "Just Before Daybreak."

Jingles (inst.).   By James P. Johnson.   Copyright October, 1926 by
    Clarence Williams, ASCAP.

Joy-Mentin' (inst.).   By James P. Johnson.   Mills Music, ASCAP, 1925.

Jungle Nymphs (novelette; inst.).   By James P. Johnson.   Copyright February, 1924 by Jack Mills Inc., ASCAP.

Just an Ordinary Guy (song).   Possibly by James P. Johnson, lyrics by Langston Hughes.   Mentioned by Hughes in correspondence, 1943.

Just Before Daybreak (inst.).   By James P. Johnson.   Copyright August, 1946 by Mills Music.

Kangaroo (song).   Music by James P. Johnson, lyrics by Henry Creamer.   From A La Carte.

Keep 'Em Guessing (song).   Music by James P. Johnson, lyrics by Flournoy Miller.   From Sugar Hill, 1949.   Copyright 1949 by Mills Music, ASCAP.

Keep Moving.   By James P. Johnson.   From Runnin' Wild.

Keep Movin'.   Recorded as a piano solo in 1945, Folkways FJ2850.

Keep Off the Grass (inst.).   By James P. Johnson.   First appeared as phonograph recording, Okeh OK 4495, October, 1921. Copyright September, 1926 by Clarence Williams, ASCAP.

Kitchen Mechanics Parade (song).   By Jimmie Johnson, words by Andy Razaf.   From Kitchen Mechanic's Revue.   Copyright March, 1930 by Joe Davis Inc.

Left All Alone with the Blues (song).   By Jimmie Johnson, words by Spenser Williams.   Copyright May, 1930 by Clarence Williams.

Liberty March (inst.).   By James P. Johnson, Mills Music, ASCAP, 1926.

Lindy Lou (song).   By James P. Johnson, lyrics by Flournoy Miller. From Kitchen Opera.   Mills Music, ASCAP, 1947.

Little Ham (song).   Possibly music by James P. Johnson, lyrics by Langston Hughes.   Mentioned by Hughes in correspondence, 1938.

Liza Jane's Weddin' (song).   Composed by Perry Bradford and James P. Johnson.   Part of "Dixieland Echoes" set.   Copyright December, 1927 by Perry Bradford.

Lock and Key (song).   By James P. Johnson, words by Henry Creamer.   Copyright April, 1947 by Henry Creamer.   Mills Music, ASCAP.

Lonesome Reverie (inst.).   By James P. Johnson.   Copyright February, 1940 by Bregman, Vocco & Conn.

Love (song).   Music by James P. Johnson, lyrics by Flournoy Miller. From Kitchen Opera.   Mills Music, ASCAP, 1947.

Love Bug (song).   By Cecil Mack and Jimmy Johnson.   From Runnin' Wild.   Copyright September, 1923 by Harms, Inc.

Love Don't Need a Referee (song).   Music by James P. Johnson, lyrics by Flournoy Miller. Mills Music, ASCAP, 1948.

Lovin' Ain't My Aim (song).   Music by James P. Johnson, lyrics by Flournoy Miller. Mills Music, ASCAP, 1948.

Lucy Brown (song).   By James P. Johnson, words by Stella Unger. Copyright November, 1962 by Bregman, Vocco and Conn. ASCAP.

Mad Manhattan (song).   Words and melody by Jo Trent and James P. Johnson. Copyright October, 1934 by Southern Music Pub.

Madame T.N.T. (song).   By James P. Johnson, words by Andy Razaf. From Harlem Hotcha.   Copyright September, 1932 by Handy Bros. Music.

Mama's Blues (song).   [Also known as "Mama's and Papa's Blues".] By William H. Farrell and James P. Johnson. Copyright May, 1917 by F.B. Haviland.

Mammy Land (song).   By Jimmie Johnson, words by Andy Razaf. From Kitchen Mechanic's Revue.   Copyright March, 1930 by Joe Davis.

Mandy's Blessing (song).   By James P. Johnson, lyrics by Flournoy Miller. From Kitchen Opera. Mills Music, ASCAP, 1947.

Misery (song).   By Jimmy Johnson, lyrics by Andy Razaf.   Copyright June, 1931 by Shapiro, Bernstein & Co.

Mistah Jim (song).   By James P. Johnson, words by Cecil Mack. Possibly from Moochin' Along.   Copyright September, 1925 by Irving Berlin.

Mister Deep Blue Sea (song).   Words and music by Gene Austin and Jimmie Johnson.   From Klondike Annie.   Copyright 1936 by Paramount Productions Music assigned to Famous Music Corp.

Modernistic (inst.).   By James P. Johnson. Copyright January, 1934 by Clarence Williams.

Monkey Hutch [Hunch] (song).   Music by James P. Johnson, lyrics by Will Farrell.   Jerry Vogel, ASCAP, 1917.   First appeared as 1917 piano roll.

Mound Bayou (song).   Music and lyrics by James P. Johnson.   Mills Music, ASCAP, 1945.

Mr. Dumbell and Mr. Tough (song).   Music by James P. Johnson, lyrics by Flournoy Miller. Mills Music, ASCAP, 1948.

Mule Walk (inst.).   By James P. Johnson. Copyright February, 1940 by Bregman, Vocco and Conn.

My Headache (song).   By James P. Johnson, words by Andy Razaf. From Harlem Hotcha.   Copyright November, 1932 by Handy Bros. Music.

My Heart Is Yours, Mi Amor E Tus (song).   Words and music by
    Leroy C. Lovett, Jimmy Johnson and Frank Bossone.   Copyright
    January, 1954 by Harvard Music Co.

My Idea of Love (song).   Lyrics and music by Stella Unger, Harold
    Stern and Jimmy Johnston [sic].   From Three Little Maids.
    Copyright March, 1930 by Shubert Theater Corp.

My Sweet Hunk O'Trash (song).   Music by James P. Johnson, lyrics
    by Flournoy Miller.   From Sugar Hill, 1949.   Copyright 1949,
    Mills Music, ASCAP.

Never Mind (song).   Lyrics and music by Stella Unger, Harold Stern
    and Jimmy Johnston [sic].   From Three Little Maids.
    Copyright March, 1930 by Shubert Theater Corp.

Nighttime in Dixieland (song).   By James P. Johnson.   Mentioned by
    Johnson, composed circa 1914.

Nobody Knows De Trouble I've Seen (song).   Music by James P.
    Johnson, lyrics by Henry Creamer.   Mills Music, ASCAP, 1962.

Now That I've Lost You (song).   By James P. Johnson, words by Nel-
    son Logan.   Copyright December, 1962 by the Estate of James
    P. Johnson.

Now, Right Now (song).   By James P. Johnson, words by Leo Israel.
    Copyright July, 1944 by Israel, Leo and Johnson, James P.

Ode to Dorie Miller (song).   Music by James P. Johnson, lyrics by
    Andy Razaf.   Performed at Carnegie Hall, 1945.

Oh, Georgie Look What You've Done to Me (song).   By Henry
    Creamer and Jimmy Johnson.   Copyright March, 1927 by M.
    Witmark, ASCAP.

Oh Malinda (song).   By Jimmy Johnson, words by Andy Razaf.
    Copyright July, 1927 by Bud Allen Music Co.

Old Fashioned Love (song).   By Cecil Mack and Jimmy Johnson.
    From Runnin' Wild.   Copyright September, 1923 by Harms Inc.,
    ASCAP.

On the Levee (song).   Music by James P. Johnson, words by Henry
    Creamer.   From Keep Shufflin'.

On the Level with You (song).   By Jimmie Johnson, words by Andy
    Razaf.   From Kitchen Mechanic's Revue.   Copyright March,
    1930 by Joe Davis.

Open Your Heart (song).   By Cecil Mack and Jimmy Johnson.   From
    Runnin' Wild.   Copyright September, 1923 by Harms Inc.,
    ASCAP.

Over the Bars (inst.).   By James P. Johnson.   First appeared on 1917
    piano roll.   Copyright March, 1939 by Clarence Williams,
    ASCAP.

Peace, Sister, Peace (song).   Music by James P. Johnson, lyrics by
Flournoy Miller.   From Sugar Hill, 1949.   Copyright 1949 by
Mills Music, ASCAP.

Poem of Love (inst.).   By James P. Johnson.   Copyright March, 1951
by Mills Music, ASCAP.

Porter's Love Song to a Chambermaid (song).   By Jimmie Johnson,
words by Andy Razaf.   From Kitchen Mechanic's Revue.
Copyright May, 1930 by Joe Davis.

Prologue (song).   Music by James P. Johnson, lyrics by Louis
Douglass.   From Policy Kings.   Copyright December, 1938 by
Joe Davis.

Psychology (song).   Music by James P. Johnson, lyrics by Henry
Creamer.   Mills Music, ASCAP, 1962.

Riffs (inst.).   By Jimmy Johnson.   Copyright August, 1930 by Acme
Music.   Pickwick Music, ASCAP.

Rosita (song).   By Jimmy Johnson, words by Henry Creamer.
Copyright August, 1961 by James P. Johnson Jr., Lillie Mae
Johnson Jr., Arceola J. Glover and Henry Creamer Jr. ASCAP.

Rumba Rhythm (song).   By Jimmie Johnson, words by Stella Unger.
From Earl Carroll's Vanities, 8th ed.   Copyright July, 1930 by
Remick Music Corp.

Sambo's Syncopated Russian Dance (song).   By Jimmie Johnson, words
by Andy Razaf.   From Kitchen Mechanic's Revue.   Copyright
March, 1930 by Joe Davis.

Scalin' the Blues (inst.).   By James P. Johnson.   Copyright September,
1926 by Clarence Williams, ASCAP.

Scoutin' Around (inst.)   By James P. Johnson.   Part of "Jazzapation;
A Study in Jazz".   Copyright October, 1927 by Perry Bradford
Inc.   Alfred Music, ASCAP.

Sender (song).   Music by James P. Johnson, lyrics by Flournoy Miller.
From Sugar Hill, 1949.   Mills Music, ASCAP, 1948.

Sepia Fashion Show (song).   Music by James P. Johnson, lyrics by
Flournoy Miller.   From Sugar Hill, 1949.   Mills Music, ASCAP,
1948.

Shake Your Duster (song).   By Jimmie Johnson, words by Andy Razaf.
From Kitchen Mechanic's Revue.   Copyright March, 1930 by
Joe Davis.

She's the Hottest Gal in Tennessee (song).   By Jimmy Johnson, words
by Henry Creamer.   Copyright November, 1926 by Shapiro,
Bernstein & Co.

'Sippi (song).   By Jimmy Johnson, words by Con Conrad and Henry
Creamer.   From Keep Shufflin'.   Copyright March, 1928 by
Harms Inc., ASCAP.

Skiddle-De-Scow (song).   By Jimmy Johnson, lyrics by Perry Bradford.
From Messin' Around.   Copyright April, 1929 by M. Witmark &
Sons, ASCAP.

Slippery Hips (song).   By Jimmie Johnson, words by Andy Razaf.
From Kitchen Mechanic's Revue.   Copyright March, 1930 by
Joe Davis, Inc.

Smilin' Through My Tears (song).   Music by James P. Johnson, lyrics
by Flournoy Miller.   From Sugar Hill, 1949.   Mills Music,
ASCAP, 1948.

Snowy Morning Blues (inst.).   By James P. Johnson.   Copyright April,
1927 by Perry Bradford Inc.   Pickwick Music, ASCAP.

So Sorry (song).   Melody by Jimmy Johnson, words by Perry Bradford.
Copyright December, 1930 by Blues Music Co., Jamaica, L.I.,
N.Y.

Solution (song).   Music by James P. Johnson, lyrics by Flournoy
Miller.   From Kitchen Opera.   Mills Music, ASCAP, 1947.

Something's Gonna Happen to Me and You (song).   By Jimmy Johnson,
words by Jo Trent.   From Sugar Hill, 1931.   Copyright
January, 1932 by Harms Inc., ASCAP.

Sorry That I Strayed Away from You (song).   Music by Jimmy
Johnson, lyrics by Perry Bradford.   From Messin' Around.
Copyright April, 1929 by M. Witmark & Sons, ASCAP.

Spanish in My Eyes (song).   By Enric Madriguera and Jimmy (J.P.)
Johnson.   Copyright May, 1934 by F.B. Haviland.   Jerry Vogel,
ASCAP.

Sparkling Drink (song).   Music by James P. Johnson, lyrics by Flournoy Miller.   Mills Music, ASCAP, 1950.

Spring Cleaning (song).   Music by James P. Johnson, lyrics by Flournoy Miller.   From Kitchen Opera.   Mills Music, ASCAP, 1947.

Stay Out of the Kitchen (song).   Music by James P. Johnson, lyrics
by Flournoy Miller.   From Sugar Hill, 1949.   Copyright 1949 by
Mills Music, ASCAP.

Steeplechase Rag (inst.).   Music by James P. Johnson.   Recorded as a
piano roll in 1917.   This is the same tune as "Over the Bars."

Stop It (song).   By William Farrell and James P. Johnson.   This is
the same tune as "Stop It, Joe."   Copyright 1917 by F.B.
Haviland.   Jerry Vogel, ASCAP.

Stop That Dog (song).   Music by James P. Johnson, lyrics by Andy
Razaf.   From Harlem Hotcha.   Copyright September, 1932 by
Handy Bros., ASCAP.

Summer Was Made for Lovers (song).   Music by James P. Johnson,
lyrics by Andy Razaf.   From Harlem Hotcha.   Copyright
September, 1932 by Handy Bros., ASCAP.

Summer Was Made for Lovers, Why Let It Go Rolling By (song). By
James P. Johnson, words by Andy Razaf. Copyright July, 1949
by Handy Bros.

Sun Will Be Shinin' for You (song). Music by James P. Johnson,
words by Cecil Mack. From The Dreamy Kid. Performed at
Heckscher Theater, 1942.

Sunny Side (song). By Jimmy Johnson, words by Saul Bernie & Stella
Unger. Copyright July, 1929 by Saul Bernie, Inc., ASCAP.

Swanee Fashion Plate (song). By Jimmie Johnson, words by Andy
Razaf. From Kitchen Mechanic's Revue. Copyright March,
1930 by Joe Davis.

Sweet Mistreater (song). By James P. Johnson, words by Henry
Creamer. Copyright April, 1927 by Henry Creamer, ASCAP.

Swinga-Dilla Street (song). Words and music by Andy Razaf, James
P. Johnson and Abner Silver. Copyright January, 1940 by Joe
Davis Inc.

Swingin' at the Lido (inst.). By James P. Johnson and Willie Smith.
Copyright February, 1940 by Bregman, Vocco and Conn.

Taking My Lessons in Rhythm (song). By Jimmy Johnson, words by
Jo Trent. Copyright July, 1932 by Alfred Music Co.

That Was Then (song). Music by James P. Johnson, lyrics by Flournoy Miller. From Sugar Hill, 1949. Mills Music, ASCAP, 1944.

That's the Stuff You Got to Watch (song). By James P. Johnson and
Bud Allen, words by Walter Bishop. Copyright February, 1945
by Allen, Bud.

Theme in Two Voices (inst.). By James P. Johnson. Copyright 1944
by Mills Music, ASCAP.

There Was a Little Frog (song). Music by James P. Johnson, lyrics
by Henry Creamer. ASCAP, 1962.

There's No Two Ways About Love (song). By James P. Johnson and
Irving Mills, words by Ted Koehler. From Stormy Weather.
Copyright June, 1943 by Mills Music.

Thinkin' Bout Home (inst.). By Jimmy Johnson. Part of "Jimmy
Johnson's Boogie Woogie" set. Copyright December, 1943 by
Mills Music, ASCAP.

Thumpin' n Bumpin' (song). Words and music by Harry White, Andy
Razaf, Jimmy Johnson, arr. by Teddy Raph. Copyright August,
1931 by Southern Music, ASCAP.

To Do What We Like (song). By James P. Johnson, words by Louis
Douglass. From Policy Kings. Copyright December, 1938 by
Joe Davis Inc.

Toddlin' (inst.).   By James P. Johnson.   From "Jazzapation; A Study
    In Jazz."   Copyright October, 1927 by Perry Bradford Inc.
    Blues Publ., ASCAP.

Toussaint l'ouverature (poem).   Music by James P. Johnson and Eubie
    Blake, poem by Andy Razaf.   Copyright July, 1944 by Handy
    Bros., ASCAP.

Toy Piper (inst.).   By James P. Johnson.   Copyright July, 1946 by
    Mills Music, ASCAP.

Twelfth Avenue (inst.).   By Jimmy Johnson.   Part of "Jimmy
    Johnson's Boogie Woogie" set.   Copyright December, 1943 by
    Mills Music, ASCAP.

Twilight Rag (inst.).   By James P. Johnson.   Exists on two
    recordings, first on 1917 piano roll.

Ukulele Blues (song).   Melody by James P. Johnson, words by Merton
    Bories, arr. by H. Qualli Clark.   From Plantation Days.
    Copyright April, 1922 by Sphinx Music.

Uncle Sammy Here I Am (song).   By James P. Johnson, words by
    F.E. Miller and Clarence Williams.   Copyright October, 1941 by
    Clarence Williams.

Until You Are Caught (song).   Music by James P. Johnson, lyrics by
    Flournoy Miller.   From Sugar Hill, 1949.   Mills Music, ASCAP,
    1948.

Vampires in the Dusk (song).   Words and melody by Jo Trent and
    James P. Johnson.   Copyright October, 1934 by Southern Music.

Victory Stride (song).   By James P. Johnson, words by Leo Israel and
    Max Margulis.   Copyright August, 1944 by Margulis, Max.   Mills
    Music, ASCAP, 1945.

Wait Until We Get Alone (song).   Words and melody by S. Williams
    and Jimmy Johnson.   Copyright November, 1930 by Spencer
    Williams.

Walkin' the Bass (inst.).   By Jimmy Johnson.   Part of "Jimmy
    Johnson's Boogie Woogie" set.   Copyright December, 1943 by
    Mills Music, ASCAP.

Walking My Baby Back Home (song).   By James P. Johnson, words by
    Louis Douglass.   From Policy Kings.   Copyright December, 1938
    by Joe Davis Inc.

Waltz Martinique (song).   By James P. Johnson, lyrics by Henry
    Creamer.   ASCAP, 1962.

Wandering (song).   Music by James P. Johnson, words by Mercer
    Cook.   Performed at Heckscher Theater, 1942.

Way Over in Jordan (song).   By James P. Johnson, lyrics by Henry
    Creamer.   ASCAP, 1962.

We're Going to Blitz the Ritzes (song). Music by James P. Johnson, lyrics by Flournoy Miller. From <u>Sugar Hill</u>, 1949. Mills Music, ASCAP, 1948.

Weepin' Blues (inst.). Melody by James P. Johnson. Copyright July, 1923 by Perry Bradford. Blues Pub., ASCAP.

What Could I Do with a Man Like That (song). Music and lyrics by James P. Johnson and Clarence Williams. Listed in MCA Publishing files, ca. 1929.

What If We Do (song). Words and melody by Clarence Williams and Jimmy Johnson. Copyright February, 1930 by Clarence Williams.

What Kind O'Tune Did Old Nero Play (song). Music by James P. Johnson, lyrics by Flournoy Miller. From <u>Sugar Hill</u>, 1949. Mills Music, ASCAP, 1948.

What's the Use of Lovin' (Without Love) (song). Music and lyrics by James P. Johnson and Clarence Williams. Listed in MCA Publishing files, ca. 1929.

When I Can't Be with You (song). Words and music by Andy Razaf and Jimmy Johnson. Copyright June, 1931 by Southern Music Publ, ASCAP.

When Stella Did the Rumba (song). By James P. Johnson, words by Nelson Cogan. Copyright December, 1962 by Estate of James P. Johnson, ASCAP.

Where Is the Handy Man (song). Music by James P. Johnson, lyrics by Flournoy Miller. From <u>Kitchen Opera</u>. Mills Music, ASCAP, 1947.

Whiskers (song). Music by James P. Johnson, lyrics by Henry Creamer. From <u>A La Carte</u>.

Whisper Sweet (song). Words and melody by Jo Trent and James P. Johnson. Copyright December, 1934 by Southern Music.

Who Loves You Now (song). Music by James P. Johnson, lyrics by Henry Creamer and G. McKinley Coleman. ASCAP, 1936.

Why Did Minnie Ha-Ha (song). By Jimmy Johnson, words by Henry Creamer. Copyright October, 1926 by Shapiro, Bernstein & Co., ASCAP.

Wipe 'Em Off (song). Words and melody by Clarence Williams and Jimmy Johnson. Copyright February, 1930 by Clarence Williams.

Worried and Lonesome Blues (inst.). Melody by James P. Johnson. Copyright July, 1923 by Perry Bradford, ASCAP.

Ya Gotta Be Versatile (song). By Jimmie Johnson, words by Andy Razaf. From <u>Kitchen Mechanic's Revue</u>. Copyright March, 1930 by Joe Davis.

Yamekraw Blues (from Negro Rhapsody). By Jimmie Johnson, arr. by
Ken Macomber. Copyright July, 1931 by Alfred Music Co.

Yes, I Love You Honey (song). By Jimmy Johnson, words by Jo
Trent. From Sugar Hill, 1931. Copyright December, 1931 by
Harms Inc., ASCAP.

You Always Can Come Back to Me (song). By Jimmy (J.P.) Johnson
and Don Redmon, words by Andy Razaf. Copyright July, 1934
by F.B. Haviland. Jerry Vogel, ASCAP, 1935.

You Can't Lose a Broken Heart (song). By James P. Johnson, lyrics
by Flournoy Miller. From Sugar Hill, 1949. Copyright 1949,
by Mills Music, ASCAP.

You Done Me Dirty (song). Music and lyrics by James P. Johnson,
Cecil Mack and Irving Mills. Listed in Berwin-Mills files, contract date ca. 1933.

You for Me, Me for You from Now On (song). By Cecil Mack and
James P. Johnson. Possibly from Mooching Along. Copyright
January, 1926 by Clarence Williams. Pickwick Music, ASCAP,
1926.

You Just Can't Have No One Man By Yourself (song). By Mercedes
Gilbert and James P. Johnson. Copyright June, 1924, by
Clarence Williams.

You Know--I Know (song). By James P. Johnson, lyrics by Henry
Creamer. ASCAP, 1962.

You Said You Wouldn't But You Done It (song). By Jimmy Johnson,
words by Henry Creamer. Copyright June, 1923 by Jack Mills
Inc.

You're My Rose (song). By James P. Johnson, lyrics by Flournoy
Miller. From Sugar Hill, 1949. Mills Music, ASCAP, 1948.

You've Got to Be Modernistic (song). By Jimmy Johnson. Copyright
January, 1930 by Clarence Williams. Pickwick Music, ASCAP,
1930.

You've Got What I've Been Lookin' For (song). By James P. Johnson,
words by Merton Bories. Copyright June, 1921 by Merton
Herman Bories; Copyright Nov., 1922 by Sphinx Music, ASCAP.

You've Lost Your Lovin' Baby Now (song). Words and music by
Henry Creamer and Jimmy Johnson. Copyright March, 1927 by
M. Witmark & Sons, ASCAP.

You Don't Understand (song). By Clarence Williams, James P.
Johnson and Spencer Williams. Copyright October, 1929 by
Clarence Williams.

Your Love I Crave (song). By Jimmy Johnson, lyrics by Perry
Bradford. From Messin' Around. Copyright April, 1929 by M.
Witmark & Sons, ASCAP.

Your Love Is All That I Crave (song). By Jimmy Johnson, lyrics by
    Al Dubin and Perry Bradford. From <u>Show of Shows</u>.
    Copyright October, 1929 by M. Witmark & Sons, ASCAP.

Yours All Yours (song). By James P. Johnson, lyrics by Andy Razaf.
    From <u>Harlem Hotcha</u>. Copyright September, 1932 by Handy
    Bros., ASCAP.

The following compositions are listed in the catalogue of copyright
entries as having been composed by one or more men by the name
of James Johnson. They are not thought to be compositions of
James P. Johnson.

Big Trunk Blues	12/03/29	James Johnson, N.Y.
Uncle Joe	12/03/29	James Johnson, N.Y.
Duck's Yas-Yas-Yas	04/24/29	James Johnson, St. Louis
You Can't Stay Here No More	02/15/30	James Johnson
Squablin'	06/05/30	James Johnson, State St. Music Publ., Chicago
Leavenworth Blues	06/05/30	James Johnson, State St. Music Publ., Chicago
Daddy You're a Low Down Man	06/14/30	James Johnson, N.Y.
Unhappy Blues	06/14/30	James Johnson, N.Y.
Good Sugar Blues	07/03/30	James Johnson, State St. Music Publ., Chicago
Rafe King Murder Case	1931	Jim Johnson, Southern Music Publ.
Wobble It a Little	02/10/32	James Johnson, N.Y.

BIBLIOGRAPHY

Afro-American music and black culture.

Allen, William Francis, Charles Pickard Ware, and Lucy McKim Garrison. Slave Songs of the United States. Peter Smith, 1951 reprint, © 1867.

Berlin, Edward A. Ragtime--A Musical and Cultural History. Berkeley and Los Angeles, University of California Press, 1980.

Blesh, Rudi. Shining Trumpets--A History of Jazz, 2nd Ed. New York, Da Capo, 1958.

Blesh, Rudi. Classic Piano Rags--Complete Original Music for 81 Rags. New York, Dover Publications, 1973.

Blesh, Rudi, and Harriet Janis. They All Played Ragtime. 4th Ed. New York, Oak Publications, 1971.

Buerkle, Jack V., and Danny Barker. Bourbon Street Black. New York, Oxford, 1973.

Charters, Samuel, and Leonard Kunstadt. Jazz: A History of the New York Scene. Garden City, N.Y., Doubleday, 1962.

Cone, James H. The Spirituals and the Blues. New York, Seabury, 1972.

Courlander, Harold. Negro Folk Music, U.S.A. New York, Columbia University Press, 1969.

Davie, Maurice R. Negroes in American Society. New York, McGraw-Hill, 1949.

Edey, Mait. "Boogie-Woogie Rarities; 1927-1932." Record album notes, Milestone Records, MLP 2009, 1969.

Epstein, Dena J. Sinful Tunes and Spirituals. Chicago, University of Illinois Press, 1977.

Foreman, Ronald Clifford. "Jazz and Race Records, 1920-1932." University of Illinois, 1969, doctoral dissertation.

Gammond, Peter. Scott Joplin and the Ragtime Era. New York, St. Martin's, 1975.

Goldberg, Isaac. Tin Pan Alley. New York, Frederick Ungar, 1961.

Harris, Rex. The Story of Jazz. New York, Grosset and Dunlap, 1960.

Hennessey, Thomas Joseph.   "From Jazz to Swing: Black Jazz Musicians and Their Music, 1917-1935."   Northwestern University, 1973, doctoral dissertation.

Hentoff, Nat.   "Garvin Bushell and New York Jazz in the 1920s." The Jazz Review, 2:1 (January 1959), pp. 11-13; 2:2 (February 1959), pp. 9, 10, 41; 2:3 (April 1959), pp. 16, 17, 40.

Hoefer, George.   "The Sound of Harlem."   Record album booklet, Columbia, Jazz Odyssey vol. III, C3L-33.

Huggins, Nathan Irvin.   Harlem Renaissance.   New York, Oxford, 1971.

Jackson, James A.   "Recent [Blues] Craze Bringing Another Big Publishing House to the Fore."   New York Amsterdam News, (Wednesday, July 11, 1923), entertainment section.

Jasen, David A., and Trebor Jay Tichenor.   Rags and Ragtime--A Musical History.   New York, Seabury, 1978.

Johnson, James Weldon.   The Autobiography of An Ex-Colored Man, 18th printing.   New York, Avon Books, 1965, © 1927.

Johnson, James Weldon.   Black Manhattan.   New York, Atheneum Edition, 1977, © 1930.

Jones, LeRoi.   Blues People.   New York, Morrow/Quill Paperbacks, 1963.

Katz, Bernard, ed.   The Social Implications of Early Negro Music in the United States.   New York, Arno Press and The New York Times, 1969.

Keepnews, Orrin, and Bill Grauer, Jr.   A Pictorial History of Jazz. New York, Crown, 1955.

Leab, Daniel J.   From Sambo to Superspade.   Boston, Houghton Mifflin, 1975.

Lipskin, Mike.   "Fats Waller Piano Solos."   Record album notes, New York, Bluebird (RCA), AXM2-5518, 1977.

Lomax, Alan.   Mister Jelly Roll.   Berkeley, University of California Press, 1950.

Lyttelton, Humphrey. The Best of Jazz--Basin Street to Harlem.   New York, Taplinger, 1978.

Montgomery, Michael, and Trebor Tichenor.   "Scott Joplin--1916." New York, Biograph, BLP 1006Q, 1971.

Parrish, Lydia.   Slave Songs of the Georgia Sea Islands.   New York, Creative Age Press, 1942.

"Phonograph Company Changes Name and Increases."   New York Amsterdam News, (Wednesday, February 14, 1923), entertainment section.

Schafer, William J., and Johannes Riedel. The Art of Ragtime. New
York, Da Capo, 1973.

Southern, Eileen. The Music of Black Americans. New York, Norton,
1971.

Thurman, Wallace. The Blacker the Berry. New York, Collier Books,
1970, © 1929.

Tichenor, Trebor Jay. Ragtime Rarities--Complete Original Music for
63 Piano Rags. New York, Dover Publications, 1975.

Tirro, Frank. Jazz--A History. New York, Norton, 1977.

Waldo, Terry. This Is Ragtime. New York, Hawthorn Books, 1976.

Williams, Martin T. The Art of Jazz. New York, Oxford, 1959.

Biographical Information

Albertson, Chris. "Backwater Blues." Record album notes, New
York, Riverside Records, RLP 151, 1961.

Andrews, Bill. "James P. Johnson: The Great Influencer." Daily
World (NY), (October 15, 1976), p. 8.

Bechet, Sidney. Treat It Gentle. New York, Twayne Publishers, Cas-
sell and Company, 1960.

Blesh, Rudi. "Esquire's Second Swing Concert." The Jazz Record,
(February 1945), p. 8.

"Boston Is Jumping." The Jazz Record, (March 1943), p. 2.

"Boston Jazz Season." The Jazz Record, (June 1946), p. 12.

Bradford, Perry. Born With the Blues. New York, Oak Publications,
1965.

Bradford, Perry, and Noble Sissle. "Yamekraw--Negro Rhapsody."
New York, Folkways Records, FJ2842, 1962.

Brenner, Alfred J. "Writes Our Songs." Equality, (June 1940).

Brown, Ken. "James P. Johnson." Piano Jazz no. 2, edited by
Albert McCarthy and Max Jones. London, Jazz Music Books,
1945.

Butts, Jimmy. "Harlem Speaks." The Jazz Record, (September 1943),
p. 2.

Butts, Jimmy. "Harlem Speaks." The Jazz Record, (October 1943),
p. 10.

Chilton, John. Who's Who of Jazz. Time-Life Records Special
edition, 1978.

Collins, Chester.   "Black Jazz Film Shorts."   Record album notes,
      Biograph, BLP-M3, 1978.

"Condon Session Honors Fats."   The Jazz Record, (January 1944), p. 7.

Correspondence: (From Yale University--James Weldon Johnson
      Collection)

      James P. Johnson to James Weldon Johnson, n.d., (ca. 1937)

      James P. Johnson to Langston Hughes, n.d. (ca. 1937)

      Langston Hughes to James P. Johnson, January 24, 1937

      James P. Johnson to Langston Hughes, n.d. (ca. 1938)

      Langston Hughes to James P. Johnson, March 8, 1938

      James P. Johnson to Langston Hughes, October 6, 1939

      James P. Johnson to Langston Hughes, December 14, 1939

      Langston Hughes to James P. Johnson, January 5, 1943

      Langston Hughes to James P. Johnson, February 1, 1943

      Langston Hughes to James P. Johnson, November 9, 1950

Correspondence: (From Library of Congress)

      James P. Johnson to Mrs. Sprague Coolidge, n.d. (ca. mid-1930s)

Davin, Tom.   "Conversations with James P. Johnson."   Jazz Review,
      (June-September 1959; March/April 1960).

"Davison Goes to Ryan's."   The Jazz Record, (March 15, 1943), p. 7.

"Davison Wakes Up Boston."   The Jazz Record, (February 15, 1943),
      p. 3.

"Dean of Colored Theatrical Profession Honored at Dinner by
      Associates."   New York Amsterdam News, (Wednesday, July 1,
      1925), entertainment section.

Eaton, Lewis.   "James P. Johnson at Town Hall."   The Jazz Record,
      (November 1945), p. 12.

Ellington, Edward Kennedy.   Music Is My Mistress.   New York, Da
      Capo, 1973.

Giddins, Gary.   "Joe Turner--King of Stride."   Record album notes,
      New York, Chiaroscuro Records CR 147.

Hadlock, Richard.   Jazz Masters of the Twenties.   New York, Collier
      Books, 1965.

Hammond, John.   "Talents of James P. Johnson Went Unappreciated."
      Down Beat, (December 28, 1955), p. 12.

Handy, W.C.   Father of the Blues, edited by Arna Bontemps.   New
     York, Collier Books, 1941.

Harrison, H.J.   "James P.'s Jazzfest."   The Jazz Record, (June 1945),
     p. 5-6.

Hodes, Art, and Chadwick Hansen.   Selections from the Gutter.
     Berkeley, University of California Press, 1977.

Hoefer, George.   "James P. Johnson Dies, But Leaves Large Legacy."
     Down Beat, (May 5, 1954), p. 6.

Holly, Hal.   "Johnson Puts On Great Show at Coast Concert."   Down
     Beat, (July 15, 1949), p. 9.

Illidge, Cora Gary.   "Music Week Closes at 'Y'."   New York Amster-
     dam News, (Wednesday, May 14, 1930), Music News, p. 10.

Johnson, James P.   "I Like Anything That's Good."   The Jazz Record,
     (April 1947), pp. 13-14.

"James P. Johnson Alive: Report of Death Regretted."   Down Beat,
     (May 19, 1954), p. 7.

"James P. Johnson, Jazz Pianist, Dies."   The New York Times,
     (November 18, 1955).

"James P. Johnson Suffers Stroke."   Down Beat,   vol. 7, no. 17
     (September 1, 1940), p. 2.

"J.P. Johnson Dies; Wrote 'Charleston'."   New York Herald Tribune,
     (November 18, 1955).

"J.P. Johnson Feted in N.Y."   Down Beat, (March 15, 1942), p. 4.

"J.P. Johnson Takes Sullivan Nitery Stand."   Down Beat, 7:12 (June 7,
     1940), p. 11.

"Jazzorama."   The Jazz Record, (April 1947), p. 18.

"The Jazz Record Jamboree," advertisement.   The Jazz Record (May
     1947), p. 38.

Listings from the Jazz Record:

          What Musicians are Doing--May 15, 1943
          What Musicians are Doing--June 1, 1943
          I Thought I Heard--November 1943
          I Ran Into--November 1943
          I Thought I Heard--December 1943
          I Ran Into--December 1943
          I Ran Into--January 1944
          I Thought I Heard--June 1944
          I Thought I Heard--August 1944
          I Ran Into--August 1944
          I Ran Into--November 1944
          I Ran Into--December 1944
          I Thought I Heard--January 1945

Around The Town--August 1946
I Ran Into--September 1946
I Ran Into--April 1947
Boston's Jordan Hall--November 1947

"Jimmie." Time Magazine, (December 27, 1943), p. 41.

Kammerer, Rafael. "They Called Him the Father of the Stride Piano." American Record Guide, (January 1963), pp. 340-341.

Kappler, Frank, Dick Wellstood, and Willa Rouder. Record album booklet, "Giants of Jazz--James P. Johnson." Time-Life Records, 1981.

Lattimore, George W., to unknown individual. Announcement of Carnegie Hall "Pop" Concert. (May 1945) Schomburg Center--JPJ file.

Maltz, Bob, to Langston Hughes. Advertisement postcards for weekly jam sessions (June 25, 1948-February 24, 1949), Yale University, James Weldon Johnson Collection, JPJ file.

McAdory, Mildred. "Noted Blues Composer Writes Ode to Hero." Daily Worker, (Wednesday, May 3, 1945), p. 11.

McGraw, James. "Fats Waller and James P." The Jazz Record, (January 1944), pp. 8-9.

McIntyre, Lillie Mae. Interview at her home. Thursday, November 12, 1981.

Mezzrow, Milton "Mezz," and Bernard Wolfe. Really The Blues. New York, Random House, 1946.

Middleton, Tony. "The Second Esquire Concert." Record album notes, Saga Records 6924, 1974.

New Jersey Department of Health, Trenton. Microfilm copy of birth record, J40, 1894.

Pease, Sharon A. "Johnson, Now Ailing, Sustained by Royalties." Down Beat, (May 20, 1953), p. 20.

Peck, Seymour. "PM Visits: The Dean of Jazz Pianists." PM, (Friday, April 27, 1945), p. 20.

PM, (February 27, 1947). Brief about James P. Johnson.

Richardson, Pat. "Of Jazz and Intellectuals." The Jazz Record, (May 1944), p. 10.

Rose, Al. Eubie Blake. New York, Schirmer, 1979.

Russell, Ross. "Grandfather of Hot Piano ... James P. Johnson." Jazz Information, (November 1941), pp. 20-24.

Shapiro, Nat, and Nat Hentoff. Hear Me Talkin' To Ya. New York, Dover Edition, 1966.

Smith, Charles Edward, and John Hammond. "From Spirituals to Swing." Record album notes, New York Vanguard USD 47/48, 1973.

Smith, Willie "The Lion," with George Hoefer. Music On My Mind. New York, Da Capo, 1964.

Foster, Pops, as told to Tom Stoddard. Pops Foster. Berkeley, University of California Press, 1971.

"Stroke Fells Hit Composer." Down Beat, (November 1955).

Town Hall benefit committee to unknown individual. Announcement of benefit for Johnson, September 1953. Rutgers Institute of Jazz Studies, JPJ file.

Turner, Joe. "The Pianists In My Life." Melody Maker, 29:1023 (April 25, 1953), p. 2.

Vance, Joel. Fats Waller--His Life and Times. Chicago, Contemporary Books, 1977.

Waller, Maurice, and Anthony Calabrese. Fats Waller. New York Schirmer, 1977.

Waters, Ethel, with Charles Samuels. His Eye Is On the Sparrow. Garden City, N.Y., Doubleday, 1951.

"Where the Bands are Playing." Down Beat, 7:1-12 (January 1, 1940-June 7, 1940), p. 22.

Words and Music, "With Our Song Writers Along Tin Pan Alley." New York Amsterdam News, (Wednesday, March 26, 1930), entertainment section.

Musical theater, stage shows and concerts

Burton, Jack. The Blue Book of Broadway Musicals. New York, Century House, 1952.

Hughes, Langston, and Milton Meltzer. Black Magic--A Pictorial History of Black Entertainers in America. New York, Bonanza Books, 1967.

Hyman, Dick, and Robert Kimball. "Charleston." Record album notes, Columbia Records M33706, 1975.

Jablonski, Edward, and Lawrence D. Stewart. The Gershwin Years. Garden City, N.Y., Doubleday, 1973.

Kimball, Robert, and William Bolcom. Reminiscing with Sissle and Blake. New York, Viking, 1973.

Lewine, Richard, and Alfred Simon. Songs of the American Theater. New York, Dodd, Mead, 1973.

Sampson, Henry T. Blacks In Blackface. Metuchen, N.J. Scarecrow
     Press, 1980.

Concert Programs (in chronological order)

"Happy Rhone and his Versatile Orchestra of 50 musicians." April 22,
     1921. Manhattan Casino. Reprinted in Record Research, no.
     39 (November 1961), p. 6.

"The Coterie of Friends"--Social Evening. At the Adelphi Rooms,
     London, Sunday, May 13, 1923.

"W.C. Handy's Orchestra and Jubilee Singers." April 27, 1928, Car-
     negie Hall. Reprinted in Southern, Music of Black Americans.

"The Federal Theater Negro Unit in 'Macbeth'." April 14, 1936,
     Lafayette Theater.

"Concert of Symphonic Works by James P. Johnson." March 8, 1942,
     Heckscher Theater.

"Jazzfest and Pop Concert Presenting James P. Johnson." May 4,
     1945, Carnegie Hall.

"James P. Johnson in a piano recital." October 25, 1945, Town Hall.

"Mura Dehn and the Jazz Dancers." April 13, 1947, Local
     Auditorium.

Information on shows   (reviews, programs, etc. in chronological order)

Plantation Days

"Plantation Days' Is Carnival of Jazz." Toledo Blade, (December 18,
     1922).

"Florence Mills Show Held Over At Lafayette." New York Amster-
     dam News, (Wednesday, February 14, 1923), entertainment
     section.

"At the Lafayette Theater." New York Age, (Saturday, February 17,
     1923), entertainment section.

"Sleuth Acting For 'Shuffle Along' Spike 'Plantation'." New York
     Amsterdam News, (Wednesday, February 28, 1923), entertainment
     section.

"Theatrical Jottings." New York Age, (Saturday, March 3, 1923), en-
     tertainment section.
"An Earful From Variety--Wherein The White Theatrical Publication
     Tells Us a Few Things Ament Colored Artists and Colored
     Shows." New York Amsterdam News, (Wednesday, March 28,
     1923), entertainment section.

"Plantation Days Next Week." New York Amsterdam News,
     (Wednesday, March 28, 1923), entertainment section.

"This Week's Offering." New York Amsterdam News, (Wednesday, April 4, 1923), entertainment section.

"Harper and Blanks Issue First Statement of 'Plantation Days' in London," by Harper and Blanks. New York Amsterdam News, (Wednesday, June 13, 1923), entertainment section.

"Florence Mills and Co. Made Big Hit in London." New York Age, (Saturday, June 23, 1923), entertainment section.

"Broadway At Its Best Has Nothing On Connie's Inn." New York Amsterdam News, (Wednesday, July 25, 1923), entertainment section.

"Harper and Blanks at Lincoln Theater." New York Amsterdam News, (Wednesday, August 1, 1923), entertainment section.

"Theatrical Jottings." New York Age, (Saturday, August 4, 1923), entertainment section.

"'Plantation Revue,' With Florence Mills, To Close In London, End of Aug." New York Age, (Saturday, September 1, 1923), entertainment section.

Raisin' Cain

"Lafayette Theater Announces New Show." New York Amsterdam News, (Wednesday, July 4, 1923), entertainment section.

Advertisement for Lafayette Theater. New York Age, (Saturday, July 7, 1923), entertainment section.

Runnin' Wild

Programs

Colonial Theater. Week Beginning Monday Evening, December 24, 1923.

Bronx Opera House. Week Beginning Monday Evening, January 19, 1925.

Reviews

Dale, Alan. New York American, (October 31, 1923). Review of N.Y. production.

Gillette, Don Carle. Billboard, (September 15, 1923). Review of Boston production.

Legitimate, (August 30, 1923). Review of Washington production.

Mantle, Burns. New York News, (November 2, 1923). Review of N.Y. production.

Meakin.   Variety,   (August 30, 1923).   Review of Washington
        production.

New York Evening Post, (October 30, 1923).   Review of N.Y.
        production.

New York Sun and Globe, (October 31, 1923).   Review of N.Y.
        production.

New York Times, (October 30, 1923).   Review of N.Y. production.

New York Tribune, (October 30, 1923).   Review of N.Y. production.

New York World, (October 31, 1923).   Review of N.Y. production.

Sinnott, James P.   New York Telegram, (October 30, 1923).   Review
        of N.Y. production.

Whyte, Gordon.   Billboard, (November 10, 1923).   Review of N.Y.
        production.

Sunshine Sammy

Preview

" 'Sunshine Sammy' At Head of Splendid Show."   New York Amster-
        dam News, (September 9, 1925), entertainment section.

Moochin' Along

Preview

" 'Mootchin' [sic] Along' by Jesse Shipp,   Underlined For Early
        Showing."   New York Amsterdam News, (December 2, 1925),
        entertainment section.

Review

"They're 'Moochin' Along' At the Lafayette Theater All This Week."
        New York Amsterdam News, (December 9, 1925), entertainment
        section.

Advertisement for Lafayette Theater, New York Amsterdam News,
        (December 9, 1925), entertainment section.

A La Carte

Programs

Martin Beck Theater.   Beginning Wednesday Evening, August 17, 1927.

Tremont Theater.   Week Beginning Monday, July 25, 1927.

Review

Watts, Richard Jr., New York Herald Tribune, (August 18, 1927).

Keep Shufflin'

Programs

Daly's 63rd St. Theater.   Week Beginning Monday Evening, February 27, 1928.

Windsor Theater.   Week Beginning Monday Evening, September 3, 1928.

Reviews

Dale, Alan.   New York American, (March 1, 1928).

Dudley, B.   New York Evening World, (February 28, 1928).

"Ibee."   Variety, (March 7, 1928).

Leland, Gordon M.   Billboard, (March 10, 1928).

Littell, Robert.   New York Post, (February 28, 1928).

New York Journal of Commerce, (February 29, 1928).

New York Times, (February 28, 1928).

Rathburn, Stephen.   New York Sun, (February 28, 1928).

Wall Street Journal, (March 2, 1928).

Winchell, Walter.   New York Graphic, (February 28, 1928).

Woolcott, Alexander.   New York World, (February 28, 1928).

Van Dycke, Thomas.   New York Telegraph, (February 28, 1928).

Messin' Around

Program

Hudson Theater.   Week Beginning Monday Evening, April 29, 1929.

Reviews

Fitzgerald, John C.   New York Evening World, (April 23, 1929).

King, William G.   New York Evening Post, (April 23, 1929).

New York Sun, (April 23, 1929).

Watts, Richard Jr.   New York Tribune, (April 23, 1929).

A Great Day In N'Orleans

"A Great Day In N'Orleans" Chicago Defender, (January 4, 1930), p. 6.

Shuffle Along of 1930

"Belated Discovery Made That Miller and Lyle Did Not Head Brooklyn Show." New York Amsterdam News, (Wednesday, April 30, 1930), entertainment section.

Fireworks of 1930

"The Lafayette Next Week." New York Amsterdam News, (Wednesday, June 25, 1930), entertainment section.

Sugar Hill (1931)

King, William G. New York Evening Post, (December 26, 1931).

New York Times, (December 26, 1931).

Variety, (December 29, 1931).

Harlem Hotcha

New York Sun, (November 12, 1932).

"Bledsoe to Head Lafayette Bill--Capable Cast in Connie's Inn Revue at the Same House this Week." New York Amsterdam News (Wednesday, March 8, 1933), entertainment section.

Advertisement for Lafayette Theater. New York Amsterdam News (Wednesday, March 1, 1933), entertainment section.

Policy Kings

Brown, Herrick. New York Sun, (December 31, 1938).

Drake, Herbert. New York Herald Tribune, (December 31, 1938).

Hobe. Variety, (January 11, 1939).

New York Post, (December 29, 1938).

New York Times, (December 31, 1938).

New York Times, (January 8, 1939).

New York World Telegram, (December 31, 1938).

TAC Cabaret

"New Cabaret TAC."   New York Herald Tribune, (October 6, 1939).

Sugar Hill (1949)

Variety, (July 27, 1949).

Others

Exhibitor's Campaign Book, by United Artists.   The Emperor Jones, 1933.

The Organizer--two drafts of libretto by Langston Hughes.   Schomburg Center--Langston Hughes file.

Musical Analysis

Balliett, Whitney.   "Supreme Tickler."   The New Yorker, (May 11, 1963), pp. 153-156.

Berlin, Edward A.   "Ragtime and Improvised Piano: Another View." Journal of Jazz Studies, 4:2 (Spring/Summer 1977).

Francis, Henry.   "Musical Aspects of Stride Piano."   Storyville 42 (August-September 1972), pp. 213-216.

Harrison, Max.   "James P. Johnson."   A Jazz Retrospect.   Boston, Crescendo Publishing Co., 1976.

Napoleon, Art, and Dick Sudhalter.   "Record Review--Parlour Piano Solos 1917-1921, Bio. vol. 1."   Jazz Journal, 23:12 (December 1970), p. 35.

Newberger, Eli H.   "The Development of New Orleans and Stride Piano Styles."   Journal of Jazz Studies, 4:2 (Spring/Summer 1977), pp. 43-70.

Newberger, Eli H.   "The Transition From Ragtime To Improvised Piano Styles."   Journal of Jazz Studies, 3:2 (Spring 1976), pp. 3-18.

"Record Review of The Father of Stride Piano."   Jazz Monthly, no. 177 (November 1969), p. 14.

Schuller, Gunther.   Early Jazz--Its Roots and Musical Development. New York, Oxford, 1968.

Taylor, William E.   "The History and Development of Jazz Piano: A New Perspective for Educators."   University of Massachusetts, 1975, doctoral dissertation.

Wellstood, Dick.   "Donald Lambert--Harlem Stride Classics."   Record album notes.   Miami, Pumpkin Productions, 1977.

Wellstood, Dick. "Reviews: Recordings--W.C. Handy Blues acc. by James P. Johnson." The Jazz Review, 1:2 (December 1958), pp. 34-35.

Wildman, Joan M. "The Function of the Left Hand in The Evolution of the Jazz Piano." Journal of Jazz Studies, 5:2 (Spring/Summer 1979).

Williams, Martin, and Dick Wellstood. "Waller to Wellstood to Williams to Chaos." The Jazz Review, 3:7 (August 1960), p. 11.

Wilson, John S. "The Jazz Panorama." Hi-Fi Review Supplement, Ziff Davis Publ. Co. 2 (April 1959), pp.67-82.

Discographical Information

Albertson, Chris. "Bessie Smith--Any Woman's Blues." Record album notes, New York, Columbia G 30126.

Brigaud, Dominique. "Piano In Style--1926-30." Record album notes, New York, MCA Records, MCA 1332, 1980.

Cooke, Roland. "Fats Waller--Vol. 3, 1927-1929." Record album notes, France, RCA, 741.076, 1973.

Cooke, Roy. "Fats Waller--Vol. 5, 1929." France, RCA 741.094, 1973.

Dance, Stanley. "James P. Johnson--Father of the Stride Piano." Record album notes, New York, Columbia, CL 1780, 1962.

Davis, Charles B. Jr. "James P. Johnson--On Record." The Mississippi Rag, (August 1977), pp. 8-9.

Driggs, Frank. "Ethel Waters' Greatest Years." Record album notes, New York, Columbia PG 31571, 1972.

"Edmond Hall Records for B.N." The Jazz Record, (February 1944), p. 10.

Feather, Leonard. "Art Tatum and James P. Johnson." Record album notes, New York, MCA Records, MCA2-4112, 1977.

Feather, Leonard. "Original Blue Note Jazz--Vol. II." Record album notes, California, Blue Note B-6506.

Hodes, Art. "Jazz Classics-Original Blue Note Jazz, Vol. I." Record album notes, California, Blue Note B-6504.

Hoefer, George. "Jazz of the Forties." Record album notes, New York, Folkways, FJ 2841, 1961.

"James P. Johnson on Blue Note." The Jazz Record, (December 1943), p. 10.

"James P. Johnson; 1921-1926." New York, Olympic Records 7132.

Janis, Harriet and Rudi Blesh. "Jazz A' La Creole." Record album notes, South Carolina, GMB Records, GMB50.

Jasen, David A. Recorded Ragtime, 1897-1958. Hamden, Ct., Archon Books, 1973.

Jasen, David A. "Striding In Dixieland." Record album notes, New York, Folkways, 1981.

"Jazz on LP's." Westport, Ct., Greenwood Press, 1978. Reprint of Decca Record Co. 1955 ed.

Jepsen, Jorgen Grunnet. Jazz Records, 1942-1968. Vol. 4c. Denmark, Tastrup Reklametryk, 1970.

Montgomery, Michael. "James P. Johnson Rollography." Record Research, 16:20 (Nov.-Dec. 1958), p. 16.

Montgomery, Michael. "James P. Johnson, 1917-1921." Record album notes, New York, Biograph BLP-1003Q, 1970.

Montgomery, Michael. "James P. Johnson, 1917, Vol. 2." Record album notes, New York, Biograph BLP 1009Q, 1973.

Montgomery, Michael. Parlor Piano." Record album notes, New York, Biograph BLP 1001Q, 1970.

Montgomery, Michael. "Thomas 'Fats' Waller, 1923-1924." Record album notes, New York, Biograph BLP 1002Q, 1970.

Morgenstern, Dan. "The Eddie Condon Concerts." Record album notes, New York, Chiaroscuro CR 113.

Morgenstern, Dan. "Classics-Volume I." Record album notes, California, Blue Note B-6509.

Morgenstern, Dan. "Yank Lawson." Record album notes, New York, Bob Thiele Music BBMI-0941.

"Red Allen & James P. Johnson." Meritt Record Society, 5.

Reitz, Rosetta. "Mean Mothers--Independent Women's Blues, Vol. I." Record album notes, New York, Rosetta Records, RR 1300, 1980.

Rust, Brian. Jazz Records, 1897-1942, vol. I & II. Arlington House, 1978.

Simmen, Johnny. "Crystal Clear." Coda 11:12 (October 1974), p. 25.

Smith, Charles E. "James P. Johnson; New York Jazz." Record album notes, Stinson SLP 21, 1963.

Smith, Charles Edward. "Young Louis--The Side Man." Record album notes, New York, Decca Records DL 9233.

Smith, Charles Edward, and David A. Jasen. "The Original James P.
    Johnson."   Record album notes, New York, Folkways FJ 2850,
    1973.

"Swing Combos; 1935-1941."   Swing Fan 1018, limited edition.

"Swing Street, Vol. 3."   Sweden, Tax m8034.

"The 'This Is Jazz' Broadcasts," vol. I & II.   England, Rarities, nos.
    33 and 35.

Trolle, Frank H.   James P. Johnson--Father of the Stride Piano.
    Netherlands, Micrography, 1981.

Libraries and Archives

Library of Congress, Music Division, Main Reading Room, Catalogue
    of Copyright Entries.

New York Public Library, Schomburg Center, Rogers and Hammerstein
    collection of the performing arts.

Rutgers University, Institute of Jazz Studies.

Yale University, Sterling Memorial Library, Music Library, Beinecke
    Rare Book and Manuscript Library.

INDEX

Letters printed in bold face refer to the special photo insert, which has letters in lieu of page numbers.

Part II

THE RECORDED WORKS OF JAMES P. JOHNSON: A DISCOGRAPHY

by Robert Hilbert

INTRODUCTION

This discography would not have been possible without the work of many pioneers. Charles Delaunay, Orin Blackstone, Brian Rust, Robert M.W. Dixon, John Godrich, Jorgen Grunnet Jepsen and Walter Bruyninckx are some of the major figures who pulled together the many threads of recorded jazz with their comprehensive works. Each built on the work of others, in many cases re-examining some of the same source material with surprisingly different results. Musicians' memories, contemporary newspaper and magazine articles, letters and journals, agents' pay receipts, recording company files and, of course, the discs themselves are among the sources of original disographical research.

It is not surprising that the field of discography has attracted so many researchers around the world. Jazz has often been defined as a spontaneous, improvised music which, by its very nature, is ephemeral. Without the invention of the phonograph, nearly coinciding with the birth of jazz in the late 19th century, the entire record of this music would have been lost, and in all probability its development would have been stunted.

Many jazz musicians and most fans first experienced the thrill of the music through the phonograph record. And the first thing the fans wanted to know was the names of the musicians on those discs. Even today, however, many of the names are still unknown to us. But with each new discography, the curtain is raised a little higher.

So it is with James P. Johnson's recordings. There are still many unanswered questions, many sessions which require clarification, many issues unknown and, one hopes, still more music which has been preserved to discover. The noted piano roll collector, researcher and pianist Michael Montgomery has contributed much to the knowledge of Johnson's piano roll recording activities and has been responsible for recording many of the rolls and seeing to their issue on phonograph records. Montgomery's work was included in Frank Trolle's pioneering discography, James P. Johnson: Father of Stride Piano (published by Micrography in two volumes in 1981). It is hoped that the new information contained in the present work will add as much to the sum of knowledge about Johnson's recorded career as did the Trolle-Montgomery work.

Research contained in some specialized discographies also helped to shed light on some areas of Johnson's recordings, especially Clarence Williams by Tom Lord; Boy From New Orleans: Louis Armstrong by Hans Westerberg; McKinney's Music by John Chilton; The Eddie Condon Town Hall Broadcasts by Bozy White; Hendersonia by Walter C. Allen; Negro Bands on Film, Vol. 1 by Klaus Strateman; Jazz in the Movies by David Meeker; Edmond Hall: A Discography by Manfred Selchow and Karsten Lohmann; The Columbia 13/14000 Series: A Numerical Listing by Dan Mahony, Clarence Williams on Microgroove by Dick Bakker, and This Is Jazz by Jack Litchfield.

I was fortunate in having access to Storyville Files (Josephine Beaton, Howard Rye, Laurie Wright) for information concerning Columbia and Vocalion recording sessions, and in having the assistance of Kurt Andersen, Larry Appelbaum, Mark Borowsky, James L. Collier, Michael Cuscuna, John R. T. Davies, Wendell Echols, John Featherstone, John Fell, Milt Gabler, Luvenia George, Robert Graf, Jeffrey P. Green, John Hammond, John Holley, Carl Kendziora, Peter Kennedy, Shirley Klett, Karl Emil Knudsen, Floyd Levin, Frank K. Lorenz, Tina McCarthy, Dan Morgenstern, David Niven, Ken Nobel, Gerald E. Parsons, Martin Rand, Willa Rouder, Richard Sears, Joe Showler, Johnny Simmen, Jack Sohmer, Dr. Klaus Stratemann, Mike Sutcliffe, Bill Thompson, Jack Towers, Jerry Valburn, Julian Vein, Howard Waters and Dick Wellstood. Dan Morgenstern and the staff and resources of the Institute of Jazz Studies at Rutgers' University provided invaluable information. I would also like to express my thanks to my wife, Betsy, and daughter, Miriam, for the many years of help and encouragement.

It should be pointed out that transfers of piano rolls to discs result in different "performances" of the roll each time it is dubbed. The rolls can be played at differing tempos and some of the disc issues are from "uncorrected" rolls. The Biograph series was "pumped" by Michael Montgomery in 1970 and represent the most realistic-sounding issues to date. Riverside and London issues use identical transfers, done in the early 1950's. Most of the "bootleg" issues, such as Kings of Jazz and Monkey, were copied from from the Riverside releases.

Some early Columbia sessions include information regarding the number of labels printed. The figures are for the initial pressing orders (both East and West coast) only. In case of popular records, such as Bessie

Smith's "Back Water Blues," additional pressings
were made. Other items which did not sell well
might not be as common as the figures suggest.
Nevertheless, the figures provide a guide to
realtive rarity.

A word about "take" numbers. Starting in
the late 1930s, most major record companies
began to record entire sessions. They employed
several turntables to preserve all the music. A
16-inch acetate disc at 33 1/3 rpm would take
down virtually everything that took place in the
studio, including all false starts, breakdowns,
and incomplete takes. This was called the
"safety." Yet another 16-inch acetate, usually
at 78 rpm, would be used for all attempts at
master takes. Simultaneously, a 10-inch disc
might be cut and perhaps used for a master right
away. By the 1940s, the smaller labels that
began to proliferate often cut corners and
dubbed the selected master take directly from
the safety. Usually, a "take 1" would be
assigned for the take first chosen for issue,
indicating order of preference rather than
sequence of recording (this had long been the
practice at Victor, by the way). Thus much
confusion has resulted, especially in the case
of more recent LP issues of previously rejected
takes. I have listed the correct sequence of
recording when known, regardless of the take
number assigned to the issued 78 rpm discs.

Robert Hilbert
Coral Gables, Florida

ABBREVIATIONS

8T   8-track tape

AFC   Association Francaise des Collectionneurs
de Disques du Jazz
AFRS   Armed Forces Radio Service
AMA   Amadeo
(Arg)   Argentina
AoH   Ace of Hearts
Ari   Ariston
(Au)   Australia

Bb   Bluebird
Bcy   Barclay
Bio   Biograph
BlSt   Blue Star
Bm   Biltmore
BN   Blue Note
Br   Brunswick
BS   Black Swan
BW   Black and White

(C)   Canada
CA   Crispus Attucks
CBS   Columbia Broadcasting System
Ccl   Collectors' Classics
CD   Compact disc
Cdm   Chant du Monde
Cent   Century
CID   Compagnie Ind. du Disque
Club   Club Internacional del Disco
Cir   Circle
CJM   Classic Jazz Masters
Clmx   Climax
Col   Columbia
Com   Commodore

Con	Contemporary
Cor	Coronet
Crl	Coral
CT	cassette tape
Cto	Cleartone
(D)	Denmark
Dec	Decca
(Du)	Dutch
(E)	England
EBW	Edison Bell Winner
Elec	Electrola
Emb	Ember
ESC	ESC
Esq	Esquire
Ev	Everest
(Eu)	European
(F)	France
Fam	Family
Fats	Fats Waller Memorial Show
FDC	For Discriminate Collectors
Fest	Festival
Fon	Fontana
(G)	German
GdJ	Guide de Jazz
Harm	Harmony
Her	Herwin
HJCA	Hot Jazz Clubs of America
HMV	His Master's Voice
HRS	Hot Record Society
HT	Hy-Tone
(I)	Italy
(J)	Japan
Jazz	Jazzology

JC   Jazz Collector
JD   Jazz Document
JLC   Jazz Live (Cicala)
JPa   Jazz Parade
JPi   Jazz Piano
JSe   Jazz Selection
JSo   Jazz Society
JU   Jazz Unlimited
Jzt   Jazztone

KoJ   Kings of Jazz

Lon   London

MFP   Music for Pleasure
Mon   Monkey
Msd   Musidisc

NWR   New World Records

Od   Odeon
OFC   Only For Collectors
OJC   Original Jazz Classics
OK   Okeh
Oly   Olympic
ONS   One Night Stand

PA   Pathe Actuelle
Ph   Philips
Para   Paramount
Per   Perfect
Pur   Puritan

Rar   Rarities
RCA   Radio Corporation of America
Reg   Regal
Riv   Riverside
RT   reel tape

SE   Special Editions

Sig   Signature
Smith Smithsonian
Sto   Storyville
Sun   Sunbeam
Sw   Swing
(Swe) Sweden
(Swi) Switzerland

TR   Top Rank
TX   transcription

(Ur)   Uruguay

Van   Vanguard
Vic   Victor
VJM   Vintage Jazz Mart
Voc   Vocalion

1.   James P.   Johnson - William A. Farrell,
piano roll duet.

                          NYC, May, 1917
          After Tonight
                Piano Roll: Universal 2191
                LP: Bio BLP 1009Q

2. James P. Johnson, piano rolls
                          NYC, May, 1917

          Caprice Rag
                Piano Roll: Metro Art 203176

                LP: Riv RLP 1046, RLP (12) 151,
                Bio BLP 1009Q, Ldn(E) AL 3540,
                Msd (F) 30JA 5120

          Steeplechase Rag
                Piano Roll: Universal 203179
                LP: Bio BLP 1009Q, Msd (F) 30JA
                5120

NOTE: "Steeplechase Rag" is the same tune as
"Over The Bars."

3. James P. Johnson, piano rolls
                          Orange,   N.J.,
                          June, 1917
          When It's Cherry Time in Tokio (sic)
                Piano Roll: Perfection 87019
                LP: Bio BLP 1009Q, Sounds LP
                1204, KoJ (I) KLJ 20008

          After To-Night
                Piano Roll: Perfection 87020
                LP: Bio BLP 1009Q, Sounds LP
                1204, Msd (F) 30JA 5120, KoJ (I)

KLJ 20008

NOTE: "When It's Cherry Time in Tokio" as
"Cherry Time Blues" on Sounds, KoJ.

4. James P. Johnson, piano roll
                              Orange,   N.J.,
                              July, 1917
            Caprice Rag
                Piano Roll: Perfection 87023
                LP: Riv RLP 1046, Bio BLP 1009Q,
                Lon (E)AL 3540

5. James P. Johnson, piano roll
                              NYC, July, 1917
            Daintiness Rag
                Piano Roll: Universal 203107
                LP: Riv RLP 1046, RLP (12) 151,
                Bio BLP 1009Q, Lon (E) AL 3540

            Monkey Hunch
                Piano Roll: Universal 2235

6. James P. Johnson, piano roll
                              Newark,   N.J.,
                              July, 1917
            Mama's Blues
                Piano Roll: Artempo 12286

7. James P. Johnson, piano roll
                              Belleville, N.J.,
                              July, 1917
            Mamma's Blues (sic)
                Piano Roll: Rythm E17933

8.   James P. Johnson, piano roll
                              Belleville,   N.J.,
                              August, 1917
          Stop It
             Piano Roll: Rythm H100253

NOTE: "Stop It" is the same tune as "Stop It,
Joe."

9.   James P. Johnson, piano roll
                              NYC, August, 1917
          Stop It
             Piano Roll: Universal 203205
             LP: Bio BLP 1009Q, Sounds LP
             1204, KoJ (I) KLJ 20008

10. James P. Johnson, piano roll
                              NYC,   September,
                              1917
          Fascination
             Piano Roll: Universal 203227
             LP: Bio BLP 1009Q, Msd (F) 30JA
             5120

11.   James P. Johnson – Edwin E. Wilson, piano
roll duet
                              NYC,   September,
                              1917
          Mama's Blues
             Piano Roll: Universal 2335
             LP: Bio BLP 1009Q, Msd (F) 30JA
             5120

12.   James P. Johnson, piano roll
                              Orange,   N.J.,
                              September, 1917

Mama's Blues
Piano Roll: Arto 228X
LP: Bio BLP 1009Q

13. James P. Johnson, piano roll
NYC, October, 1917
Innovation
Piano Roll: Universal 203255
LP: Bio BLP 1009Q

14. James P. Johnson - Edwin E. Wilson, piano roll duet

NYC,   November, 1917
Twilight Rag
Piano Roll: Universal 203275
LP: Bio BLP 1009Q, Msd (F) 30JA 5120

15. James P. Johnson, piano rolls
Newark,   N.J., February, 1918
Carolina Shout
Piano Roll: Artempo 12975
LP: Bio BLP 1003Q, BLP 1009Q

Eccentricity
Piano Roll: Artempo 12997
LP: Bio BLP 1001Q, BLP 1009Q

16. James P. Johnson, piano rolls
NYC, May, 1921
Carolina Shout
Piano Roll: QRS 100999, Q129
LP: Riv RLP 1046, RLP 12-105,

Bio BLP 1003Q, Oly OL 7132, Lon
(E) AL 3540, Emb (E) CJS 853, Msd
(F) 30JA 5120, Joker (I) SM 3108,
Monkey (F) MY 40023, Vogue (F)
DP.36, Vogue/Swing (F) 000103
RT: Riv RT 5-2

Eccentricity
Piano Roll: QRS 101000, Q 131
LP: Riv RLP 12-105, Bio BLP
1003Q, Oly OL 7132, Emb (E) CJS
853, Joker (I) SM 3108, Monkey
(F) MY 40023

Don't Tell Your Monkey Man (Monkey Man
Blues)
Piano Roll: QRS 1338
78: Cent 4023, JSo (F) AA 610
LP: Riv RLP 1046, RLP (12) 151,
Bio BLP 1003Q, Sounds LP 1204,
Lon (E) AL 3540, Msd (F) 30JA
5120, KoJ (I) KLJ 20008

It Takes Love To Cure The Heart's
Disease
Piano Roll: QRS 1339
LP: Riv RLP 1011, RLP (12) 151,
Sounds LP1204, Bio BLP 1003Q, Lon
(E/Au) AL 3511, KoJ (I) 20008
RT: Riv RT 5-2

Loveless Love (A "Blues" Ballad)
Piano Roll: QRS 1340
LP: Riv RLP 1011, RLP (12) 131,
Bio BLP 1003Q, Sounds LP 1204,
Lon (E/Au) AL 3511, Msd (F) 30JA
5120, KoJ (I) KLJ 20008, Monkey
(F) My 40023, Joker (I) SM 3948
RT: Riv RT 5-2

                    CT: Joker (I) MC 3948

NOTE: "Don't Tell Your Monkey Man" as "Monkey
Man Wiggle" on Century and Jazz Society. "Old
Fashioned Love" is interpolated into this title.
"Loveless Love" on Joker SM 3948 lists the
artist as "James Pete Johnson."

17. James P. Johnson, piano rolls
                              NYC, June, 1921
            Doctor Jazzes Raz-Ma-Taz
                  Piano Roll: QRS 1473
                  LP: Folkways RBF RF-7, Bio BLP
                  1003Q, Msd (F) 30JA 5120

            Roumania
                  Piano Roll: QRS 1479
                  78: Lon (E) L 808
                  LP: Bio BLP 1003Q

18.   Alice   Leslie   Carter, acc. by Jimmie
Johnson's Jazz Boys
                              NYC, c. August,
                              1921
Carter, vocals, June Clark, cornet; unknown
trombone, clarinet and violin; Johnson, piano;
unknown brass bass; possibly other instruments
on some sides.

            Dangerous Blues
                  78:   Arto 9086, Bell P-86,
                  Cleartone C-86, Globe 7086, HT
                  K-86

            I Want Some Lovin' Blues
                  78:   Arto 9086, Bell P-86,
                  Cleartone C-86, Globe 7086, HT
                  K-86

The Also-Ran Blues
        78:     Arto   9095,   Bell   P-95,
        Cleartone C-95,   Globe 7095, HT
        K-95

Cry Baby Blues
        78:     Arto   9095,   Bell   P-95,
        Cleartone C-95,   Globe 7095, HT
        K-95

You'll Think of Me Blues
        78:     Arto   9096,   Bell   P-96,
        Cleartone P-96,   Globe 7096, HT
        K-96

NOTE: No piano is audible on any of these recordings.

19.   Alice Leslie Carter, accompanied by Jimmie Johnson's Jazz Boys
                        NYC, c. September, 1921
Carter,   vocal;   June Clark, cornet; unknown trombone,   clarinet,   violin, Johnson, piano; unknown brass bass; possibly other instruments.

Aunt Hagar's Children Blues
        78:     Arto   9103,   Bell   P-103,
        Cleartone C-103,   Globe 7103, HT
        K-103

Down Home Blues
        78:     Arto   9103,   Bell   P-103,
        Cleartone   C-103,   Globe 7103, HT
        K-103

NOTE: No piano is audible on these recordings.

20.   Lavinia   Turner and Jas. P. Johnson's
Harmony Seven

NYC,   c.   2
September 1921

Turner,   vocal; two unknown cornets; unknown
trombone,   clarinet,   tenor sax; Johnson, piano;
unknown banjo, xylophone.

69358-2   He Took It Away From Me
            78: PA 020627, Per 12034

69359-3   If I Were Your Daddy (And You Were A
Mama to Me)
            78: PA 020627, Per 12034

NOTE: 69358 on PA 020627 labeled as accompanied
by Jas. J. (sic) Johnson's Harmony Seven. Some
copies of PA 020627 were issued with the labels
reversed.

21. Lavinia Turner and Johnson's Harmony Seven
                    NYC,   September,
                    1921

Turner, vocal; two unknown cornets, trombone,
clarinet, tenor sax, Johnson, piano, unknown
banjo.

69397-1   When The Rain Turns into Snow (Who's
Gonna Keep You Warm)
            78: PA 020878, Per 12039

69398-   Who'll Drive Your Blues Away?
            78: PA 020878, Per 12039

22. James P. Johnson, piano solo

                              NYC, c. September,
                              1921
P-151-1   The Harlem Strut
                78:    Black Swan 2026, Para 12144,
                14009, JC (E) L-60
                LP: Bio BLP 12047, VJM (E)VLP 6,
                CBS (F) 85387
                CT: CBS (F) 40-85387

23. James P. Johnson, piano roll
                              NYC,   September,
                              1921
            If You've Never Been Vamped By a Brown
            Skin, You've Never Been Vamped At All
                Piano Roll: QRS 1644
                LP: Bio BLP 1003Q

24. James P. Johnson, piano roll
                              NYC, October, 1921
            Arkansas Blues
                Piano Roll: QRS 1670
                LP: Riv RLP 12-105, Bio BLP
                1003Q, Oly OL 7132, Emb (E) CJS
                853, Msd (F) 30JA 5120, Joker (I)
                SM 3108

            Cry Baby Blues
                Piano Roll: QRS 1673
                LP: Riv RLP 12-105, Bio BLP
                1003Q, Oly OL 7132, Emb (E) CJS
                853, Msd (F) 30 JA 5120, Joker
                (I) SM 3108

            Gypsy Blues
                Piano Roll: QRS 1674
                LP: Riv RLP 1046, RLP (12) 151,
                Lon (E) AL 3540

NOTE: "Cry Baby Blues" as "Baby Blues" on Msd.

25. Jimmie Johnson's Jazz Boys
                              NYC,   c. October,
                              1921
Unknown   cornet   (June   Clark?),   trombone,
clarinet, alto sax, soprano sax; Johnson, piano;
unknown banjo, brass bass, drums.

           Carolina Shout
                78:    Arto   9096;   Bell   P-96,
                Cleartone C-96, Globe 7096, HT
                K-96
                LP: Folkways RBF RF-25; CJM (Swe)
                CJM-1

NOTE: On Arto as by Blue Flame Syncopators.

26. James P. Johnson, piano solos
                              NYC,   18   October
                              1921

S-70159-D   Keep Off The Grass
                78: OK 4495, JSo (F) AA 504
                LP: Col C3L 33   (Cl 2160), Her
                405, CBS (Eu) 67257, Time-Life
                STL-J18, Time-Life (Au) STL-J18,
                Col C 32355, CBS (F) 85387
                CT: Time-Life 4TL-J18, CBS (F)
                40-85387
                8T: Time-Life 8TL-J18

S-70160-C   Carolina Shout
                78: OK 4495, JSo (F) AA-504
                LP: Col   CL 1780, Smith P-11892,
                CBS (Eu) BPG 62090, Parl (E) PMC
                1174,   Odeon   (E)   PPMC   1174,
                Time-Life STL-J18, Time-Life (Au)

STL–J18,   I   Grande   del   Jazz (I)
85,   CBS   (F)   85387,   CBS   (F)   66403,
CBS (F) 66425
CT: Time–Life   4TL–J18,   CBS   (F)
40–85387
8T: Time–Life 8TL–J18

NOTE: CBS   67257   lists   the   title for matrix
S–70159–D as "Keep Out of the Grass."

27.   Eddie   Gray,   accompanied   by Jas. P.
Johnson's Harmony Eight
                                        NYC,   c.   early
                                        November, 1921
Gray,   vocal;   possibly   Gus Aiken, trumpet;   Bud
Aiken,   Jake   Frazier   or   Charlie   Irvis,
trombones;   unknown alto;   Walter Watkins, tenor
sax; Johnson, piano; unknown bass and drums.

P–159–   You've Got What I'm Looking For
                78: BS 2020, Para 12138

Add ukelele, probably played by Gray.

P–160–   Ukelele Blues
                78: BS 2020, Para 12138

NOTE: The   matrix   numbers surrounding this
session   pose   some   difficulties.   Ivan H.
Browning is credited with the preceeding numbers
(P   157,   "Christians   Awake"   and P 158, "My
Task"),   issued   on Black Swan 2033 and Paramount
1020.   Although   the accompaniment on the record
label   is   credited   to the Black Swan Orchestra,
only   a   piano   can   be heard, probably played by
Fletcher   Henderson.   The   matrix   numbers
following   the   Gray   session are by Trixie Smith
(P   161,   "Desperate   Blues,"   a   Johnson
composition,   and P 162, "Trixie's Blues.")   The

orchestral accompaniment sounds similar to the
band on the Gray session, with a violin added
and perhaps one of the reeds omitted. To
further complicate matters, matrix numbers P
160, P 161 and P 162 were all used on two other
Black Swan releases as by Ethel Waters' Jazz
Masters. Despite the name, none of the three
titles ("Frisco Jazz Band Blues," "Royal Garden
Blues" and "Bugle Blues") have vocals. That
band, according to Walter Allen's Hendersonia ,
included Gus Aiken, trumpet, Bud Aiken,
trombone; Garvin Bushell, clarinet; probably Joe
Elder, sax and clarinet; Fletcher Henderson,
piano; "Bill D.C." or "C. Mosby," bass sax.
There is no piano audible on any of the sides,
including the Eddie Gray session, and while the
band sound on each is very similar, that could
be due to the extremely poor recording quality
as well as to contemporary musical conventions.

28.   Alice Leslie Carter, accompanied by Jimmie
Johnson's Jazz Boys

                          NYC, c. November,
                          1921
Carter, vocal; June Clark, cornet; unknown
trombone, clarinet, tenor sax, violin; Johnson,
piano; unknown brass bass; possibly other
instruments.

          Decatur Street Blues
               78:   Arto 9112, Bell P-112,
               Cleartone C-112, Globe 7112, HT
               K-112

          Got To Have My Daddy Blues
               78:   Arto 9112, Bell P-112,
               Cleartone C-112, Globe 7112, HT
               K-112

NOTE: No piano is audible on this session.

29. Trixie Smith, accompanied by Jas. P. Johnson's Harmony Eight

NYC, c. November, 1921

Smith, vocal; unknown cornet, trombone, clarinet; probably Walter Watkins, tenor sax; unknown violin, Johnson, piano; unknown banjo.

P-282-1-2 You Missed A Good Woman When You Picked All Over Me
78: BS 2044, Para 12162

P-283-2 Long Lost, Weary Blues
78: BS 2044, Para 12162

NOTE: No piano is audible on this session. Some copies of BR 2044 have matrix P-282 pressed on both sides.

Some sources have identified some Black Swan issues, labeled as "Johnson's All Star Orchestra" as James P. Johnson items. Titles are "Suez" and "Cock-a-Doddle Do," on Black Swan 2102; "All Muddled Up (Down in Maryland)" and "Apple Sauce" on Black Swan 2111, and "Baby Girl" and "New Moon" on Black Swan 10082. It is extremely doubtful that any of these are James P. Johnson items.

30. Lavinia Turner and Jas. P. Johnson's Harmony Seven (sic)

NYC, November, 1921

Turner, vocals; Johnson, piano; only, despite label.

69521-   Watch Me Go
                     78: PA 020705, Per 12005

69522-   You Never Miss A Good Thing Till It's
Gone
                     78: PA 020705, Per 12005

NOTE: Ms. Turner's first name given as Lavina
on the Pathe issue of 69522.

31.   James P. Johnson's Harmony Eight
                               NYC,   5   December
                               1921
Two   unknown   cornets;   unknown   trombone,
clarinet, alto sax; possibly Walter Watkins,
alto and tenor sax; Johnson, piano; unknown
banjo, drums.

S-70350-B   Dear Old Southland
                     78:   OK/Apex 4504, Starr Gennett
                     (C) 16006
                     LP: Arcadia 2009

S-70351-C   Bandana Days (introducing Love Will
Find a Way)
                     78:   OK/Apex 4504, Starr Gennett
                     (C) 16006
                     LP: Arcadia 2009

NOTE: No piano is audible on this session.
32.   James P. Johnson, piano roll
                               NYC,   December,
                               1921
              I Ain't Givin' Nothin' Away
                 Piano Roll: QRS 1724
                 LP: RCA Victor LPM 2058

33. James P. Johnson, piano roll
                                NYC,   December,
                                1921
        Baltimore Buzz
                Piano Roll: QRS 1738
                LP: Riv RLP 1046, RLP (12) 151,
        Lon (E) AL 3540

34. James P. Johnson, piano solo
                                NYC,   23   January
                                1922
        Four A.M. Shout
                78: Victor Test (Unissued)

35. James P. Johnson, piano rolls
                                NYC,   February,
                                1922
        The Down Home Blues
                Piano Roll: QRS 1797
                LP: Riv RLP 12-105, Oly OL 7132,
                Sounds LP 1204, Emb (E) CJS 853,
                Joker (I) SM 3108, KoJ (I) KLJ
                20008

        I've Got My Habits On
                Piano Roll: QRS 1804
                LP: Riv RLP 1011, RLP (12) 151,
                Sounds LP 1204, Lon (E/Au) AL
                3511, KoJ (I) KLJ 20008
                RT: Riv RT 5-2

NOTE: "I've Got My Habits On" as "Got My Habits
On" on KoJ and Sounds.

36. James P. Johnson, piano rolls.
                                NYC, March, 1922

Joe Turner Blues
        Piano Roll: QRS 1830
        LP: Sounds LP 1204, KoJ (I) KLJ
        20008

Look What A Fool I've Been
        Piano Roll: QRS 1831
        LP: Riv RLP 12-105, Oly OL 7132,
        Emb (E) CJS 853, Joker (I) SM
        3108

Nervous Blues
        Piano Roll: QRS 1833, QRS Q-128

Ole Miss Blues
        Piano Roll: QRS 1834, QRS Q-132
        LP: Riv RLP 12-105, Oly OL 7132,
        Emb (E) CJS 853, Joker (I) SM
        3108

Vampin' Liza Jane
        Piano roll: QRS 1836
        LP: Riv RLP 1011, RLP (12) 151,
        Sounds LP 1204, Lon (E/Au) AL
        3511
        RT: Riv RT 5-2

37.   James P. Johnson, Piano Roll
                          NYC, April, 1922

Muscle Shoals Blues
        Piano Roll: QRS 1888
        LP: Riv RLP 12-105, Oly OL 7132,
        Emb (E) CJS 853, Joker (I) SM
        3108

38.   James P. Johnson, Piano Roll
                          NYC, June, 1922

      Harlem Strut
         Piano Roll: QRS 101014, QRS Q-130
         LP: Riv RLP 1011, RLP 12-115,
         SDP-11   (5-LP   set), Sounds LP
         1204, Lon (E/Au) AL 3511, KoJ (I)
         KLJ 20008, Ariston (I) 12020
         RT: Riv RT 5-2

39. James P. Johnson, Piano Roll
                       NYC, August, 1922
      Buzz Mirandy
         Piano Roll: QRS 1952

40. James P. Johnson, Piano Roll
                       NYC,   September,
                       1922
      Birmingham Blues
         Piano Roll: QRS 1994

41. James P. Johnson, Piano solos
                       NYC, 28 February,
                       1923
80877-2   Papa Blues
         Columbia unissued

80878-3   Railroad Blues
         Columbia Unissued

80879-3   Caprice Rag
         Columbia Unissued

80880-3   Glory Shout
         Columbia Unissued

42. James P. Johnson, Piano Rolls
                    NYC, May, 1923

Don't Mess With Me
Piano Roll: QRS 2202, Q-135
LP: Sounds LP 1204, KoJ (I) KLJ
20008

Farewell Blues
Piano Roll: QRS 2244, Q-134

43.   James P. Johnson, Piano solos
                                   NYC, 28 June 1923
81099-2   Weeping Blues
               78: Col A-3950
               LP: Col CL 1780, CBS (Eu) BPG
               62090, Philips (E) BBL 7511, (E)
               R47121L, I Grande del Jazz (I)
               85, CBS (F) 85387
               CT: CBS (F) 40-85387

81100-2   Worried and Lonesome Blues
               78: Col A-3950
               LP: Col CL 1780, CBS (Eu) BPG
               62090, I Grande del Jazz (I) 85,
               CBS (F) 85387
               CT: CBS (F) 40-85387

NOTE: Three takes of each title were recorded.
Columbia files show the first title as "Weeping
Blues (An Improvisation)."

44.   James P. Johnson, Piano solos
                                   Camden,   N.J.,   17
                                   July 1923
B-28196-3   You Can't Do What My Last Man Did
                 Vic rejected

B-28197-3   Bleeding Hearted Blues
                 Vic rejected

45. James P. Johnson, Piano solos
                              Camden,   N.J.,   25
                              July 1923
B-28196-4   You Can't Do What My Last Man Did
                   78: Vic 19123
                   45: HMV (E) 7EG 8164
                   LP: Folkways FJ 67, FJ 2807, RCA
                   (F) 741.118/119

B-28197-6   Bleeding Hearted Blues
                   78: Vic 19123
                   45: HMV (E) 7EG 8164, Vic WEJ-7
                   LP: Vic   LEJ-7,   Murray Hill
                   927942, RCA (F) 741.118/119

NOTE: Vic LEJ-7 liner notes list "Thou Swell"
by Louisiana Sugar Babes as included on the LP.
Some copies, however, play Johnson's "Bleeding
Hearted Blues" instead. The label indicates the
correct title, but gives Louisiana Sugar Babes
as the artist credit.

46. James P. Johnson, Piano Roll
                              NYC, August, 1923
          Railroad Man
                   Piano Roll: QRS 2302
                   LP: Riv RLP 1046, RLP (12) 151,
                   Bio BLP 1001Q, Lon (E) AL 3540

47. James P. Johnson, Piano solos
                              NYC, 8 August 1923
S-71741-A   Scouting Around
                   78: OK 4937
                   LP: Herwin 402, CBS (F) 85387
                   CT: CBS (F) 40-85387

S-71742-A   Toddlin'

354 James P. Johnson

           78: OK 4937
           LP: CBS (F) 85387
           CT: CBS (F) 40-85387

48. James P. Johnson, Piano Roll
                      NYC,   November,
                      1923
        Black Man (Be On Your Way)
           Piano Roll: QRS 2351
           LP: Sounds LP 1204, JPi (D) JP
           5002

49. James P. Johnson, Piano Rolls
                      NYC, March, 1924
        "Runnin' Wild" Medley
        a. Charleston
        b. Old Fashioned Love
        c. Open Your Heart
        d. Love Bug
           Piano Roll: QRS 101027
           LP: Riv RLP 1070, RLP 12-105,
           Oly OL 7132, Lnd (E) AL 3553, Emb
           (E) CJS 853, Joker (I) SM 3108

50. James P. Johnson, Piano Roll
                      NYC, June, 1925
        Charleston
           Piano Roll: QRS 3143, QRS Q-133
           78: Century 4023, JSo (F) AA
           610, Sto (D) KB-102
           LP: Riv RLP 1011, RLP (12) 151,
           Lon (E/Au) AL 3511, KoJ (I) KLJ
           20008, Sounds 1204, Monkey (F) MY
           40023
           RT: Riv RT 5-2

51. Perry Bradford's Jazz Phools
                              NYC,   7   October
                              1925
Possible personnel: Louis Armstrong, cornet;
Charlie   Green,   trombone,   Buster   Bailey,
clarinet; Don Redman, alto sax; Johnson, piano;
Sam   Speede or Charlie Dixon, banjo; Kaiser
Marshall, drums

E-1434/6 Lucy Long
              Voc rejected

E-1437/9 I Ain't Gonna Play No Second Fiddle
              Voc rejected

52. Perry Bradford's Jazz Phools
                              NYC,   2 November
                              1925
Louis   Armstrong, cornet; possibly Charlie Green,
trombone; Buster Bailey, clarinet.; Don Redman,
alto sax; Johnson, piano; Sam Speede or Charlie
Dixon, banjo; Kaiser Marshall, drums; Bradford,
vocal; unknown second vocal on Lucy Long.

E-1580w   Lucy Long
              78:   Voc 15165, HJCA 604, Voc (E)
              V 1030, JD (F) JD 011
              45: Crl (G) 94201 EPC
              LP: Dec DL 9233, DL 79233, MCA
              (F) 510010; Crl (G) COPS 2879, Br
              (Du) 373 271 BOY; MCA (J) MCX 5,
              Swaggie (Au) JCS 33740, Dec (Ur)
              MCA 85044, Smith 15790

E-1583   I Ain't Gonna Play No Second Fiddle
              78:   Voc 15165, HJCA 604, Voc (E)
              V 1030, JD (F) JD 011
              45: Crl (G) 94201 EPC
              LP: Decca DL 9233, DL 79233, C-A

PB 101, MCA (F) 510010, Crl (G)
COPS 2879, Br (Du) 373 271 BOY;
MCA (J) MCX 5, Swaggie (Au) JCS
33740, Dec (Ur) MCA 85044, NWR NW
269, Smith 15790, Folkways FJ
2863

NOTE: HJCA 604, a 12-inch disc, is labeled
"Louis Armstrong with Perry Bradford's Jazz
Phools."

New Hot Discography, by Charles Delaunay, lists
two sessions as by "Jimmy Johnson's Rebels," c.
mid-1926. Titles are "Horses" and "Poor Papa,"
issued on Paramount 20449, and "Show That Fellow
the Door," and "What a Man," issued on Paramount
20452 and Puritan 11452. These are almost
certainly not genuine James P. Johnson items.

53. James P. Johnson, Piano Roll
                              NYC, July 1926
        Harlem Choc'late Babies On Parade
            Piano Roll: QRS 3526
            LP: Riv RLP 1011, RLP 12-105,
            Oly OL 7132, Lon (E/Au) AL 3511,
            Emb (E) CJS 853, Joker (I) SM
            3108, Vogue (F) DP.36
            RT: Riv RT 5-2

54. James P. Johnson, Piano Roll
                              NYC,   September,
                              1926
        Make Me a Pallet On The Floor
            Piano Roll: QRS 3626, Jazz
            Classics 1006
            78: Century 4001, JC (E) L-60,
            AFC (F) A 021

                   LP: Riv RLP 1011, RLP (12) 151,
                   Lon (E/Au) AL 3511
                   RT: Riv RT 5-2

55. James P. Johnson, Piano Roll
                           NYC,   October,
                           1926
            He's My Man Blues
            Piano Roll: QRS 3676

56. Sadie Jackson
                           NYC,   29   October
                           1926
Sadie Jackson, vocal, accompanied by James P.
Johnson, piano

W-142889-3   Original Black Bottom Dance
              78: Col rejected

W-142890-3 Nobody Worries 'Bout Me
              78: Col rejected

57. James P. Johnson, Piano Roll
                           NYC,   November,
                           1926
          Sugar (That Sugar Baby o' Mine)
            Piano Roll: QRS 3705
            LP: Riv RLP 12-105, Oly OL 7132,
            Emb (E) CJS 853, Joker (I) SM
            3108, Vogue (F) DP 64, Vogue (F)
            400064

58. Sadie Jackson
                           NYC,   20 November
                           1926
Sadie Jackson, vocal, accompanied by James P.

Johnson, piano.

W-142889-6   Original Black Bottom Dance
                   78: Col 14181-D

W-142890-5   Nobody Worries 'Bout Me
                   78: Col 14181-D

NOTE: Three   takes   of each title were recorded
at this remake session. Columbia files indicate
a total of 8,725 labels for Col 14181-D were
printed.

59. James P. Johnson, Piano Roll
                              NYC,   February,
                              1927
            Black Bottom Dance
                 Piano Roll: QRS 3792
                 LP: Sounds LP 1202, Sandy Hook
            SH 2069, Swaggie (Au) 825

60.   James P. Johnson - Fats Waller, piano roll
duet
                              NYC,   February,
                              1927
            Cryin' For My Used To Be
                 Piano Roll: QRS 3800

61. Perry Bradford and His Gang
                              NYC,   16 February
                              1927

Jimmy   Wade,   cornet;   Bill Dover, trombone;
unknown clarinet and alto sax; Johnson, piano;
Stanley   Wilson, banjo; Walter Wright, brass
bass; possibly Ed Jackson, drums;   Bradford,
vocal.

W-80429-C   All That I Had Is Gone
                78: OK 8450, Od (G) A-189104

W-80430-B   Lucy Long
                78: OK 8450, Od (G) A-189104

62. Bessie Smith   Piano accomp. by Jimmy
Johnson
                          NYC,   17 February
                          1927
Smith, vocal, Johnson, piano.

W-143490-2   Preachin' The Blues
                78:    Col 14195-D, 35842, Parl (E)
                R-2483, Parl (Swe) B-71094
                45: Col G 4-8
                LP: Col GL 506, ML 4810, CL 858,
                KG 31093, Ph (Eu) 807005L, Ph (E)
                BBL 7049, CBS (Eu) BPG 62380,
                67232, Cor (Au) KLP 617, Jolly
                Roger   5003,   Time-Life STL-J18,
                (Au) STL-J18
                CT: Time-Life 4TL-J18
                8T: Time-Life 8TL-J18
W-143491-1   Back-Water Blues
                78:    Col 14195-D, 3176-D, HJCA HC
                105,   Parl (E) R-2481, Parl (Swi)
                PZ-11174, Parl (Au) A-7588
                45: Col G 4-8
                LP: Col GL 506, ML 4810, CL 858,
                KG 31093, Ph (Eu) 807005L, Ph (E)
                BBL 7049, CBS (Eu) BPG 62380,
                67232, Cor (Au) KLP 617, Parl (I)
                B71227,   Jolly   Roger   5002,
                Time-Life STL-J18, (Au) STL-J18,
                Franklin Mint Jazz 55

                    CT: Time-Life 4TL-J18
                    8T: Time-Life 8TL-J18

NOTE: Col 3176-D was issued in a special
unnumbered album entitled "Bessie Smith Album."
Three takes of each title were recorded at this
session.   Columbia files indicate a total of
19,325 copies of labels for Col 14195-D were
printed.

63. James P. Johnson, piano solos
                              NYC,   25 February
                              1927

W-143531-3   All That I Had Is Gone
             Col rejected

W-143532-3   Snowy Morning Blues
             Col rejected

64.   James P. Johnson - Fats Waller, piano roll
duet
                         NYC, March, 1927
             If I Could Be With You
             Piano Roll: QRS 3818, Q-152
             LP: Bio BLP 1005-Q, Sounds LP
             1202, Monkey (F) MY 40023, MY
             40018,   Sandy   Hook   SH   2069,
             Musical Heritage Society 4937Y,
             Swaggie (Au) 825

NOTE: The roll is played on a Compton Theater
Organ on the Musical Heritage Society release.

65. Jimmy Johnson, piano solos
                         NYC, 7 March 1927
W-143531-5   All That I Had Is Gone

                    78: Col 14204-D
                    LP: Col CL 1780, CBS (Eu) BPG
                    62090,   Time-Life   STL-J18,
                    Time-Life (Au) STL-J18, I Grande
                    del Jazz (I) 85, CBS (F) 85387
                    CT: Time-Life 4TL-J18, CBS (F)
                    40-85387
                    8T: Time-Life 8TL-J18

W-143532-6   Snowy Morning Blues
                    78: Col 14204-D
                    LP: Col CL 1780, CBS (Eu) BPG
                    62090,   Time-Life   STL-J18,
                    Time-Life (Au) STL-J18, I Grande
                    del Jazz (I) 85, CBS (F) 85387
                    CT: Time-Life 4TL-J18, CBS (F)
                    40-85387
                    8T: Time-Life 8TL-J18

NOTE: Four takes of the first title and three
takes of the second were recorded at this remake
session.   Columbia files indicate a total of
8,075 labels of Col 14204-D were printed.

A Laura Smith unissued OK session has been
listed as possibly including James P. Johnson,
due to an article in the Chicago Defender of
April 16, 1927, which reported the session had
been recorded a few weeks earlier with Smith,
Shakey,   Todd   and   Holland,   accompanied by
Johnson.   The article may refer to the unissued
session of March 9, 1927, at which "Home"
(matrix 80510-B) and "If Anybody Here Wants A
Real Kind Mama" (matrix 80511-B) were cut. No
tests have been available from this session.

66. Original Jazz Hounds

                                    NYC 15 March 1927
Louis Metcalf, cornet; Jake Frazier, trombone;
Bob Fuller, clarinet; James P. Johnson, piano;
unknown banjo; possibly Harry Hull, brass bass;
unknown drums and chimes; Perry Bradford,
vocal.

W-143657-2   All That I Had Is Gone (P.B.,
vocal)
                    78:   Col 14207-D
                    LP: VJM (E) VLP 45

W-143658-3   Lucy Long (P.B., vocal)
                    78:   Col 14207-D
                    LP: VJM (E) VLP 45, Time-Life
              STL-J18, Time-Life (Au) STL-J18
                    CT: Time-Life 4TL-J18
                    8T: Time-Life 8TL-J18

NOTE: Three takes of each title were recorded.
Band name originally entered in the Columbia
files was "Perry Bradford & His Band." A total
of 9,150 labels of Col 14207-D were printed.

67. Bessie Smith   Piano accomp. by Jimmy
Johnson
                             NYC, 1 April 1927
Smith, vocal, Johnson, piano

W-143735-3   Sweet Mistreater
                    78:   Col 14260-D
                    LP: Col G 30818, CBS (Eu) 66264

W-143736-3   Lock and Key
                    78:   Col 14232-D
                    LP: Col G 30818, CBS (Eu) 66264,
              Time-Life STL-J28, Prestige P
              24113, ABC (Au) L 38266, BBC (E)
              REB 590

```
          CT:   Time-Life  4TL-J28, ABC (Au)
          C 38266, BBC (E) ZCF 590
          8T:   Time-Life 8TL-J28
          CD:   BBC (E) CD 590
```

NOTE: Johnson receives label credit on Col
14232-D as shown above, but not on Col 14260-D.
Three takes of each title were recorded. A
total of 13,075 labels of Col 14232-D and
15,650 of Col 14260-D were printed.

Discographies list an intriguing item under the
name of Sara Lawrence (Oriole 894.)   Titles
listed are "Don't Love Me" and "If You Don't
Like My Potatoes," and the accompaniment given
as by ?Tommy Ladnier, cornet, and James P.
Johnson, piano.   Researcher Carl Kendziora
recently turned up a copy of Oriole 894 by Sara
Lawrence, with the titles "Don't You Leave Me
Here," control number 813-1, and "If You Don't
Like Potatoes," control number 814-2. The first
title features the same vocalist and
accompanists (although an alternate take) as
Plaza matrix number 7130 by Laura Smith and was
released under her name on Banner 1977, Domino
3948 and Regal 8304.   The second title
apparently was not released on the Plaza labels,
but sounds as though it was recorded at the same
session and with the same personnel as the first
title.   The pianist does not resemble James P.
Johnson, and is addressed by Ms. Smith as
"Mike."   The cornetist is addressed as "Tom,"
but Tom Morris is a more likely choice than
Ladnier.   Mike Jackson has been suggested as the
pianist.   Interestingly, Rust in Jazz Records
1897-1942 (revised edition, 1969, and fourth
edition) lists the first title also under Laura
Smith's name and gives the accompaniment as Tom
Morris, cornet, Lukie Johnson, piano. At any

rate Johnson is not present.

68. Evelyn Thompson
                              NYC,   c.   April,
                              1927

Thompson, vocal, possibly Joe Smith, cornet; Bob Fuller or Ernest Elliot, clarinet; possibly Johnson, piano.

E-4786   Looking for the Sunshine, Walking Around in the Rain
           78: Voc 15548

NOTE: Johnson's presence is very doubtful.

69. Evelyn Thompson
                              NYC, May, 1927

Thompson, vocal; possibly Joe Smith, cornet; Bob Fuller or Ernest Elliot, clarinet; possibly Johnson, piano.

E-4941   One Sweet Letter From You
           78: Voc 15548

NOTE: Johnson's presence is very doubtful.

70. Rosa Henderson, accompanied by James P. Johnson
                              NYC, mid May, 1927

Henderson, vocals; Johnson, piano.

107545   Black Snake Moan
           78:   PA 7529, Per 129

107546   Fortune Teller Blues
           78:   PA 7529, Per 129

        Gay Cattin' Daddy
            78:   PA 7534, Per 134

        I'm Saving It All For You
            78:   PA 7534, Per 134

NOTE: "Back Water Blues" was issued as a Piano Roll on Imperial 06522, and on Riverside RLP 1046, RLP (12) 151 and London (E) AL 3540 LPs as by James P. Johnson. This roll was arranged by J. Lawrence Cook, who probably also played it.

71. James P. Johnson, piano roll
                          NYC, August 1927
        Wasn't It Nice
           Piano Roll: QRS 3996

72. Johnson's Jazzers
                     NYC,   2 September 1927
Louis Metcalf, cornet, Johnson, piano; Perry Bradford, vocal

W-144621-2 Skiddle-De-Scow
              78: Col 14247-D
              LP: Arcadia 2009

W-144622-2 Can I Get It Now?

              78: Col 14247-D
              LP: Arcadia 2009

NOTE: Two takes of 144621 and three takes of 144622 were recorded. Columbia files confirm

personnel. A total of 7,200 labels were printed
of Col 14247-D.

73. James P. Johnson, piano solos
                              NYC,   3   February
                              1928
BVE-42409-1   Mournful Thoughts
                 78: Victor rejected

BVE-42410-1   Ebony Dreams
                 78: Victor rejected

74. Dunn's Original Jazz Hounds
                         NYC, 26 March 1928

Johnny   Dunn, cornet; possibly Herb Fleming,
trombone;   possibly Garvin Bushell, clarinet,
alto   sax;   unknown alto sax; Johnson, Fats
Waller, pianos; possibly John Mitchell, banjo.

E-7232/3   What's The Use Of Being Alone?
                 78: Voc 1176
                 LP: Arcadia   2009,   Time-Life
                 STL-J18, Time-Life (Au) STL-J18
                 CT: Time-Life 4TL-J18
                 8T: Time-Life 8TL-J18

E-7234/5   Original Bugle Blues
                 78: Voc 1176
                 LP: Arcadia 2009

75. Louisiana Sugar Babes
                         Camden,   N.J.,   27
                         March 1928
Jabbo   Smith,   cornet; Garvin Bushell, clarinet,
alto   sax   or bassoon; Johnson, piano; Fats
Waller, organ.   Bushell plays bassoon on 42567

and 42569 only.

BVE-42566-1   Willow Tree
                78: Vic 21348
                LP: RCA (F) 86.413, (F) 741.076,
                New World Records NW 256

BVE-42566-2   Willow Tree
                45: HMV (E) 7EG 8215
                LP: RCA (F) 741.076

BVE-42566-3   Willow Tree
                78: Vic test

BVE-42567-1   'Sippi
                78: Vic 21348
                LP: RCA (F) 86.413, (F) 741.076,
                Collectors (Swiss) 12-7

BVE-42567-2   'Sippi
                78: BB B-10260
                45: HMV (E) 7EG 8215
                LP: RCA (F) 741.076

BVE-42568-1   Thou Swell
                78: BB B-10260
                45: Vic WEJ-7, HMV (E) 7EG 8215
                LP: Vic   LEJ-7, Folkways FJ
                2823, RFB RF-3, Camden CAL 328,
                (E) CDN 118, (I) LCP 54, RCA (F)
                741.076

BVE-42568-2   Thou Swell
                78: Vic 21346
                LP: RCA (F) 86.413, (F) 741.076,
                Collectors (Swiss) 12-7

BVE-42569-1   Persian Rug
                78: Vic 21346, HMV (E) EA 397
                45: HMV (E) 7EG 8215

LP: RCA (F) 86.413, (F) 741.076

NOTE: A test of 42566-3 was offered in a Vintage Jazz Mart auction in 1983. It is not known if this is identical with the take issued as 42566-2 on microgrooves or an additional take. Although "Thou Swell" is listed on the liner and label for Vic LEJ-7 and WEJ-7, some of the pressings inspected play James P. Johnson's solo recording of "Bleeding Hearted Blues" from July 25, 1923 (see session 45).

76. Martha Copeland
                                  NYC, 8 June 1928
Copeland, vocal; Clarence Adams, clarinet; Johnson, piano

W-146417-1 Somethin' Goin' On Wrong
            78: Col 14352-D

NOTE: Two takes of this title were recorded.

77. Martha Copeland
                                  NYC, 9 June 1928
Copeland, vocal; Clarence Adams, clarinet; Johnson, piano and speech.

W-146420-3 Desert Blues
            78: Col 14352-D
            LP: CBS (Eu) 66232

NOTE: Three takes of this title were recorded. A total of 5,600 copies of the label for Col 14352-D were printed.

The Roy Evans session for Columbia of June 15, 1928, has been listed as a James P. Johnson session. Titles cut were "My Old Lady" and "The New St. Louis Blues." However, Roy Evans accompanied himself.

78. Jimmy Johnson and His Orchestra
                              NYC, 18 June 1928
Cootie Williams, Ward Pinkett, trumpets; unknown trombone; possibly Charlie Holmes, clarinet, soprano and alto sax; unknown clarinet and tenor sax; Johnson, Fats Waller, pianos; Joe Watts, string bass; Perry Bradford, speech.

W-146539-3   Chicago Blues (PB speech)
                78: Col 14334-D
                45: Pirate (Swe) MPC 514
                LP: Arcadia 2009,   Time-Life
                STL-J18, Time-Life (Au) STL-J18
                CT: Time-Life 4TL-J18
                8T: Time-Life 8TL-J18

W-146540-1   Mournful Tho'ts
                78: Col 14334-D
                45: Pirate (Swe) MPC 514
                LP: Arcadia 2009

NOTE: Three takes of each title were recorded. Col 14334-D was also issued on "Royal Blue" pressings. A total of 6,300 labels of Col 14334-D were printed.

A remake session for Columbia by Roy Evans of "The New St. Louis Blues" on July 20, 1928, was thought to have accompaniment by James P. Johnson. However, the accompaniment is by Evans himself.

79. Roy Evans
                              NYC, 20 June 1928

Evans, vocal; Garvin Bushell, clarinet; Johnson,
piano.

W-146558-1   How Long Is That Train Been Gone?
                78: Col 2257-D
                LP: Crispus-Attucks   PB   101,
                Folkways FJ 2863

Bushell switches to bassoon and alto sax.

W-146559-2   Georgia's Always On My Mind
                78: Col 1449-D
                LP: Folkways FJ 2842

NOTE: Three takes of the first title were
recorded. Columbia files list J. C. Johnson as
the pianist, but Perry Bradford used the first
title to illustrate James P. Johnson's style in
his narration on the Crispus-Attucks/Folkways
issues. The pianist sounds like James P.
Johnson.

80. Clarence Williams   Piano Accomp. By
Jimmy Johnson
                              NYC, 20 July 1928
Williams, vocal; Johnson, piano.

W-146761-3   My Woman Done Me Wrong (As Far As I
Am Concerned)
                78: Col 14341-D
                LP: Natchez (Arg) NLP 3002

W-146762-3   Farm Hand Papa
                78: Col 14341-D
                LP: Natchez (Arg) NLP 3002

NOTE: Three takes were recorded of each title.
A total of 6,300 labels were printed of Col
14341-D.

81.   Roy Evans
                                    NYC, 26 July 1928

Evans, vocals; Arthur Whetsol, cornet; Johnson,
piano.

W-146811-2 So Sorry
            78: Col 2257-D

W-146812-3 Syncopated Yodelin' Man
            78:    Col 1559-D, 14359-D, (E)
            01360, Reg (E) G-9271

NOTE: Three takes of each title were recorded.
A total of 8,025 labels were printed of Col
14359-D.

82.   Ethel Waters   Piano Accomp. by James P.
Johnson
                                    NYC,   21   August
                                    1928
Waters, vocal; Johnson, piano.

W-146871-1 Lonesome Swallow
            78: Col 14411-D
            LP: Col KG 31571

W-146872-2 Guess Who's In Town
            78: Col 14353-D
            LP: Col KG 31571, Time-Life
            STL-J18, Time-Life (Au) STL-J18,
            Franklin Mint Jazz 7
            CT: Time-Life 4TL-J18, Franklin
            Mint Jazz 7

8T: Time-Life 8TL-J18

W-146873-1   My Handy Man
             78: Col 14353-D, SE 1514-S
             LP: Col   KG 31571, Time-Life
             STL-J18, Time-Life (Au) STL-J18
             CT: Time-Life 4TL-J18
             8T: Time-Life 8TL-J18

W-146874-2   Do What You Did Last Night
             78: Col 14380-D, SE 1514-S
             LP: Col C3L 33 (CL 2161)

NOTE: Two takes were recorded of each title.
Total of 8,950 labels of Col 14411-D, 12,625 of
Col 14353-D, and 6,925 of Col 14380-D were
printed.   "Royal Blue" pressings exist of Col
14353-D and 14380-D.

A recording of "My Baby Sure Knows How to Love"
by   Ethel   Waters   has   been   listed   as   having
accompaniment by James P. Johnson.   The pianist
is not James P. Johnson; J.C. Johnson has been
suggested.

83.   Roy Evans, Piano accomp. by Jimmy Johnson
                              NYC,   4 September
                              1928

Evans, vocals; Johnson, piano.

W-146941-1   Take Your Tomorrow (And Give Me
Today)
             78: Col rejected

W-146942-2   Jazbo   (sic)   Dan and His Yodelin'
Band
             78:    Col 1559-D, 14359-D, (E)

01360, Reg (E) G-9271

NOTE: Three takes of both titles were recorded.
A total of 8,025 labels were printed of Col
14359-D.

84. The Gulf Coast Seven

Possibly   Louis   Metcalf,   cornet;   unknown
trombone;   possibly Emmett Matthews, soprano sax;
possibly   Barney Bigard,   tenor   sax;   possibly
Johnson, piano; drums; Perry Bradford, vocal.
                              NYC,   19   October
                              1928

W-147151-1 Daylight Savin' Blues
                    78: Col 14373-D
                    LP: Historical ASC 5829-6, VJM
                    (E) VLP 45

W-147152-1 Georgia's Always On My Mind (PB,
vocal)
                    78: Col 14373-D
                    LP: Historical ASC-5829-6; VJM
                    (E) VLP 45

NOTE: Three takes of each title were recorded.
A total of 5,175 labels were printed of Col
14373-D.

Although Annette Hanshaw herself reportedly
remembered that she was accompanied by James P.
Johnson on her Columbia session of October 19,
1928, the accompaniment sounds nothing like
Johnson. Titles are "If You Want The Rainbow,"
and "My Blackbirds Are Bluebirds Now."

85. James P. Johnson, piano solos
                                    NYC,   29   January
                                    1929
W-401565-B   Riffs
                78:   OK 8770, Parl (E) R-1072,
                Col (E) DB 3495; Od (G) A-286052,
                028598, Parl (Swe) B-71220
                45:   Fon   (E) TFE 17246, Philips
                (E) BBL 7511, (E) R 47121L, Col
                (E) SCM 5127
                LP: Epic LN 3295, Col KG 31564,
                CBS (Eu) 67273, Electrola (G) 1C
                054   0631M,   Time-Life STL-J18,
                Time-Life (Au) STL-J18, CBS (F)
                85387
                CT: Time-Life 4TL-J18, CBS (F)
                40-85387
                8T: Time-Life 8TL-J18

W-401566-A   Feelin' Blue
                78:   OK 8770, Col (E) DB 3495
                45:   Fon   (E) TFE 17246, Col (E)
                SCM 5127
                LP: Epic   LN   3295, CBS   (F)
                40-85387
                CT: CBS (F) 85387

NOTE: "Feelin' Blue" as "Feeling Blues" on Col
(E) DB 3495. Two takes of each title were
recorded.

86. Clarence Williams' Jazz Kings
                                    NYC,   5   February
                                    1929

Ed Allen, cornet; Albert Socarras, flute (on
matrix 147928 only), clarinet and alto; Arville
Harris, clarinet, tenor sax; Johnson, piano;
possibly Leroy Harris, banjo; Williams, vocal

and possibly additional piano on 147726-4

W-147726-4   If You Like Me Like   I Like You
(C.W., vocal)
                78: Col 1735-D
                LP: VJM   (E) VLP 37, Ariston (I)
                Ar/LP 12063; Natchez (Arg) 3001
                CT: Neovox (E) 764

W-147928-3   Have You Ever Felt That Way (C.W.,
vocal)
                78: Col 1735-D
                LP: VJM   (E) VLP 37, Ariston (I)
                AR/LP 12063; Natchez (Arg) 3001
                CT: Neovox (E) 787

NOTE: Some copies of Col 1735-D exist on "Royal
Blue" wax pressings.

87.   Jimmy Johnson and His Band
                        NYC, 5 March 1929
Louis Metcalf, cornet; unknown trombone; Ernest
Elliot, clarinet; unknown clarinet and tenor
sax; Johnson, piano; Perry Bradford, Gus
Horsley, vocals.

W-148015-1   Put Your Mind Right On It (P.B.,
G.H. vocal)
                78: Col 14417-D
                LP   Arcadia 2009

W-148016-3 Sorry (Horsley, vocal only)
                78: Col rejected

NOTE: Someone hits a cymbal at the end of
148015-1 but there is no evidence elsewhere of a
drummer. It has been suggested that Bradford
hit the cymbal. Three takes of each title were
recorded.   Col 14417-D was also issued on a

"Royal Blue" pressing. A total of 5,875 labels
were printed of Col 14417-D.

88. Jimmy Johnson and His Band
                          NYC 20 March 1929
Louis Metcalf, cornet; probably Geechie Fields,
trombone;   Ernest   Elliot, clarinet; Johnson,
piano; Perry Bradford, vocal

W-148108-3 Fare Thee Honey Blues
                78: Col 14417-D
                LP: Arcadia   2009,   Time-Life
                STL-J18, Time-Life (Au) STL-J18
                CT: Time-Life 4TL-J18
                8T: Time-Life 8TL-J18

NOTE: Three takes of this title were recorded.
Col 14417-D was also issued on a "Royal Blue"
pressing.   A total of 5,875 labels were printed
for Col 14417-D.

Some discographies have listed James P. Johnson
as being the pianist on Gladys Bentley's Okeh
session of March 26, 1929, but the pianist does
not   sound like Johnson.   It has also been
suggested the piano might be played by Bentley
herself or by J.C. Johnson.   Titles recorded
were "Big Gorilla Man" and "Red Beans and Rice."

89. "St. Louis Blues" film soundtrack
                          Astoria,   Long
                          Island, New York,
                          late June 1929

Bessie Smith, vocal, the Hall Johnson Chior (40
mixed voices) and James P. Johnson's Orchestra:

Joe Smith, Sidney DeParis, trumpets; unknown
trombone; unknown clarinet; unknown tenor sax;
Johnson, piano; possibly Charlie Dixon, banjo;
possibly Harry Hull, brass bass; Kaiser
Marshall, drums.

Band introduction
LP: Empress (G) 10006, JLC (I)
BLJ 8025, Sto (D) SLP 702, Sandy
Hook S.H. 2068

(NY-39) St. Louis Blues, part 1
78: Circle J-1016
LP: Empress (G) 10006, JLC (I)
BLJ 8025, Sto (Dan) SLP 702, Bio
BLP M-3, Sandy Hook S.H. 2068

(NY-40) St. Louis Blues, part 2
78: Circle J-1016
LP: Riv RLP 1032, RLP 12-113,
RLP 12-121, SDP-11 (5-LP set),
Bio BLP M-3, London (E) AL 3530,
Empress (G) 10006, JLC (I), BLJ
8001, BLJ 8025; Joker (I) SM
3098, Sto (D) SLP 702, Sandy
Hook S.H. 2068

(NY-41) St. Louis Blues, part 3
78: Circle J-1017
LP: Empress (G) 10006, JLC (I)
BLJ 8025, Sto (D) SLP 702, Bio
BLP M-3, Sandy Hook S.H. 2068

(NY-42) St. Louis Blues, part 4
78: Circle J-1017
LP: Empress (G) 10006, JLC (I)
BLJ 8025, Sto (Dan) SLP 702, Bio
BLP M-3, Sandy Hook S.H. 2068

NOTE: The matrix numbers, shown as they appear

on the Circle 78 rpm issues, are control numbers
only. Bio BLP M-3 contains all four parts of
the original Circle issues. Only part 2
appeared on Riverside and London issues. The
entire soundtrack was issued on Empress,
Storyville, Sandy Hook and JLC 8025. Circle
J-1016 and J-1017 were issued in album S-16.
The film, directed by Dudley Murphy, briefly
shows James P. Johnson on screen as the pianist.
A brief excerpt from the film, as it was used on
the CBS televisin program, "Chicago and All That
Jazz," was issued on the soundtrack LP, Sounds
Great SG-8007.

90. Bessie Smith   Piano accomp. by James P.
Johnson
                              NYC,   20 August
                              1929

Smith, vocal, Johnson, piano.

W-148901-3 My Sportin' Man
              78: Col rejected

W-148902-2 He's Got Me Goin'
              78: Col 14464-D
              45: Ph (E) bbe 12231, (Du) 429
              224BE, Col G 4-8
              LP: Col ML 4810, GL 506, CL 858,
              G 30126, Ph (Eu) B 07005L, Ph (E)
              BBL 7049, CBS (Eu) BPG 62380,
              66262, Cor (Au) KLP 617, Swaggie
              (Au) S 1264

W-148903-2 When My Baby Comes
              78: Col rejected

W-148904-1 It Makes My Love Come Down
              78: Col 14464-D, Bm 1038

                    LP: Swaggie   (Au)   33767, Col G
                    30126,   CBS   (Eu)   66262, CC1 (D)
                    CC 31

NOTE: Swaggie (Au) 33767 is a 7-inch 33 1/3 rpm
disc.   Two takes of 148903 were recorded. Three
takes were recorded of the other titles. A
total of 7,375 labels of Col 14464-D were
printed.

91. Clara Smith
                              NYC,   4 September
                              1929

Smith, vocal, Ed Allen, cornet; possibly Benny
Morton, trombone; possibly Johnson, piano.

W-148970-2 Papa I Don't Need You Now
                78: Col 14462-D
                LP: Rosetta RR 1306

W-148971-2 Tired Of The Way You Do
                78: Col 14462-D

W-148972-3 Breath and Breeches
                78: Col rejected

NOTE: Three takes were recorded of each title.
A total of 5,635 labels were printed of Col
14462-D.

92. Clara Smith   Piano accomp. by James P.
Johnson
                              NYC, 12 September
                              1929
Smith, vocal; Johnson, piano.

W-148994-2   Oh, Mr. Mitchell
                78: Col 14536-D
                LP: Col C3L 33 (CL 2161)

W-148995-3   Where Is My Man?
                78: Col 14536-D

NOTE: Three takes were recorded of each title.
Columbia files show the first title as "Oh! Mr.
Mitchell (I'm Crazy 'Bout Sweet Poontang)." A
total of 1,355 labels were printed of Col
14536-D.

93. Bessie Smith   James P. Johnson at the
Piano.
                              NYC,   1 October
                              1929
Smith, vocal; Johnson, piano.

W-149074-3   Wasted Life Blues
                78: Col 14476-D, Bm 1038
                LP: Swaggie (Au) JCS 33767, Col
                G 30126, CBS (Eu) 66262, CCl (D)
                CC 31

W-149075-1   Dirty No-Gooder's Blues
                78: Col 14476-D
                LP: Col G 30126, CBS (Eu) 66262,
                CCl (D) CC 31, Time-Life STL-J28
                CT: Time-Life 4TL-J28
                8T: Time-Life 8TL-J28

NOTE: Three takes were recorded of each title.
A total of 7,595 labels were printed of Col
14476-D, which also was issued on "Royal Blue"
pressings.

94. Bessie Smith   Accomp. by Jimmy Johnson

                                    NYC,   11   October
                                    1929
Smith, vocal; Johnson, piano.

W-149134-3   Blue Spirit Blues
                    78:   Col 14527-D, Bm 1039
                    45:     Ph   (E)   BBE   12233,   (Du)
                    429120BE, Col G 4-8
                    LP: Col ML 4810, GL 506, CL 858,
                    G 30126, Ph (Eu) B 07005L, Ph (E)
                    BBL 7049, CBS (Eu) BPG 62380,
                    66262, Cor (Au) KLP 617, Swaggie
                    (Au) S 1264, Franklin Mint Jazz
                    55

W-149135-3   Worn Out Papa Blues
                    78:   Col 14527-D, Bm 1041
                    LP: Col G 30126, CBS (Eu) 66262,
                    CCl (D)   CC 31

W-149136-2   You Don't Understand
                    78:   Col 14487-D
                    45:   Pirate (Swe) MPC 503
                    LP: Col G 30126, CBS (Eu) 66262,
                    CCl   (D)   CC 31,   Time-Life
                    STL-J28, (Au) STL-J28
                    CT: Time-Life 4TL-J28
                    8T: Time-Life 8TL-J28

W-149137-2   Don't Cry Baby
                    78:   Col 14487-D
                    45:   Pirate (Swe) MPC 503
                    LP: Col G 30126, CBS (Eu) 66282,
                    CCl (D)   CC 31

NOTE: Three takes were recorded of each title.
Totals   of 6,275 labels for Col 14487-D and 2,995
labels   for   Col   14527   were printed. Col 14527
was   also   issued   on   "Royal Blue" pressings.
Labels   for   Col   14487-D state: James P. Johnson

at the Piano," while the labels for Col 14427-D
list the credit as above.

James P. Johnson has been listed as the pianist
on the McKinney's Cotton Pickers sessions of
November 5, 6 and 7, 1929. The pianist was
Leroy Tibbs on the November 5 session and Fats
Waller on the other sessions.

95. King Oliver and His Orchestra
                              NYC,   6 November
                         1929
Oliver, Dave Nelson, trumpets; unknown trombone;
possibly Glyn Pacque, clarinet, alto sax; Hilton
Jefferson, alto sax; possibly Charles Frazier,
tenor sax; Johnson, piano; Arthur Taylor, banjo;
Clinton Walker, brass bass, Edmund Jones, drums.
Loren L. Watson, director.

BVE-57527-1   I'm Lonesome Sweetheart (Dave
Nelson, vocal)
                78: Vic 23029
                45: Pirate (Swe) MPC 512
                LP: RCA LPV 529, RCA (F)
                430.709, 741.055, PM 42.411, RCA
                (G) LPM 10017

BVE-57528-1   I Want You Just Myself
                78:   Vic V-38101, Vic (Arg)
                V-38101, HMV (VDP) (I) R-14433
                LP: HMV (E) DLP 1096, RCA (F)
                130.276,   430.592,   730.557,   PM
                42.411, Fam (I) SFR-DP 657,
                Camden (Arg) CAL 2957

BVE-57529-1   I Can't Stop Loving You
                78: Vic 23029, HMV (E) B-4844
                LP: HMV (E) DLP 1096, RCA (F)

430.709, 741.055, PM 42.411, RCA
(G) LPM 10017, Fam (I) SFR-DP
657, Camden (Arg) CAL 2957

96. Jimmy Johnson and His Orchestra
                          NYC,   18 November
                          1929
King Oliver, Dave Nelson, trumpets; Jimmy
Archey, trombone, two unknown clarinet and alto
sax, Charles Frazier, tenor sax; Johnson, Fats
Waller, pianos; Teddy Bunn or Bernard Addison,
banjo, guitar; Harry Hull, string bass; unknown
drums, "Keep Shufflin' Trio," vocal.

BVE-57701-2   You Don't Understand
              78:   Vic   V-38099,   Vic (Arg)
              V-38099, HMV (VDP) (I) R-14398
              45: HMV (E) 7EG 8164
              LP: RCA (F) 741.094, Jass (Du)
              603

BVE-57702-2   You've Got To Be Modernistic
              78:   Vic   V-38099,   Vic (Arg)
              V-38099, HMV (VDP) (I) R-14398
              45: HMV (E) 7EG 8164
              LP: RCA (F) 741.094, PM 43259,
              Jass (Du) 603

NOTE: "The Keep Shufflin' Trio" might include
Fats Waller, James P. Johnson and Teddy Bunn.
Jass (Du) 603 is a 7-inch disc.

97. Clarence Williams' Washboard Band
                          NYC,   19 November
                          1929
Charlie Gaines, trumpet; unknown clarinet and
alto sax; Johnson, piano and celeste; Williams,
piano, vocal; Floyd Casey, washboard.

W-403280-C You Don't Understand
                78: OK 8752, Parl (E) R-2243
                LP: Swaggie (Au) S 1282, Natchez
                (Arg) NLP 3002

W-403281-A (Oh Baby) What Makes Me Love You So?
                78: OK 8752, Parl (E) R-2147
                45:   Parl (E) GEP 8733, Odeon (G)
                41287
                LP: CC1 (D) CC 44, Swaggie (Au)
                S 1282

NOTE: Williams plays piano until just before
the vocal on each side at which point James P.
Johnson takes over. Williams also plays piano
behind the celeste on "You Don't Understand."
Three takes were recorded of each title.

98. Clarence Williams and His Jazz Kings
                          NYC,   3   December
                          1929
Leonard Davis, unknown, trumpet; possibly
Geechie Fields, trombone; possibly Don Redman,
clarinet, alto sax; Arville Harris, clarinet,
tenor sax; possibly Johnson, piano; Leroy
Harris, banjo; possibly Richard Fullbright,
string bass; Eva Taylor, vocal, Williams,
director.

W-149665-4 Zonky
                78: Col 14488-D, OK 8918
                LP: VJM (E) VLP 47, OFC (Arg)
                OFC 43

W-149666-3 You've Got To Be Modernistic
                78: Col 14488-D, OK 41561
                LP: VJM (E) VLP 47, OFC (Arg)
                OFC 43

NOTE: OK 8918 (mx. 405107-A), and OK 41561 (mx. 405184-A) as by the Shreveport Sizzlers. Three takes were recorded of each title. A total of 4,825 labels were printed of Col 14488-D, which was also released on "Royal Blue" pressings.

On December 4, 1929, Annette Hanshaw recorded "I'm A Dreamer - Aren't We All" (matrix 149676-2) and "If I Had A Talking Picture Of You" (matrix 149677-4) for Harmony. Miss Hanshaw recalled James P. Johnson as being on the date but the pianist does not sound like Johnson.

99. Eva Taylor

NYC,   16 December 1929

Taylor, vocal, Ed Anderson, cornet; Clarence Williams and Johnson, pianos.

BVE-57782-2   What Makes Me Love You So?
                78: Vic V-38575
                LP: RCA (F) 741.058

BVE-57783-1   You Don't Understand
                78: Vic V-38575
                LP: RCA (F) 741.058

100. Great Day New Orleans Singers

NYC,   19 December 1929

Unknown vocal group; Johnson, piano.

W-403533-B   You've Got To Be Modernistic
                78: OK 8755

W-403534-B Shout On
            78: OK 8755

NOTE: OK   8755   labeled: Directors: Jimmy
Johnson   and   Clarence   Williams.   Johnson   only
plays   piano.   Williams   can   be heard as one of
the   singers.   The   vocal   group   may have had a
connection with the revue "Messin' Around."

101. Lonnie Johnson and Spencer Williams
                              NYC,   8   January
                          1930
Vocal   duet   by   Lonnie   Johnson   and   Williams,
Lonnie Johnson, guitar; Johnson, piano.

W-403596-C Once Or Twice
            78: OK 8812

Lonnie   Johnson,   vocal;   Spencer   Williams   and
Clarence   Williams,   vocal duet; James P. Johnson,
piano; Spencer Williams, scraper.

W-403597-B Monkey and The Baboon
            78:     OK 8762, Voc 03013, Col
            30058, 37681
            LP: Queen Disc (I) Q-043

Lonnie   Johnson   and   Clarence   Williams,   vocal
duet,   James   P.   Johnson,   piano;   Lonnie Johnson,
guitar;   Spencer   Williams,   scraper;   Clarence
Williams, woodblocks.

W-403598-B Wipe It Off
            78:     OK 8762, Voc 03013, Col
            30058, 37681.
            LP: Queen Disc (I)Q-043

NOTE: Mx.   403598   issued on Columbia   and Okeh

as by Lonnie Johnson and Clarence Williams.
Three takes were recorded of W-403596 and two
takes were recorded of the other titles.

102. Clarence Williams Orchestra
                         NYC,   15 January
                         1930
Possibly Charlie Gaines   trumpet;   unknown
trombone; possibly Ben Whittet, alto sax;
Arville Harris, clarinet and tenor sax; possibly
Johnson, piano; Cyrus St. Clair, brass bass;
Floyd Casey, cymbals.

W-403630-B Left All Alone With The Blues
            78: OK 8763, Col (E) DB-3513
            LP: Ari (I) AR/LP 12063, Natchez
            (Arg)   NLP   3001, Swaggie (Au)
            S-1282

W-403631-A I've Found A New Baby
            78: OK 8763, Parl (E) R-2225
            LP: Parl (E) PMC 1166, Col (I)
            CO62-041447,   Od   (G)   83248,
            Swaggie (Au) S 1282, S 1301

NOTE: Three takes were recorded of each title.

103. James P. Johnson, piano solos
                         NYC,   21 January
                         1930

E-31956 Crying For the Carolines
            78: Br 4712, Br (G) A-8663
            LP: MCA (F) 510.109, MCA 1332
            CT: MCA 1332

E-31957 What Is This Thing Called Love?

78:    Br 4712, Br (G) A-8663, JU
11
LP: NWR NW 274, MCA (F) 510.109,
MCA   1332,   Time-Life   STL-J18,
Time-Life (Au) STL J-18
CT: Time-Life 4TL-J18, MCA 1332
8T: Time-Life 8TL-J18

E-31958   You've Got To Be Modernistic
78:      Br   4762, 80032, Br (F)
500203, Br (G) A-8718
45: Br 9-80032
LP: Br BL 58022, BL 54015, Dec
DL 8398, Folkways RBF RF 33, MCA
2-4061, MCA 1332, Vogue/Coral (E)
LRA   10022,   MCA   (F) 510.109,
Time-Life STL-J18, Time-Life (Au)
STL-J18,   Festival (Au) CFR 10
440, (Au) F AL 1, Franklin Mint
Jazz 77
CT: Time-Life 4TL-J18, MCA 1332
8T: Time-Life 8TL-J18

E-31359   Jingles
78:      Br   4762, 80032, Br (F)
500203, Br (G) A-8718
45: Br 9-80032
LP: Br BL 58022, Br 54015, Her
405, Vogue/Coral (E) LRA 10022,
MCA   1332,   MCA   (F)   510.109,
Time-Life STL-J18, Time-Life (Au)
J-18, Festival (Au) CFR 10 440
CT: Time-Life 4TL-J18, MCA 1332
8T: Time-Life 8TL-J18

NOTE: Br 80032 issued in Brunswick album B-1008

104.   Jimmy Johnson and Clarence Williams (with
Their Two Pianos.)

NYC   31   January
1930

Piano duet and speech by James P. Johnson and
Clarence Williams

W-149951-1 How Could I Be Blue?
            78: Col 14502-D
            LP: Col CL 1780, CBS (E) BPG
            62090,   Time-Life   STL-J18,
            Time-Life (Au) STL-J18, I Grande
            del Jazz (I) 85, CBS (F) 85387
            CT: Time-Life 4TL-J18, CBS (F)
            40-85387
            8T: Time-Life 8TL-J18

W-149952-2 I've Found A New Baby
            78: Col 14502-D
            LP: Natchez (Arg) NLP 3002, CBS
            (F) 85387
            CT: CBS (F) 40-85387

NOTE: Three takes of each title were recorded.
A total of 1,885 labels were printed of Col
14502-D.

105. Lonnie Johnson and Clarence Williams
                        NYC,   7   February
                        1930
Lonnie   Johnson and Clarence Williams, vocal
duets;   James P. Johnson, piano; Lonnie Johnson,
guitar; Clarence Williams, gourd.

W-403749-B The Dirty Dozen
            78: OK 8775

W-403750-A Keep It To Yourself
            78: OK 8812

NOTE: Mx. 403750 issued as Lonnie Johnson and Spencer Williams. Three takes were recorded of the first title and two takes of the last.

106. "Yamakraw" Film Soundtrack
                              NYC, late February
                              1930
The film, Vitaphone 1009, presents the James P. Johnson composition, performed by a studio band, Hugo Marianni and His Mediterraneans. Marianni was a white conductor under contact to CBS at the time of filming. Actors included Jimmy Mordecai, who appeared in the Bessie Smith film, "St. Louis Blues," Louise "Jota" Cook and Margaret Sims. James P. Johnson does not appear in the film nor does he play piano on the soundtrack. The film was reviewed in Variety on April 30, 1930, and was copyrighted on June 9.

107. Teddy Bunn and Spencer Williams
                              NYC, 2 June 1930
Teddy Bunn and Spencer Williams, vocal duets; James P. Johnson, piano; Bunn, guitar; Bruce Johnson, washboard.

BVE-62178-2   Goose And Gander
                 78: Vic V-38602

BVE-62179-2   The New Goose and Gander
                 78: Vic V-38617

BVE-62180-2   Clean It Out
                 78: Vic V-38602

BVE-62181-1   Blow It Up
                 78: Vic V-38617

108.   Bessie Smith and The Bessemer Singers
                              NYC, 9 June 1930
Smith, the Bessemer Singers, (four male voices)
vocal; Johnson, piano.

W-150574-4   On   Revival   Day   (A   Rhythmic
Spiritual)
                78: Col 14538-D, HJCA HC-29
                45: Col G 4-8
                LP: Col ML 4810, GL 506, CL
                858, GP 33, Ph (Eu) B 07005L, Ph
                (E) BBL 7049, CBS (Eu) BPG 62380,
                66258, Cor (Au) KLP 617, Swaggie
                (Au) S 1264, Time-Life STL-J28
                CT: Time-Life 4TL-J28
                8T: Time-Life 8TL-J28

W-150575-4   Moan Mourners
                78: Col 14538-D, HJCA HC 29
                45:    Ph   (E)   BBE   12231,   (Du)
                429224 BE, Col G 4-8
                LP: Col ML 4810, GL 506, CL
                858, GP 33, Ph (Eu) B 07005L, Ph
                (E) BBL 7049, CBS (Eu) BPG 62380,
                66258, Cor (Au) KLP 617, Swaggie
                (Au) S 1264

NOTE: Four takes were recorded of each title.
W-150575 is labeled "Moan Mourners" on Col
14538-D and as "Moan, You Mourners" on most
subsequent issues. A total of 4,095 labels were
printed of Col 14538-D.

The McKinney's Cotton Pickers sessions of July
28, 29, 30 and 31, 1930, have been listed
frequently in discographies as including James
P. Johnson among the personnel. However, the
pianist is Todd Rhodes.

109. Jimmy Johnson and His Orchestra
                        NYC, 25 March 1931
Ward   Pinkett,   trumpet   and   vocal; unknown
trumpet; possibly Fernando Arbello, trombone;
Fred Skeritt, Henry L. Jones, alto sax; Bingie
Madison,   clarinet and tenor sax; Johnson, piano;
Goldie Lucas, guitar; Richard Fullbright, string
bass; Bill Beason, drums; Andy Razaf, vocal.

W-151457-2 Go Harlem (A.R., vocal)
                78: Col 2448-D
                LP: Time-Life STL-J18, Time-Life
                (Au) STL-J18, Stash ST 124
                CT: Time-Life 4TL-J18
                8T: Time-Life 8TL-J18

W-151459-2   A   Porter's Love Song (To A
Chambermaid) (A.R., vocal)
                78: Col 14668-D

W-151460-3   Just A Crazy Song (Hi-Hi-Hi) (A.R.,
W.P., vocal)
                78: Col 2448-D

NOTE: Col 2448-D and Col 14668-D exist on
"Royal Blue" pressings. Three takes of each
title were recorded. A total of 400 labels were
printed of Col 14668-D.

110. Rosa Henderson
                        NYC,   19   August
                        1931
Henderson, vocal; Johnson, piano.

W-151739-1 Doggone Blues
                78: Col 14627-D
                CT: Neovox (E) 807

W-151740-1 Can't Be Bothered With No Sheik
                    78: Col 14627-D
                    LP: Rosetta RR 1300
                    CT: Neovox (E) 807

NOTE: Two takes were recorded of each title. A
total of 650 labels were printed of Col 14627-D.

Two   sessions   with   singer Ora Alexander on
January 8 and March 15, 1932, have been listed
as   having   accompaniment by James P. Johnson.
The pianist on both sessions is Milton Davage.

111. "The Emperor Jones" Film Soundtrack
                              Astoria,   Long
                              Island, New York,
                              c. July 1933

This   feature   film,   starring Paul Robeson,
includes "St. Louis Blues" played by Johnson,
solo   piano   behind   dialogue,   and "Toot It,
Brother Armstrong," sung by an unknown "blues"
singer with possible accompaniment by Johnson.
Johnson is seen on screen for a few seconds, but
only from the back.   The film was directed by
Dudley Murphy and was copyrighted September 29,
1933.   Included in the cast were Frank Wilson,
Fredi Washington, Rex Ingram, Jimmy Mordechai,
Dudley Diggs, Ruby Elzy, Harold Nicholas, The
Hall-Johnson Choir (Billie Holiday appeared as
an extra in a crowd scene.) J. Rosamund Johnson
received   credit   for   the   musical   score.
According to "Variety," production began on July
1.   The film took seven weeks to complete and
cost $263,000.   Robeson was reported to have
earned $30,000 for his role in the film.

112.   Clarence Williams and His Orchestra
                              NYC,   6   December
                        1933
Ed   Allen,   cornet   and vocal;   Cecil   Scott,
clarinet   and   tenor   sax;   Johnson,   piano;
Williams,   second piano on "St. Louis Blues"; Roy
Smeck,   guitar;   Cyrus   St.   Clair,   brass   bass;
Floyd Casey, washboard; Chick Bullock, vocal.

14423-1   Ooh! Looka-There, Ain't She Pretty
(CB, vocal)
                   45: Col (E) SEG 7545

14423-2   Looka-There,   Ain't   She   Pretty   (CB,
vocal)
                   78: Voc 2616, Br (G) A-86051
                   LP: Ph   (E)   BBL   7521,   Ph (Eu)
                   13653,   CJM   (Swe) CJM 15, Swaggie
                   (Au) 812

14425-1   How Can I Get It? (EA, vocal)
                   78: Voc 2630
                   LP: CJM   (Swe)   CJM 15, Swaggie
                   (Au) 812

14425-2   How Can I Get It? (EA, vocal)
                   78: Voc 2630
                   LP: JSo (Swe) LP 17, CJM (Swe)
                   CJM 15, Swaggie (Au) 812

NOTE: Two additional tunes cut at this session
do not include Johnson.   Voc 2630 erroneously
credits   the   vocal   to   Henry   Allen. Two takes
were recorded of each title.

113.   Clarence Williams and His Orchestra
                              NYC,   10   January
                        1934
Ed   Allen,   cornet;   Cecil   Scott,   clarinet;

Johnson, piano; Williams, second piano; Roy
Smeck, steel guitar; Cyrus St. Clair, brass
bass; Floyd Casey, washboard; Chick Bullock,
vocal.

14571-1   On The Sunny Side of the Street (CB,
vocal)
              78: Voc 2630
              45: Col (E) SEG 7545
              LP: CJM (Swe) CJM 15, Swaggie
              (Au) 812

14571-2   On The Sunny Side Of The Street (no
vocal)
              LP: CJM (Swe) CJM 15, Swaggie
              (Au) 812

14572-1   Won't You Come Over and Say "Hello"
(CB, vocal)
              78: Voc 2718
              LP: CJM (Swe) CJM 15

NOTE: Two other tunes cut at this session do
not include James P. Johnson.

114. Clarence Williams and His Orchestra
                            NYC,   17   January
                            1934
Ed Allen, cornet; Cecil Scott, clarinet;
Johnson, piano; Roy Smeck, guitar and steel
guitar; Cyrus St. Clair, brass bass; Floyd
Casey, washboard; Williams, Dick Robertson,
vocal.

14611-1   Jimmy Had A Nickel (DR, vocal)
              78: Voc 2629
              LP: CJM (Swe) CJM 16, Swaggie
              (Au) 813

14612-1   He's A Colonel From Kentucky (DR, vocal)
                78:   Voc 2629, EBW (E) W-121
                LP: Ph (E) BBL 7521, Ph (Eu)
                13653, CJM (Swe) CJM 16, Swaggie
                (Au) 813

14630-1   Pretty Baby, Is It Yes or No? (CW, vocal)
                78:   Voc 2718
                LP: CJM (Swe) CJM 16, Swaggie
                (Au) 813

14631-1   Mister, Will You Serenade? (CW, vocal)
                78:   Voc 2676, Br (G) A-86050
                LP: CJM (Swe) CJM 16, Swaggie
                (Au) 813

NOTE: Matrices   14613-14629   are   by   other
artists.

115. Clarence Williams and His Orchestra
                                NYC,   7   February
                                1934
Ed Allen, cornet; unknown trombone; Cecil Scott,
clarinet; Johnson, piano; Williams, vocal and
second piano on matrix 14806; Roy Smeck, guitar;
Cyrus St. Clair, brass bass.

14804-1   I Got Horses And Got Numbers On My
Mind (CW, vocal)
                78: Voc 2654
                LP: CJM (Swe) CJM 16, OFC (Arg)
                OFC 15, Swaggie (Au) 813

14805-1   New Orleans Hop Scop Blues (CW, vocal)
                78: Voc 2654
                LP: JSo (Swe) LP 17, CJM (Swe)
                CJM 16, OFC (Arg) OFC 15, Swaggie

                    (Au) 813

14806-1   Let's Have A Showdown
                78: Voc 2759
                LP: CJM (Swe) CJM 16, OFC (Arg)
                OFC 15, Swaggie (Au) 813

NOTE: Despite the label on Voc 2759, there is
no vocal on this side. Two takes each of the
first two titles and one take of the last title
were recorded.

116. Clarence Williams And His Orchestra
                            NYC, 23 March 1934
Charles Gaines, trumpet and vocal; Ed Allen,
cornet; Cecil Scott, clarinet and tenor sax;
Louis Jordan, alto and possibly tenor sax,
vocal; unknown third sax added on last two
titles; James P. Johnson, piano; Cyrus St.
Clair, brass bass; Floyd Casey, washboard;
Williams, Chick Bullock, vocal.

14989-1   I Can't Dance, I Got Ants In My Pants
(CG, LJ, band, vocal)
                78: Voc 2689
                LP: CJM (Swe) CJM 16, Swaggie
                (Au) 813

14990-1   Christmas Night in Harlem (CB, vocal)
                78: Voc 2689
                LP: CJM (Swe) CJM 16, Swaggie
                (Au) 813

14991-1   Ill Wind (You're Blowin' Me No Good)
(CB, vocal)
                78: Voc 2674, EBW (E) W-142
                LP: CJM (Swe) CJM 16, Swaggie
                (Au) 813

14992-1   As Long As I Live (CB, vocal)
                78: Voc 2674, EBW (E) W-142
                LP: CJM (Swe) CJM 16, Swaggie
            (Au) 813

NOTE: Matrix 14989 was remade, or perhaps
simply dubbed, on March 30, 1934, but it is not
known if the results were issued. Four takes of
14989 were recorded.

117. Clarence Williams and His Orchestra
                        NYC, 6 July 1934
Ed   Allen,   cornet; Cecil   Scott, clarinet;
Johnson,   piano;   Floyd   Casey,   washboard,
Williams, Eva Taylor, vocal.

15398-1   Jerry The Junker (CW, vocal)
                78: Voc 2854
                LP: Stash ST 100, CJM (Swe) CJM
            17, Swaggie (Au) 813

15399-1   Organ Grinder's Blues (CW, ET , vocal)
                78: Voc 2871, Br (G) A-86009
                LP: CJM (Swe) CJM 17, Swaggie
            (Au) 813

15400-1   I'm Getting My Bonus In Love (CW,
vocal)
                78: Voc 2889, Br (G) A-86004,
            A-86052
                LP: CJM (Swe) CJM 17, Swaggie
            (Au) 813

15401-1   Chizzlin' Sam (CW, ET and band, vocal)
                78: Voc 2854
                LP: CJM (Swe) CJM 17, Swaggie
            (Au) 814

15401-2   Chizzlin' Sam (CW, ET and band,

vocal)
                78:   Voc 2854
                LP: CJM (Swe) CJM 17, Swaggie
                (Au) 814

NOTE: Though Williams addresses the cornet
player as "Big Fat Red Allen" on matrix 15399-1,
it is Ed Allen, not Henry "Red" Allen. Two
takes of each title were recorded.

118. House Party with Fats Waller
                          NYC,   c. April-May,
                          1937
Piano solo by Fats Waller with talking by James
P. Johnson, Eubie Blake, Willie "The Lion" Smith
and Waller.

        The Gathering
                LP: Ristic (E) 22/23 (2 LP set)

NOTE: Other titles recorded at this party,
presumably at Waller's home, are by Waller,
piano and vocal; Gene Sedric, tenor; Andy Razaf
and Mrs. James P. Johnson, vocals.

119. James P. Johnson, piano solo
                          Fats   Waller's
                          Home, New York, c.
                          May 1937
        Liza
                LP: Ristic (E) 22/23 (2 LP set)

120. James P. Johnson
                          CBS   Broadcast,
                          NYC, 2 July 1938
Johnson, Fats Waller, piano; Waller, vocal.

I Found A New Baby (FW, vocal)
      45: MA 1
      LP: Fanfare LP 17-117

NOTE: From the CBS Broadcast, "The Saturday
Night Swing Club." Johnson does not appear on
the other title by Fats Waller, "Hold My Hand."
MA 1 is a single-sided disc without a label
name.

121. Pee Wee Russell's Rhythmakers
                            NYC,   31   August
                            1938
Max Kaminsky, trumpet; Dicky Wells, trombone;
Russell,   clarinet; Al Gold, tenor; Johnson,
piano; Freddie Green, guitar; Wellman Braud,
string bass; Zutty Singleton, drums, vocal.

P-23391-1   Baby, Won't You Please Come Home
              78: HRS 1000, Mdsc (E) 1137
              45: Atlantic EP 529
              LP: Atlantic ALR 126, Riv RLP
              (12)   141,   OJC-1708,   BYG (F)
              529.066,   Joker   (I)   SM 3096,
              Time-Life STL-J17, (Au) STL-J17
              CT: Time-Life 4TL-J17
              8T: Time-Life 8TL-J17
              TX: AFRS DB 347, DB 420

P-23391-2   Baby, Won't You Please Some Home
              78: HRS 17

P-23392-1   There'll Be Some Changes Made
              78:   HRS 1001, Esq (E) 10-051,
              JSe (F) 524
              45: Atlantic EP 529
              LP: Atlantic ALR 126

P-23392-2   There'll Be Some Changes Made

                78:   HRS 1001
                LP: Riverside   RLP   (12)   141,
         OJC-1708,   BYG   (F) 529.066, Joker
         (I) SM 3096, Meritt 9
                TX: AFRS DB 299

P-23393-1   Horn Of Plenty Blues (Z.S., vocal)
                78:    HRS 1001, Esq (E) 10-051,
                JSe (F) 524
                LP: Atlantic ALR 126, Riv RLP
                (12)   141,   OJC-1708,   BYG   (F)
                529.066, Joker (I) SM 3096, ESC
                101
                TX: AFRS DB 357

P-23394-1   Dinah
                78:   HRS 1000, Mdsc (E) 1137
                LP: Atlantic ALR 126, Riv RLP
                (12)   141,   OJC-1708,   BYG   (F)
                529.066, (F) DALP 2 1910, Joker
                (I) SM 3096, Time-Life STL-J18,
                (Au) STL-J18
                CT: Time-Life 4TL-J18
                8T: Time-Life 8TL-J18
                TX: AFRS DB 372

Pee Wee, Zutty and James P.
                        Same session.
Pee Wee Russell, clarinet;   James P. Johnson,
piano; Zutty Singleton, drums.

P-23395-1   I've Found A New Baby
                78:   HRS 1002, Mdsc (E) 1144
                45:   Atlantic EP 529
                LP: Atlantic ALR 126, Riv RLP
                (12)   141,   OJC-1708,   BYG   (F)
                529.066,   Joker   (I)   SM 3096,
                Time-Life STL-J17, (Au) STL-J17
                CT: Time-Life 4TL-J17
                8T: Time-Life 8TL-J17

                        TX: AFRS DB 298, DB345, DB 417

P-23396-2   Everybody Loves My Baby
                        78:   HRS 1002, Mdsc (E) 1144
                        45:   Atlantic EP 529
                        LP: Atlantic ALR 126, Riv RLP
                        (12)   141,   OJC-1708,   BYG (F)
                        529.066,   Joker   (I)   SM 3096,
                        Time-Life STL-J18, (Au) STL-J18
                        CT: Time-Life 4TL-J18
                        8T: Time-Life 8TL-J18

NOTE: Mx. 23395 and 23396 issued as by "The
Rhythmakers" on JSe, and as James P. Johnson
Trio on Mdsc. 23395 was also issued as by James
P. Johnson Trio on Time-Life releases. "Horn
Of Plenty" retitled as "Zutty's Hootie Blues" on
the brown issue of HRS 1001 and on microgrooves.
Later issues of HRS 1002 show 23395-2 in the
wax, but the performance is identical to
23395-1. The red HRS label issues are from the
original stampers while the brown label HRS
issues are dubbings. P-23392-1 was issued on
the   red HRS label and has a trumpet solo
following the opening ensemble while P-23392-2,
issued on the brown HRS label, has a piano solo
following the opening ensemble.

122. Mezz Mezzrow and His Orchestra
                                    NYC   21   November
                                    1938
Tommy Ladnier, Sidney DeParis, trumpet; Mezzrow,
clarinet; Johnson, piano; Teddy Bunn, guitar;
Elmer James, string bass; Zutty Singleton,
drums.

BS-028988-1 Revolutionary Blues
                        78:   BB B-10088, HVM (E) B-9470,
                        HMV (VSM) (F) SG-350, Sw (F) 78,

HMV (VDP9 (I) HN-2953, HMV (Swi)
JK-2174, HMV (Au) EA-3333
45: HMV (E) 7EMF39
LP: RCA LPV 542, X LVA 3027, HMV
DLP 1110, RCA (E) RD 7887, RCA
(F) 730.509, FXM1 7132; RCA (I)
LPM 34042, Electrola (G) E 83045,
RCA (J) RA 5324, Jazz Panorama LP
1814, ESC 101, RCA Special
Products DMM4-0456 (Neiman-Marcus
Fourth Series), RCA (F) PM 45728
CT: Joker (I) MC 3949

BS-028989-1 Comin' On With The Come On, part 1
78:   BB B-10085, HMV (E) B-9468,
HMV (VSM) (F) SG 353, Sw (F) 47,
HMV (Au) EA-2336
45: HMV (E) 7EMF 39
LP: RCA LPV 542, X LVA 3027,
Jazz Panorama LP 1814, HMV (E)
DLP 1110, RCA (E) RD 7887, RCA
(F) 730.509, FXM1 7132, RCA (I)
LPM 34042, Electrola (G) E 83045,
RCA (J) RA 5324, RCA (F) PM 45728

BS-028990-1 Comin' On With The Come On, part 2
78:   BB B-10085, HMV (E) B-9468,
HMV (VSM) (F) SG-353, Sw (F) 47,
HMV (Au) EA-2336
45: HMV (E) 7EMF 39
LP: RCA LPV 542, X LVA 3027,
Jazz Panorama LP 1814, HMV DLP
1110, RCA (E) RD 7887, RCA (F)
730.509, FXM1 7132, RCA (I) LPM
34042, Electrola (G) E 83045, RCA
(J) RA 5324, RCA (F) PM 45728

BS-028991-1 Swingin' For Mezz
LP: Jazz Archives JA 40, RCA (F)
PM 45728

NOTE: "Swingin' For Mezz," mx 028991-2 was also
released on Jazz Archives JA 40 and RCA (F) PM
45728, but that take does not include Johnson.
"Swingin' For Mezz" is another title for
"Careless Love." RCA (F) PM 45728 labels
028991-1 as "Careless Love (Swingin' for Mezz)."
Zutty Singleton discusses this session on ESC
101.

123   James P. Johnson, piano solos
                                Carnegie   Hall,
                                NYC,   23 December
                                1938
        Mule Walk
                LP: Van VSD 47/48, VRS 8523/4;
                Fon   (E)   TFL   5187/8;   TR (E)
                35064/65; Vogue (E) VJD 550; GdJ
                (F) J 1248/9; Vox (F) VST
                26340/350; Jzt (G) J 1248/9; Fon
                (Du) FJL 401/2; Ama (Austria)
                AVRS 9014/5, Van (J) VY 504/4;
                Club (Arg) SJ 1/2

        Carolina Shout
                LP: Van VSD 47/48; VRS 8523/4;
                Fon   (E)   TFL   5187/8;   TR (E)
                35064/65; Vogue (E) VJD 550; GdJ
                (F) J 1248/9; Vox (F) VST
                26340/350; Jzt (G) J 1248/9; Fon
                (Du) FJL 401/2; Ama (Austria)
                AVRS 9014/5; Van (J) VY 503/4;
                Club (Arg) SJ 1/2

New Orleans Feetwarmers
                                Same   date   and
                                location.
Tommy Ladnier, trumpet; Dan Minor, trombone;

Sidney Bechet, clarinet and soprano sax; Johnson, piano; Walter Page, bass; Jo Jones, drums.

Weary Blues
LP: Van VSD 47/48; VRS 8523/4; Fon (E) TFL 5187/8; TR (E) 35064/65; Vogue (E) VJD 550; GdJ (F) J 1248/9; Vox (F) VST 26340/350; Jzt (G) J 1248/9; Fon (Du) FJL 401/2; Ama (Austria) AVRS 9014/5; Van (J) VY 503/4; Club (Arg) SJ 1/2, Ariston (I) 12020

I Wish I Could Shimmy Like My Sister Kate
LP: Van VSD 47/48; VRS 8523/4; Fon (E) TFL 5187/8; TR (E) 35064/65; Vogue (E) VJD 550; GdJ (F) J 1248/9; Vox (F) VST 26340/350; Jzt (G) J 1248/9; Fon (Du) FJL 401/2; Ama (Austria) AVRS 9014/5; Van (J) VY 503/4; Club (Arg) SJ 1/2; Ariston (I) 12020

NOTE: These recordings are from the first "Spirituals to Swing" concert.

124. James P. Johnson, piano solos
                              Havers   Studio,
                              NYC, 24 December
                              1938
Johnson, piano, vocal and speech, interviewed by Alan Lomax for the Library Of Congress.

2490-B-1 Low Down Blues (James P. Johnson, vocal)

                              78:     Library   of   Congress,
                              unissued.

2490-B-2 Stop It, Joe (James P. Johnson, vocal)
                              78:     Library   of   Congress,
                              unissued

2490-B-3 Ethel Waters' Blues
                              78:     Library   of   Congress,
                              unissued

2490-B-4 Snowy Morning Blues
                              78:     Library   of   Congress,
                              unissued

2496-B-1 Monologue On Early Life
                              78:     Library   of   Congress,
                              unissued

2496-B-2   The   Bull   Diker's   Dream   (James   P.
Johnson, vocal)
                              78:     Library   of   Congress,
                              unissued

2496-B-3 Pork and Beans
                    LP: Library of Congress LCB-14

125. Frankie Newton and His Orchestra
                              NYC,   13   January
                              1939
Newton, trumpet; Mezz Mezzrow, clarinet; Pete
Brown, alto sax; Johnson, piano; Albert Casey,
guitar; John Kirby, bass; Cozy Cole, drums.

BS-031460-1   Rosetta
                    78: BB B-10176, Sw (F) 53
                    45: RCA EJC-1006 (947-0174)
                    LP: RCA LJM 1006, LPV 542, RCA
                    (E) RD 7887, RCA (F) 730.509,

741.117, RCA (I) LPM 10131, LPM
34042, Time-Life STL-J18, (Au)
STL-J18, RCA (F) PM 45728
CT: Time-Life 4TL-J18
8T: Time-Life 8TL-J18

BS-031461-   Minor Jive
                78: BB B-10186, Sw (F) 53, HMV
                (Au) EA-2671
                45: RCA EJC 1006 (947-0174)
                LP: RCA LJM 1006, LPV 578, RCA
                (F) 741.046, RCA (I) LPM 10131,
                RCA (F) PM 45728

BS-031462-   The World Is Waiting For The
Sunrise
                78: BB B-10176, Sw (F) 198
                45: RCA EJC 1006 (947-0175)
                LP: RCA LJM 1006, LPV 542, RCA
                (E) RD 7887, RCA (F) 730.509,
                741.117, RCA (I) LPM 10131, LPM
                34042, Folkways FP 75, FJ 2811,
                RCA (F) PM 45728

BS-031463-1   Who?
                78: BB B-10216, HMV (E) B 8927,
                Sw (F) 68
                45: RCA EJC 1006 (947-0175)
                LP: RCA LJM 1006, LPV 542, RCA
                (E) RD 7887, RCA (F) 730.509,
                741.117, RCA (I) LPM 10131, LPM
                34042, Time-Life STL-J18, (Au)
                STL-J18, RCA (F) PM 45728
                CT: Time-Life 4TL-J18
                8T: Time-Life 8TL-J18

BS-031464-1   The Blues My Baby Gave To Me
                78: test pressing

BS-031464-2   The Blues My Baby Gave To Me

78: BB B-10216, Sw (F) 198
45: RCA EJC 1006 (947-0175)
LP: RCA LJM 1006, LPV 578, RCA
(F) 741.046, RCA (I) LPM 10131,
RCA (F) PM 45728, Franklin Mint
89

BS-031465-   Rompin'
78:   BB B-10186, HMV (E) B 8927,
B 9154, Sw (F) 68, HMV (Au) EA
2671
45: RCA EJC 1006 (947-0175)
LP: RCA LJM 1006, LPV 578, RCA
(F) 741.046, RCA (I) LPM 10131,
RCA Special Products DMM4-0342
(Neiman-Marcus Second Series),
RCA (F) PM 45728

NOTE:

126. Rosetta Crawford, accompanied by James P.
Johnson's Hep Cats

NYC,   1   February
1939

Crawford, vocal; Tommy Ladnier, trumpet; Mezz
Mezzrow, clarinet; Johnson, piano; Teddy Bunn,
guitar; Elmer James, bass; Zutty Singleton,
drums.

64970-A   I'm Tired Of Fattenin' Frogs for
Snakes
78:   Dec 7584, Voc (E) S-247, Br
(E) 03461
LP: Br 10-662, Swaggie (Au) S
1215, Decca DL 79230, DL 9230,
MCA 1353, Coral CP 58, MCA (F)
510.111, Kings of Jazz (I)
NLJ-18018

Discography 409

64971-A   Stop It, Joe
          78:   Decca 7567, Voc (E) S-240,
          V-1002, Br (G) A-82738, Br (Swi)
          88062
          LP: Br 10-662, MCA-Coral (G)
          820404 (4-LP set), Swaggie (Au) S
          1215,   Coral   CP   58,   MCA (F)
          510.111, Kings of Jazz   (I)
          NLJ-18018

64972-A   My Man Jumped Salty On Me
          78:   Dec 7567, Voc (E) S-240,
          V-1002, Br (G) A-82738
          LP: Br 10-662, Dec DL 4434, AoH
          (E) AH 72, MCA-Coral (G) 820404
          (4-LP set), (G) 6.30106, Swaggie
          (Au) S 1215, MCA 1352, Coral CP
          58, MCA (F) 510.111, Kings of
          Jazz (I) NLJ-18018

64973-A   Double Crossin' Papa
          78:   Decca 7584, Voc (E) S-247,
          Br (E) 03461, Br (Swi) 88062
          LP: Br 10-662, Swaggie (Au) S
          1215,   Coral   CP   58,   MCA (F)
          510.111, Kings of Jazz   (I)
          NLJ-18018

NOTE: On Br (E) 03461 as "Vocal accompanied by
Jimmy Johnson's Band."

127. Jimmy Johnson And His Orchestra
                      NYC, 9 March 1939
Henry   Allen,   trumpet;   J.C.   Higginbotham,
trombone; Gene Sedric, tenor sax; Johnson,
piano; Albert Casey, guitar; Johnny Williams,
bass; Sid Catlett, drums; Anna Robinson, Ruby
Smith, vocal.

W-24205-1   Harlem Woogie (AR, vocal)
             78:   Voc 4768, Parl (E) R-2863,
             Od   (G)   A-2352,   Parl   (Swi)
             PZ-11117
             LP: Col KG 30788, Swingfan (G)
             1018, CBS (Du) 67203, Tax (Swe)
             m-8034

W-24205-2   Harlem Woogie (AR, vocal)
             78:   test pressing
             LP: Meritt 5, Everybody (Swe)
             1000

W-24206-1   Hungry Blues (AR, vocal)
             LP: Col CL 1780, CBS (Eu) BPG
             62090,   Time-Life   STL-J18,   (Au)
             STL-J18, I Grande del Jazz (I) 85
             CT: Time-Life 4TL-J18
             8T: Time-Life 8TL-J18

W-24207-1   Back Water Blues (RS, vocal)
             78:   Voc 4903
             LP: Col KG 30788, Fon (E) TFL
             5123, Fon (Du) 682.073, CBS (Du)
             67203, Tax (Swe) m-8034

W-24207-2   Back Water Blues (RS, vocal)
             78:   test pressing
             LP: Meritt 13/14

W-24208-1   He's Mine, All Mine (RS, vocal)
             78:   Voc 4903
             LP: Tax (Swe) m-8034

W-24209-1   After Tonight
             78:   Voc 4768, Parl (E) R-2863,
             Parl (Swi) PZ-11117
             LP: Epic LN 3295, Swingfan (G)
             1018, Tax (Swe) m-8034, Time-Life
             STL-J18, (Au) STL-J18

```
                    CT:  Time-Life 4TL-J18
                    8T:  Time-Life 8TL-J18
```

NOTE: Voc 4903 as by Ruby Smith with Jimmy Johnson and His Orchestra.

128. James P. Johnson, piano solos
                              NYC, 14 June 1939

```
W-24757-A    If Dreams Come True
                    LP:  Col CL 1780, CBS (Eu) BPG
                    62090,  Time-Life STL-J18, (Au)
                    STL-J18, I Grande del Jazz (I)
                    85, CBS (F) 85387
                    CT:  Time-Life 4TL-J18, CBS (F)
                    40-85387
                    8T:  Time-Life 8TL-J18

W-24757-B    If Dreams Come True
                    78:  Test pressing

W-24758-A    Fascination
                    LP:  Col CL 1780, Bio BLP 1009Q,
                    CBS (Eu) BPG 62090, I Grande del
                    Jazz (I) 85, CBS (F) 85387
                    CT:  CBS (F) 40-85387

W-24759-A    A-Flat Dream
                    78:  Col 37333, C-6330
                    45:  Col B-2047
                    LP:  Col CL 685, Harm HL 7104,
                    Fon  (E)  TFL  6018, Time-Life
                    STL-J18,  (Au) STL-J18, Queen Disc
                    (I) Q-056, Murray Hill M-61358
                    (P-16991), CBS (F) 85387
                    CT:  Time-Life 4TL-J18, CBS (F)
                    40-85387
                    8T:  Time-Life 8TL-J18
```

W-24760-A   The Mule Walk
                      LP: Col CL 1780, CBS (Eu) BPG
                      62090, I Grande del Jazz (I) 85,
                      CBS (F) 85387
                      CT: CBS (F) 40-85387

W-24761-A   Lonesome Reverie
                      LP: Col CL 1780, CBS (Eu) BPG
                      62090, I Grande del Jazz (I) 85,
                      CBS (F) 85387
                      CT: CBS (F) 40-85387

W-24762-A   Blueberry Rhyme
                      LP: Col CL 1780, CBS (Eu) BPG
                      62090, Time-Life STL-J18, (Au)
                      STL-J18, I Grande del Jazz (I)
                      85, CBS (F) 85387
                      CT: Time-Life 4TL-J18, CBS (F)
                      40-85387
                      8T: Time-Life 8TL-J18

NOTE: Col 37333 (Mx. 24759) was issued in album
C-130.

129.   James P. Johnson and His Orchestra
                              NYC 15 June 1939
Henry   Allen,   trumpet;   J.C.   Higginbotham,
trombone;   Gene   Sedric,   tenor sax; Johnson,
piano; Eugene Fields, guitar; Pops Foster, bass;
Sid Catlett, drums.

W-24776-1   Memories of You
                      LP: Meritt 5, Everybodys (Swe)
                      1000

W-24776-2   Memories of You
                      LP: Col CL 1780, CBS (Eu) BPG
                      62090, I Grande del Jazz (I) 85

W-24777-1   Old Fashioned Love
             LP: Meritt 5, Everybodys (Swe)
             1000

W-24777-2   Old Fashioned Love
             78: Col (Swiss) DZ-545
             LP: Col CL 1780, CBS (Eu) BPG
             62090,   Time-Life STL-J18,   (Au)
             STL-J18, I Grande del Jazz (I) 85
             CT: Time-Life 4TL-J18
             8T: Time-Life 8TL-J18

W-24778-1   Swingin' At The Lido (breakdown)
             78: unissued, test exists

W-24778-2   Swingin' At The Lido
             78: unissued, test exists

W-24778-3   Swingin' At The Lido (breakdown)
             78: unissued, test exists

W-24778-4   Swingin' At The Lido
             LP: Col CL 1780, CBS (Eu) BPG
             62090, I Grande del Jazz (I) 85

W-24778-5   Swingin' At The Lido
             LP: Meritt 5, Everybodys (Swe)
             1000

W-24779-1   Havin' A Ball
             LP: Meritt 5, Everybodys (Swe)
             1000

W-24779-2   Havin' A Ball (breakdown)
             78: unissued, test exists

W-24779-3   Havin' A Ball
             LP: Meritt 5, Everybodys (Swe)
             1000

W-24779-4   Havin' A Ball
                    LP: Col CL 1780, CBS (Eu) BPG
                    62090, I Grande del Jazz (I) 85

W-24780-1   Hungry Blues (unknown female vocal)
                    LP: Meritt 5, Everybodys (Swe)
                    1000

NOTE: The titles "Swingin' At The Lido" and
"Havin' A Ball" are reversed on Col CL 1780. W
24777   on Col DZ 545 as by Jimmy Johnson and his
Orchestra.   Ruby Smith has been suggested as the
vocalist on matrix W-24780-1.

130.   Ida Cox, accompanied by Her All Star Band
                                   NYC,   31   October
                                   1939
Cox, vocals; Hot Lips Page, trumpet; J. C.
Higginbotham, trombone; Edmond Hall, clarinet;
Johnson, piano; Charlie Christian, electric
guitar; Artie Bernstein, bass; Lionel Hampton,
drums.

25509-1   Deep Sea blues (false start)
                    78: unissued, acetate exists.

25509-2   Deep Sea Blues (false start)
                    78: unissued, acetate exists.

25509-3   Deep Sea Blues
                    78: unissued, acetate exists.

25509-4   Deep Sea Blues
                    LP: Meritt   5,   Collectors
                    Classics (Swiss) CC 56

25509-5   Deep Sea Blues (breakdown)
                    LP: unissued, acetate exists.

25509-6   Deep Sea Blues
                78: Voc 05336
                45:   Fontana (E) TFE 17137, (H)
                467025 TE
                LP: Queen Disc (I) Q-048

Omit J.C. Higginbotham, trombone; Ed Hall, clt.,
and Lionel Hampton, drums.

22510-1   Death Letter Blues
                78: unissued, acetate exists.

22510-2   Death Letter Blues
                78: unissued, acetate exists.

22510-3   Death Letter Blues (breakdown)
                78: unissued, acetate exists.

25510-4   Death Letter Blues
                LP: Meritt   5,   Collectors
                Classics (Swiss) CC 56

25510-5   Death Letter Blues
                78: Voc 05336, Parl (E) R-2974,
                Parl   (I) B-71097, Parl (Swiss)
                PZ 11023
                LP: Queen   Disc   (I)   Q-048,
                Collectors Classics (Swiss) CC 56

Add Higginbotham, Hall and Hampton.

25511-1   One Hour Mama
                LP: Rosetta RR 1300

25511-2   One Hour Mama (breakdown)
                78: unissued, acetate exists.

25511-3   One Hour Mama

                                     78:   unissued   fragment,   acetate
                                     exists.

25511-4   One Hour Mama
                   LP: Collectors   Classics   (Swiss)
                   CC 56

25511-5   One Hour Mama (breakdown)
                   LP: Collectors   Classics   (Swiss)
                   CC 56

25511-6   One Hour Mama
                   LP: Meritt   5,   Collectors
                   Classics (Swiss) CC 56

25511-7   One Hour Mama (breakdown)
                   78:   unissued, acetate exists.

NOTE: This   sequence   is   accurate   despite the
differences   in   the   "take"   numbers   indicated on
the   original 78 rpm and LP issues. On Collectors
Classics   CC 56, 25509-4 is listed as take 3.   On
Meritt   5, 25510-4 is shown as take 2 and 25511-6
is   shown   as take 1.   Voc 05336 shows "take" 1
on   each   side.   An   unknown   take   of "One Hour
Mama"   was scheduled to be released on Voc 05232,
but the record was never issued.

131.   Ida Cox and Band
                                     Carnegie   Hall,
                                     NYC,   24 December,
                                     1939.

Cox,   vocal; Shad Collins, trumpet; Dickie Wells,
trombone;   possibly   Buddy   Tate,   tenor   sax;
Johnson,   piano; Walter Page, bass; Jo Jones,
drums.

            Four Day Creep

LP: Van   Vsd   47/48, VRS 8523/4;
Fon   (E)   TFL   5187/8; TR (E)
35064/65; Vogue (E) VJD 550; GdJ
(F) J   1248/9;   Vox   (F) VST
26340/350; Jzt (G) 1248/9, Ama
(Austria) AVRS 9014/5; Van (J) VY
503/4; Club (Arg) SJ 1/2

Low Down Dirty Shame
    LP: GdJ   (F) J1248/9, Jzt (G)
    1248/9

NOTE: Recorded at the second "Spirituals to
Swing" concert.   Acetate discs of other Johnson
performances from this event may exist.

132. Clarence Williams' Blue Five
                      NYC,   22   October
                      1941

Williams, vocal; Johnson, piano; Grace Harper,
Nathan Barlow, guitar; Wellman Braud, bass; Eva
Taylor, vocal.

BS-071198-1   Uncle Sammy Here I Am (ET and CW,
vocal)
           78: RCA unissued test

BS-071198-2   Uncle Sammy Here I Am (ET and CW,
vocal)
           78: BB B-11368
           LP: RCA (F) 741.058

NOTE: Johnson does not appear on the other
title   recorded   at   this session, "Thriller
Blues."

133.   James P. Johnson, piano solos
                          NYC, 2 July 1942

300   Boogie Woogie Stride
                78: Asch 1001
                LP: Stinson SLP 29, Queen Disc
                (I) Q-056

301-   Impressions
                78: Asch 1001
                LP: Stinson SLP 29, Queen Disc
                (I) Q-056

322-   Snowy Morning Blues
                78: Asch 350-3
                LP: Stinson SLP 20

322-alt. Snowy Morning Blues
                LP: Xtra (E) 1024

NOTE: Asch 1001, a 12-inch disc, is contained
in Asch album S456. The Stinson LPs were issued
in both 10 inch and 12 inch formats; however,
the   content   of   each   is   identical.   Two
additional   takes   of "Snowy Morning Blues",
recorded   by   Asch,   were   issued.   See   the
following   session   for   details.   The actual
recording date of these two versions of "Snowy
Morning Blues" is not known. These two
versions, however, sound as if they were
recorded at one session, and the two versions
listed in the next session also sound as if they
were recorded at one date. Asch files indicate
this   session   was   recorded on October 17, 1943,
but this may be the date the masters were
processed. The sequence of recording is not
known.

134.   James P. Johnson, piano solos

NYC, possibly July
1943.
Daintiness Rag
LP: Folkways FJ 2850

Snowy Morning Blues
LP: Folkways FP 71, FJ 2809,
Queen Disc (I) Q-056

Snowy Morning Blues (alternate)
LP: Folkways FJ 2850

NOTE: Folkways FP 71 indicates recording date
was November 17, 1943, the same as the following
Blue Note session! A search of the Blue Note
files, however, does not reveal any information
about these titles. See notes for the preceding
session. The sequence of recording for this
session is not known.

135. James P. Johnson, piano solos
NYC, 17 November
1943

BN 777   J. P. Boogie
78: BN 24
LP: BN (G) 667.787, (J)
K23P-6725, (J) K23P 9281, Mosaic
MR6-109

BN 778   Back Water Blues
78: BN 25, JSe (F) 647
LP: BN BLP 7011, Queen Disc (I)
Q-056, BN (J) K23P 9281, Mosaic
MR6-109

BN 779   Carolina Balmoral
78: BN 25, JSe (F) 647
LP: BN BLP 7011, Queen Disc (I)

Q-056,   Time-Life STL-J18, (Au)
STL-J18, Mosaic MR6-109
CT: Time-Life 4TL-J18
8T: Time-Life 8TL-J18

BN 780   Gut Stomp
           78: BN 24
           LP: BN BLP 7011, Mosaic MR6-109

NOTE: BN 78 rpms and JSe are 12-inch discs.
Recorded at WOR studios.

136. Eddie Condon's Barrelhouse Gang
                              NYC,   20 November
                              1943
Yank Lawson, trumpet; Brad Gowans, valide
trombone; Pee Wee Russell, clarinet; Johnson,
piano; Condon,   guitar; Bob Haggart, bass; Tony
Spargo, drums.

T1901   Squeeze Me
           78: Sig 28130
           LP: Riv RLP 2509, Bob Thiele
           BBM1-0941, Doctor Jazz FW 40064,
           Joker (I) SM 3244
           CT: Doctor Jazz FWT 40064

T1902   That's A Plenty
           78: Sig 28130
           LP: Riv RLP 2509, Bob Thiele
           BBM1-0941, Doctor Jazz FW 40064,
           Joker (I) SM 3244
           CT: Doctor Jazz FWT 40064

Yank Lawson's Jazz Doctors
                              Same session
Same personnel.

T1903   Yank's Blues

                    LP: Riv RLP 2509, RLP 12-116,
                    SPD-11 (5-LP set), Bob Thiele
                    BBM1-0941, Doctor Jazz FW 40064,
                    Joker (I) SM 3244
                    CT: Doctor Jazz FWT 40064

Ray Eckstrand, clarinet, added.

T1904   Old Fashioned Love
                    LP: Riv RLP 2509, Bob Thiele
                    BBM1-0941, Doctor Jazz FW 40064,
                    Joker (I) SM 3244
                    CT: Doctor Jazz FWT 40064

NOTE: All microgroove issues issued as by Yank
Lawson.   The valide trombone was a modified
trombone made by Gowans.

137. Edmond Hall's Blue Note Jazz Men
                              NYC,   29 November
                              1943
Sidney   DeParis,   trumpet; Vic   Dickenson,
trombone; Hall, clarinet; Johnson, piano; Jimmy
Shirley, guitar; Israel Crosby, bass; Sidney
Catlett, drums.

BN901-1   High Society (alternate take #1)
                    LP: Mosaic MR6-109

BN901-2   High Society #2
                    LP: BN B-6504, Mosaic MR6-109

BN901-3   High Society
                    78: BN 28
                    LP: BN 7007, B-6504, B-6509, (J)
                    NR-8102,   (J) K23P-9287, Mosaic
                    MR6-109

BN903-1   Blues At Bluenote (alternate take)

                    LP: Mosaic MR6-109

BN903-2   Blues At Bluenote
                    78: BN 28
                    LP: BN   7007,   B-6504,   (J)
                    NR-8102,   (J) K23P-9287, Mosaic
                    MR-106

BN905-1   Night Shift Blues (alternate take)
                    LP: Mosaic MR6-109

BN905-2   Night Shift Blues
                    78:    BN   29, JSe (F) 646, Vogue
                    (E) V 2045
                    45: Vogue (E) EPV 1164
                    LP: BN BLP 7007, B-6504, B-6509,
                    (J)   NR-8102,   (J)   K23P-9287,
                    Mosaic MR6-109

BN907-1   Royal Garden Blues (alternate take)
                    LP: BN B-6504, (J) NR-8102, (J)
                    K23P 9287, Mosaic MR6-109

BN907-2   Royal Garden Blues
                    78:    BN   29, JSe (F) 646, Vogue
                    (E) V 2045, (J) K23P-9287
                    45: Vogue (E) EPV 1164
                    LP: BN BLP 7007, Mosaic MR6-109

                    Blue Note Boogie
                    LP: BN   (G)   667.787,   (J)
                    K23P-9287, Mosaic MR6-109

NOTE: The above comprises the entire session.
On BN 6504, BN 905-2 is incorrectly listed as an
alternate   take.   On   BN   6509, BN901-3 is
incorrectly listed as an alternate take. The 78
rpm issues are 12 inch discs. Recorded at WOR
studios.

138.   James P. Johnson, piano solos
                                    NYC,   15   December
                                    1943
BN781   Mule Walk (Stomp)
                78: BN 27
                LP: BN BLP 7011, BST 89902, BN
                LA-158-2,   BN   (G)   667.787,
                Time-Life   STL-J18,   (Au) STL-J18,
                Queen Disc (I) Q-056, EMI-Liberty
                LCSP   101,   BN   (J)   K23P 9281,
                Mosaic MR6-109
                CT: Time-Life 4TL-J18
                8T: Time-Life 8TL-J18

BN782   Arkansas Blues
                78: BN 27
                LP: BN   BLP   7011, Time-Life
                STL-J18,   (Au)   STL-J18,   Queen
                Disc (I) Q-056, BN (J) K23P 9281,
                Mosaic MR6-109
                CT: Time-Life 4TL-J18
                8T: Time-Life 8TL-J18

BN783   Caprice Rag
                78: BN 26
                LP: BN BLP 7011, Herwin 403,
                Mosaic MR6-109

BN   784   Improvisation on Pinetop's Boogie
Woogie
                78: BN 26
                LP: Mosaic MR6-109

NOTE: The 78 rpm issues are 12 inch discs.
Recorded at WOR studios.

139.   Yank Lawson's Jazz Band
                                    NYC,   18   December

1943

Lawson, trumpet; Miff Mole, trombone; Rod Cless,
clarinet; Johnson, piano; Bob Haggart, bass;
George Wettling, drums.

T1909-2   Squeeze Me
                  78: Sig 28103, Br 80180
                  LP: Br BL 58035, Bob Thiele
          BBM1-0941, Doctor Jazz FW 40064
                  CT: Doctor Jazz FWT 40064

T1910-   When I Grow Too Old To Dream
                  78: Br 80174
                  LP: Br BL 58035

T1911-2   Too Many Times
                  78: Sig 28107, Br 80179
                  LP: Br BL 58035, Bob Thiele
          BBM1-0941, Doctor Jazz FW 40064
                  CT: Doctor Jazz FWT 40064

T1912-2   The Sheik of Araby
                  78: Sig 28103
                  LP: Br BL 58035, Bob Thiele
          BBM1-0941, Doctor Jazz FW 40064
                  CT: Doctor Jazz FWT 40064

James P. Johnson, piano solos
                              same   location and
                              date

T1913   Old Fashioned Love
                  Signature unissued.

T1914   Blueberry Rhyme
                  78: Sig 28105
                  LP: Doctor Jazz FW 38851, (J)
          K25P 6288
                  CT: Doctor Jazz FWT 38851, PRT

        (E) ZCAS 802

T1915   Blues for Fats
                78: Sig 28105
                LP: Doctor Jazz FW 38851, (J)
                K25P 6288
                CT: Doctor Jazz FWT 38851, PRT
                (E) ZCAS 802

T1916   Over the Bars
                Signature unissued.

NOTE: T1913 and T1916 apparently have been
lost.

140. James P. Johnson's Blue Note Jazz Men
                        NYC, 4 March 1944
Sidney   DeParis,   trumpet; Vic Dickenson,
trombone; Ben Webster, tenor; Johnson, piano;
Jimmy   Shirley,   guitar; John Simmons, bass;
Sidney Catlett, drums.

BN 950-1 Blue Mizz
                78: BN 32, JSe (F) 541
                LP: BN B-6506, (J) NR-8104, (J)
                K23P 9286, Mosaic MR6-109

BN 950-2 Blue Mizz
                LP: Mosaic MR6-109

BN 951-2 Victory Stride
                LP: Mosaic MR6-109

BN 951-3 Victory Stride
                78: BN 32, JSe (F) 541
                LP: BN B-6506, (J) NR-8104, (J)
                K23P 9286, Mosaic MR6-109

BN 952-2 Joy-Mentin'
            78: BN 33, JSe (F) 547
            LP: BN B-6506, (J) NR-8104, (J)
            K23P 9286, Mosaic MR6-109

BN 953-2 After You've Gone
            78: BN 33, JSe (F) 547
            LP: BN BLP 7012, B-6505, BST
            89902,   LA-158-2,   Time-Life
            STL-J18, (Au) STL-J18, (J) K23P
            9286, Mosaic MR6-109
            CT: Time-Life 4TL-J18
            8T: Time-Life 8TL-J18

NOTE: 78 RPM issues are 12-inch discs. Recored
at WOR studios.

141. Eddie Condon
                          NYC,   12   March
                          1944

Wild Bill Davison, cornet; George Lugg,
trombone; Ed Hall, Pee Wee Russell, clarinets;
Johnson, piano; Condon, guitar; Pops Foster,
bass; Kansas Fields, drums. Jimmy Rushing,
vocal

            Blues (Rushing, vocal)
            LP: Aircheck 31

            I Ain't Gonna Give Nobody None of My
            Jelly Roll #1
            LP: Aircheck 31

            I Ain't Gonna Give Nobody None of My
            Jelly Roll #2
            LP: Aircheck 31

NOTE: This session was recorded for V-Disc at
Columbia Records' studios, 799 Seventh Avenue.
"Honeysuckle   Rose,"   also   recorded at this
session, has Joe Bushkin replacing Johnson.
Other titles may have been recorded at this
session as well. Manfred Selchow and Karsten
Lohmann in Edmond Hall: A Discography, indicate
additional titles that include "Baby, Won't You
Please Come Home," "Someday Sweetheart," and a
piano duet by Johnson and Bushkin of "Old
Fashioned Love." These titles have not been
found.

142. James P. Johnson, piano solos
                              NYC, 12 April 1944
71979-A   I've Got A Feelin' I'm Fallin'
(N-2062)
                    LP: Dec DL 5228, MCA 2-4112, Br
                    (E) LA 8662, JPi (D) JP 5004,
                    Swaggie (Au) S 1211, CID (F)
                    US-223567, Festival (Au) CFR10
                    398

71980-A   My Fate Is In Your Hands
(N-2063)
                    LP: Dec DL 5228, MCA 2-4112, Br
                    (E) LA 8662, JPi (D) JP 5004,
                    Swaggie (Au) S 1211, CID (F)
                    US-223567, Festival (Au) CFR10
                    398

71981-A   Ain't Misbehavin'
(N-2064)
                    LP: Dec DL 5228, MCA 2-4112, Br
                    (E) LA 8662, JPi (D) JP 5004,
                    Swaggie (Au) S 1211, CID (F)
                    US-223567, Festival (Au) CFR10
                    398

71982-A   Blue Turning Grey Over You
(N-2065)

>LP: Dec DL 5228, MCA 2-4112, Br
>(E) LA 8662, JPi (D)   JP 5004,
>Swaggie   (Au) S 1211, CID (F)
>US-223567,   MCA   (F)   510.204,
>Festival (Au) CFR10 398

NOTE: Matrix numbers shown in parentheses are
World   transcription   numbers,   although   this
session   was   never   released   on   World.   World
files   list the date of this session as March 12,
1944.

143.   James P. Johnson, piano solos
                                    NYC, 20 April 1944

72007-A   I'm Gonna Sit Right Down (and Write
Myself A Letter)
(N-2118)

>LP: Dec DL 5228, MCA 2-4112, Br
>(E) LA 8662, JPi (D)   JP 5004,
>Swaggie   (Au) S 1211, CID (F)
>US-223567, Festival (Au) CRF10
>398

72008-A   Keepin' Out Of Mischief Now
(N-2119)

>LP: Dec DL 5228, MCA 2-4112, Br
>(E) LA 8662, JPi (D)   JP 5004,
>Swaggie   (Au) S 1211, CID (F)
>US-223567, Festival (Au) CRF10
>398

72009-A   Squeeze Me
(N-2120)

>LP: Dec DL 5228, MCA 2-4112, Br
>(E) LA 8662, JPi (D)   JP 5004,
>Swaggie   (Au) S 1211, CID (F)

                    US-223567,   Festival   (Au)   CFR10
                    398

72010-A   Honeysuckle Rose
(N-2121)
                    LP: Dec   DL 5228, MCA 2-4112, Br
                    (E) LA 8662, JPi (D) JP 5004,
                    Swaggie (Au) S 1211, CID (F)
                    US-223567,   Festival   (Au)   CFR10
                    398

NOTE: Matrix numbers in parentheses are World
transcription numbers, although this session was
never released on World.

144. Eddie Condon Town Hall Concert
                            Town Hall, NYC, 20
                            May 1944
Johnson, piano solo

                Carolina Shout
                unissued

NOTE: While this title is reported to have been
broadcast on this date, no recording of it is
known to exist.

145. Eddie Condon Town Hall Concert
                            Town Hall, NYC, 3
                            June 1944
Hot Lips Page, trumpet; Johnson, piano; others
uncertain.

                The Joint Is Jumpin'
                unissued

NOTE: Although no transcription of this concert
is known to exist, either on acetates or AFRS

transcription in the Eddie Condon Town Hall
series, this title is believed to have been
broadcast.

146. Will Bradley-Yank Lawson All Stars
                              NYC, 7 June 1944
Lawson,   trumpet;   Bradley,   trombone;   Ray
Eckstrand,   clarinet; Johnson, piano; Carl Kress,
guitar;   Bob   Haggart,   bass; Chauncey Morehouse,
drums.

BT 101-   I've Found A New Baby
              78: Signature 28120

BT 102-1 Jazz Me Blues
              78: Signature 28120

              Noteworthy Blues
                 78:   Br 80180
                 LP: Br BL 58035

              Oh, Lady Be Good
                 LP: Br BL 58035

NOTE: The last two titles have been listed
previously as being recorded on August, 1944.
Br BL 58035 liner notes give that date as the
recording date.   However, it is felt that these
two   titles   are from the June 7, 1944, session.
"Oh, Lady Be Good" on V-Disc 437, reported to be
the above performance,   is by a very different
band without Johnson.

147.   James P. Johnson, piano solos
                              NYC 8 June 1944
Johnson, piano; Eddie Dougherty, drums.

72233-A   I've Got A Feeling I'm Falling

(N-2288)

TX: World   Feature   Jam   Session
JS-21
78:   Dec 23593, Dec (F) 60045
LP: MCA (F) 510.085

72234-A   Honeysuckle Rose
(N-2289)

TX: World   Feature   Jam   Session
JS-20, World Disc R-570
78:   Dec 23593, Dec (F) 60045
LP: MCA (F) 510.085

72235-A   Keepin' Out Of Mischief Now
(N-2290)

TX: World   Feature   Jam   Session
JS-20, World Disc 388, World Disc
R-570
78:   Dec 23594, Dec (F) 60046
LP: MCA (F) 510.085

72236-A   My Fate Is In Your Hands
(N-2291)

TX: World   Feature   Jam   Session
JS-21
78:   Dec 23595, Dec (F) 60046
LP: MCA (F) 510.085

NOTE: The US-Decca 78 rpms were issued in Decca
album A-446. World Transcription JS 20 and 21,
which were the original issues of this material,
are 16-inch 33 1/3 rpm discs. World Disc R-570
is a standard 12-inch LP.   The World matrix
numbers are shown in parentheses.   The piano
solos on the reverse of World JS-21 are labeled
as by James P. Johnson, but are performances by
Pete Johnson.   World JS-22A is labeled as by
James P. Johnson, but contains solos by Pete
Johnson.

148.   James P. Johnson's New York Orchestra
                                NYC 12 June 1944
Frank Newton, trumpet; Johnson, piano and vocal;
Albert Casey, guitar; Pops Foster, bass; Eddie
Dougherty, drums.

MA 1242   Hesitation Blues (James P. Johnson,
vocal)
                    78: Asch 551-2
                    LP: Stinson SLP 21, Asch AA 1/2,
                    Time-Life STL-J18, (Au) STL-J18
                    CT: Time-Life 4TL-J18
                    8T: Time-Life 8TL-J18

MA 1243   The Boogie Dream
                    78: Asch 551-3
                    LP: Stinson SLP 21

MA 1244   The Boogie Dream
                    78:    Asch   unissued.   Acetate
                    exists.

MA 1245   Euphonic Sounds
                    LP: Folkways FG 2850 (?)

MA 1246   Four O'Clock Groove
                    78: Asch 551-2
                    LP: Stinson SLP 21

MA 1246-? Four O'Clock Groove
                    78:    Asch   unissued.   Acetate
                    exists.

MA 1247-? The Dream (breakdown)
                    78:    Asch   unissued.   Acetate
                    exists.

MA 1247-? The Dream

                        78:   Asch   unissued.   Acetate
                        exists.

MA 1247   The Dream (Slow Drag)
                        78:   Asch 551-2
                        LP: Stinson SLP 21

MA 1248   Hot Harlem
                        78:   Asch 551-3
                        LP: Stinson SLP 21,   Time-Life
                        STL-J18, (Au) STL-J18
                        CT: Time-Life 4TL-J18
                        8T: Time-Life 8TL-J18

MA 1248-? Hot Harlem
                        78:   Asch   unissued.   Acetate
                        exists.

MA 1249   unknown title
                        78:   Asch unissued.

MA 1250   Euphonic Sounds
                        78:   Asch 551-1
                        LP: Stinson SLP 21

MA 1250-? Euphonic Sounds
                        LP: Xtra (E) 1024

NOTE: "Euphonic Sounds" on Folkways has drum
accompaniment thoughout with the band coming in
on the last chorus. The different versions on
Asch/Stinson and Xtra are without drums. On
Folkways, "Euphonic Sounds" is mislabeled "St.
Louis Blues."   Above information is from the
Asch files, which show the recording date as
June 19, 1944. This may be the mastering date.
Matrix MA 1249 is shown in the Asch files as a
question mark only.   It is not known if the
version of "Euphonic Sounds" on Folkways is MA
1245 or another alternate of MA 1250. The Asch

78 rpm issues, all 12-inch discs, are contained in Asch album A-551. The matrix numbers and/or takes of the unissued items are not known.

149. Eddie Condon Town Hall Concert
                        NYC, 17 June 1944
Hot Lips Page, trumpet, vocal; Bobby Hackett, cornet; Bill Harris, trombone; Pee Wee Russell, clarinet; Ernie Caceres, baritone; James P. Johnson, piano; unknown bass; Joe Grauso, drums.

           The Joint Is Jumpin'
           LP: Pumpkin 117

James P. Johnson, piano solos

        Willow Tree
              45: Tempo (E) EXA 65, Sto (D)
        SEP 307

        Candy Sweets
              45: Tempo (E) EXA 65, Sto (D)
        SEP 307

        I'm Crazy 'Bout My Baby
              45: Tempo (E) EXA 65, Sto (D)
        SEP 307

Same personnel as first selection.

        Impromptu Ensemble (Uncle Sam Blues)

              LP: Chiaroscuro CR 113, (J)
        ULX-54-V

NOTE: No AFRS transcription of this broadcast has been located. Other selections played at the concert do not include James P. Johnson. Eddie Condon interviews Johnson in the

introductions to each of the solos, but these do
not appear on the Tempo or Storyville releases.
Although no piano is distinctly audible, it is
possible Johnson also plays on "Squeeze Me" from
this concert. "Impromptu Ensemble" titled as
"Uncle Sam Blues" on Chiaroscuro.

150. Sidney DeParis' Blue Note Jazzmen
                              NYC, 21 June 1944
DeParis, trumpet; Vic Dickenson, trombone;
Edmond Hall, clarinet; Johnson, piano; Jimmy
Shirley, guitar; John Simmons, bass; Sidney
Catlett, drums.

BN 981-0 Everybody Loves My Baby
               78: BN 40, JSe (F) 544, Clmx (G)
               BN-40
               LP: BN BLP 7012, B-6506, (J)
               K23P-9287, Mosaic MR6-109

BN 981-1 Everybody Loves My Baby
               LP: BN 6501, 6506, (J) NR-8102,
               K23P-9287, Mosaic MR6-109

BN 982-0 Ballin' The Jack
               78: BN 41, JSe (F) 533, JPa (E)
               2
               LP: BN BLP 7007, B-6506, (J)
               NR-8102, (J) K23P-9287, Mosaic
               MR6-109

BN 982-0 Who's Sorry Now
               LP: Mosaic MR6-109

BN 983-1 Who's Sorry Now
               78: BN 41, JSe (F) 533, JPa (E)
               2
               LP: BN BLP 7007, B-6501, B-6506,

                (J) NR-8102 (J) K23P-9287, Mosaic
                MR6-109

BN 984-0 The Call Of The Blues
                78: BN 40, Clmx (G) BN-40
                LP: BN BLP 7012, B 6506, ST
                89902, 158-2, (J) NR-8102, (J)
                K23P-9287, Mosaic MR6-109

NOTE: BN B-6506 and (J) K23P-9287 contain both
takes of "Everybody Loves My Baby." BN 983-1 is
incorrectly listed as an alternate take on BN
6506. The 78rpm issues are 12-inch discs.
Recorded at WOR studios.

151. Max Kaminsky And His Jazz Band
                      NYC, 22 June 1944
Kaminsky,   trumpet;   Frank   Orchard,
valve-trombone; Rod Cless, clarinet; Johnson,
piano; Eddie Condon, guitar; Bob Casey, bass;
George Wettling, drums.

A-4786-   Love Nest No. 2 (sic)
                LP: Com   XFL 14940, Lon (G)
                6.24060AG

A-4786-1 Love Nest
                78: Com 595
                45: Com CEP-36
                  LP: Com FL 20019, FL 30013, XFL
                14940, Mdsc (E) MLP 12-126, Lon
                (G) 6.24060AG

A-4787-1 Everybody Loves My Baby
                78: Com 595
                45: Com CEP 37
                  LP: Com FL 20019, FL 30013, XFL
                14940, Mdsc (E) MLP 12-126, Lon
                (J) SLC 456, (G) 6.24060AG, Book

of the Month Club 10-5557
CT: Book   of   the   Month   Club
60-5561
8T: Book   of   the   Month   Club
50-5560

A-4787-2 Everybody Loves My Baby No. 2
          LP: Com   XFL   14940, Lon   (G)
          6.24060AG

A-4788-1 Eccentric (That Eccentric Rag) No. 2
(sic)
          LP: Com   XFL   14940, Lon   (G)
          6.24060AG

A-4788-2 Eccentric (That Eccentric Rag)
          78: Com 560
          45: Com CEP-36
          LP: Com   FL 20019, FL 30013, XFL
          14940, Mdsc (E) MLP 12-126, Lon
          (G) 6.24060AG, Book of the Month
          Club 10-5557
          CT: Book   of   the   Month   Club
          60-5561
          8T: Book   of   the   Month   Club
          50-6650

A-4789- Guess Who's In Town No. 2 (sic)
          LP: Com   XFL   14940, Lon   (G)
          6.24060AG

A-4789-1 Guess Who's In Town
          78: Com 560
          45: Com CEP-37
          LP: Com   FL 20019, FL 30013, XFL
          14940, Mdsc (E) MLP 12-126, Lon
          (G) 6.24060AG

NOTE: The above recording sequence is believed

to be accurate despite the indicated take
numbers and titles. Recorded at WOR studios,
1440 Broadway.

152. James P. Johnson, piano solos
                              NYC 28 June 1944
Johnson, piano; Eddie Dougherty, drums.

72311-A   Blue Turning Grey Over You
(N-2375)
               TX: World Feature Jam Session JS
               21, World Disc R-570
               78: Dec 23596, Dec (F) 60052
               LP: MCA (F) 510.085

72312-A   Squeeze Me
(N-2376)
               TX: World Feature Jam Session JS
               20, World Disc R-570
               78: Dec 23596, Dec (F) 60052
               LP: MCA (F) 510.085

72313-A   I'm Gonna Sit Right Down (and Write
Myself A Letter)
(N-2377)
               TX: World Feature Jam Session JS
               20, World Disc 388, World Disc
               R-570
               78: Dec 23595, Dec (F) 60047
               LP: MCA (F) 510.085

72314-A   Ain't Misbehavin'
(N-2378)
               TX: World Feature Jam Session JS
               21
               78: Dec 23594, Dec (F) 60046
               LP: MCA (F) 510.085

NOTE: The US Decca 78 rpms were issued in Decca

album A-446. World transcription matrix numbers
are shown in parentheses. World files list the
recording date as June 26, 1944. World Jam
Session JS 20, JS 21 and World Disc 388 are
16-inch transcriptions while World Disc R-570 is
a standard 12-inch issue.

153. Eddie Condon Town Hall Concert
                         NYC,   12   August
                         1944
Johnson, piano solos.

            Just Before Daybreak
                  TX: AFRS EC 11
                  45:   Tempo (E) EXA 65, Sto (D)
                  SEP 307
                  LP: Chiaroscuro   CR 113,   (J)
                  ULX-54-V, KoJ (I) KLJ 20028

            Caprice Rag
                  TX: AFRS EC 11
                  45:   Tempo (E) EXA 65, Sto (D)
                  SEP 307
                  LP: Chiaroscuro   CR 113,   (J)
                  ULX-54-V, KoJ (I) KLJ 20028

NOTE: Tempo (E) EXA 65 and Sto (D) SEP 307 list
first title as "Just Before Dawn."

154. James P. Johnson, piano solos
                         NYC 15 August 1944
Johnson, piano, Eddie Dougherty, drums.

72386-A   Snowy Morning Blues
(N-2655)
                  TX: World Feature Jam Session JS
                  35, World Disc R-726
                  45: VJM (E) VEP 28

                    LP: Dec DL 5190, Br (E/Au) LA
                    8548, MCA (F) 510.085, JPi (D) JP
                    5004, Swaggie (Au) S 1211, CID
                    (F) UM-233066

72387-A   The Carolina Shout
(N-2656)
                    TX: World Feature Jam Session JS
                    35, World Disc R-726
                    45: VJM (E) VEP 28
                    LP: Dec DL 5190, Br (E/Au) LA
                    8548, MCA (F) 510.085, JPi (D) JP
                    5004, Swaggie (Au) S 1211, CID
                    (F) UM-233066, Yazoo 1070

72388-A   Keep Off The Grass
(N-2657)
                    TX: World Feature Jam Session JS
                    35
                    45: VJM (E) VEP 28
                    LP: Dec DL 5190, Br (E/Au) LA
                    8548, MCA (F) 510.085, JPi (D) JP
                    5004, Swaggie (Au) S 1211, CID
                    (F) UM-233066

72389-A   Old Fashioned Love
(N-2658)
                    TX: World Feature Jam Session
                    JS-35
                    45: VJM (E) VEP 28
                    LP: Dec DL 5190, Br (E/Au) LA
                    8548, MCA (F) 510.085, JPi (D) JP
                    5004, Swaggie (Au) S 1211, CID
                    (F) UM-233066

NOTE: World matrix numbers are shown in
parentheses. World files list the recording
date as September 15, 1944. World Jam Session
JS 35 is a 16-inch transcription.

155. Rod Cless Quartet

NYC 1 September 1944

Sterling Bose, trumpet; Cless, clarinet; Johnson, piano; Pops Foster, bass

BW 33   Froggy Moore
           78:   BW 29
           LP: Jazztone J 1019, Jazztone
           (G) J 1019, GdJ 1039

BW 34   Make Me A Pallet On the Floor
           78: BW 8, 30
           LP: Jazztone J 1019, Jazztone
           (G) J 1019, GdJ (F) J 1039, CA PB
           101, Folkways FJ 2863, Time-Life
           STL-J18, (Au) STL-J18
           CT: Time-Life 4TL-J18
           8T: Time-Life 8TL-J18

BW 35   I Know That You Know
           78:   BW 30
           LP: Jazztone J 1019, Jazztone
           (G) J 1019, Time-Life STL-J18,
           (Au) STL-J18
           CT: Time-Life 4TL-J18
           8T: Time-Life 8TL-J18

BW 36   Have You Ever Felt That Way?
           78:   BW 29
           LP: Jazztone J 1019, Jazztone
           (G) J 1019, GdJ (F) 1039

NOTE: BW 33 is titled "Froggy More" on Jazztone J 1019, which was issued as by James P. Johnson Quartet. The issue on Black and White 8 is a 12-inch vinyl pressing.

442   James P. Johnson

156. James P. Johnson, piano solos
                              NYC   22 September
                              1944
Johnson, piano, Eddie Dougherty, drums.

72390-A   If I Could Be With You
(N-2694)
                    TX: World Feature   Jam Session
                    JS 36, World Disc R-726
                    LP: Decca DL 5190, Br (E/Au) LA
                    8548, MCA (F) 510.085, JPi (D) JP
                    5004, Swaggie (Au) S 1211, CID
                    (F)   UM   233066,   MCA   2-4112,
                    Time-Life STL-J18, (Au) STL-J18
                    CT: Time-Life 4TL-J18
                    8T: Time-Life 8TL-J18

72391-A   A Porter's Love Song
(N-2695)
                    TX: World Feature Jam Session JS
                    36, World Disc R-726
                    LP: Dec DL 5190, Br (E/Au) LA
                    8548, MCA (F) 510.085, JPi (D) JP
                    5004, Swaggie (Au) S 1211, CID
                    (F) UM 233066, MCA 2-4112

72392-A   Over The Bars
(N-2696)
                    TX: World Feature Jam Session JS
                    36, World Disc R-726
                    LP: Dec DL 5190, Br (E/Au) LA
                    8548, MCA (F) 510.085, JPi (D) JP
                    5004, Swaggie (Au) S 1211, CID
                    (F) UM 233066, MCA 2-4112

72393-A   Riffs
                    LP: Dec DL 5190, Br (E/Au) LA
                    8548, MCA (F) 510.085, JPi (D) JP
                    5004, Swaggie (Au) S 1211, CID
                    (F) UM 233066, MCA 2-4112

(N-2697)   Riffs
              TX: World Feature Jam Session JS
              36, World Disc R-726

NOTE: World transcription matrix numbers are
shown in parentheses. The take of "Riffs"
issued on World JS 36 and World Disc R-726 is
different from that issued on LPs. World JS 36
is a 16-inch transcription while World Disc
R-726 is a standard 12-inch LP.

157. Eddie Condon Town Hall Concert
                        NYC   23 September
                        1944
James P. Johnson, piano solos

              Euphonic Sounds
                 TX: AFRS EC 17

              If Dreams Come True
                 LP: Pumpkin 117

NOTE: "If Dreams Come True" exists on acetate
recordings from the broadcast, but was not
issued on AFRS.

158. James P. Johnson's Blue Note Jazzmen
                        NYC, 26 October
                        1944
Sidney DeParis, trumpet; Vic Dickenson,
trombone; Ed Hall, clarinet; Johnson, piano;
Jimmy Shirley, guitar; Al Lucas, bass; Arthur
Trappier, drums.

BN 993-0   Tishomingo Blues
              LP: Mosaic MR6-109

BN 993-2   Tishomingo Blues
           LP: BN BLP   7012, B-6506,   (J)
           NR-8102,   (J) K23P-9287, Mosaic
           MR6-109

BN 994-0   Walkin' the Dog
           LP: Mosaic MR6-109

BN 994-1   Walkin' The Dog
           LP: BN BLP 7012, BN (G) 667.787,
           Queen   Disc   (I)   Q-020,   BN   (J)
           NR-8102, (J) K23P-9287

BN 995-0   Easy Rider
           LP: BN   (G)   667.787,   (J)
           K23P-9287, Mosaic MR6-109

BN 996-0   At the Ball
           LP: Mosaic MR6-109

BN 996-3   At The Ball
           LP: BN BLP 7012, Queen Disc (I)
           Q-020,   Time-Life STL-J18, (Au)
           STL-J18,   BN   (J) NR-8102,   (J)
           K23P-9287, Mosaic MR6-109
           CT: Time-Life 4TL-J18
           8T: Time-Life 8TL-J18

NOTE: Recorded at WOR studios.

159.   Katherine Handy, accompanied by James P.
Johnson
                            NYC, possibly 1944
Katherine Handy Lewis, vocal; Johnson, piano

           Yellow Dog Blues
           LP: Folkways FG 3540

           Memphis Blues

LP: Folkways FG 3540

Loveless Love
    LP: Folkways FG 3540

Chantez Les Bas
    LP: Folkways FG 3540

Joe Turner Blues
    LP: Folkways FG 3540

St. Louis Blues
    LP: Folkways FG 3540

NOTE: The sequence of recording of these titles
is not known.

160.   James P. Johnson, piano solos
                              NYC, possibly 1944

Blue Moods 1
    LP: Folkways FG 3540

Blue Moods 2
    LP: Folkways FG 3540, Xtra (E)
    1024

Blue Moods, Sex
    LP: Folkways FG 3540, Xtra (E)
    1024

NOTE: "Blue Moods, Sex" on Xtra labeled as
"Theme." "Blue Moods 2" on Xtra is labeled as
"Blue Moods." Two false starts exist on acetate
of "Blue Moods 1."   The sequence of recording
for these titles is not known.

161.   James P. Johnson, piano solos

NYC, possibly 1944

Yamekraw - A Negro Rhapsody (in four movements)

Part 1 (2:27)
    LP: Folkways FJ 2842

Part 2 (2:51)
    LP: Folkways FJ 2842

Part 3, take 1 (2:19)
    78: Asch unissued.   Acetate exists

Part 3, take 2 (breakdown)
    78: Asch unissued.   Acetate exists

Part 3, take 3 (2:39)
    LP: Folkways FJ 2842

Part 4 (3:25)
    LP: Folkways FJ 2842

NOTE: Folkways FJ 2842 has the four parts spliced together. The timings have been included to indicate where each part ends on the LP issue. The sequence of recording for these titles is not known.

162. Louis Armstrong's Jazz Foundation Six
                          New Orleans, 17
                          January 1945
Louis Armstrong, trumpet and vocals; J.C. Higginbotham, trombone; Sidney Bechet, soprano sax, clarinet; James P. Johnson, piano; Richard Alexis, bass; Paul Barbarin, drums.

Back O' Town Blues (L.A., vocal)
TX: AFRS ONS 489, ONS 916
LP: Sun SB 219, Palm (E) 30-15,
Saga (E) 6924, FDC (I) 1008/9;
Delta (G) DA 50104, Elec (J) KV
301, Jazz Club (F) 2M126-64480

James P. Johnson, piano, Richard Alexis, bass

Arkansas Blues
TX: AFRS ONS 489, ONS 916
LP: Sun SB 219, Palm (E) 30-15,
Saga (E) 6924, FDC (I) 1008/9,
Delta (G) DA 50104, Elec (J) KV
301, Jazz Club (F) 2M126-64480

Full band personnel

I'm Confessin' (L.A., vocal)
TX: AFRS ONS 489, ONS 916
LP: Sun SB 219, Palm (E) 30-15,
Saga (E) 6924, FDC (I) 1008/9,
Delta (G) DA 50104, Elec (J) KV
301, Jazz Club (F) 2M126-64480

Dear Old Southland
TX: AFRS ONS 489, ONS 916
LP: Sun SB 219, Palm (E) 30-15,
Saga (E) 6924, FDC (I) 1008/9,
Delta (G) DA 50104, Elec (J) KV
301, Jazz Club (F) 2M126-64480

Add Bunk Johnson, trumpet. Bechet plays
clarinet only.

Basin Street Blues (L.A., vocal)
TX: AFRS ONS 489, ONS 916
LP: Sun SB 219, Palm (E) 30-15,
Saga (E) 6924, FDC (I) 1008/9,
Delta (G) DA 50104, Elec (J) KV

301, Jazz Club (F) 2M126-64480

NOTE: This session was part of the second
Esquire All-American Jazz Concert, broadcast
from the Municipal Auditorium. The sequence of
tunes listed above is the sequence in which they
appear on the AFRS transcriptions and presumably
were played at the concert. Although "Perdido
Street Blues" was announced, the band played
"Back O' Town Blues" instead. Apparently,
"Perdido Street Blues" was not performed. At
least, none of the issues to date contain it,
although Sunbean and Delta list the title on
their labels. "Basin Street Blues" is
incomplete on the broadcast. "Dear Old
Southland" is a feature for Higginbotham.

163. Tribute To Fats Waller

                                NYC, 4 February
                                1945, 7 P.M. to
                                7:30 P.M.
(WNEW "Second Anniversary Swing Festival"
broadcast)

James P. Johnson, piano solo

            Old Fashioned Love
               unissued acetate

            Ed Kirkeby interviews Johnson
               unissued acetate

Add Art Trappier, drums.

            Carolina Shout
            LP: Pumpkin 117

Herman Autrey, trumpet; Tommy Dorsey, trombone;
Gene Sedric, clarinet, tenor sax; Johnson,

piano; Al Casey, guitar; Cedric Wallace, bass,
Art Trappier, drums.

Ain't Misbehavin'

LP: Pumpkin 117

Add Pat Flowers, speech, Jerry Marshall,
announcer.

Ain't Misbehavin' (incomplete)
            LP: Fats MA-2

164. The Carnival Three
                              NYC,   22 February
                              1945
Omer Simeon, clarinet, Johnson, piano; Pops
Foster, bass

D 205   Lorenzo's Blues
            78: Disc 6001, Tempo (E) A-15
            45: Tempo (E) EXA 46
            LP: Folkways FP 53, FJ 2801, FJS
            2816,   Pax LP 6006, Jazztone
            J-734,   Xtra (E) 1024, Queen Disc
            (I) Q-056

D 206   Harlem Hotcha
            78: Disc 6001, Tempo (E) A-15
            45: Tempo (E) EXA 46
            LP: Folkways FJS 2816, Jazztone
            J-734, Asch AA 1/2, Pax LP 6006,
            Queen Disc (I) Q-056, Time-Life
            STL-J18, (Au) STL-J18
            CT: Time-Life 4TL-J18
            8T: Time-Life 8TL-J18

D 207   Bandana Days
            78: Disc 6002, Tempo (E) A-27

                        45: Tempo (E) EXA 46
                        LP: Folkways FJS 2816, Jazztone
                        J-734, Pax LP 6006, Queen Disc
                        (I) Q-056

D 208   Creole Lullaby
                        78: Disc 6002, Tempo (E) A-27
                        45: Tempo (E) EXA 46
                        LP: Folkways FJS 2816, Jazztone
                        J-734, Pax LP 6006, Queen Disc
                        (I) Q-056

NOTE: Disc issues were in album 708. Tempo and
Pax issued as Omer Simeon Trio. Jazztone J-734,
a 7-inch disc at 33 1/3 rpm, was issued as James
P. Johnson.

165. James P. Johnson, piano solos
                                    NYC,   possibly
                                    April, 1945
            Blues For Jimmy (breakdown)
                        78: Asch unissued. Acetate
                        exists.

            Blues For Jimmy
                        78: Selmer (F) Y 7218, Cupol
                        9001
                        LP: Folkways FJ 2850

            Jersey Sweet, take 1
                        LP: Folkways FJ 2850

            Jersey Sweet, take 2
                        LP: Folkways FJ 2850

            Keep Movin'
                        LP: Folkways FJ 2850

            Keep Movin' (alternate take)

LP: Xtra (E) 1024

Jungle Drums
LP: Folkways FJ 2850

Twilight Rag
LP: Folkways FJ 2850

Twilight Rag (alternate take)
LP: Xtra (E) 1024

Carolina Balmoral, take 1
78: Asch unissued. Acetate
exists.

Carolina Balmoral, take 2
78: Asch unissued. Acetate
exists.

Jazzamine Concerto, part 1 (5:15)
78: Asch unissued. Acetate
exists.

Jazzamine Concerto, part 2 (2:35)
78: Asch unissued. Acetate
exists.

NOTE: Sequence of recording for these titles is
not known. "Keep Movin'" on Xtra 1024 is
labeled as "Rag." Selmer and Cupol issues
reported to be labeled as by James Pete Johnson.
"Blues for Jimmy" is a portion of the second
movement of the Jazzamine Concerto. "Jersey
Sweet" is another title for "Just Before
Daybreak." "Carolina Balmoral" and the
"Jazzamine Concerto" recordings may be from
this session or another Asch session around this
time.

166.   James P. Johnson, piano solos
                              NYC,   possibly May,
                              1945

        Liza
              LP: Folkways FJ 2850, Time-Life
              STL-J18, (Au) STL-J18
              CT: Time-Life 4TL-J18
              8T: Time-Life 8TL-J18

        Liza (alternate take)
              LP: Xtra (E) 1024

        Aunt Hagar's Blues
              LP: Folkways FJ 2850

        Aunt Hagar's Blues (alternate take)
              LP: Xtra (E) 1024

        The Dream (#1) (3:41)
              Unissued. Acetate exists.

        The Dream (#2) (2:24)
              LP: Possibly issued on Xtra (E)
              1024 in a speeded-up dub which
              runs for 2:07

        The Dream (#3) (breakdown)
              Unissued. Acetate exists.

        The Dream (#4) (2:28)
              LP: Possibly issued on Folkways
              FJ 2850 in a speeded-up version
              (2:13)

        St. Louis Blues
              LP: Folkways FJ 2850

        Sweet Lorraine - Take 2 (sic)
              LP: Folkways FJ 2850

> Sweet Lorraine (alternate take)
>> 78:   Selmer   (F) Y 7218,   Cupol
>> 9001
>> LP: Xtra (E) 1024

NOTE: On Folkways FJ 2850, "The   Dream" is
labeled   as   "Memphis   Blues,"   and   "St.   Louis
Blues"   is   labeled   as   "Euphonic Sounds."   The
sequence of recording for these titles is not
known.   Selmer and Cupol were reportedly issued
as by James Pete Johnson.

167. Eddie Condon Jazz Concert
>> NYC, c. 1945
Bobby Hackett,   cornet; unknown trombone; Joe
Dixon,   clarinet;   Harry   Carney,   baritone sax;
Johnson,   piano;   Sid Weiss,   bass; possibly Joe
Grauso, drums.

DS-172   Oh, Lady Be Good
>> TX: Voice of America American
>> Jazz #27
>> LP: Pumpkin 117

168. Eddie Condon and His Orchestra
>> NYC 17 July 1946

Max Kaminsky,   trumpet; Fred Ohms, trombone; Joe
Dixon, clarinet; Johnson, piano; Condon, guitar;
Jack Lesberg, bass; Dave Tough, drums.   John
"Bubbles" Sublett, vocal.

73647-A   Just You, Just Me
>> 78:   Dec 23720, Br (E) 03793, Dec
>> (Swi) 03793, Dec (Au) Y-6041
>> LP: Dec DL 5218, DL 8281, Br (E)
>> LA 8577, Dec (F) MU 60027, Br (G)

                        87008 LPBM, MCA (F) 510.206, MCA
                        2-4071, 2-4112

73648-A   Atlanta Blues (J.B., vocal)
                        78:    Dec 23720, Br (E) 03793, Dec
                        (Swi) 03793, Dec (Au) Y-6041
                        LP: Dec DL 5218, DL 8281, Br (E)
                        LA 8577, Dec (F) MU 60027, Br (G)
                        87008 LPBM, MCA (F) 510.206, MCA
                        2-4071

NOTE: Two additional titles from this session
have Gene Schroeder on piano. Dec 23720 is
contained in Decca album A-490.

169. Concert At Town Hall
                                    NYC, 21 September
                                    1946
Sidney Bechet, soprano sax; Johnson, piano; Pops
Foster, bass; Baby Dodds, drums.

            China Boy
                        45: Sto (Da) SEP 380
                        LP: Folkways FJ 2841, Sto SLP
                        4028, (Da) 109, 671.199, Fest.
                        (F) SLP 1091, FLPZ 420, 139,
                        Musidisc CCV 2522, Score/Encore
                        (F) SCO 8976, (all edited); Xtra
                        (E) 1003, HMV (Au) OXLP 7503
                        (unedited)

            Dear Old Southland
                        45: Sto (Da) SEP 380
                        LP: Folkways FJ 2841, Sto SLP
                        4028, (Da) 109, 671.199, Fest.
                        (F) SLP 1091, FLPZ 420, 139,
                        Musidisc CCV 2522, Score/Encore
                        (F) SCO 8976, (all edited); Xtra
                        (E) 1003, HMV (Au) OXLP 7503

(unedited)

Johnson, piano; Pops Foster, bass; Baby Dodds, drums.

> Maple Leaf Rag
>> LP: Folkways   FJ   2841, Xtra (E) 1003, HMV (Au) OXLP 7503

> Snowy Morning Blues
>> LP: Folkways   FJ   2841 (edited); Xtra (E) 1003, HMV (Au) OXLP 7503 (unedited)

Johnny Windhurst, trumpet; Mezz Mezzrow, clarinet; Johnson, piano; Pops Foster, bass; Baby Dodds, drums.

> She's Funny That Way
>> LP: Folkways   FJ   2841 (edited); Xtra (E) 1043 (unedited)

Add Miff Mole, trombone.

> Sister Kate
>> LP: Folkways   FJ   2841 (edited), Xtra (E) 1043 (unedited)

> I've Found A New Baby
>> LP: Folkways   FJ   2841 (edited), Xtra (E) 1043 (unedited)

Add Pee Wee Russell, clarinet; Art Hodes, piano.

> The Blues
>> LP: Folkways   FJ   2841 (edited), Xtra (E) 1043 (unedited)

NOTE: All titles, except for "Maple Leaf Rag" are heavily edited on the Folkways release. It

is believed that the complete versions appear
only on the Xtra and Australian HMV issues.
Following is an examination of the differences:

Snowy Morning Blues   Folkways 1:05, Xtra 2:21

Dear   Old   Southland   Folkways   deletes
Johnson's intro.

China   Boy   Folkways deletes the bass
solo.

She's Funny That Way   Folkways 1:30, Xtra 2:26.
Deleted is part of Windhurst's solo.

Sister   Kate   Folkways   3:55,   Xtra
11:09.   Deleted are solos by Johnson, Mole,
Mezzrow, Windhurst.

I Found A New Baby   Folkways 3:50, Xtra 4:46.
Deleted are Johnson's intro and the first
ensemble chorus.

The   Blues   Folkways 5:14, Xtra
13:40.   Deleted are solos by Mezzrow, Mole,
Russell and Mezzrow, Mezzrow again, Windhurst,
Mole and Johnson, in that order.

The   sequence of tunes as presented in the
concert is not known.   Art Hodes played other
tunes at the concert in place of Johnson. Both
the Xtra and HMV issues give October, 1948, as
the date of this concert.

170. Bechet-Mezzrow Feetwarmers
                              NYC,   15 February
                        1947
Vernon Brown, trombone; Mezz Mezzrow, clarinet;
Sidney Bechet, soprano sax; Johnson, piano;

Bernard Addison, guitar; Pops Foster, bass.

>   Royal Garden Blues
>   LP: Wax LP 201, Sto SLP 4028,
>   (Da) SLP 671.199, Festival (F)
>   139,   Musidisc   (E)   CCV 2522,
>   Score/Encore (F) SCO 8976.
>
>   Slow Blues
>   LP: Wax LP 201, Sto SLP 4028,
>   (Da) SLP 671.199, Festival (F)
>   139,   Musidisc   (E)   CCV 2522,
>   Score/Encore (F) SCO 8976
>
>   Old Fashioned Love
>   LP: Wax LP 201, Sto SLP 4028,
>   (Da) SLP 671.199, Festival (F)
>   139,   Musidisc   (E)   CCV 2522,
>   Score/Encore (F) SCO 8976
>
>   Fast Blues
>   LP: Wax LP 201, Sto SLP 4028,
>   (Da) SLP 671.199, Festival (F)
>   139,   Musidisc   (E)   CCV 2522,
>   Score/Encore (F) SCO 8976
>
>   Bugle Blues
>   LP: Wax LP 201, Sto SLP 4028,
>   (Da) SLP 671.199, Festival (F)
>   139,   Musidisc   (E)   CCV 2522,
>   Score/Encore (F) SCO 8976

Johnson, piano solo.

>   Maple Leaf Rag
>   LP: Wax LP 201

171. This Is Jazz
                          NYC, 1 March 1947

33

Johnson, piano solo.

Caprice Rag
LP: Rar (D) 33, Little Gem (Swe)
33
Full band personnel.

Charleston
LP: Riv RLP (12) 149, Jazz J-35,
Rar (D) 33, Fon (E) FJL 122, Fon
(Du) 683272JCL, Riv (J) R-5027,
KoJ (I) KLJ 20004, Little Gem
(Swe) 33

Theme (Way Down Yonder In New Orleans)
LP: Rar (D) 33, Little Gem (Swe)
33

NOTE: "Blues Improvisation" is titled "Slow
Blues" on Fontana and "Blues" on Rarities.
Rarities 33 and Little Gem 33 contain the
entire broadcast including producer Rudi
Blesh's narration. The program was broadcast as
part of the "This Is Jazz" series on Mutual, and
was written and hosted by Blesh.

172. This Is Jazz
NYC 19 April 1947
Wild   Bill   Davison, cornet; George Brunies,
trombone;   Albert   Nicholas, clarinet; Sidney
Bechet, soprano sax and clarinet; Bob Wilber,
clarinet and soprano sax; Johnson, piano, Danny
Barker, guitar; Pops Foster, bass; Baby Dodds,
drums.

Theme (Way Down Yonder in New Orleans)

Muggsy Spanier, cornet; George Brunies, trombone
and vocal; Sidney Bechet, clarinet, soprano sax;
Albert Nicholas, clarinet; Johnson, piano; Danny
Barker, guitar; Pops Foster, bass; Baby Dodds,
drums.

Theme (Way Down Yonder in New Orleans)
LP: Rarities (D) 33, Little Gem
(Swe) 33

That's A Plenty
LP: Circle L-423, Rarities (D)
33, Fon (E) FJL 122, Fon (Du)
683272JCL, Kings of Jazz (I) KLJ
20004, Little Gem (Swe) 33

Baby, Won't You Please Come Home (GB,
vocal)
LP: Riv RLP 12-138/139, Rar (D)
33, Fon (E) FJL 122, BYG (F)
529.064, Mon (F) MY 40010, Fon
(Du) 683272JCL, Sagapan (E) PAN
6900, Saga (E) SAGA 6900, Kings
of Jazz (I) KLJ 20004, Little Gem
(Swe) 33

I Know That You Know
LP: Rar (D) 33, Fon (E) FJL 122,
Fon (Du) 683272JCL, KoJ (I) KLJ
20004, Little Gem (Swe) 33

Omit Spanier and Brunies.

Blues Improvisation
LP: Riv RLP 12-138/139; Rar (D)
33, Fon (E) 122; BYG (F) 529.064,
Fon (Du) 683272JCL, Sagapan (E)
PAN 6900, Saga (E) SAGA 6900, KoJ
(I) KLJ 20004, Little Gem (Swe)

         LP: Rar (D) 35, Little Gem (Swe)
         35

Maple Leaf Rag
         LP: Rar (D) 35, Little Gem (Swe)
         35

Basin Street Blues
         LP: Rar (D) 35,   Little Gem
         (Swe) 35,   MFP (F) 64.846

Polka Dot Stomp Rag
         LP: Rar (D) 35, Little Gem (Swe)
         35,   MFP (F) 64.846, KoJ (I) KLJ
         20033

Kansas City Man
         LP: After Hours (G) J-1201, Rar
         (D) 35, Little Gem (Swe) 35,   MFP
         (F) 64.846, KoJ (I) KLJ 20033

Jazz Me Blues
         LP: Rar (D) 35, Little Gem (Swe)
         35

Rudy Blesh interviews James P. Johnson
         LP: Rar (D) 35, Little Gem (Swe) 35

Johnson, piano, Baby Dodds, drums.

         Carolina Shout
         TX: Office of International
         Information OII-61, VOA 61
         LP: FDC (I) 1012, Rar (D) 35,
         Little Gem (Swe) 35

Full band personnel.

         Panama March (Rag)
         LP: Rar (D) 35, Little Gem (Swe)

35

Theme (Way Down Yonder in New Orleans)
LP: Rar (D) 35, Little Gem (Swe)
35

NOTE: Rarities 35 and Little Gem 35 contain
the entire broadcast, including narration. From
the Mutual broadcast. "Kansas City Man" labeled
as "Kansas City Man Blues" on Rarities (E) 35.

173. Hamilton College Concert
                        Alumni   Gymnasium,
                        Clinton, N.Y., May
                        3, 1947
Max Kaminsky, trumpet; Miff Mole, trombone; Tony
Parenti, clarinet; Johnson, piano; Jimmy Butts,
bass; Danny Alvin, drums.

        Muskrat Ramble
            unissued acetate

        Squeeze Me
            unissued acetate

        At The Jazz Band Ball
            unissued acetate

Tony Parenti, clarinet; Johnson, piano; Danny
Alvin, drums.

        Maple Leaf Rag
            unissued acetate

        Black and Blue
            unissued acetate

Johnson, piano solos.

Back Water Blues
    LP: Pumpkin 117

Liza
    LP: Pumpkin 117

Snowy Morning Blues
    unissued acetate

Carolina Shout
    unissued acetate

Private Party at fraternity house after the
concert (same date.)

Johnson, piano solos.

Liza
    unissued acetate

Hallelujah
    unissued acetate

Medley: Boogie Woogie Stride and Tea
for Two
    unissued acetate

Squeeze Me
    unissued acetate

Medley: Ain't   Misbehavin',   Just
Before Daybreak, I Can't Get Started
    unissued acetate

Keepin' Out Of Mischief
    unissued acetate

NOTE: Some of the tunes from this concert have
been listed with an unknown date, 1949. The
college student newspaper, "The Hamiltonews,"

gives the date as above. The Concert was a
benefit for the Cancer Fund and was promoted by
Art Hodes, who appears on all selections except
those listed above. Johnson was listed in the
newspaper account as the intermission pianist.

174. This Is Jazz
                              NYC, 24 May 1947
Wild Bill Davison, cornet; George Brunies,
trombone and vocal; Sidney Bechet, clarinet and
soprano sax; Albert Nicholas, clarinet; Johnson,
piano, Danny Barker, guitar; Pops Foster, bass;
Freddie Moore, drums.

> Theme (Way Down Yonder In New Orleans)
> unissued

> I'm Crazy 'Bout My Baby (GB, vocal)
> LP: Pumpkin 117

Sidney Bechet, soprano sax; Johnson, piano.

> Wild Cat Blues
> LP: Riv RLP (12) 149, Jazz J-35,
> KoJ (I) KLJ 20033, Riv (J) R-5027

Full band personnel.

> Squeeze Me
> LP: Storyville (D) SLP 4068

> Ain't Misbehavin'
> LP: Riv RLP (12) 149, Jazz J-35,
> KoJ (I) KLJ 20033, Riv (J) R-5027

Johnson, piano solo.

> Chocolate Bar

                    LP: Pumpkin 117

Full band personnel.

              Blue Turning Grey Over You
                    LP: Riv RLP (12) 149, Jazz J-35,
                    KoJ (I) KLJ 20033, Riv (J) R-5027

NOTE: This was a special edition of the This Is
Jazz series, dedicated to Fats Waller. Johnson
plays "Honeysuckle Rose" behind Rudi Blesh's
narration between tunes throughout the program.
Band joins in to play a chorus of "Honeysuckle
Rose" prior to the closing theme.   A brief
interview by Blesh of Johnson preceeds
"Chocolate Bar."

175.   James P. Johnson, piano solos
                              NYC, 5 June 1947

NY 29   Daintiness Rag
                    78:   Circle 3005, Esq (E) 10-149,
                    BlSt (F) 198, Cir (F) 3005, CdM
                    (F) 29638
                    LP: Her 403

NY 30   Mama and Papa Blues
                    LP: Riv   RLP   1056, Lon (E)
                    HB-U1057

NY 31   Ain't 'Cha Got Music
                    78:   Circle 3005, Esq (E) 10-149,
                    BlSt (F) 198, Cir (F) 3005, CdM
                    (F) 29638
                    LP: Riv RLP 1056, Lon (E) HB-U
                    1057

NY 32   Old Fashioned Love
                    LP: Riv RLP 1056, Lon (E) HB-U

1057

NY 33   I'm Crazy 'Bout My Baby
           LP: Riv RLP 1056, Lon (E) HB-U
           1057

NY 34   Wild Cat Rag
           unissued.   78   rpm   metal   part
           exists.

NOTE: Above matrix   numbers are as listed in
Circle files.

176. This Is Jazz
                        NYC, 7 June 1947
Wild   Bill Davison, cornet; Albert Nicholas,
clarinet   and   vocal;   Johnson, piano; Danny
Barker,   guitar;   Pops Foster, bass; Freddie
Moore, drums, washboard and vocal.

           Theme (Way Down Yonder In New Orleans)
           LP: Manhattan (I) 503

           I Wish I Could Shimmy Like My Sister
           Kate (FM, vocal)
           LP: Manhattan (I) 503

           Ad Lib Blues (FM, vocal)
           LP: Manhattan (I) 503

           Poor Butterfly
           TX: OIICA 24
           LP: Manhattan (I) 503

Johnson, piano solo.

           Snowy Morning Blues
           TX: OIICA 24
           LP: Manhattan (I) 503

Full band personnel.

        Creole Song (AN, vocal)
           LP: Manhattan (I) 503

        I'm Confessin'
           TX: OIICA 24
           LP: Circle L-405, Manhattan (I)
        503

        Big Butter and Egg Man
           TX: OIICA 24
           LP: Manhattan   (I)   503,
        Storyville (D) SLP 4067

        Theme (Way Down Yonder In New Orleans)
           LP: Manhattan (I) 503

NOTE: Manhattan   503   contains   the   entire broadcast, including narration by Rudi Blesh. OIICA 24 is a 16-inch transcription issued by the   Office of International Information and Cultural Affairs.

177. Nick and His Creole Serenaders
                        NYC 12 June 1947
Nicholas, clarinet and vocal, Johnson, piano; Danny Barker, guitar and vocal; Pops Foster, bass;

NY 35B   Salee Dame (AN, vocal)
              78: Cir J-1018
              45: Riv (I) REP 116
              LP: Riv RLP 12-216, GHB 50, Lon
        (E) HA-U 2035

NY 36   Mo Pas Lemme Ca (AN, DB, vocal)
              78: Cir J-1018

                        45: Riv (I) REP 116
                        LP: Riv RLP 12-216, GHB 50, Lon
                        (E) HA-U 2035

NY 37   Les Ognons (AN, DB, vocal)
                        78: Cir J-1019, Cir (Au) C-104
                        45: Riv (I) REP 116
                        LP: Riv RLP 12-216, GHB 50, Lon
                        (E) HA-U 2035

NY 38   Creole Blues (AN, vocal)
                        78: Cir J-1019, Cir (Au) C-104
                        LP: Cir (I) ES 40020, GHB 50

NOTE: Circle J-1018 and J-1019 in Circle Album
S-13, "Jazz a la Creole." The Circle files show
NY35 as "Mo Pas Lemma Ca" and NY 36 as "Salee
Dame, BonJour."   The discs, however, indicate
matrix numbers as listed above. Circle (Aus)
C-104 exists on a vinyl pressing.

178.   This Is Jazz
                             NYC 14 June 1947
Wild   Bill   Davison,   cornet;   Jimmy   Archey,
trombone; Albert Nicholas, clarinet; Johnson,
piano; Danny Barker, guitar; Pops Foster, bass;
Baby Dodds, drums; Alberta Prime, vocal.

            Theme (Way Down Yonder In New Orleans)
                LP: Manhattan (I) 504

            Fidgety Feet
                LP: Manhattan (I) 504

            Ain't Gonna Give Nobody None Of My
            Jelly Roll (AP, vocal)
                LP: Manhattan (I) 504

Sugar
LP: Manhattan (I) 504

Muskrat Ramble
LP: Manhattan (I) 504

Theme (Way Down Yonder In New Orleans)
LP: Manhattan (I) 504

NOTE: Manhattan 504 contains the entire program, including Rudi Blesh's narration. From the Mutual broadcast. Leadbelly (Huddie Ledbetter) also appeared on the broadcast and perfromed "Green Corn" and "John Henry." Baby Dodds also performed a drum solo "Drum Improvisation."

179. This Is Jazz
                              NYC 21 June 1947
Wild Bill Davison, cornet; Jimmy Archey, trombone; Albert Nicholas, clarinet; Johnson, piano; Danny Barker, guitar; Pops Foster, bass; Baby Dodds, drums.

Theme (Way Down Yonder In New Orleans)
LP: Manhattan (I) 504

Panama Rag
LP: Manhattan   (I)   504,
Storyville (D) SLP 4067

Trombone Preachin' Blues
LP: Riv RLP 2514, S-1, Manhattan
(I) 504

Johnson, piano solo.

Ain't Cha Got Music
LP: Manhattan (I) 504, Pumpkin

117

Full band personnel.

Sensation Rag
LP: Manhattan   (I)   504,
Storyville (D) SLP 4067

When It's Sleepy Time Down South
LP: Manhattan   (I)   504,
Storyville (D) SLP 4067

NY 69   St. Louis Blues
78: Circle J-1041, BlSt (F) 159
LP: Circle   L-402,   Riv   RLP
12-211, Vogue (E) LDE 020, Lon
(E) LTZ-U 15068, BlSt (F) BLP
6803, Chant du Monde (F) 29611,
Manhattan (I) 504

NOTE: Manhattan   504   contains   the   entire
program, including Rudi Blesh's narration. From
the Mutual broadcast.

Johnson is reported to have appeared on the
Eddie Condon television series, "Floor Show"
during 1948-49 but no specific information has
surfaced regarding his appearances in the
series.

180.   Sidney Bechet and His Circle Seven
NYC   27   January
1949.
Albert   Snaer,   trumpet;   Wilbur   De   Paris,
trombone;   Buster   Bailey,   clarinet;   Bechet,
soprano sax; Johnson, piano; Walter Page, bass;
George Wettling, drums.

NY 83D   I Got Rhythm
                    78:    Circle   J-1058,   Esq   (E)
                    10-075, BlSt (F) 188
                    45: Bcy (F) EP 74002
                    LP: Riv RLP 2516, 12-138/139;
                    Con 2516 LP, Ev FS 228; Fon (E)
                    FJL 122, Bcy (F) 820119, BYG (F)
                    529.064, Mon (F) MY 40010, Fon
                    (Du) JCL 663272

NY 84C   September Song
                    78:    Circle   J-1057,   Esq   (E)
                    10-076, BlSt (F) 180
                    45: Bcy (F) EP 74002
                    LP: Riv RLP 2516, 12-138/139,
                    Con 2516 LP, Fon (E) FJL 122, Mon
                    (F)   MY   40010,   Fon (Du) JCL
                    683272, BYG (F) 529.064

NY 85B   Who?
                    78:    Circle   J-1057,   Esq   (E)
                    10-076, BlSt (F) 180
                    45: Bcy (F) EP 74002
                    LP: Riv RLP 2516, 12-138/139;
                    Con 2516 LP, Ev FS 228, Fon (E)
                    FJL 122, Bcy (F) 820119, Mon (F)
                    MY 40010, Fon (Du) JCL 683272

NOTE: "Casbah," also recorded at this session,
has James Tolliver in place of Johnson. Session
date as listed in Circle files.

181. Kid Ory
                              Los Angeles, Ca.,
                              28 June 1949

possibly Teddy Buckner, trumpet; Ory, trombone;
unknown clarinet; Johnson, piano; Ed Garland,
bass; Minor Hall, drums.

D-56736   Four or Five Times
                    TX: AFRS END 143-12, part 2

NOTE: Apparently, James P. Johnson sat in with
the band on this one tune, replacing regular
pianist Buster Wilson. The regular clarinetist
with   the   band,   Joe   Darensbourg, was also
replaced on this title.   Andrew Blakeney has
also been suggested as the trumpet player.
Broadcast by KGFJ from the Beverly Cavern.

182.   James P. Johnson, piano solos
                            Privately   recorded
                            in   Los   Angles,
                            Ca.,   Probably
                            September, 1949.

        Sugar
            LP: Pumpkin 117

        Sugar Hill Theme (You Can't Lose A
        Broken Heart)
            LP: Pumpkin 117

        Steeplechase Rag
            LP: Pumpkin 117

        Old Fashioned Love (incomplete)
            unissued tape

NOTE: Tape also contains speech Johnson and
Floyd Levin.

183.   Sidney Bechet Stompers
                            Vernon   Hall,   NYC,
                            5 March 1950

Max   Kaminsky, trumpet; Munn Ware, trombone;
Bechet, soprano sax; Johnson, piano; unknown
bass; Art Trappier, drums.

> Someday Sweetheart
> unissued acetate

> Muskrat Ramble
> unissued acetate

> Tin Roof Blues
> unissued acetate

Sidney Bechet, soprano sax; Johnson, piano; Art
Trappier, drums.

> Summertime
> unissued acetate

Johnnson, piano solo.

> Old Fashioned Love
> unissued acetate

Full band personnel

> Jazz Me Blues
> unissued acetate

> I Found A New Baby
> unissued acetate

Sidney Bechet, soprano sax; Johnson, piano; Art
Trappier, drums.

> Dear Old Southland
> unissued acetate

Full band personnel.

High Society
 unissued acetate

NOTE: The location of this concert has also
been   given   as Yale University, New Haven,
Connecticut, but the Vernon Hall location is
believed to be correct. These are the last
performances known to have been preserved by
James P. Johnson.

Following is a very selective listing of recordings of compositions by James P. Johnson which he never recorded himself. The listing is not comprehensive nor inclusive, but is meant only as a guide to locating some of his more obscure compositions.

Alabama Stomp
>Dixie Stompers (Fletcher Henderson)
>Red and Miff's Stompers
>Red Nichols

April in Harlem (from Harlem Symphony)
>William Albright

Chicago Stomp Down
>Duke Ellington

Concerto Jazz-A-Mine (second movement)
>William Albright

Desperate Blues
>Trixie Smith

Doin' What I Please
>Don Redman

Don't Never Tell Nobody What Your Good Man Can Do
>Maggie Jones
>Clara Smith

Elevator Papa-Switchboard Mama
                    Butterbeans and Susie

Everybody's Doing That Charleston Now
                    Original Indiana Five

Ginger Brown
                    Dick Hyman

Give Me the Sunshine
                    Roger Wolfe Kahn

Harlem Symphony (see April in Harlem)

How Could You Put Me Down
                    Willie "The Lion" Smith

I Don't Love Nobody But You
                    Phil   Baxter   and   His
                    Orchestra

I Need Lovin'
                    Alabama Washboard Stompers
                    Blanche Calloway
                    Coon-Sanders Orchestra
                    Fletcher Henderson
                    Jimmie Noone

Ivy
                    Original Memphis Five

Keep 'Em Guessing
                    Monette Moore

Misery
                    Blanche Calloway

My Sweet Hunk O' Trash

Louis Armstrong and Billie
Holiday

Oh Malinda

Te Roy Williams and His
Orchestra

Peace, Sister, Peace
Monette Moore

Poem of Love
Ken Werner

Stop That Dog
State Street Aces

Swinga-Dilla Street
Fats Waller

That Gets It, Mr. Joe
Fats Waller

There's No Two Ways About Love
Lena Horne
Teddy Weatherford

Thumpin' and Bumpin'
Eubie Blake

What If We Do?
Eva Taylor

Whisper Sweet
Bob Howard
Valaida Snow

You for Me, Me for You From Now On
Dixie Washboard Band
Alberta Hunter

You Just Can't Have No One Man By Yourself
                    Sara Martin

You You You
                    Dick   Wellstood   and   Bob
                    Wilber

    There have been many recordings of James P.
Johnson compositions through the years. Some of
the more interesting albums currently available
dedicated to his works are listed below.

CHARLESTON: THE SONG THAT MADE THE TWENTIES
ROAR (Columbia M 33706)

Arranged, conducted and performed by Dick Hyman.
Includes Charleston; If I Could Be with You One
Hour   Tonight;   Caprice Rag; Selections from
"Running   Wild"   including Ginger Brown, Old
Fashioned Love, Love Bug, Charleston, and Open
Your Heart; Snowy Morning Blues; Steeplechase
Rag; Eccentricity; Carolina Balmoral; Just
Before Daybreak; Jingles, Carolina Shout and
You've Got to Be Modernistic.

MUSIC OF FATS WALLER AND JAMES P. JOHNSON
(SMITHSONIAN N 021)

Smithsonian Jazz Repertory Ensemble. Includes
Caprice Rag; Old Fashioned Love; Carolina
Shout-Snowy Morning Blues; You've Got to Be
Modernistic; If I Could Be with You; Willow
Tree.

OLD FASHIONED LOVE: A TRIBUTE TO JAMES P.
JOHNSON (EUPHONIC ESR-1222)

Jim   Turner, piano solos. Includes Carolina
Shout; If I Could Be with You One Hour Tonight;

Fascination; Charleston; Jersey Sweet; Snowy
Morning Blues; Old Fashioned Love; Keep Off the
Grass; Eccentricity Waltz; Lonesome Reverie.

SCOTT JOPLIN AND JAMES P. JOHNSON; RAGTIME BACK
TO BACK (MUSICAL HERITAGE SOCIETY MHS 4022)

William Albright, piano solos.   Includes Mule
Walk Stomp; Eccentricity; You've Got to Be
Modernistic; Snowy Morning Blues and Carolina
Shout.

KEN   WERNER   PLAYS   THE PIANO MUSIC OF BIX
BEIDERBECKE,   DUKE ELLINGTON, GEORGE GERSHWIN AND
JAMES P. JOHNSON (FINNADAR SR 9019)

Ken Werner, piano solos. Includes Caprice Rag,
Poem of Love, Daintiness Rag.

THE SYMPHONIC JAZZ OF JAMES P. JOHNSON (MUSICAL
HERITAGE SOCIETY MHS 4888W)

William   Albright, piano solos.   Includes
Yamekraw (Negro Rhapsody); Fascination; April in
Harlem (from Harlem Symphony); Keep Off the
Grass; Concerto Jazz-A-Mine (second movement);
A-Flat Dream.

TITLE INDEX

Numbers   refer to the recording session listed in
the discography section.

PERSONNEL INDEX

Numbers refer to the recording session listed in the discography section.